Bilingual Course of Approaches and Methods in Second Language Teaching

第二语言教学法流派概要
双语教程

匡昕　主编

北京体育大学出版社

策划编辑　佟　晖
责任编辑　佟　晖
责任校对　潘海英
版式设计　联众恒创

图书在版编目（CIP）数据

第二语言教学法流派概要双语教程 = Bilingual Course of Approaches and Methods in Second Language Teaching：汉、英 / 匡昕主编 . -- 北京：北京体育大学出版社，2024.12
ISBN 978-7-5644-4096-1

Ⅰ.①第… Ⅱ.①匡… Ⅲ.①第二语言—外语教学—教学法—双语教学—高等学校—教材—汉、英 Ⅳ.① H09

中国国家版本馆 CIP 数据核字（2024）第 107118 号

第二语言教学法流派概要双语教程　　　　匡昕　主编

DI-ER YUYAN JIAOXUEFA LIUPAI GAIYAO
SHUANGYU JIAOCHENG

出版发行：北京体育大学出版社
地　　址：北京市海淀区农大南路 1 号院 2 号楼 2 层办公 B-212
邮　　编：100084
网　　址：http://cbs. bsu. edu. cn
发 行 部：010-62989320
邮 购 部：北京体育大学出版社读者服务部 010-62989432
印　　刷：三河市国英印务有限公司
开　　本：787mm×1092mm　1/16
成品尺寸：185mm×260mm
印　　张：23.75
字　　数：608 千字
版　　次：2024 年 12 月第 1 版
印　　次：2024 年 12 月第 1 次印刷
定　　价：90.00 元

（本书如有印装质量问题，请与出版社联系调换）
版权所有·侵权必究

编 委 会

主　编　匡　昕

编　委　（按姓氏笔画排序）

　　　　王　辰　项　英

前言

◎ 为什么编写这样一本双语教材？

随着经济全球化步伐的日益加快，我国在国际社会中的地位和影响力都得到了极大提高，需要在越来越多的国际领域开展交流与合作，这就对我国的高等教育提出了新的挑战，即如何培养出既具有扎实的专业功底又具有良好外语交流能力的国际型人才。面对这一情况，教育部早在 2001 年《关于加强高等学校本科教学工作提高教学质量的若干意见》中便提出"积极推动使用英语等外语进行教学"的号召。由此，全国各高校相继开设双语课程，开展双语教学工作。为了进一步推动双语教学的发展，2007 年根据《教育部　财政部关于实施高等学校本科教学质量与教学改革工程的意见》，教育部决定启动双语教学示范课程建设项目。截至 2010 年共支持建设了 500 门双语教学示范课程。2018 年，《关于高等学校加快"双一流"建设的指导意见》中又指出，高校要以"一带一路"倡议为引领，加大双语种或多语种复合型国际化专业人才培养力度。双语课程建设与双语教学推行已成为高校"双一流"建设、"国际化"办学的重要评估指标。双语课程在提高学生外语专业词汇量和外文水平，增进了解学科前沿动态知识，引入国外先进教学理念与方法，培养学科认知、思维及创新能力，提高教师队伍整体素质等方面都具有极大的促进作用。从当前高校实施双语教学的实际情况来看，我国高校的双语教学还处于起步阶段，受到师资、授课对象、教材、教学理念、教学方法、教育技术等多种因素的制约。双语教学效果不理想，亟待加大研究力度，推行教学改革，开展教学实践，提高教学效果以达到开展双语教学的教育目标。

"语言教学法"是北京体育大学汉语国际教育本科专业 2018 级培养方案中的一门专业核心双语课程，于 2019—2020 学年秋季学期面向 2018 级汉语国际教育本科专业学生实施了第一轮课程教学。在双语教学过程中，我们采用的是"全英文原版教材＋全英文课件

+70% 中文讲授"的授课方式。授课结束后，我们对学生进行了双语课程学习调查，调查内容涉及学生的英语水平，双语课程开设的学期、目的及必要性，教材、课件及教师授课语言的中英文比例，双语授课的方法，学生学习双语课程的投入、效果、期望及负担等。从学生的反馈结果可以看出，学生对双语课程的开设目的，即学习专业知识、提升学术英语能力的双重教学目标具有一定的认知度。由于学生自身专业英语水平、专业理论知识以及学习投入时间、精力上的限制，部分学生对双语课程的效果及满意度不高，认为双语课程教学的设置，尤其是全英文原版教材和全英文课件的使用成为理解专业知识的障碍。所以，学生对中英双语教材的渴望与需求极高。

本着"为教学建教材，用教材促课改，借课改提质量"的思路，我们在全面调研、总结与反思后，形成了双语教材与双语课程教学的改革思路。恰逢其时，北京体育大学教务处启动了双语教材申报项目。经个人申报、学院推荐、教学指导与教材建设委员会专家评审等程序，《第二语言教学法流派概要双语教程》于 2018 年 12 月正式被立项为北京体育大学双语课程教材建设项目。教材的设计、撰写直至成稿经历了 2019—2022 年四年的教学实践。我们在教学中反思，在反思中凝练，在凝练后成书，并期望通过教材建设与课程改革共同提高汉语国际教育专业教学法类课程双语教学的质量与效果。

◎这本双语教材有何特色?

本教材具有三个突出特色:

1. 科学性: 遵循先进的教育及学习理论

教材以建构主义学习观为基础理论，在体例设计和教学内容编排上由浅入深、由易到难。在体例设计上，基于维果茨基"最近发展区"理论与"支架式"教学理论，以实现双语课程教学"专业 + 语言"的双重目标为导向，紧紧围绕学生认知发展和语言能力提升，聚焦知识重点难点，通过分解认知与语言双重学习任务，分层、分项、分步、分类搭建学习支架，如案例支架、问题支架、向导支架和图表支架等，形成对学生知识建构的"援助"，达到简化、易化教材难度，引导学生开展课程学习，完成新知识内化的目的。在教学内容编排上，基于教学法理论框架，对教学内容进行知识解构，将知识点细粒化，通过述渊源、给示例、讲理论、阐原则、论方法、说影响等环节，为学生构建语言教学法理论分析框架，培养科学思维，提升学术能力。

2. 实用性: 多元化内容板块设计，增强可读性

教材主要章节采取统一内容板块设计，即章节内容提要、词语热身、教学法概述、教学示例、教学原则与教学过程、活动与练习、拓展阅读等。以词云图的形式呈现专业英语词汇，从生动的教学示例入手解读教学法理论，通过多样化的活动与练习，巩固所学、深化知识，最后选录经典英文文献或相关学术论文，提升学生对理论知识的理解，强化学术英语能力。其编排设置在理论阐述和学生英语能力的培养方面，环环相扣、层层推进，大大降低了教材理论知识及学术英文理解的难度，提高了教材的可教性、可读性及实用性。

3. 针对性：专业特色鲜明，教学实践性强

教材以汉语国际教育本科专业 2018 级培养方案专业核心双语课程"语言教学法"教学大纲为依据，教材内容契合大纲设置，对学生学习该课程有针对性指导作用。作为汉语国际教育专业的核心课程，"语言教学法"双语课程讲授汉语国际教育教学技能的基础理论，在教材内容编写及案例选用上，选择英语或汉语教学示例，在活动与练习中，针对汉语教学设置多样化的教学案例，引导学生在审视中发现、在发现中提高，通过教案讨论与纠错，显化专业特色，实践理论应用，达到学而能思、学有所用的教学目标。

◎这本双语教材的章节编排是怎样的？

在内容编排及体例设计方面，教材包括 11 章、附录和参考文献。第 1 ~ 10 章是教材的主体部分，采用中英双语的形式呈现，内容设计上分章介绍语言教学发展历史上的 10 个重要的第二语言教学法流派，分别为语法翻译法（The Grammar-Translation Method）、直接法（The Direct Method）、听说法（The Audiolingual Method）、全身反应法（Total Physical Response）、社团语言学习法（Community Language Learning）、沉默法（The Silent Way）、暗示法（Suggestopedia）、交际法（Communicative Language Teaching）、内容教学法（Content-Based Instruction）和任务型教学法（Task-Based Language Teaching）等。

第 11 章采用中英双语的形式呈现。内容上，对第 1 ~ 10 章所涉及的教学法进行全面总结与系统的知识构建。通过对各类教学法横向、纵向梳理比较分析，从历史论未来，从实践炼理论，促使学生在教学法历史发展变迁中，在基于一个个教学法案例的感性经验积累中，提炼体悟语言教学的理论内蕴，感受教育教学的"初心"，服务语言类应用型师资的培养。

附录为全英文补充文献，供学生开展拓展阅读。内容包括情景法（Situational Language Teaching）、多元智能法（Multiple Intelligences）、词汇法（The Lexical Approach）、自然法（The Natural Approach）、合作学习语言法（Cooperative Language Teaching）、能力导向型教学法（Competency-Based Language Teaching）、基于项目的教学法（Project-Based Learning）和翻转课堂教学法（Flipped Classroom Approach）等 8 个教学法，帮助学生进一步开阔学科视域，增加专业知识，强化文献阅读能力，为专业学习拓展更广阔的视野。

◎这本双语教材的主体部分内容体例是怎样设计的？

教材的主体部分第 1 ~ 10 章采用统一的体例设计。在内容上分项介绍各历史时期的共计 10 个重要的教学法，编写体例上具有同一性，旨在切实服务师生的教与学。每章分为内容提要、词语热身、主体内容、活动与练习等板块，详见表 1。

内容提要板块以中英双语的形式就本章知识内容进行概括，以明晰章节学习目标，导航学习要点。

表 1　教材第 1～10 章内容板块设计表

教材板块	英文部分		中文部分	设计意图
内容提要	Contents		内容提要	提要中英章节主要知识点
词语热身	Wordle		—	呈现英文词云图，导入重点专业术语，主题热身
主体内容	1 Introduction		一、教学法概述	概述教学法的产生背景、代表人物等信息要素
	2 Teaching Cases		二、教学示例	呈现 1 到 2 个完整的教学案例，建立感性认知
	3 Teaching Principles and Teaching Procedures		三、教学原则与教学过程	分述教学法的理论基础、教学原则、教学方法等，讲授教学法理论知识
	4 Conclusion		四、小结	总结并评价教学法的意义与影响等
活动与练习	Activities and Exercises	Understanding and Thinking	（理解与思考）	【研】摘录教学法相关的重要论述、学者评论，供课堂研讨
		Teaching Design	（教学设计）	【用】呈现两例教学设计，第 1 例为经典样例，服务学生理论理解与学习模仿；第 2 例为真实的教案设计作业，以改促研，提升实践能力
		Further Readings	（拓展阅读）	【读】选录教学法经典英文论文或相关文献重要内容，提升学术英语水平
		Knowledge Table	（知识表格）	【炼】以表格填写的形式辅助搭建知识框架
		Mind Map	（思维导图）	【思】以思维导图形式促进学生思考并形成知识网络，提升思维能力

　　词语热身板块以英文词云图的形式呈现。词云图包含该章教学法涉及的重点专业术语，帮助学生扫除生词障碍，为预习、学习及复习本章主题及内容提供知识图谱。

　　主体内容板块分为教学法概述（Introduction）、教学示例（Teaching Cases）、教学原则与教学过程（Teaching Principles and Teaching Procedures）和小结（Conclusion）四部分内容，采用中英双语的形式，是教材的重点理论内容。第一部分概述教学法的产生背景、代表人物、重要意义等。第二部分教学示例引用国内外知名经典教学案例，将教学法立体化、生动化、叙事化地呈现出来，为学生建立对教学法的感性认知。第三部分教学原则与教学过程立足各教学法的特点，解读其理论基础、教学原则与特色、教学过程与方法、教学步骤、特殊教具及教学技巧等内容，在教学案例的感性认识基础上进一步解读教学法理论体系及实践方法。第四部分小结在实践与理论学习的基础上进行总结与反思，归纳教学法的意义与影响、优势与不足，强化学生反思、评价的理论应用能力与思维能力。

　　活动与练习板块是做中学、练中思的部分，体现了教材的特征——讲练结合、学思互促。这个板块设置了理解与思考（Understanding and Thinking）、教学设计（Teaching Design）、拓展阅读（Further Readings）、知识表格（Knowledge Table）、思维导图（Mind Map）五类内容，通过一系列拓展练习，如观点阐述与分析、教学案例研讨与修改、文献阅读、知识提炼与统合等方式，以思考题、学术文献、教案、表格、思维导图等形式，促进学生对章节内容的理解掌握、吸收内化与应用转化。第一类理解与思考聚焦"研"，通过提出问题或提供材料，促使师生研学讨论，加深对该章教学法的理解。第二类教学设计聚焦"用"，以教学示例和教案的形式呈现两例教学设计：第 1 例为经典样例，进一步丰富教学法案例，服务学生理论理解与学习模仿；第 2 例援引真实的学生教案设计作业（均有删改加工），该教案在语言表述、设计思路、方法应用等方面存在或多或少的问题，供师生结合教学法理论开展研讨与修改活动，提升教学实操能力。第三类拓展阅读聚焦"读"，选录教学法经典英文论文或节选相关文献重要内容，完整、系统地拓深教学法相关知识，同时提升学生的学术英语水平，尤其是专业英语阅读理解能力。第四类知识表格聚焦"炼"，以表格填写的形式引导学生复习提炼本章知识点，搭建教学法知识框架。第五类思维导图聚焦"思"，需要学生在本章知识点的基础上，思考知识点之间的逻辑关系，形成知识结构网，并绘制思维导图，促进学生知识的网络化、系统化与可视化，加强记忆，促进知识的巩固内化。

◎怎样使用这本双语教材？

教材可供应用语言学、教育学及语言教育类本、硕师生教学或自主学习使用。在使用中，我们建议：

英文为主、中文为辅，多读英文，以提升学术英语能力。

知识为体，语言为用，专业知识与语言能力、思维能力互促互进，共同推进。

案例先行，研读拓展，围绕教材中的教学示例还原教学现场，研析教学法理论，在用中学。

充分利用教材活动与练习部分的内容，通过思考题研讨、教学设计案例分析、填表画图、阅读文献或论文等活动促进教学法理论的理解，整合专业知识，提升中英语言能力及批判思维能力。

勇于结合案例教学、混合式教学、项目教学、合作学习、翻转课堂等多元教学理念与现代教育技术，提升学习兴趣与学习效果。

◎这本双语教材的编写历程

这本双语教材的编写经历了近 5 年的时间，是所有编写者共同努力的成果。教材内容具体分工为匡昕老师策划并构建教材编写体例，编撰第 1 ~ 8 章、第 11 章及附录、参考文献的内容，项英老师编撰第 9 章，王辰老师编撰第 10 章。

在教材的编写过程中，北京体育大学教务处、北京体育大学出版社及北京体育大学人文学院等单位给予了大力的支持。北京体育大学出版社佟晖编审多次审校教材，付出了极大的心血，并提出了宝贵的修改建议，在此特致谢忱！

匡昕

2023 年 7 月 1 日

CONTENTS

目录

Chapter 1　The Grammar-Translation Method

第 1 章　语法翻译法

○ Contents

○ **Wordle**

1 Introduction

The Grammar-Translation Method can be regarded as the oldest teaching method in second language teaching. At one time it had been called the Classical Method or Traditional Method since it was first used in the teaching of the classical languages the Ancient Greek and Latin in the early 1500s. But after the language died out, the Grammar-Translation Method was still used to teach French, Italian, English and had a great influence on modern European language teaching. It is this method that dominated foreign language teaching from the 1840s to the 1940s, and in modified form it continues to be widely used in some parts of the world today.

In grammar-translation classes, students learn grammatical rules and expressions as well as enormous vocabulary lists, then apply those rules and words by translating sentences between the target language and the native language. Advanced students may be required to translate whole texts word-for-word. The method has two main goals: to enable students to read and translate literature written in the target language, and to further students' general intellectual development.

一、教学法概述

语法翻译法被认为是第二语言教学领域最古老的教学法。早在 16 世纪初期，它便被用于古希腊语和拉丁语的教学，因此语法翻译法也称"古典法"或"传统法"。当古代欧洲语言消亡后，语法翻译法仍被用于法语、意大利语、英语的教学，并对现代欧洲语言教学产生了巨大影响。19 世纪 40 年代到 20 世纪 40 年代的一百年间，语法翻译法在外语教学界占据主导地位，时至今日，一些地区仍在广泛使用该教学法的变体进行语言教学。

在语法翻译法教学的语言课程中，学生学习语法规则、语言表达方式以及大量的词汇，然后使用这些语法及词汇，进行母语和目的语之间的句子翻译练习。教师可以要求外语水平较高的学生逐字逐句地翻译整篇文章。使用这种方法主要有两个目的：一是使学生能够阅读并翻译用目的语撰写的文学作品；二是促进学生的智力发展。

2 Teaching Case[①]

The class using the Grammar-Translation Method is a high-intermediate level English class at a university in Columbia. There are 42 students in the class. Two-hour classes are conducted three times a week. The teaching procedures are as follows:

Now, the class is in the middle of reading a passage in their textbook. The passage is an excerpt entitled "The Boys' Ambition" from Mark Twain's *Life on the Mississippi*. Each student is called on to read a few lines from the passage. After the student has finished reading, he is asked to translate a few lines he has just read into Spanish. The teacher helps him with new vocabulary items. When the students have finished reading and translating the passage, the teacher asks them in Spanish if they have any questions. One girl raises her hand and says, "What is paddle wheel?" The teacher replies, "*Esuna rueda de paletas.*" Then she continues in Spanish to explain how it looked and worked on the steamboats which moved up and down the Mississippi River during Mark Twain's childhood. Another student says, "I don't understand 'gorgeous'." The teacher translates, "*primoroso.*"

After the students finish questions, the teacher asks them to write the answers to the comprehension questions which appear at the end of the excerpt. The questions are in English, and the students are instructed to write the answers to them in English as well. They do the first one together as an example. A student reads out loud, "When did Mark Twain live?" Another student replies, "Mark Twain lived from 1835 to 1910." "*Bueno.*" says the teacher, and the students begin working quietly by themselves.

In addition to questions that ask for information contained within the reading passage, the students answer two other types of questions. For the first type, they have to make inferences based on their understanding of the passage. For example, one question is: "Do you think the boy was ambitious? Why or why not?" The other type of question requires the students to relate the passage to their own experience. For example, one of the questions based on this excerpt asks them, "Have you ever thought about running away from home?"

After one-half hour, the teacher, speaking in Spanish, asks the students to stop and check their work. One by one, each student reads a question and then reads his or her response. If the answer is correct, the teacher calls on another student to read the next question. If the student is incorrect, the teacher selects a different student to supply the correct answer, or the teacher herself gives the right answer.

Announcing the next activity, the teacher asks the students to turn over the page in their text.

① LARSEN-FREEMAN D, ANDERSON M. Techniques and Principles in Language Teaching [M]. Oxford: Oxford University Press, 2011: 13–17.

There is a list of words there. The introduction to the exercise tells the students that these are words taken from the passage they have just read. The students see the words "ambition" "career" "wharf" "tranquil" "gorgeous" "loathe" "envy" and "humbly". They are told that some of these are review words and that others are new to them. The students are instructed to give the Spanish word for each of them. The class does this exercise together. If no one knows the Spanish equivalent, the teacher gives it. In Part 2 of this exercise, the students are given English words like "love" "noisy" "ugly" and "proudly" and are directed to find the opposites of these words in the passage (Figure1-1).

Exercise 2A

These words are taken from the passage you have just read. Some of them are review words and others are new. Give the Spanish translation for each of them. You may refer back to the reading passage.

ambition	gorgeous	career	loathe
wharf	envy	tranquil	humbly

Exercise 2B

These words all have antonyms in the reading passage. Find the antonym for each.

| love | ugly | noisy | proudly |

Figure 1-1 An Example of a Grammar-Translation Exercise

When they have finished this exercise, the teacher reminds them that English words that look like Spanish words are called cognates. "The English '-ty,'" she says, "for example, often corresponds to the Spanish endings '-dad' and '-tad'." She calls the students attention to the word "possibility" in the passage and tells them that this word is the same as the Spanish "*posibilidad*". The teacher asks the students to find other examples in the excerpt. Hands go up; A boy answers, "Obscurity." "*Bien*." says the teacher. When all of these cognates from the passage have been identified, the students are told to turn to the next exercise in the chapter and to answer the question, "What do these cognates mean?" There is a long list of English words (curiosity, opportunity, liberty, etc.) which the students translate into Spanish.

The next section of the chapter deals with grammar. The students follow in their books as the teacher reads a description of two-word (phrasal) verbs. This is a review for them as they have encountered phrasal verbs before. Nevertheless, there are some new two-word verbs in the passage the students haven't learned yet. These are listed following the description, and the students are asked to translate them into Spanish. Then they are given the rule for use of a direct object with two-word verbs:

If the two-word verb is separable, the direct object may come between the verb and its particle. However, separation is necessary when the direct object is a pronoun. If the verb is inseparable, then there is no separation of the verb and particle by the object. For example:

John put away his book.   or   John put his book away/John put it away.

but not

*John put away it. (because "put away" is a separable two-word verb)

The teacher went over the homework.

but not

*The teacher went the homework over. (because "go over" is an inseparable two-word verb)

After reading over the rule and the examples, the students are asked to tell which of the following two-word verbs, taken from the passage, are separable and which inseparable. They refer to the passage for clues. If they cannot tell from the passage, they use their dictionaries or ask their teacher.

turn up	wake up	get on	take in	run away
fade out	lay up	go away	break down	turn back

Finally, they are asked to put one of these phrasal verbs in the blank of each of the 10 sentences they are given. They do the first two together.

① Mark Twain decided to _____ because his parents wouldn't let him get a job on the river.

② The steamboatmen _____ and discharge freight at each port on the Mississippi River.

When the students finished this exercise, they read their answers aloud.

At the end of the chapter, there is a list of vocabulary items that appear in the passage. The list is divided into two parts: the first contains words, and the second, idioms like "to give someone the cold shoulder". Next to each is a Spanish word or phrase. For homework, the teacher asks the students to memorize the Spanish translation for the first 20 words and to write a sentence in English using each word.

In the two remaining lessons of the week, the students will be asked to:

① Write out the translation of the reading passage in Spanish.

② State the rule for the use of a direct object with two-word verbs, and apply it to other phrasal verbs.

③ Do the remaining exercises in the chapter that include practice with one set of irregular past participle forms. The students will be asked to memorize the present tense, past tense, and past participle forms of this irregular paradigm:

drink	drank	drunk
sing	sang	sung
swim	swam	swum
ring	rang	rung
begin	began	begun

④ Write a composition in the target language about an ambition they have.

⑤ Memorize the remaining vocabulary items and write sentences for each.

⑥ Take a quiz on the grammar and vocabulary of this chapter. They will be asked to translate a Spanish paragraph about steamboats into English.

二、教学示例

本示例中，语法翻译法被应用于哥伦比亚一所大学的高级英语课堂中。本班共 42 名学生，每周 3 节课，每节课时长为 2 小时。具体教学过程如下：

现在，全班学生正在阅读课本上的一个段落。这篇文章节选自马克·吐温《密西西比河上的生活》中的"逐梦的少年"。老师先让每个学生都朗读文章中的几行。一名学生读完后，老师便请这名学生把刚才读的几行翻译成西班牙语。不认识的词汇老师会给予帮助。当学生们读完并翻译了这篇文章后，老师用西班牙语问他们是否有疑问。一名女生举起手问道："什么是'paddle wheel'？"老师回答说："桨轮。"然后老师继续用西班牙语解释马克·吐温童年时见到的在密西西比河上往返的汽船的外观和工作原理。另一名学生说："我不明白'gorgeous'是什么意思。"老师翻译道："华丽的。"

在确认学生们没有其他问题之后，老师让他们完成选文后面的综合思考题，并写出自己的答案。这些思考题是用英文撰写的，学生们也需要用英文作答。作为示范，老师带着学生们一起完成了第一题。一名学生大声念道："马克·吐温生活在哪个时代？"另一名学生回答说："马克·吐温生活在 1835 年到 1910 年间。"老师对学生的答案予以肯定，说："很好。"示范后，学生们开始自己作答，不发出声音。

思考题除了就文章内容所包含的信息进行提问外，还有另外两种类型。一类是让学生根据自己对文章的理解进行推断或概括。例如，其中一个问题是："你认为这个男孩有志气吗？说明理由。"另一类问题是要求学生联系自己的实际经历进行回答。例如，基于这段节选的一个问题是："你曾想过离家出走吗？"

半小时后，老师用西班牙语让学生们停止作答，随后老师进行检查。学生们依次朗读问题并说出自己的答案。如果回答正确，老师就叫下一名学生回答问题。如果学生的答案不正确，老师会让另一名学生提供正确答案，或者老师自己给出正确答案。

老师宣布开始下一个课堂活动，并让学生把课本翻至相应的页数。在这一页上有一个词汇表。"练习说明"部分提示学生，这些单词选自他们刚才读过的文章。学生们可以看到"志向""事业""码头""宁静的""华丽的""厌恶""妒忌""谦逊地"等词语。这些词中一部分是之前学过的词，再次出现是为了进行复习，另一部分是本课出现的新词。学生们要把每个单词都翻译成西班牙语。这个练习要求全体学生一起完成。假如一个单词，没有任何一名学生知道这个词用西班牙语怎么翻译，老师就会给出答案。在本练习的第二部分，会给出英语单词，例如"爱""吵闹的""丑陋的""骄傲的"，要求学生从课文中找出这些单词的反义词（图 1–1）。

练习 2A

下列单词选自你们刚读过的文章。其中一部分是学过的单词，另一部分是新单词。请将所给单词翻译成西班牙语。你可以参考所阅读的文章进行翻译。

志向	华丽的	事业	厌恶
码头	嫉妒	宁静的	谦逊地

练习 2B

课文中出现了下列单词的反义词，请找出每个单词的反义词。

爱	丑陋的	吵闹的	骄傲的

图 1-1　语法翻译法练习示例

学生们完成这个练习后，老师告诉他们那些看起来像西班牙语单词的英语单词叫作同源词。然后老师一边引导一边解释道：“例如，以‘ty’结尾的英语单词通常与西班牙语中以‘dad’和‘tad’结尾的单词对应。”老师提醒学生们注意文章中“possibility”这个词，并告诉学生们这个词等同于西班牙语中的“posibilidad”。随后，老师让学生们在选文中寻找其他的例词。一名男生举起手说：“Obscurity。”老师肯定了他的答案，说：“可以。”学生们将文章中所有的同源词都找出来之后，老师让学生们进行本章下一个练习，并问学生：“这些同源词是什么意思？”学生需要将包含“好奇”“机会”“自由”等英语单词的词汇表翻译成西班牙语。

下一个教学环节是讲授语法。本课所学的语法内容是由动词和小品词构成的短语动词。学生翻开书，一边看语法释义，一边听老师朗读释义。释义下面是短语动词，这些词语有的学过，有的还没学，但均已出现在了新课文中。老师让学生们把这些短语动词翻译成西班牙语。随后，老师给学生们讲解了短语动词在搭配宾语时的语法规则及用法：

如果短语动词是可分离的，搭配宾语时宾语可以放在动词和小品词之间。但是，当宾语是代词时，短语动词必须分开，即必须放在动词和小品词之间。如果短语动词是不可分离的，那么搭配宾语时，动词与它后面的小品词不能分开。例如：

可以说：John put away his book. 或 John put his book away/John put it away.

但是不可以说：*John put away it.（因为短语动词 put away 是可分离的）

可以说：The teacher went over the homework.

但是不可以说：*The teacher went the homework over.（因为短语动词 go over 是不可分离的）

朗读完语法规则和例句之后，老师从文章中摘出一些短语动词，让学生们说出哪些是可分离的，哪些是不可分离的。学生们可以通过重读课文找到线索，进行回答。如果无法从文章中找到线索，他们可以查阅词典或者向老师求助。

这些短语动词是：

出现	醒来	上车	带走	离开
淡出	放置	走开	损坏	返回

最后，学生要用所给的 10 个短语动词进行填空练习。老师带领学生们一起完成前两个题目。

①马克·吐温决定_____，因为他的父母不让他在河上找工作。

②汽船工人_____并在密西西比河上的每个港口卸货。

学生们完成这个练习后，他们一起大声朗读句子。

在本章的最后，列出了一个词汇表，表中是选文中出现过的词汇。词汇表分为两部分：一部分是单词，另一部分是习语，比如"冷落某人"。所有词语旁边配有用西班牙语书写的单词或短语翻译。老师布置的作业就是让学生们记住前 20 个单词的西班牙语翻译，并用每一个单词造一个英语句子。

在本周后续的两次课中，学生将完成：

①将这篇文章翻译成西班牙语。

②阐述短语动词与宾语搭配时的规则用法，并将该语法规则用到其他短语动词中。

③完成本章的后续练习，包括进行不规则动词的过去分词形式的练习。学生需要记住下列不规则动词的一般现在时、一般过去时以及过去分词这三种形式。

drink	drank	drunk
sing	sang	sung
swim	swam	swum
ring	rang	rung
begin	began	begun

④用目的语（英语）写一篇关于自己志向的作文。

⑤记住词汇表中剩下的生词并进行造句。

⑥进行一个本章词汇和语法的小测验。这个测验要求学生将一段关于汽船的文章翻译成英语。

3 Teaching Principles and Teaching Procedures

3.1 Background and the Theoretical Basis of the Grammar-Translation Method

Today, English is the world's most widely studied foreign language, while more than 500 years ago it was Latin, for it was the dominant language of education, commerce, religion, and government in the Western world. In the sixteenth century, however, French, Italian, and English gained in importance as a result of political changes in Europe, and Latin gradually became displaced as a language of spoken and written communication. The study of Latin in the school curriculum took on a different function. The study of classical Latin and an analysis of its grammar and rhetoric became the model for foreign language study from the seventeenth to the nineteenth centuries.

As "modern" languages began to enter the curriculum of European schools in the eighteenth century, they were taught using the same basic procedures that were used for teaching Latin. Textbooks consisted of statements of abstract grammar rules, lists of vocabulary, and sentences for translation. Speaking a foreign language was not the goal, and oral practice was limited to students reading aloud the sentences they had translated. These sentences were constructed to illustrate the grammatical system of the language and consequently bore no relation to the language of real communication. By the nineteenth century, this approach based on the study of Latin had become the standard way of studying foreign languages in schools. And the approach to foreign language teaching became known as the Grammar-Translation Method.

The linguistic basis of Grammar-Translation Method is Historical Comparative Linguistics. The result of comparison between different languages indicated that the classical languages such as Greek and Latin were very much similar to the modern Indo-European languages. Some linguists believed that all languages originated from one language and were ruled by common grammar. In foreign language teaching, the target language was primarily interpreted as a system of rules to be observed in texts and sentences and to be related to the first language rules and meanings. The first language was maintained as the reference system in the acquisition of the target language.

The theory of language learning underlying the Grammar-Translation Method was Faculty Psychology founded by C. Wolff, a German philosopher in the 18th century. The Faculty Psychologists believed that the mind of human beings had various faculties which could be trained separately. Understanding and memorization of complicated grammatical rules of languages were regarded as important means of developing mentality. Latin grammar was then considered as the most logical and well-organized grammar.

3.2 Teaching Principles of the Grammar-Translation Method

The principal characteristics[①] of the Grammar-Translation Method were these:

① The goal of foreign language study is to learn a language in order to read its literature or in order to benefit from the mental discipline and intellectual development that result from foreign language study. Grammar Translation is a way of studying a language that approaches the language first through detailed analysis of its grammar rules, followed by application of this knowledge to the task of translating sentences and texts into and from the target language. It hence views language learning as consisting of little more than memorizing rules and facts in order to understand and manipulate the morphology and syntax of the foreign language.

② Reading and writing are the major focus; little or no systematic attention is paid to

---

① RICHARDS J C, RODGERS T S. 语言教学的流派 [M]. 2 版 . 北京：外语教学与研究出版社，2008：5-6.

speaking or listening.

③ Vocabulary selection is based solely on the reading texts used, and words are taught through bilingual word lists, dictionary study, and memorization. In a typical Grammar-Translation text, the grammar rules are presented and illustrated, a list of vocabulary items is presented with their translation equivalents, and translation exercises are prescribed.

④ The sentence is the basic unit of teaching and language practice. Much of the lesson is devoted to translating sentences into and from the target language, and it is this focus on the sentence that is a distinctive feature of the method. Earlier approaches to foreign language study used grammar as an aid to the study of texts in a foreign language. But this was thought to be too difficult for students in secondary schools, and the focus on the sentence was an attempt to make language learning easier.

⑤ Accuracy is emphasized. Translation is the main means of teaching, practice and evaluation in grammar-translation class. Students are expected to attain high standards in translation.

⑥ Grammar is taught deductively — that is, by presentation and study of grammar rules, which are then practiced through translation exercises. In most grammar-translation texts, a syllabus is followed for the sequencing of grammar points throughout a text, and there is an attempt to teach grammar in an organized and systematic way.

⑦ The student's native language is the medium of instruction. It is used to explain new items and to enable comparisons to be made between the foreign language and the student's native language.

3.3 Teaching Procedures of the Grammar-Translation Method

The main procedures for a typical lesson of the Grammar-Translation Method can be divided into three phases. The activities in each phase are described below:

Phase One

① The teacher reads and explains the new words and expressions in the first language. Students listen to the teacher, take notes and repeat after the teacher.

② The teacher teaches the new grammar with a deductive method. Students listen to the teacher and take notes.

Phase Two

③ Students are asked to read a few sentences out aloud and translate them into the first language. The teacher corrects the mistakes in students' pronunciation and translation.

④ The teacher analyses some difficult sentences and translates them into their native language first literally and then freely. Students listen to the teacher and take notes. They may be asked to do some analysis or translation.

⑤ Students read the studied part of the passage silently and ask the teacher questions they can not answer by themselves.

Phase Three

⑥ Students are asked to write the answers to the questions about the reading passage. The teacher checks students' work.

⑦ Students are asked to do other written work that is meant to reinforce the new grammar items and vocabulary.

三、教学原则与教学过程

1. 语法翻译法的产生背景与理论基础

英语是当今世界上最为普及的外语学习语种。而 500 多年前，西方世界的主要语言还是拉丁语。因为拉丁语是当时西方教育、商业、宗教和政府所使用的主流语言。然而，到了 16 世纪，由于欧洲的政治格局发生变化，法语、意大利语和英语的重要性逐渐提升，取代了拉丁语的地位，成了人们口头和书面交流的主要语言。拉丁语在学校课程中的作用也发生了功能性的变化。古典拉丁语的学习方法和拉丁语语法与修辞的分析方法，成为17 世纪至 19 世纪外语教学的范式。

在 18 世纪，"现代"语言开始进入欧洲学校的课程体系，它们的教学沿用了与拉丁语教学相同的基本教学过程。教科书包括抽象的语法规则释义、词汇列表和句子翻译练习。口语不是外语教学的目标，口语练习仅限于学生大声朗读他们翻译的句子。这些用于翻译练习的句子是为了说明语言的语法体系，因此，练习的句子与日常交流的语言表达严重脱节。到了 19 世纪，这种以学习拉丁语为基础的教学方法已经成为学校学习外语的标准范式。而这一外语教学法即人们熟知的语法翻译法。

语法翻译法的语言学基础是历史比较语言学。不同语言之间的比较结果表明，希腊语、拉丁语等古典语言与印欧语系的众多现代语言非常相似。一些语言学家认为，所有的语言都起源于一种语言，并受一种共同的语法支配。在外语教学中，目的语被认为是一套语法规则体系，在语篇和句子中都要遵守。另外，这套规则体系与第一语言的语法规则和意义相联系。在学习目的语的过程中，第一语言被认为是学习过程的参照系。

支撑语法翻译法的语言学习理论是 18 世纪的官能心理学，其创始人是德国哲学家沃尔夫。官能心理学认为，人的心智可以划分为多种不同的官能或能力，各种不同的官能可以分别施以专门训练，以促其发展。对语言中复杂的语法规则的理解和记忆被认为是发展思维的重要手段。拉丁语的语法，结构合理，逻辑严密，在当时看来，正是适合发展智力的语法。

2. 语法翻译法的教学原则

语法翻译法的主要特点是：

①外语学习的目的是通过学习掌握一门语言，阅读其目的语作品，或从中训练心智，

发展智力。语法翻译法是学习一门语言的方法，即先对目的语的语法规则进行详细分析，然后运用这些语法知识将目的语的句子、课文进行翻译。因此，语法翻译法认为语言学习就是通过记忆语法规则和语言事实，理解和掌握外语的词法与句法。

②阅读和写作是教学的重点，较少或没有系统地对听说进行关注。

③词汇的选择完全基于所选用的阅读文本，通过双语词表、词典和强记的方式教授词汇。在一篇使用语法翻译法的典型课文中，将列出语法规则及其释义，以及对译的词汇表，并设置翻译练习。

④句子是语言教学和运用的基本单位。课程的大部分内容都是把句子从母语翻译成目的语或从目的语翻译成母语。关注句子是语法翻译法的一个显著特征。早期的外语学习方法把语法作为学习外语课文的辅助手段。但人们认为这对中学生来说太难了，把注意力放在句子上会让语言学习更容易一些。

⑤强调准确性。翻译是语法翻译法课堂的主要教学手段、练习手段和测评方式。因此，语法翻译法课堂要求学生在翻译方面达到较高的水平。

⑥语法教学采用演绎法，即先学习语法规则，然后通过翻译练习来理解和运用这些规则。在大多数语法翻译法课文中，教学大纲是按照语法点在课文中的出现顺序进行编排的，语法项目尽可能做到系统有序。

⑦学生的母语是教学媒介语。学生的母语用来解释新的教学项目，并进行目的语和母语之间的比较。

3. 语法翻译法的教学过程

一节典型的语法翻译法课程的主要教学过程可分为三个阶段。每个阶段的教学活动如下：

阶段一

①老师朗读并用学生母语解释新课的生词和短语。学生边听老师讲课，边记笔记，随后跟着老师复述。

②老师用演绎法讲授新课语法。学生听讲并做笔记。

阶段二

③学生大声朗读句子，并把句子翻译成母语。老师纠正学生的发音和翻译练习中的错误。

④老师先就一些难句、长句进行分析讲解，然后从字面上翻译句子，之后再完善翻译，通达句义。学生听老师讲课，记笔记。老师也有可能要求学生进行一些句子分析或翻译练习。

⑤学生默读课文中所学的部分，遇到不懂的问题，向老师提问。

阶段三

⑥学生阅读文章后，根据问题，写出答案。老师检查学生的答案。

⑦学生完成其他书面作业，以便巩固新课的语法点和生词。

4 Conclusion

The Grammar-Translation Method is the first comprehensive teaching system in the history of second language teaching. It emphasizes the mastery of grammar rules, the development of students' intelligence, and the cultivation of reading ability and translation ability. This method has the longest history and strong vitality.

The Grammar-Translation Method has obvious disadvantages, mainly neglecting oral teaching and phonetic teaching, lacking the training of listening and speaking ability, relying too much on students' native language and translation, attaching the high priority of grammar, memorizing grammar rules mechanically without meanings, etc. These shortcomings resulted in the type of Grammar-Translation classes remembered with distaste by thousands of school learners, for whom foreign language learning meant a tedious experience of memorizing endless lists of unusable grammar rules and vocabulary and attempting to produce perfect translations of stilted or literary prose. Although the Grammar-Translation Method often creates frustration for students, it makes few demands on teachers. Consequently, it may be true to say that the Grammar-Translation Method is widely practiced, but it has no high appreciation and advocates.

四、小结

语法翻译法是第二语言教学法历史上第一个完整的教学法体系。它强调对语法规则的掌握，注重学生智力的发展，能较好地培养阅读能力和翻译能力。该教学法历史最久，有很强的生命力。

语法翻译法也存在明显的局限性，主要是忽视口语教学和语音教学，缺乏听说能力的训练，过分依赖母语和翻译手段，过分重视语法，死记硬背语法规则，不注重语义等。这些不足之处导致了成千上万的学生对语法翻译法的课堂留有的仅仅是厌恶的记忆，对他们来说，外语学习意味着一种枯燥的经历，既要记住无数枯燥的语法规则和词汇，又要对高深艰涩的文学文献进行完美的翻译。语法翻译法虽然经常带给学生们挫折感，但对教师的要求却相对较低。因此，尽管语法翻译法一直被广泛使用，却没能获得人们的高度赞誉和大力提倡。

○ Activities and Exercises

● Understanding and Thinking

1. Based on the following materials or your own English learning experiences, please state the teaching principles and main characteristics of the Grammar-Translation Method.

Scott Thornbury describes: "When I was a student of French at secondary school in New Zealand in the 1960s, the curriculum was based on a textbook called A New French Course. *The story-line followed the (fairly uneventful) life of the Ravel family, dramatized as short dialogues, but the syllabus was organized around a graded list of grammatical structures, one or two per unit. The English equivalents of these structures were provided, along with a list of thematically-related words. Exercises involving translating sentences from French into English, and then the reverse, provided the bulk of the practice."*

2. Guy Cook points out: "It may be particularly well suited to those teachers who are themselves not wholly proficient in the language they are teaching and/or too overworked to undertake extensive preparation." This is one of the Grammar-Translation's merits and may be one of the main reasons for its enduring appeal.

To be a new language teacher, if you were asked to teach a second language, would you give priority to the Grammar-Translation Method? Please talk about how you feel when you use the Grammar-Translation Method in language teaching.

3. What role do you think grammar and translation plays in language teaching and learning? Please give examples of your views.

● Teaching Design

1. Please study the characteristics of the Grammar-Translation Method intensively, choose a text, design the teaching details, and then make a teaching demonstration in group.

Prator and Murcia in Setiyadi list the major characteristics of Grammar-Translation Method, as follows:

① *Classes are taught in the mother tongue, with little active use of the target language;*

② *Much vocabulary is taught in the form of lists of isolated words;*

③ *Long elaborate explanations of the intricacies of grammar are given;*

④ *Grammar provides the rules for putting words together, and instruction often focuses on the form and inflection of words;*

⑤ Reading of difficult classical texts began early;

⑥ Little attention is paid to the content of texts, which are treated as exercises in grammatical analysis;

⑦ Often the only drills are exercises in translating disconnected sentences from the target language into the mother tongue;

⑧ Little or no attention is given to pronunciation;

⑨ The focus is on accuracy, and not fluency.

2. Please read the following teaching plan carefully, point out the inappropriate places according to the theory and principles of the Grammar-Translation Method, then revise and improve it.

(1) Students Review

Students should write the words by heart and recite the passage.

(2) Teach New Words

The teacher lists the new words, phonetic symbols and explanations of the mother tongue on the blackboard, and explains them word by word. Then read the new words "ten," "time," "smile," and "flower." For example, the teacher reads "ten," the students say "十," the teacher says: "ten students," students translate: "十个学生," and so on.

(3) Teaching Grammar

Explain grammatical meaning and relevant rules, such as: "sb./sth.+will+do+sth." in mother tongue, with the student explaining the grammatical meaning: "will" said things will happen in the future. Then ask the students to make sentences in their mother tongue and translate them. If the answers are wrong, the teacher should correct them in time.

(4) Explain the Text

The teacher reads the text sentence by sentence, lists the relevant vocabulary on the blackboard, and the students translate the text according to the grammar rules. Students are then asked to analyse the grammar and translate it into their mother tongue.

(5) Consolidation of the New Lesson

Students and teachers read the text sentence by sentence. The teacher asks questions according to the text and the students answer according to the text.

(6) Homework to Set

Write the new words by heart and recite the text. Next class, write the new words and sentences by dictation.

● **Further Reading**

Grammar-Translation Method[①]

1. Preamble

The Grammar-Translation Method is one of the key methods applied to the teaching of foreign languages. It is a derivation of the classical (sometimes called traditional) method of teaching Greek and Latin. According to this method, students learn grammatical rules and then apply those rules to translating sentences between the target language and their native language. Advanced students may be required to translate whole texts word-for-word.

2. History and Philosophy

While studying the history of teaching methods, we come to know that the Grammar-Translation Method originated from the practice of teaching Latin. In the early 1500s, Latin was the most widely-studied foreign language due to its prominence in government, academia, and business. However, during the course of the century, the use of Latin dwindled, and it was gradually replaced by English, French, and Italian.

After the decline of Latin, the purpose of learning it in schools changed. Whereas previously students had learned Latin for the purpose of communication, it came to be learned as a pure academic subject.

Throughout Europe in the past two centuries, the education system was formed primarily around a concept called faculty psychology. This theory dictated that the body and mind were separate and the mind consisted of three parts: the will, emotion, and intellect. It was believed that the intellect could be sharpened enough to eventually control the will and emotions. The way to do this was through learning the classical literature of the Greeks and Romans, as well as mathematics. Additionally, an adult with such an education was considered mentally prepared for the world and its challenges.

At first, it was believed that teaching modern languages was not useful for the development of mental discipline and thus they were left out of the curriculum. When modern languages did begin to appear in school curriculums in the 19th century, teachers taught them with the same Grammar-Translation Method as was used for classical Latin and Greek and subsequently textbooks were prepared for the modern language classroom.

3. Goals and Principles

As for the goals, the Grammar-Translation Method stresses upon two main objectives.

---

① ABDULLAH S S. A Contrastive Study of the Grammar Translation and the Direct Methods of Teaching [C]// 3rd International Conference on Business, Economics, Management and Behavioral Sciences (ICBEMBS' 2013) January 26-27, 2013 Hong Kong (China). 124–127.

One is to develop students' reading ability to a level where they can read literature in the target language. The other is to develop students' general mental discipline.

As cited in Richards and Rodgers:

When once the Latin tongue had ceased to be a normal vehicle for communication, and was replaced as such by the vernacular languages, then it most speedily became a "mental gymnastic," the supremely "dead" language, a disciplined and systematic study of which was held to be indispensable as a basis for all forms of higher education.

As far as the principals of this method are concerned, they can be listed as follows:

The main principles on which the Grammar-Translation Method is based are the following:

① Translation interprets the words and phrases of the foreign languages in the best possible manner.

② The phraseology and the idioms of the target language can best be assimilated in the process of interpretation.

③ The structures of the foreign languages are best learned when compared and constrasted with those of first languages.

4. Method

Grammar-Translation classes are usually conducted in the students' native language. Grammar rules are learned deductively; students learn grammar rules by rote, and then practice the rules by doing grammar drills and translating sentences to and from the target language. More attention is paid to the form of the sentences being translated than to their content. When students reach more advanced levels of achievement, they may translate entire texts from the target language. Tests often consist of the translation of classical texts.

There is not usually any listening or speaking practice, and very little attention is placed on pronunciation or any communicative aspects of the language. The skill exercised is reading, and then only in the context of translation.

5. Scope of the Grammar-Translation Method

The method by definition has a very limited scope. Because speaking or any kind of spontaneous creative output was missing from the curriculum, students would often fail at speaking or even letter writing in the target language. A noteworthy quote describing the effect of this method comes from Bahlsen, who was a student of Plötz, a major proponent of this method in the 19th century. In commenting about writing letters or speaking, he said he would be overcome with "a veritable forest of paragraphs, and an impenetrable thicket of grammatical rules."

According to Richards and Rodgers, the Grammar-Translation Method has been rejected as a legitimate language teaching method by modern scholars:

Though it may be true to say that the Grammar-Translation Method is still widely practiced, it has no advocates. It is a method for which there is no theory. There is no literature that offers a rationale or justification for it or that attempts to relate it to issues in linguistics, psychology, or educational theory.

6. Chief Features of Grammar-Translation Method

In the following part, the main features of the Grammar-Translation Method will be briefly introduced.

(1) Roles of Teacher and Students in the Grammar-Translation Method

Teacher has authority: students follow instructions to learn what teacher knows.

Teaching/Learning Process: Students learn by translating from one language to the other, often translating reading passages in the target language to the native language. Grammar is usually learned deductively on the basis of grammar rules and examples. Students memorize the rules, then apply them to other examples. They learn paradigms such as verb conjugations, and they learn the native language equivalents of vocabulary words.

(2) Interaction: Student-Teacher & Student-Student

Most interaction is teacher-to-student; student-initiated interaction and student-student interaction is minimal.

(3) Aspects of Language

The approach emphasizes vocabulary and grammar; reading, writing are primary skills; pronunciation and other speaking/listening skills are not emphasized.

(4) Role of Students' Native Language

Native language is used freely in class as it provides key to meanings in the target language.

(5) Means for Evaluation

Tests require translation from native to target and target to native language, applying grammar rules, answering questions about foreign culture.

(6) Response to Students' Errors

Heavy emphasis is placed on correct answers; teacher supplies correct answers when students cannot.

7. Merits of the Grammar-Translation Method

Merits of this method can be listed as follows.

(1) The Target Language Is Quickly Explained

Translation is the easiest way of explaining meanings or words and phrases from one language into another. Any other method of explaining vocabulary items in the second language is found time-consuming. A lot of time is wasted if the meanings of lexical items are explained through definitions and illustrations in the second language. Further, learners acquire some short of accuracy in understanding synonyms in the source language and the target language.

(2) Teacher and Students Are Easy to Communicate/It Does Not Need Native Language

Teacher's labor is saved. Since the textbooks are taught through the medium of the mother tongue, the teacher may ask comprehension questions on the text taught in the mother tongue. Pupils will not have much difficulty in responding to questions on the mother tongue. So, the teacher can easily assess whether the students have learned what he has taught them. Communication between the teacher and the learners does not cause linguistic problems. Even teachers who are not fluent in English can teach English through this method. That is perhaps the reason why this method has been practiced so widely and has survived so long.

(3) The Students Can Understand Easily Because of Grammatical Lessons

ESL students taught successfully under the Grammar-Translation Method will have the ability to translate even difficult texts from their native language into English. They possess a thorough knowledge of English grammar, including verb tenses. These students will be familiar with several classical pieces of English literature, which are used for grammatical analysis and exercises.

This method requires few specialized skills on the part of teachers. Grammar rules and translation tests are easy to construct and can be objectively scored. Many standardized tests of foreign languages still do not attempt to test communicative abilities, so students have little motivation to go beyond grammar analogies, translations and other written exercises.

8. Demerits of the Grammar-Translation Method

Every method and every technique has its own advantages and disadvantages. The advantages of the Grammar-Translation Method have been explained on the passage above. Here are some of its disadvantages:

(1) No Scope for Effective Communication and Very Tedious for Learners

Direct translation is widely regarded as an inefficient way of becoming fluent in any language. For example, translating a sentence word-for-word from Spanish to English might not result in a sentence with the same meaning because so little attention is paid in class to listening and speaking. Students with years of English lessons through this method are often unable to hold even a basic conversation in English because classes with this method are usually taught in a lecture style, with the teacher mostly speaking the students' native language rather than English, and the class can be dull and cause students to lose interest.

(2) Ineffective Method

It is the teaching method that studies a foreign language in order to read its literature, focusing on the analysis of its grammar rules, and to translate sentences and texts into and from the target language. In the Grammar-Translation Method the teaching of the second language starts with the teaching of reading. Little attention is paid to the content of texts, which are treated as exercises in grammatical analysis. Thus, the learning process is reversed.

(3) More Importance on Grammar Rules than on Meaning

Exact translation is not possible. Translation is, indeed, a difficult task and exact translation from one language to another is not always possible. A language is the result of various customs, traditions, and modes of behavior of a speech community and these traditions differ from community to community. There are several lexical items in one language, which have no synonyms/equivalents in another language. For instance, the meaning of the English word "table" does not fit in such expression as the "table of contents" "table of figures" "multiplication table" "timetable" and "table the resolution" etc. English prepositions are also difficult to translate. Consider sentences such as "We see with our eyes" "Bombay is far from Delhi" "He died of cholera" "He succeeded through hard work". In these sentences "with" "from" "of" "through" can be translated into the Hindi preposition "*se*" and vice versa. Each language has its own structure, idiom and usage, which do not have their exact counterparts in another language. Thus, translation should be considered an index of one's proficiency in a language.

(4) Slow Learning Rate and Making Learners Think in L1

It does not give pattern practice. A person can learn a language only when he internalizes its patterns to the extent that they form his habit. But the Grammar-Translation Method does not provide any such practice to the learners of a language. It rather attempts to teach a language through rules and not by use. Researchers in linguistics have proved that it is impossible to speak any language, whether native or foreign, exactly according to the rules. Language learning means acquiring certain skills, which can be learned through practice and not by just memorizing rules. People who have learned a foreign or second language through this method find it difficult to give up the habit of first thinking in their mother tongue and then translating their ideas into the second language. Therefore, their proficiency in the second language is not close to that of the first language. The method, therefore, suffers from certain weaknesses for which there is no remedy.

9. Conclusion

The Grammar-Translation Method was originally developed for the study of "dead" languages and to facilitate access to those languages' classical literature. That's the way it should stay. English is certainly not a dead or dying language, so any teacher that takes "an approach for dead language study" into an English language classroom should perhaps think about taking up Math or Science instead. Rules, universals and memorized principles apply to those disciplines — pedagogy and communicative principles do not.

● **Knowledge Table**

Table 1-1　Summary of Characteristics of the Grammar-Translation Method

Key Points	The Grammar-Translation Method
Period	
Representatives	
Background	
Theory of Language	
Theory of Language Learning	
Objectives	
The Syllabus	
Types of Learning and Teaching Activities	
Teacher's Roles	
Learner's Roles	
The Role of Students' Native Language and Target Language	
The Role of Instructional Materials and Textbook	
Others	
Summary	

● **Mind Map**

Chapter 2　The Direct Method

第 2 章　直接法

⬤ Contents

- ◆ Teaching Case of the Direct Method
- ◆ Teaching Cases of Gouin's "Series" and of Berlitz's Method
- ◆ The Reform Movement and the Background of the Direct Method
- ◆ Teaching Principles of the Direct Method
- ◆ Techniques of the Direct Method
- ◆ Comments on and Significance of the Direct Method
- ◆ Activities and Exercises

- ◆ 直接法教学示例
- ◆ 古安"系列法"与贝立子教学法的教学示例
- ◆ 改革运动与直接法的产生背景
- ◆ 直接法的教学原则
- ◆ 直接法的教学技巧
- ◆ 直接法的重要意义及其评价
- ◆ 活动与练习

Wordle

1 Introduction

The Direct Method is a method of teaching language directly establishing a direct or immediate association between learners' experience and expression, between the target language word, phrase or idiom and its meaning through demonstration, dramatization without the use of learners' native language. It was established in Germany and France around the 19th century. The Reform Movement in language teaching at that time is regarded as the forerunner of Direct Method. The German foreign language educator Wilhelm Viëtor (1850–1918) is regarded as the main founder of the Reform Movement and the Direct Method. Other important specialists who had great influence on the production of Direct Method are F. Gouin (1831–1896), Berlitz (1852–1921), L. Sauveur (1826–1970) and Henry Sweet (1845–1912).

The Direct Method was an answer to the dissatisfaction with the older Grammar-Translation Method, which teaches students grammar and vocabulary through direct translations and thus focuses on the written language. It is designed to take the learner into the domain of the target language in the most natural manner and intends for students to learn how to communicate in the target language. This method is based on the assumption that the learner should experience the new language in the same way as he/she experienced his/her mother tongue. There are some teaching essentials, such as no translation; concepts are taught by means of objects or by natural contexts; oral training helps in reading and writing; grammar is taught indirectly, etc.

一、教学法概述

直接法是一种不依赖学习者母语，而通过演示、表演等方式在学习者的经验与表达，目的语词汇、短语或习语与其所表达的意义之间直接建立联系的教学方法。直接法产生于19世纪的德国和法国。当时的教学改革运动被认为是直接法的先导。德国外语教育学家威廉·维耶托（1850–1918）被认为是教学改革运动的领导者以及直接法的主要奠基人。对直接法的产生有重要影响的人物还包括古安（1831–1896）、贝力子（1852–1921）、索维尔（1826–1970）及亨利·斯威特（1845–1912）等。

直接法是对当时现存的语法翻译法的一种逆反。语法翻译法通过直接翻译来教授学生语法和词汇，侧重书面语言；而直接法旨在以最自然的方式将学习者带入目的语的世界，并帮助学生学习如何用目的语进行交际。这种方法基于这样一个假设：学习者应该以他（她）体验母语的方式来体验新的语言。因此，直接法的教学要素包括：不翻译；概念是通过实物或自然语境传授的；口语训练有助于阅读和写作；间接地教授语法等等。

2 Teaching Cases

2.1 Case of the Direct Method①

The Direct Method is used by an English teacher in a lower-level secondary school class in Italy. The class has 30 students who attend English class for one hour, three times a week. The class of this teaching case is at the end of its first year of English language instruction.

The teacher has placed a big map of the U.S. in front of the classroom. He asks the students to open their books to a certain page number. The lesson is entitled "Looking at a Map." As the students are called on one by one, they read a sentence from the reading passage at the beginning of the lesson. The teacher points to the part of the map the sentence describes after each has read a sentence. The passage begins:

> We are looking at a map of the United States of America. Canada is the country to the north of the United States, and Mexico is the country to the south of the United States. Between Canada and the United States are the Great Lakes. Between Mexico and the United States is the Rio Grande River. On the East Coast is the Atlantic Ocean, and on the West Coast is the Pacific Ocean. In the east is a mountain range called the Appalachian Mountains. In the west are the Rocky Mountains.

After the students finish reading the passage, they are asked if they have any questions. A

① LARSEN-FREEMAN D, ANDERSON M. Techniques and Principles in Language Teaching [M]. Oxford: Oxford University Press, 2011: 25–28.

student asks what a mountain range is. The teacher turns to the whiteboard and draws a series of inverted cones to illustrate a mountain range. The student nods and says, "I understand." Another student asks what "between" means. The teacher replies, "You are sitting between Maria Pia and Giovanni. Paolo is sitting between Gabriella and Cettina. Now do you understand the meaning of 'between'?" The student answers, "Yes, I understand."

After all of the questions have been answered, the teacher asks some of his own, "Class, are we looking at a map of Italy?"

The class replies in chorus, "No!"

The teacher reminds the class to answer in a full sentence.

"No, we aren't looking at a map of Italy," they respond.

The teacher asks, "Are we looking at a map of the United States?"

"Yes. We are looking at a map of the United States."

"Is Canada the country to the south of the United States?"

"No. Canada isn't the country south of the United States."

"Are the Great Lakes in the North of the United States?"

"Yes. The Great Lakes are in the North."

"Is the Rio Grande a river or a lake?"

"The Rio Grande is a river."

"It's a river. Where is it?"

"It's between Mexico and the United States."

"What color is the Rio Grande on the map?"

"It's blue."

The teacher points to a mountain range in the west. "What mountains are they?"

"They are the Rocky Mountains."

The question and answer session continues for a few more minutes. Finally, the teacher invites the students to ask questions. Hands go up, and the teacher calls on students to pose questions one at a time, to which the class replies. After several questions have been posed, one girl asks, "Where are the Appalachian Mountains?" Before the class has a chance to respond, the teacher works with the student on the pronunciation of "Appalachian." Then he includes the rest of the class in this practice as well, expecting that they will have the same problem with this long word. After insuring that the students' pronunciation is correct, the teacher allows the class to answer the question.

Later another student asks, "What is the ocean in the West Coast?" The teacher again interrupts before the class has a chance to reply, saying, "What is the ocean in the West Coast? … or on the West Coast?" The student hesitates, then says, "On the West Coast."

"Correct," says the teacher. "Now, repeat your question."

"What is the ocean on the West Coast?"

The class replies in chorus, "The ocean on the West Coast is the Pacific."

After the students have asked about 10 questions, the teacher begins asking questions and making statements again. This time, however, the questions and statements are about the students in the classroom, and contain one of the prepositions "on," "at," "to," "in," or "between," such as, "Antonella, is your book on your desk?" "Antonio, who is sitting between Luisa and Teresa?" "Emanuela, point to the clock." The students then make up their own questions and statements and direct them to other students.

The teacher next instructs the students to turn to an exercise in the lesson which asks them to fill in the blanks. They read a sentence out loud and supply the missing word as they are reading, for example:

The Atlantic Ocean is _____ the East Coast.

The Rio Grande is _____ Mexico and the United States.

Edoardo is looking _____ the map.

Finally, the teacher asks the students to take out their notebooks, and he gives them a dictation. The passage he dictates is one paragraph long and is about the geography of the United States.

During the remaining two classes of the week, the class will:

① Review the features of United States geography.

② Following the teacher's directions, label blank maps with these geographical features. After this, the students will give directions to the teacher, who will complete a map on the board.

③ Practice the pronunciation of "river," paying particular attention to the /ɪ/ in the first syllable (and contrasting it with /i:/) and to the pronunciation of /r/.

④ Write a paragraph about the major geographical features of the United States.

⑤ Discuss the proverb "Time is money". Students will talk about this in order to understand the fact that Americans value punctuality. They will compare this attitude with their own view of time.

2.2 Case of Gouin's "Series"

Frenchman F. Gouin (1831–1896) developed an approach to teaching a foreign language based on his observations of children's use of language. He believed that language learning was facilitated through using language to accomplish events consisting of a sequence of related actions. His method used situations and themes as ways of organizing and presenting oral language — the famous Gouin "series," which includes sequences of sentences related to such activities as chopping wood and opening the door. Here is one of the series, called "The girl chops some wood."

The Girl Chops Some Wood

The girl goes and seeks a piece of wood.	goes and seeks
She takes a hatchet.	takes
She draws near to the block.	draws near
She places the wood on this block.	places
She raises the hatchet.	raises
She brings down the hatchet.	brings down
The blade strikes against the wood.	strikes against
The blade penetrates the wood.	penetrates
The blade cleaves the wood.	cleaves
The pieces fall right and left.	fall
The girl picks up one of the pieces,	picks up
places it upon the block,	places
raises her hatchet,	raises
brings down her hatchet,	brings down
and chops the piece of wood.	chops
She chops another piece and then another.	chops
She chops up all the wood.	chops up
She puts down her hatchet,	puts down
gathers up the pieces into her,	gathers up
takes one or two logs and some,	takes
and carries them to the stove.	carries

2.3 Case of Berlitz's Method

This is lesson 1 and lesson 2 in Volume 1 of *Method for Teaching Modern Language* written by Berlitz.

We call the teacher's attention to our large colored wall-pictures, which we have had designed by a renowned artist. These pictures represent everything referring to the topics of daily conversation. They will be a great help in making even the elementary lessons interesting and effective, and give the teacher a better opportunity to illustrate different objects, colors, dimensions, places, positions, etc.

Lesson 1

the pencil	the pen	the table	the book	the box
the door	the paper	the chair	the window	

What is this? The pencil, the book, etc.

Is this the pencil? Yes, it is. / No, it is not.

Clothing: the coat, the hat, the glove, the boot, the dress, the necktie, the cuff, the collar, the handkerchief, the pocket.

Lesson 2

Colors: red, blue, yellow, green, black, white, gray, brown.

The pencil is green. The book is blue. The ruler is yellow. The necktie is red. The boot is black. The coat is gray. The hat is brown.

Is the pencil green? Yes, it is. Is the table green? No, it is not.

What color is the table? It is brown. What color is the pencil? It is green.

What color is the book? The book is blue and yellow. What color is the box? The box is blue and white.

The black pencil is long. The red pencil is not long; it is short.

Which pencil is long? What color is the long pencil? Which pencil is short? Which pencil is black? etc. Is this pencil long or short?

The brown book is wide (broad). The black book is not wide; it is narrow.

Which book is wide? Which book is narrow? What color is the wide book? What color is the narrow book? Is the window wide or narrow?

The red book is long and wide; it is large. The gray book is short and narrow; it is small.

Which book is large? Which book is small? Is the gray book large or small? Is the small book black or gray? Is the red book large? Is the large book red? Which book is small? etc.

二、教学示例

1. 直接法教学示例

本示例中，直接法被一名意大利教师应用于一个中学课堂中。该班级共有 30 名学生，学生英语水平为初级，每周 3 次英语课，每课时长 1 小时。这个教学示例为中学英语教学第一学期期末所上的课程。

上课前，老师在教室前挂了一张美国地图。课上，老师让学生把书翻到"看地图"的那一课，并让学生大声朗读课文，学生每读完一句话，老师就指向地图上相应的地方。课文原文如下：

> 我们正在观看美利坚合众国的地图。加拿大在美国北边，墨西哥在美国南边。加拿大和美国之间是五大湖区。在墨西哥和美国之间是里奥格兰德河。美国的东海岸是大西洋，西海岸是太平洋。东边是一座山脉，叫作阿巴拉契亚山脉。西边是落基山脉。

学生读完课文后，老师问他们有没有什么问题。一名学生询问："mountain range"的意思。于是老师在白板上画了一些连绵的山，向他说明山脉的意思。学生点点头，说："我明白了。"另一名学生问"between"是什么意思。老师解释道："你坐在玛丽亚·皮亚和乔瓦尼之间。保罗坐在加布里埃拉和塞蒂娜之间。现在你明白'between'的意思了吗？"学生回答："我明白了。"

学生问完之后，老师又向学生提出了一系列问题："同学们，我们看的是意大利地图吗？"

全班同学齐声回答："不是！"

老师提醒全班学生用完整的句子回答。

"不是，我们看的不是意大利地图。"他们回答说。

老师问："我们在看美国地图吗？"

"是的。我们正在看美国地图。"

"加拿大在美国南边吗？"

"不，加拿大不在美国南边。"

"大湖区在美国北边吗？"

"是的，大湖区在北边。"

"里奥格兰德是河流还是湖泊？"

"里奥格兰德是一条河。"

"里奥格兰德是一条河。它在哪里？"

"它在墨西哥和美国之间。"

"地图上的里奥格兰德河是什么颜色的？""是蓝色的。"

老师指向西边的山脉，问："它们是什么山？"

"它们是落基山脉。"

问答环节持续了几分钟后，老师让学生们自行提问。学生们举起手来，老师逐个请学生提问，然后全班回答。问过几个问题后，有个女生问道："阿巴拉契亚山脉在哪里？"老师示意大家先不要回答，转而对这名学生的"阿巴拉契亚"这个单词的发音进行了纠正。然后老师让全班学生一起练习这个词的发音，因为老师认为有可能其他学生也会在这个长单词的发音上存在问题。在确保全班学生都掌握了正确发音后，老师才示意学生们继续回答这个问题。

之后，另一名学生问道："（美国）西海岸的海洋是什么？"老师又打断了全班学生的回答，示意大家安静，然后问那名学生："西海岸的海洋是什么？用 in the west coast 还是 on the west coast？"那位学生犹豫片刻，说道："On the west coast."

"对了！"老师肯定道："现在，请你再重复一遍你的问题。"

那位学生又重复了一遍问题："（美国）西海岸的海洋是什么？"

然后全体学生一起回答："（美国）西海岸的海洋是太平洋。"

大概 10 名学生提问完之后，老师开始进行提问和表达练习。在这次练习中，问题都是关于学生个人的，而且问题中包含"in""on""at""to""between"等介词。例如："安东妮拉，你的书在桌子上吗？""安东尼奥，谁坐在路易莎和特雷莎之间？""伊曼纽拉，请指钟。"然后学生们编出自己的问题和表达，并请其他同学回答。

之后，老师指导学生完成课后的介词填空练习。全班学生大声朗读句子，并在朗读时补全答案。例如：

大西洋_____东海岸。

格兰德河_____墨西哥和美国。

爱德华多正在看_____地图。

最后，老师让全班学生拿出笔记本进行听写。老师听写的是关于美国地理的一小段话。

在本周后续的两次课中，课程内容安排如下：

①复习美国地理的特点。

②学生们根据老师的指示在空白地图上标注地理特征。之后，老师根据学生们的指示，在黑板上画出地图。

③练习 river 的发音，要特别注意第一个音节中 /ɪ/ 的发音（并与 /i:/ 做对比）和 /r/ 的发音。

④写一篇有关美国主要地理特征的文章。

⑤讨论谚语"时间就是金钱"。讨论这句谚语是为了让学生们了解这句谚语包含的"美国人重视准时"这一价值观，并且让学生将这一观点与他们自己的时间观念进行比较。

2. 古安"系列法"教学示例

法国人古安（1831—1896）通过对儿童使用语言的观察，提出了一种教授外语的方法。他认为，语言学习是通过使用语言来完成一项任务，而这项任务将由一系列相关动作组成。因此，他提出了著名的古安"系列法"。该方法利用如砍柴、开门等活动情景和主题组成一系列相关的句子，呈现并教授口语。下面便是"系列法"中的"系列"之一："女孩劈木头"。

女孩劈木头	
女孩去找木头。	去找
她拿起一把斧子。	拿
她走近一块砧板。	走近
她把木头放在砧板上。	放
她举起斧子。	举起
她落下斧子。	落下
斧刃触到木头。	触到
斧刃劈进木头。	劈进
斧刃劈开木头。	劈开
劈开的木头倒向两边。	倒
女孩拾起一块劈开的木头，	拾起
把它放在砧板上，	放
举起斧子，	举起
落下斧子，	落下
劈这块木头。	劈

<table>
<tr><td colspan="2" align="center">女孩劈木头</td></tr>
<tr><td>她劈另一块木头，接着又劈另一块。</td><td>劈</td></tr>
<tr><td>她劈碎所有的木头。</td><td>劈碎</td></tr>
<tr><td>她放下斧子，</td><td>放下</td></tr>
<tr><td>把碎木块拾拢到围裙里，</td><td>拾拢</td></tr>
<tr><td>手拿一两块大劈柴和一些碎木片，</td><td>拿</td></tr>
<tr><td>把它们送到炉边。</td><td>送</td></tr>
</table>

3. 贝力子学校语言教学法教学示例

以下是贝力子编写的《现代语言教学方法》第一册中第 1、2 课的课文。

请老师们注意挂在墙上的彩色挂图，挂图是由一位著名艺术家设计的。这些图片涵盖了日常对话的主题。它们将有助于使基础课程变得既有趣又有效，还能帮助教师更好地说明不同的物体、颜色、尺寸、地点、方位等。

第 1 课
铅笔　钢笔　桌子　书　盒子　门　纸　椅子　窗户

这是什么？这是铅笔、书等。

这是铅笔吗？是的，是铅笔。不，不是铅笔。

服饰：外套、帽子、手套、靴子、连衣裙、领带、袖口、领子、手帕、口袋。

第 2 课
颜色：红色、蓝色、黄色、绿色、黑色、白色、灰色、棕色。

铅笔是绿色的。书是蓝色的。尺子是黄色的。领带是红色的。靴子是黑色的。外套是灰色的。帽子是棕色的。

铅笔是绿色的吗？是的。桌子是绿色的吗？不，不是。

桌子是什么颜色的？它是棕色的。铅笔是什么颜色的？它是绿色的。

这本书是什么颜色的？这本书是蓝黄相间的。这个盒子是什么颜色的？这个盒子是蓝白相间的。

黑色的铅笔很长。红色的铅笔不长，它很短。

哪支铅笔长？那支长铅笔是什么颜色的？哪支铅笔短？哪支铅笔是黑色的？等等。这支铅笔是长还是短？

这本棕色的书很宽。黑色的书不宽，很窄。

哪本书宽？哪本书窄？这本较宽的书是什么颜色的？这本较窄的书是什么颜色的？窗户宽还是窄？

红皮书又长又宽，很大。灰皮的书又短又窄，很小。

哪本书大？哪本书小？这本灰皮书是大还是小？这本小书是黑色的还是灰色的？这本红皮书大吗？这本大书是红色的吗？哪本书小？等等。

3 Teaching Principles and Teaching Procedures

3.1 Background of the Direct Method

Toward the mid-nineteenth century, increased opportunities for communication among Europeans created a demand for oral proficiency in foreign languages. In Germany, England, France, and other parts of Europe, new approaches to language teaching were developed by individual language teaching specialists such as C. Marcel, T. Prendergast, and F. Gouin, each with a specific method for reforming the teaching of modern languages. The work of these individual language specialists reflects the needs and changing climate of the times. Educators also recognized the need for speaking proficiency rather than reading comprehension, grammar, or literary appreciation as the goal for foreign language programs. There was an interest in how children learn languages, which prompted attempts to develop teaching principles from observation of child language learning.

By 1886, the International Phonetic Association was founded. The design of International Phonetic Alphabet (IPA) provided a scientific analysis method of Phonetic and made the sounds of any language to be accurately transcribed. Linguists such as Henry Sweet in England, Wilhelm Viëtor in Germany, and Paul Passy in France began to provide the intellectual leadership. The Reform Movement in language teaching was laid.

In general, the reformers believed that[①]:

① The spoken language is primary and that this should be reflected in an oral-based methodology.

② The findings of phonetics should be applied to teaching and to teacher training.

③ Learners should hear the language first, before seeing it in written form.

④ Words should be presented in sentences, and sentences should be practiced in meaningful contexts and not be taught as isolated, disconnected elements.

⑤ The rules of grammar should be taught only after the students have practiced the grammar points in context — that is, grammar should be taught inductively.

⑥ Translation should be avoided, although the native language could be used in order to explain new words or to check comprehension.

These principles provided the theoretical foundations for a principled approach to language teaching, one based on a scientific approach to the study of language and of language learning. They reflect the beginnings of the discipline of applied linguistics — that branch of language

---

① RICHARDS J C, RODGERS T S. 语言教学的流派 [M].2 版 . 北京：外语教学与研究出版社，2008：10.

study concerned with the scientific study of second and foreign language teaching and learning. And this ultimately led to the development of the Direct Method.

3.2 Teaching Principles of the Direct Method

The teaching principles of the Direct Method are as follows:

① Classroom instructions are conducted exclusively in the target language.

② Only everyday vocabulary and sentences are taught during the initial phase; grammar, reading and writing are introduced in intermediate phase.

③ Oral communication skills are built up in a carefully graded progression organized around question-and-answer exchanges between teachers and students in small, intensive classes.

④ Grammar is taught inductively.

⑤ New teaching points are introduced orally.

⑥ Concrete vocabulary is taught through demonstration, objects, and pictures; abstract vocabulary is taught by association of ideas.

⑦ Both speech and listening comprehensions are taught.

⑧ Correct pronunciation and grammar are emphasized.

3.3 Techniques of the Direct Method

The typical teaching techniques of the Direct Method are as follows:

① Question/answer exercise — The teacher asks questions of any type and the student answers.

② Dictation — The teacher chooses a grade-appropriate passage and reads it aloud. Students write down what they have heard.

③ Reading aloud — The students take turns reading sections of a passage, a play or a dialogue aloud.

④ Student self-correction — When a student makes a mistake, the teacher offers him/her a second chance by giving a choice.

⑤ Conversation practice — The students are given an opportunity to ask their own questions to the other students or to the teacher. This enables both a teacher-learner interaction as well as a learner-learner interaction.

⑥ Paragraph writing — The students are asked to write a passage in their own words.

三、教学原则与教学过程

1. 直接法的产生背景

19 世纪中叶，欧洲各国人际交往机会增多，对外语口语能力提出了要求。在德国、英格兰、法国和欧洲其他地区，一些语言教学专家如马塞尔、普伦德加斯特和古安都各自创立了新的语言教学方法，他们对现代语言教学法的尝试与改革都具体而鲜明。这些语言教学专家的探索与改革反映了那一时代的需求和变化。教育工作者也开始认识到，外语课程的目标不是阅读理解、语法学习或文学鉴赏，而应该是培养口语能力。这使人们对儿童是如何学习语言的产生了兴趣，并促使人们从对儿童语言学习的观察中总结并发展语言教学的原则。

1886年，国际语音协会成立。国际音标表（IPA）的设计为语音分析提供了科学的方法，使得任何语言的声音都能进行准确的转录。英国的亨利·斯威特、德国的威廉·维耶托和法国的保罗·帕西等语言学家在理论界起了领导作用。语言教学改革运动就此展开。

一般来说，改革者们认为：

①口语是首要的，并且这一观点应该反映在以口语为基础的教育方法论中。

②语音学的研究成果应该用于语言教学和教师培训。

③学习者应先听语言的发音，再看其书写形式。

④单词应该在句子中呈现，句子应在有意义的上下文中进行练习，而不是作为孤立的、不连贯的语言元素来教授。

⑤语法规则只有在学生根据上下文练习语法点之后才能教授，也就是说，语法应该通过归纳法教授。

⑥可以用母语解释生词或检查是否理解，但应避免进行翻译。

这些原则鲜明的特点为语言教学法提供了理论基础，这种教学法的建立基于对语言及语言学习的研究。它标志着应用语言学，即对第二语言教学和外语教学的科学研究，这一语言学分支学科的开端。此外，也为直接法的最终产生奠定了基础。

2. 直接法的教学原则

直接法的教学原则如下：

①仅使用目的语进行课堂教学。

②学习的初级阶段教师只教授常用的词汇和句子；中高级阶段再引入语法、阅读和写作。

③在小班教学中，教师通过精心组织的师生问答练习，逐步培养学生的口语交际能力。

④采用归纳法进行语法教学。

⑤通过口头形式引入新的教学内容。

⑥通过展示实物、图片和演示的方式教授具体词汇；通过意义联系教授抽象词汇。

⑦教学内容包含语音和听力两部分。

⑧强调正确的发音和语法。

3. 直接法的教学技巧

直接法的典型教学方法有：

①问答练习——教师提出各种类型的问题，并让学生回答。

②听写——教师选取与所学课文水平相近的文章并大声朗读，让学生进行听写。

③大声朗读——学生轮流朗读一段文章、戏剧或对话。

④学生自我纠正——当学生犯错时，教师会给出可供选择的答案，给学生第二次机会自行纠正错误。

⑤会话练习——学生可以向其他学生或老师提问。这样既可以实现师生互动，也可以实现生生互动。

⑥写作——要求学生用自己的语言写出一篇文章。

4 Conclusion

Many claims of the Direct Method, such as direct connection with objective things, aim to communicate in the target language, imitation and self-correct, teaching grammar by induction, oral language as the basis, teaching real language etc., have broken the domination of Grammar-Translation Method in language teaching, activated academic thinking, and thus opened up the field of second language teaching method research. Therefore, the Direct Method can be regarded as the first language teaching method to have caught the attention of teachers and language teaching specialists, and it offered a methodology that appeared to move language teaching into a new era. It marked the beginning of the "methods era."

However, the Direct Method was perceived to have several drawbacks. It overemphasized and distorted the similarities between naturalistic first language learning and classroom foreign language learning and failed to consider the practical realities of the classroom. And this made it difficult to implement in public secondary school education. Besides, this method required teachers who were native speakers or who had native-like fluency in a foreign language. It was largely dependent on the teacher's skill, rather than on a textbook, and not all teachers were proficient enough in a foreign language to adhere to the principles of the method. Critics also pointed out that strict adherence to principles of the Direct Method was often counterproductive, since teachers were required to go to great lengths to avoid using the native language, when sometimes a simple, brief explanation in the student's native language would have been a more efficient route to comprehension. In addition, it lacked a rigorous basis in applied linguistic theory, and for this reason it was often criticized by the more academically based proponents of the Reform Movement.

四、小结

直接法提出了很多主张，例如：与客观事物直接联系，以使用目的语进行交际为学习目标，模仿和自我纠错，用归纳法教授语法，以口语为基础，教授真实语言等。这些主张打破了语法翻译法在语言教学中的主导地位，活跃了学术思想，从而开辟了第二语言教学法研究这一新的领域。因此，直接法可以看作引起教师和语言教学专家关注的第一个语言教学法，它为语言教学进入新时代提供了一种方法论。它标志着"方法时代"的开端。

直接法也存在一些局限性。它过分强调并扭曲了幼儿自然习得第一语言与课堂外语学习的相似性，没有考虑课堂的实际情况。这就使得它难以在公立中学教育中实施。另外，直接法还要求教师是目的语母语者或者教师的目的语掌握水平等同于母语者。这就使得教学效果很大程度上取决于教师的个人语言水平，而不是教科书。因此，并不是所有的语言教师都能达到足以贯彻直接法教学原则的熟练的外语水平。批评者还指出，严格遵守直接法教学原则往往会适得其反，因为教师必须尽最大努力避免使用学生母语，而有时用学生母语进行简单、简短的解释会是更有效的理解途径。此外，该教学法在应用语言学理论方面缺乏扎实的理论基础，因此，它也经常受到改革运动学术派学者们的批评。

○ Activities and Exercises

● Understanding and Thinking

1. Please read the following materials, discuss the significance of the establishment of the International Phonetic Association and of the design of the International Phonetic Alphabet (IPA) for the initiation of the Direct Method.

Phonetics — the scientific analysis and description of the sound systems of languages — was established, giving new insights into speech processes. Linguists emphasized that speech, rather than the written word, was the primary form of language. The International Phonetic Association was founded in 1886, and its International Phonetic Alphabet (IPA) was designed to enable the sounds of any language to be accurately transcribed. One of the earliest goals of the association was to improve the teaching of modern languages. It advocated:

① the study of the spoken language;

② phonetic training in order to establish good pronunciation habits;

③ the use of conversation texts and dialogues to introduce conversational phrases and idioms;

④ an inductive approach to the teaching of grammar;

⑤ teaching new meanings through establishing associations within the target language rather than by establishing associations with the native language.

2. The German prominent scholar Wilhelm Viëtor argued that training in phonetics would enable teachers to pronounce the language accurately. Speech patterns, rather than grammar, were the fundamental elements of language.

Please show your opinion about the basic nature of language, the goals of language teaching, or the best principles in language teaching.

3. According to the following guidelines for teaching oral language in Berlitz schools, talk about your understanding on the teaching Principles and Teaching Procedures of the Direct Method.

Never translate: demonstrate

Never explain: act

Never make a speech: ask questions

Never imitate mistakes: correct

Never speak with single words: use sentences

Never speak too much: make students speak much

Never use the book: use your lesson plan

Never jump around: follow your plan

Never go too fast: keep the pace of the student

Never speak too slowly: speak normally

Never speak too quickly: speak naturally

Never speak too loudly: speak naturally

Never be impatient: take it easy

● **Teaching Design**

1. Based on the teaching paradigms of the Direct Method intensively, choose a topic, design teaching details, and then make a teaching demonstration in groups.

Text (Lesson 3, Book 1, *Essential English*)

This is a classroom in a language school. There is a teacher in the room, and there are some other men and women who are students. There is a table in the room; the teacher is near the table. The door is behind the teacher. There are two windows in the room. The window on the left is open, but the window on the right is closed. There is a clock on the wall, near the door. The door is closed, but one window is open. There are some pencils and some flowers on the table.

Presentation

T: Please open your books and turn to page x. Let's read the text. (Students read the text sentence by sentence, following the teacher who, while reading, points at each part of the picture that matches the sentence.)

(After the students finish reading the passage, they are asked if they have any questions.)

S1: What are "men" and "women"?

T: Li Ming is a man. Wang Lin is a man. They are men. Wang Fang is a woman. Wang Lan is a woman. They are women. Now, do you understand the meaning of "men" and "women"?

S1: Yes, I understand.

S2: What does "behind" mean?

T: You are sitting behind Li Ming. Wang Lin is sitting behind you.

S3: What are pencils? I can not see them clearly in the picture.

T: (Picking up a pencil) This is a pencil.

Practice

(After the questions and answers, the teacher asks some questions about the text.)

T: Class, is there a teacher in the room?

Ss: Yes.

T: Please answer in a full sentence.

Ss: Yes, there is a teacher in the room.

T: Are there any other men and women in the room?

Ss: Yes, there are some other men and women in the room.

T: Is the teacher a man or a woman?

S4: The teacher is a men.

T: The teacher is a "men" or a "man"?

S4: The teacher is a man.

T: How many windows are there in the room?

S5: There are two windows in the room.

T: Is the window on the right closed?

S5: Yes, the window on the right is closed.

(After some more questions, the teacher invites individual students to ask the class questions.)

S6: Is the window on left open?

T: (Interrupting before the class has a chance to respond) Is the window on left? ... or on the left?

S6: On the left.

T: Right. Now, repeat your question.

S6: Is the window on the left open?

Ss: Yes, the window on the left is open.

S7: Is the door open or close?

T: (Interrupting) Is the door open or ...?

S7: Sorry, I see. Is the door open or closed?

Ss: The door is closed.

(After the students have asked some questions, the teacher begins asking questions about the students and their classroom, and pays special attention to "there be" structure and prepositions.)

T: Are there four windows in our classroom?

Ss: Yes, there are four windows in our classroom.

T: Is there a clock on the wall?

S8: Yes, there is a clock on the wall.

T: Are there any pencils on your desk?

S9: Yes, there are some pencils on my desk.

T: Who is sitting behind Wang Fang?

S10: Li Ping is sitting behind Wang Fang.

(Then the students are told to do pair work, asking each other questions with "there be" structure and prepositions.)

(The teacher next instructs the students to fill in the blanks in the sentences on the blackboard, which are covered before the students do the exercise. The students are required to read a sentence out aloud and give the missing words. The sentences are as follows:)

There _____ a teacher in the room.

There _____ two windows in the room.

The door is _____ the teacher.

The window _____ the left is open.

There is a clock _____ the wall, _____ the door.

There are some flowers _____ the table.

Consolidation

Finally, the students are given a dictation:

This is a classroom in a school. The teacher and the students are in the classroom. One student is near the open window. The other window is closed. The clock is behind the teacher. There are some flowers on the table and there is a picture on the wall under the clock.

The homework for the students is two compositions. One is Our Classroom. The other is My Bedroom.

2. Please read the following teaching plan carefully, point out the inappropriate places according to the theory and principles of the Direct Method, then revise and improve it.

Topic of This Lesson: *"What do you want to buy in the supermarket?"*

Teaching Objectives:

(1) Understand the content of the text.

(2) Memorize and master the basic sentence patterns in the text.

(3) Guide students to use this sentence pattern for basic dialogues and communication.

Content of Courses:

Text	
A：你想去超市买什么呢?	B：我想买面包和牛奶。
A：它们一共要多少钱?	B：它们一共 20 元。

Teaching Key Points and Difficulties:

Key points: Read the text skillfully and understand the meaning of the text.

Difficulty: Remember the basic sentence pattern in the text, and be able to use it to make sentences and communicate.

Teaching Process:

(1) Import New Lessons

① Where do you often go in your life?

② "Supermarket" is an indispensable place for us to buy daily necessities in our life, so today we need to learn about the communication between friends in the supermarket.

(2) Study the Text

① Lead the students to read the text.

② Let the students read the text by themselves.

③ Summarize the basic sentence patterns in the text.

A: What do you want to buy in the supermarket?

B: I want to buy ...

A: How much are they altogether?

B: They are ... Yuan in total.

④ Lead students to read and memorize sentence patterns.

(3) Communication and Connection

In pairs, use this sentence pattern to simulate dialogue.

(4) Homework After Class

① Review the sentence pattern of "shopping in the supermarket" and improve your speaking proficiency.

② Let students try to simulate other sentences and create dialogues.

● **Further Reading**

The Direct Method[①]

1. Preamble

The Direct Method is the offshoot of teaching methods which sprang in reaction to the Grammar-Translation Method and stressed on the teaching of second language in the target language. The torch bearer of this method took it as a very beneficiary one for the teaching of

---

① Abdullah S S. A Contrastive Study of the Grammar Translation and the Direct Methods of Teaching [C]. 3rd International Conference on Business, Economics, Management and Behavioral Sciences (ICBEMBS'2013) January 26-27, 2013 Hong Kong (China). 127–128.

foreign languages, though, later some serious drawbacks of this method came to light. All this is mentioned and assessed in the pages that follow.

2. The History of the Direct Method

During the middle ages, in the western world, foreign language learning was associated with the learning of Latin and Greek, both supposed to promote their speakers' intellectuality. At the time, it was of vital importance to focus on grammatical rules, syntactic structures, along with rote memorization of vocabulary and translation of literary text. There was no provision for the oral use of the languages under study; after all, both Latin and Greek were not being taught for oral communication but for the sake of their speakers' becoming "scholarly" or creating an illusion of "erudition". Late in the nineteenth century, the classical method came to be known as the Grammar-Translation Method, which offered very little beyond an insight into the grammatical rules attending the process of translating from the second to the native language.

It is widely recognized that the Grammar-Translation Method is still one of the most popular and favorite models of language teaching, which has been rather stalwart and impervious to educational reforms, remaining standard and sine qua non methodology. With hindsight, we could say that its contribution to language learning has been lamentably limited, since it has shifted the focus from the real language to a "dissected body" of nouns, adjectives and prepositions, doing nothing to enhance a student's communicative ability in a foreign language.

The last two decades of the nineteenth century ushered in a new age. In his *The Art of Learning and Studying Foreign Languages*, Francouis Gouin described his "harrowing" experiences of learning German, which helped him gain insights into the intricacies of language teaching and learning and find out that language learning is a matter of transforming perceptions into conceptions and then using language to represent these conceptions. Equipped with this knowledge, he devised a teaching method premised upon these insights. It was against this background that the series method was created, which taught learners directly a "series" of connected sentences that are easy to understand. Nevertheless, this approach to language learning was short-lived and, only a generation later, gave place to the Direct Method, posed by Charles Berlitz. The basic tenet of Berlitz's method was that second language learning is similar to first language learning. In this light, there should be lots of oral interaction, spontaneous use of the language, no translation, and little if any analysis of grammatical and syntactic structures.

3. Targets of the Direct Method

As these techniques of teaching emerged as a reaction to the Grammar-Translation Method, the main stress in it is placed on the pronunciation rather than the learning of grammar and rules.

This method is based on the direct involvement of the student when speaking, and listening to the foreign language in common everyday situations. Consequently, there is lots of oral interaction, spontaneous use of the language, no translation, and little if any analysis of grammar rules and syntax. The focus of the lessons is on good pronunciation, often introducing learners to phonetic symbols before they see standard writing examples. Briefly it can be summed up that in the Direct Method "The focus is on good pronunciation, with spontaneous use of the language, no translation, and little grammar analysis."

4. The Principles of the Direct Method

Direct Method works on the following principles:

① Classroom instruction is conducted in the target language.

② Concrete vocabulary is taught through pictures and objects, while abstract vocabulary is taught by association of ideas.

③ The learner is actively involved in using the language in realistic everyday situations.

④ Students are encouraged to think in the target language.

⑤ Speaking is taught first before reading or writing.

⑥ The printed word are kept away from the second language learner for as long as possible.

⑦ Classroom activities are carried out only in the target language. Translation is completely banished from any classroom activity.

⑧ A chain activities accompanies the verbal comments.

⑨ Grammar is taught inductively (i.e., having learners find out rules through the presentation of adequate linguistic forms in the target language).

⑩ Emphasis is put on correct pronunciation and grammar.

5. Teaching Techniques Applied in the Direct Method

Following techniques are mostly applied in the direct method:

① Reading aloud.

② Question-answer exercise.

③ Self correction.

④ Conversation practice.

⑤ Fill-in-the-blank exercise.

⑥ Dictation.

⑦ Paragraph writing.

6. The Advantages

Clearly the Direct Method is a shift away from the Grammar-Translation Method. One of its positive points is that it promises to teach the language and not about the language.

More advantages can be listed as follows:

① It is a natural method. It teaches the second language in the same way as one learns one's mother tongue. The language is taught through demonstration and conversation in context. Pupils, therefore, acquire fluency in speech. They are quick at understanding spoken English. They can converse in English with felicity and ease.

② There is no gap between active and passive vocabulary. This method does not differentiate between active and passive vocabularies. According to this method, whatever is required for understanding through English is also required for expressing through it. If English is taught through the mother tongue, the gulf between the active and passive vocabularies is widened. The learner acquires more of passive vocabulary because he concentrates on understanding English rather than expressing through it.

③ This method is based on sound principles of education. It believes in introducing the particular before general, concrete before abstract and practice before theory.

④ According to Macnee, "It is the quickest way of getting started."

7. The Disadvantages

Major fallacy of the Direct Method is the belief that the second language can be learned in the same way as the first language is acquired.

Second language learning is a determined process, whereas, the learning of the first language is the natural one, so learning of the both cannot be considered on the same lines and on the same principles.

The direct methods does not rules out the teaching of grammar; instead, it stresses upon the inductive teaching of grammar.

Some key disadvantages of this method as are follows:

① There are many words that cannot be interpreted directly in second language and much time are wasted in making attempts for this purpose.

② This method assumes that the auditory appeal is stronger than the visual, but it has been experienced that many of the learners learn more with their oral-aural sense like ears and tongue.

③ This method ignores systematic written work and reading activities, and sufficient attention is not paid to reading and writing.

④ This method does not hold well in higher classes where the Grammar-Translation Method is found more suitable.

⑤ In large classes this method is not properly applicable as it fails to meet with the needs of the students individually in such classes.

8. Conclusion

The Direct Method of teaching emerged as the reaction to the Grammar-Translation Method. It sought to immerse the learner in the same way as when the first language is learned. All teaching is done in the target language; grammar is taught inductively; there is a focus on speaking and listening, and only useful "everyday" language is taught. The weakness in the Direct Method is its assumption that a second language can be learned in exactly the same way as the first, when in fact the conditions under which a second language is learned are very different. The teacher and the students are more like partners in the teaching/learning process. The teacher is as

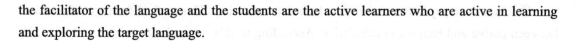
the facilitator of the language and the students are the active learners who are active in learning and exploring the target language.

● **Knowledge Table**

Table 2-1   Summary of Characteristics of the Direct Method

Key Points	The Direct Method
Period	
Representatives	
Background	
Theory of Language	
Theory of Language Learning	
Objectives	
The Syllabus	
Types of Learning and Teaching Activities	
Teacher's Roles	
Learner's Roles	
The Role of Students' Native Language and Target Language	
The Role of Instructional Materials and Textbook	
Others	
Summary	

● **Mind Map**

Chapter 3　The Audiolingual Method

第 3 章　听说法

○ **Contents**

○ **Wordle**

1 Introduction

The Audiolingual Method came into being in the 1940s, which had a great influence and impact on foreign language teaching. During the Second World War, the U.S. faced the task of training a vast number of people to equip them with foreign language speaking ability, for the purpose of military needs. In order to achieve this purpose in a short time, the framework of the Army Specialized Training Program (ASTP) appeared in 1942 and 55 American universities and hundreds of linguists, such as Leonard Bloomfield, were involved in the program by the beginning of 1943. In such courses of this training program, students studied 10 hours a day, 6 days a week. There were generally 15 hours of drill with native speakers and 20 to 30 hours of private study spread over two to three 6-week sessions. This was the system adopted by the army, and in small classes of mature and highly motivated students, excellent results were often achieved. The Army Specialized Training Program lasted only about two years, but the Teaching Principles and Teaching Procedures of its "Army Method" became the original of the Audiolingual Method.

一、教学法概述

听说法产生于 20 世纪 40 年代，它对外语教学产生了巨大的作用和影响。第二次世界大战期间，为了军事需要，美国面临着培养大量人才，使他们具备外语口语能力的任务。为了在短时间内实现这一目标，美国陆军专业训练计划（ASTP）于 1942 年提出，到 1943 年年初已有 55 所美国大学和包括伦纳德·布龙菲尔德在内的上百名语言学家参与到该计划中。在这项语言培训课程中，学生每周学习 6 天，每天学习 10 小时。课程一般有 15 个小时与母语者进行语言操练,有20～30个小时的个人学习,课程6周为一期,一般进行2～3期。这是从军队借鉴来的训练系统,加之课程采用小班授课,学生也多为上进心强的成年学生,因此,该方法收效甚佳。陆军专业训练计划虽然仅持续了两年左右,但该"陆军法"的教学原则和教学步骤成了听说法的起源。

2 Teaching Case①

The language teaching class in which the Audiolingual Method is being used is a beginning-level English class in Mali. There are 34 students, 13–15 years of age. The class meets for one hour a day, five days a week.

Now the students are attentively listening as the teacher is presenting a new dialogue, a conversation between two people. The students know they will be expected eventually to memorize the dialogue the teacher is introducing. All of the teacher's instructions are in English. Sometimes she uses actions to convey meaning, but not one word of the students' native language is uttered. After she acts out the dialogue, she says:

"All right, class. I am going to repeat the dialogue now. Listen carefully, but not talking please.

Two people are walking along a sidewalk in town. They know each other, and as they meet, they stop to talk. One of them is named Sally and the other one is named Bill. I will talk for Sally and for Bill. Listen to their conversation.

SALLY: Good morning.

BILL: Good morning, Sally.

SALLY: How are you?

BILL: Fine, thanks. And you?

SALLY: Fine. Where are you going?

BILL: I'm going to the post office.

SALLY: I am, too. Shall we go together?

BILL: Sure. Let's go.

Listen one more time. This time try to understand all that I am saying."

Now she has the whole class repeat each of the lines of the dialogue after her model. They repeat each line several times before moving on to the next line. When the class comes to the line, "I'm going to the post office," they stumble a bit in their repetition. The teacher, at this point, stops the repetition and uses a backward build-up drill (expansion drill). The purpose of this drill

---

①   LARSEN-FREEMAN D, ANDERSON M. Techniques and Principles in Language Teaching [M]. Oxford: Oxford University Press, 2011: 35–41.

is to break down the troublesome sentence into smaller parts. The teacher starts with the end of the sentence and has the class repeat just the last two words. Since they can do this, the teacher adds a few more words, and the class repeats this expanded phrase. Little by little the teacher builds up the phrases until the entire sentence is being repeated.

TEACHER: Repeat after me: post office.

CLASS: Post office.

TEACHER: To the post office.

CLASS: To the post office.

TEACHER: Going to the post office.

CLASS: Going to the post office.

TEACHER: I'm going to the post office.

CLASS: I'm going to the post office.

Through this step-by-step procedure, the teacher is able to give the students help in producing the troublesome line. Having worked on the line in small pieces, the students are also able to take note of where each word or phrase begins and ends in the sentence.

After the students have repeated the dialogue several times, the teacher gives them a chance to adopt the role of Bill while she says Sally's lines. Before the class actually says each line, the teacher models it. In effect, the class is experiencing a repetition drill where the students have to listen carefully and attempt to mimic the teacher's model as accurately as possible.

Next, the class and the teacher switch roles in order to practice a little more: The teacher says Bill's lines and the class says Sally's. Then the teacher divides the class into two halves so that each half on their own gets to try to say either Bill's or Sally's lines. The teacher stops the students from time to time when she feels they are straying too far from the model, and once again provides a model which she has them attempt to copy. To further practice the lines of this dialogue, the teacher has all the boys in the class take Bill's part and all the girls take Sally's.

She then initiates a chain drill with four of the lines from the dialogue. A chain drill gives students an opportunity to say the lines individually. The teacher listens and can tell which students are struggling and will need more practice. A chain drill also lets students use the expressions in communication with someone else, even though the communication is very limited. The teacher addresses the student nearest her with, "Good morning, Adama." He, in turn, responds, "Good morning, teacher." She says, "How are you?" Adama answers, "Fine, thanks. And you?" The teacher replies, "Fine." He understands through the teacher's gestures that he is to turn to the student sitting beside him and greet her. That student, in turn, says her lines in reply to him. When he has finished, she greets the student on the other side of her. This chain continues until all of the students have a chance to ask and answer the questions. The last student directs the greeting to the teacher.

Finally, the teacher selects two students to perform the entire dialogue for the rest of the class. When they are finished, two others do the same. Not everyone has a chance to say the dialogue in a pair today, but perhaps they will sometime later in the week.

The teacher moves next to the second major phase of the lesson. She continues to drill the students with language from the dialogue, but these drills require more than simple repetition. The first drill the teacher leads is a single-slot substitution drill in which the students will repeat a sentence from the dialogue and replace a word or phrase in the sentence with the word or phrase the teacher gives them. This word or phrase is called the cue.

The teacher begins by reciting a line from the dialogue, "I am going to the post office." Following this, she shows the students a picture of a bank and says the phrase, "the bank." She pauses, then says, "I am going to the bank."

From her example, the students realize that they are supposed to take the cue phrase ("the bank"), which the teacher supplies, and put it into its proper place in the sentence.

Now she gives them their first cue phrase, "the drugstore." Together the students respond, "I am going to the drugstore." The teacher smiles. "Very good!" she exclaims. The teacher cues, "the park." The students chorus, "I am going to the park."

Other cues she offers in turn are "the café" "the supermarket" "the bus station" "the football field" and "the library". Each cue is accompanied by a picture as before. After the students have gone through the drill sequence three times, the teacher no longer provides a spoken cue phrase. Instead, she simply shows the pictures one at a time, and the students repeat the entire sentence, putting the name of the place in the picture in the appropriate slot in the sentence.

A similar procedure is followed for another sentence in the dialogue, "How are you?" The subject pronouns "he" "she" "they" and "you" are used as cue words. This substitution drill is slightly more difficult for the students since they have to change the form of the verb "be" to "is" or "are", depending on which subject pronoun the teacher gives them. The students are apparently familiar with the subject pronouns since the teacher is not using any pictures. Instead, after going through the drill a few times supplying oral cues, the teacher points to a boy in the class and the students understand they are to use the pronoun "he" in the sentence. They chorus, "How is he?" "Good!" says the teacher. She points to a girl and waits for the class's response, then points to other students to elicit the use of "they".

Finally, the teacher increases the complexity of the task by leading the students in a multiple-slot substitution drill. This is essentially the same type of drill as the single-slot the teacher has just used. However, with this drill, students must recognize what part of speech the cue word is and where it fits into the sentence. The students still listen to only one cue from the teacher. Then they must make a decision concerning where the cue word or phrase belongs in a sentence also supplied by the teacher. The teacher in this class starts off by having the students repeat the original sentence from the dialogue, "I am going to the post office." Then she gives them the cue "she". The students understand and produce, "She is going to the post office!" The next cue the teacher offers is "to the park". The students hesitate at first; then they respond by correctly producing, "She is going to the park." She continues in this manner, sometimes providing a subject pronoun, other times naming a location.

The substitution drills are followed by a transformation drill. This type of drill asks students to change one type of sentence into another — an affirmative sentence into a negative or an active sentence into a passive, for example. In this class, the teacher uses a substitution drill that requires the students to change a statement into a yes/no question. The teacher offers an example, "I say, 'She is going to the post office.' You make a question by saying, 'Is she going to the post office?'"

The teacher models two more examples of this transformation, then asks, "Does everyone understand? OK, let's begin. 'They are going to the bank.'" The class replies in turn, "Are they going to the bank?" They transform approximately fifteen of these patterns, and then the teacher decides they are ready to move on to a question-and-answer drill.

The teacher holds up one of the pictures she used earlier, the picture of a football field, and asks the class, "Are you going to the football field?" She answers her own question, "Yes, I'm going to the football field." She poses the next question while holding up a picture of a park, "Are you going to the park?" And again answers herself, "Yes, I'm going to the park." She holds up a third picture, the one of a library. She poses a question to the class, "Are you going to the library?" They respond together, "Yes, I am going to the library."

"Very good!" the teacher says. Through her actions and examples, the students have learned that they are to answer the questions following the pattern she has modeled. The teacher drills them with this pattern for the next few minutes. Since the students can handle it, she poses the question to selected individuals rapidly, one after another. The students are expected to respond very quickly, without pausing.

The students are able to keep up the pace, so the teacher moves on to the next step. She again shows the class one of the pictures, a supermarket this time. She asks: "Are you going to the bus station?" She answers her own question, "No, I am going to the supermarket."

The students understand that they are required to look at the picture and listen to the question and answer negatively if the place in the question is not the same as what they see in the picture. "Are you going to the bus station?" The teacher asks while holding up a picture of a café. "No, I am going to the café." The class answers.

"Very good!" exclaims the teacher. After posing a few more questions that require negative answers, the teacher produces the pictures of the post office and asks, "Are you going to the post office?" The students hesitate a moment and then chorus, "Yes, I am going to the post office."

"Good!" comments the teacher. She works a little longer on this question-and-answer drill, sometimes providing her students with situations that require a negative answer and sometimes giving encouragement to each student. She holds up pictures and poses questions one right after another, but the students seem to have no trouble keeping up with her. The only time she changes the rhythm is when a student seriously mispronounces a word. When this occurs she restates the word and works briefly with the student until his pronunciation is closer to her own.

For the final few minutes of the class, the teacher returns to the dialogue with which she began the lesson. She repeats it once, then has the half of the class to her left do Bill's lines and the half of the class to her right do Sally's. This time there is no hesitation at all. The students move through the dialogue briskly. They trade roles and do the same. The teacher smiles, "Very good. Class dismissed."

The lesson ends for the day. Both the teacher and the students have worked hard. The students have listened to and spoken only English for the period. The teacher is tired from all her actions, but she is pleased for she feels the lesson went well. The students have learned the lines of the dialogue and to respond without hesitation to her cues in the drill pattern.

In lessons later in the week, the teacher will do the following:

① Review the dialogue.

② Expand upon the dialogue by adding a few more lines, such as "I am going to the post office. I need a few stamps."

③ Drill the new lines and introduce some new vocabulary items through the new lines, for example:

I am going to the supermarket.	I need a little butter.
... library.	... few books.
... drugstore.	... little medicine.

④ Work on the difference between mass and count nouns, contrasting "a little/a few" with mass and count nouns respectively. No grammar rule will ever be given to the students. The students will be led to figure out the rules from their work with the examples the teacher provides.

⑤ A contrastive analysis (the comparison of two languages, in this case, the students' native language and the target language, English) has led the teacher to expect that the students will have special trouble with the pronunciation of words such as "little," which contain /ɪ/.The students do indeed say the word as if it contained /iː/. As a result, the teacher works on the contrast between /ɪ/ and /iː/ several times during the week. She uses minimal pair words, such as ship/sheep, live/leave, and his/he's to get her students to hear the difference in pronunciation between the words in each pair. Then, when she feels they are ready, she drills them in saying the two sounds — first, the sounds on their own, and later, the sounds in words, phrases, and sentences.

⑥ Sometime towards the end of the week, the teacher writes the dialogue on the blackboard. She asks the students to give her the lines and she writes them out as the students say them.

They copy the dialogue into their notebooks. They also do some limited written work with the dialogue. In one exercise, the teacher has erased 15 selected words from the expanded dialogue. The students have to rewrite the dialogue in their notebooks, supplying the missing words without looking at the complete dialogue they copied earlier. In another exercise, the students are given sequences of words such as "I" "go" "supermarket" and "he" "need" "butter", and they are asked to write complete sentences like the ones they have been drilling orally.

⑦ On Friday, the teacher leads the class in the "supermarket alphabet game." The game starts with a student who needs a food item beginning with the letter "A." The student says, "I am going to the supermarket. I need a few apples." The next student says, "I am going to the supermarket. He needs a few apples. I need a little bread. (or "a few bananas," or any other food item you could find in the supermarket beginning with the letter "B")" The third student continues, "I am going to the supermarket. He needs a few apples. She needs a little bread. I need a little cheese." The game continues with each player adding an item that begins with the next letter in the alphabet. Before adding his or her own item, however, each player must mention the items of the previous students. If the student has difficulty thinking of an item, either the other students or the teacher helps.

⑧ A presentation by the teacher on supermarkets in the United States follows the game. The teacher tries very hard to get meaning across in English. The teacher answers the students' questions about the differences between supermarkets in the United States and open-air markets in Mali. They also discuss briefly the differences between American and Mali football. The students seem very interested in the discussion. The teacher promises to continue the discussion of popular American sports the following week.

二、教学示例

在本示例中，听说法被用于马里的一个初级水平的英语课堂上。该班共有 34 名学生，年龄在 13~15 岁。该班一周上 5 次课，每次 1 学时。

此时，老师正在引入一段新的双人对话，学生们正在专心地听。学生们知道他们最后要记住老师正在介绍的对话。老师的介绍是全英文的，有时伴随动作演示，没有一个词是用学生的母语来表达的。老师完成对话的展示后，说道：

"好，同学们，我现在要重复对话。你们认真听，请不要说话。

两个人在镇上的人行道上散步。他们彼此认识，在路上碰面后，他们停下来交谈。其中一个人叫莎莉，另一个人叫比尔。我将既扮演莎莉，也扮演比尔。现在请听听他们的对话。

莎莉：'早上好。'

比尔：'早上好，莎莉。'

莎莉：'你好吗？'

比尔：'挺好的，谢谢。你呢？'

莎莉：'我也挺好的。你要去哪里？'

比尔：'我要去邮局。'

莎莉：'我也去邮局。咱们一起去，好吗？'

比尔：'当然可以。走吧。'

请大家再听一遍，并试着理解我所说对话的意思。"

之后，老师示范朗读对话的每一行每一句，学生跟读。每一句，他们都要重复好几遍，直到开始下一句。当全班学生重复句子"我要去邮局"时，他们复述得有点儿结结巴巴。老师便在这一句上停了下来，并开始进行扩展训练。这个训练的目的是把造成学习困难的句子切分成几个组块进行练习。老师从句子的结尾处开始，先让全班学生重复句子的最后两个单词。同学们都做到后，老师就再多加几个单词，然后全班同学重复这个扩展的短语。老师一点一点地叠加扩展短语，最终学生们复述下来了整个句子。

老师："跟我重复一遍：邮局。"

全班学生："邮局。"

老师："去邮局。"

全班学生："去邮局。"

老师："要去邮局。"

全班学生："要去邮局。"

老师："我要去邮局。"

全班学生："我要去邮局。"

通过这样循序渐进的教学步骤，教师协助学生们说出了那个难句。在句子的切分练习过程中，学生们也对句子中的单词和短语进行了切分和识别。

学生们将对话重复了几次以后，老师读莎莉的台词，学生们读比尔的台词。依然是老师先做示范，然后全班学生进行重复。在这段时间里，学生们一直在进行重复练习。在重复练习中，学生们必须仔细听，并尽可能准确地模仿老师的语音语调。

之后，老师和学生们互换角色，以便进行更多的练习，即老师扮演比尔，学生们扮演莎莉。完成后，老师又把全班同学分成两组，一组扮演比尔，另一组扮演莎莉，继续操练对话中的句子。在学生们重复整个对话的过程中，一旦老师认为学生们读得有问题，她就会让全班学生停下来，自己重新示范，然后再让学生们模仿重复。为了进一步操练这个对话，老师还让班上的所有的男生扮演比尔，所有的女生扮演莎莉，再进行重复。

接下来，老师利用对话中的四个句子进行"接龙"训练。"接龙"训练可以为学生提供单独重复对话句子的机会。在练习过程中，老师通过听学生的重复，能够从中了解哪些学生还有疑问，是否还需要更多的练习。"接龙"训练还可以让学生在与他人交流时用上所学的表达句式，虽然这样的交流非常有限。老师向离她最近的学生问好："早上好！阿达马。"阿达马转过身，回答道："早上好，老师！"老师继续问："你好吗？"阿达马回答道："很好，谢谢。你呢？"老师回答："很好。"通过老师的手势，他明白接下来老师让他转向坐在他旁边的学生，并跟她打招呼。旁边的那位同学也转过身，与阿达马进行对话。完成对话后，第二位女生又跟她另一边的学生打招呼。这个训练一直持续到所有学生都完成了对话的问与答。最后一位学生直接与老师进行对话。

随后，老师选出两名学生为全班同学表演整个对话。当他们展示完之后，便由另外两名学生进行同样的对话展示。不是每名学生都有机会在今天做这个一对一的对话展示，他们有可能在本周的后续课程中进行展示。

接下来，老师过渡到第二个主要的教学环节。老师继续利用对话进行语言操练，这些操练方式不再仅仅是简单的重复了。老师引入的第一个操练是单项替换练习，在这个练习中，学生要用老师提供给他们的单词或短语，替换对话句子中的一个单词或短语，然后重复替换后的句子。给出的替换单词或短语称为"提示词"。

老师首先展示了对话中的一个句子："我要去邮局。"紧接着，老师向学生展示了一张银行的图片，并说："银行。"暂停片刻后，老师又说："我要去银行。"

通过老师的示范，学生们了解到他们需要将老师给出的提示词（"银行"）放到句中合适的位置。

老师开始为学生提供第一个提示词"药店"。学生们集体回答："我要去药店。"老师微笑，称赞道："非常好！"老师再提示："公园。"学生们齐声说："我要去公园。"

之后，老师依次提供的提示词有："咖啡馆""超市""汽车站""足球场"和"图书馆"。像之前一样，每个提示词都利用图片进行提示。在学生完成三次替换练习后，老师不再朗读提示词，而仅仅展示提示词的图片，学生依旧重复整个句子，并把图片中的处所词放到句中恰当的位置。

操练完一个句子后，他们以同样的方式练习对话中的另一个句子"你好吗？"。这个句子的替换提示词是主语位置的代词："他""她""他们"，还有"你"。这个替换练习对学生们来说稍微困难一些，因为（根据主谓一致原则）他们必须根据老师给他们的不同代词将系动词 be 随之改为 is 或者 are。很显然，学生们已经非常熟悉主语位置的代词替换练习了，因此，老师并没有使用图片进行提示。在进行了几次口头提示后，老师用手指向班里的一名男生，学生们便明白了老师让他们在句子中替换代词"他"。学生们便齐声说："他好吗？"老师回答道："很好！"老师又指向一名女生，等待学生们进行回应。之后，老师又指着其他学生，引导大家使用"他们"来进行替换。

最后，老师通过引导学生进行多项替换练习来增加课堂任务的复杂性。多项替换练习显然与刚才进行的单项替换练习属于同一类操练。在进行这个练习时，学生们必须明确提示词的词性及其在句中的位置。老师仍然一次只给出一个提示词。学生听后，首先需要确定老师给出的提示词应该放在句子的哪个位置。在这个练习中，老师首先让学生们重复对话中最原始的句子："我要去邮局。"然后老师给出提示词"她"。学生听后进行替换："她要去邮局。"之后，老师给出的提示词是"公园"。学生们起初犹豫了片刻，然后做出了正确的回答："她要去公园。"老师以这样的方式进行着这个练习，即有时提供主语位置的代词，有时提供处所名词。

替换练习之后是变换练习。这类练习要求学生将句子类型进行转换，即把一种句子变换成另一种句子，如肯定句变为否定句，主动句变为被动句。在这堂课上，老师使用了一个变换练习，即让学生将一个陈述句变为是非问句。老师首先进行示范："我说：'她要去邮局。'你们要把这个句子变成问句，所以你们要说'她要去邮局吗？'"

之后，老师又示范变换了两个句子，然后问道："大家都明白了吗？来，让我们开始练习。'他们要去银行。'"全班学生回答："他们要去银行吗？"全班进行了大约 15 个类似的变换练习，之后，老师准备进入问答练习。

老师拿起之前用过的那张足球场的图片，向全班学生提问："你要去足球场吗？"然后老师回答道："是的，我要去足球场。"老师又拿起公园的图片继续提问："你要去公园吗？"之后老师又自问自答："是的，我要去公园。"老师拿起第三张图片，这是一张图书馆的图片，向全班学生提问："你要去图书馆吗？"学生们集体回答："是的，我要去图书馆。"

老师予以肯定，道："非常好！"通过老师的行为示范和例句演示，学生们领会到要按照老师给出的模式回答问题。在接下来的几分钟里，老师用这个练习模式进行了操练。由于学生们已经掌握了这种练习方式，因此，老师开始一个接一个地对学生进行个别提问，并要求学生快速反应，不要停顿。

看到学生们都能够跟着进度进行操练，老师便进入了下一个环节。这次，老师又向学生们出示了一张图片，是超市的图片，然后问道："你要去汽车站吗？"随后老师自问自答："不，我要去超市。"

学生们马上明白了这次他们需要听问题并看图片，如果问题中的处所词与图片中的处所不同，他们应该进行否定回答。老师又举起一张咖啡馆的图片，问道："你要去汽车站吗？"全班学生回答道："不，我要去咖啡馆。"

老师对学生们的答案予以肯定："非常好！"在完成了一些要求进行否定回答的提问后，老师拿出邮局的图片，问道："你要去邮局吗？"学生们犹豫了片刻，然后齐声回答："是的，我要去邮局。"

老师再次肯定大家的答案，说道："很好！"老师在这个问答环节上又花了一些时间，时而给学生提供需要否定答案的情况，时而对学生们进行表扬和鼓励。她举着图片，一个接一个地提出问题，学生们一直跟着老师的节奏进行练习，没有任何困难和迟疑。此期间，老师唯一一次放慢了节奏，是因为一名学生出现了严重的发音错误。这种情况发生时，老师重复了一下那个单词，并与那名学生进行了简短的交流（纠正），以便使他的发音与自己的发音接近。

在本次课的最后几分钟，老师回到了她开始上课时的对话。她重复了一遍，然后让她左边的学生们扮演比尔，右边的学生们扮演莎莉。这次的集体对话顺畅无比。学生们轻轻松松地完成了对话。然后角色互换，又进行了一次对话。老师微笑道："很好。下课！"

今天的课到此为止。老师和学生都很努力。在上课期间，学生只用英语进行听和说，老师专注课堂展示和组织控制。她虽然很累，但感到很高兴，因为她觉得这次课上得不错。

学生们学会了对话的句子，并能够毫不犹豫地在语言操练中根据她的提示进行回答。

在本周的后续课程中，老师将完成如下教学任务：

①复习对话。

②在原对话的基础上再扩展一些句子，例如："我要去邮局。我需要几张邮票。"

③对新扩展出的句子进行操练，并在操练新句型时引入一些新词语，例如：

我要去超市。　　　　　　　　我需要一些黄油。

……图书馆。　　　　　　　　……一些书。

……药店。　　　　　　　　……一些药。

④辨析可数名词和不可数名词，并在名词复数与 a little 和 a few 的搭配上进行对比。在这项任务中，老师不会给学生提供任何语法规则。学生将通过老师提供的例子，并基于练习自行总结出规律。

⑤对比分析（两种语言的比较，在这个教学示例中，指的是学生的母语和目的语，也就是英语）使老师预测到学生将在诸如包含 /ɪ/ 的单词 little 的发音上有困难。而学生也确实将这个词的元音说得好像 /iː/。因此，老师在这一周将多次进行 /iː/ 和 /ɪ/ 的对比。她将利用（语音中的）最小对比对词语，如 ship 与 sheep，live 与 leave，his 与 he's，以便让学生们在听每对单词发音时体会它们之间的差异。在学生充分感知发音区别后，老师再训练他们发出这两个元音，即先进行单独的发音练习，然后通过单词、短语和句子进行发音训练。

⑥在本周最后的课程中，老师把对话写在黑板上。她让学生们把对话的句子说出来，然后她按学生们说的把对话写在黑板上。学生们把对话抄到笔记本上。他们也要完成一定的对话书写练习。比如，在一个练习中，老师从扩展的对话中删除了 15 个单词。学生们需要在不看之前抄写的完整对话的情况下，填出缺失的单词，并在本子上重写这一对话。在另一个练习中，老师给学生列出一系列单词，如"我""去""超市"，还有"他""需要""黄油"，并要求他们仿照之前进行口头练习的句子，写出完整的句子。

⑦星期五，老师带领全班学生进行"超市中的字母游戏"的活动。游戏从一个学生开始，他需要找到一个以字母 A 开头的食物。这名学生说："我要去超市。我需要一些苹果。"下一名学生说："我要去超市。他需要一些苹果。我需要一点儿面包（或者'一些香蕉'，或者任何其他能在超市里找到且以字母 B 开头的食物）。"第三名学生继续说："我要去超市。他需要一些苹果。她需要一点儿面包。我需要一点儿奶酪。"游戏继续，每名学生都添加一个以字母表中的下一个字母开头的单词。在添加自己的单词之前，每个学生都必须先复述之前所有学生说过的句子。如果有学生想不出来用什么词，其他学生或老师会进行提示帮助。

⑧游戏结束后，老师介绍了美国的超市。老师尽量用英语进行表达。老师还回答了学生关于美国超市和马里露天市场之间差异的问题。他们还简要讨论了美式足球和马里足球的区别。学生们似乎对讨论很感兴趣。因此，老师承诺下周继续与他们讨论美国流行的体育运动。

3 Teaching Principles and Teaching Procedures

3.1 Theoretical Basis of the Audiolingual Method

The theory foundations of the Audiolingual Method mainly contain two aspects: linguistics and psychology.

In the 1940s, American Structuralism or Descriptive Linguistics gained extreme popularity and reputation; the representative figures are Charles, Fries, and Bloomfield, whose linguistic theories underline the Audiolingual Method. From the Structural Linguists' view on language, structure is focused and emphasized much. Language was viewed as a system of structurally related elements for the encoding of meaning, the elements being phonemes, morphemes, words, structures, and sentence types. Another important view of structural linguistics was that the primary medium of language is oral: Speech is language. In addition, the scientific techniques of Structuralism on language analysis also provides a methodological basis for the Audiolingual Method.

Behaviorism, being the theoretical base for the Audiolingual Method from the perspective of psychology, advocated that language learning in terms of stimulus and response, operant conditioning, and reinforcement with an emphasis on successful error-free learning.

According to the above theories of Structural Linguistics and Behaviorism Psychology, W. G. Moulton, Professor of Princeton University in the United States, summarized the theoretical basis of the Audiolingual Method as follows:

① Language is speech, not writing;

② Language is what its native speaker says, not what someone thinks they ought to say;

③ Languages are different;

④ A language is a set of habits;

⑤ Teach the language, not about the language.

3.2 Teaching Principles of the Audiolingual Method

The teaching principles of the Audiolingual Method can be summarized as follows:

① Listening and speaking ability is a priority. Language skills are divided into four categories: listening, speaking, reading, and writing. Since "language is speech, not writing", so listening and speaking take the lead and should be given the top priority.

② Practice repeatedly and form a habit. That is to say, in teaching, repeated exercises and drilling are necessary, and such kind of repeated actions can pave the way for mastering language ability.

③ Teach on a sentence pattern-centered basis. Sentence is the basic unit of effective communication; sentence pattern should be focused and be the core of teaching.

④ Mother tongue is not used in classroom instruction. Imitation in Audiolingual class plays an important role. In order to give learners a pure target language environment for imitation and memorization, learners' mother tongue should be avoided.

⑤ Compare and contrast language structures to identify difficult points in teaching. By comparing the structures between learners' native language and the target language, the difference between the two languages and difficulty for learners can be found and pointed out, and thus during teaching, the difficult point will be emphasized.

⑥ Correct errors and cultivate a good language habit. When errors occur, the teacher will give the students a negative reinforcement, then the students will not repeat the mistaken action, and the errors can be prevented. According to Behaviorism, language learning is a kind of habit-forming. By repeated reinforcement and negative reinforcement, the correct language can be learned and good language habit can be formed.

⑦ Make full use of modern teaching means. In the 1950s, science and technology provided the developed teaching means for Audiolingual Method. So the tapes, language lab, MP3, videos and other teaching means should be applied in order to strengthen stimulation.

3.3 Teaching Procedures of the Audiolingual Method

Professor W. F. Twadell from Brown University made Audiolingual teaching procedures standardized in five stages: cognition, imitation, repetition, variation, and selection.

(1) Cognition

Cognition is the first step of the method, which means understanding. The students learn the material by listening to and repeating after the teacher or tape, and the teacher ought to make full use of the model structures, introduce new items and language points by the way of reviewing the learned material. Then the students may try their best to associate the new items to the learned items, thus cognition or understanding will be achieved.

(2) Imitation

Imitation is a very important concept in Behaviorism. By imitation to the native pronunciation and intonation, the students may be closer to the native speaker. Students should imitate those new sentence patterns which the teacher reads out in the target language. Since imitation means practicing and memorizing, listening is the major concern in this stage.

(3) Repetition

Repetition is the key step for habit forming. By repetition, the memory can be strengthened and with a reinforcement given by teacher, the response or the habit will be formed accordingly. Students learn to master sentence patterns by repeating the imitated and memorized items. In this section, dialogues are used for repetition and memorization. Correct pronunciation, stress, rhythm, and intonation are also emphasized.

(4) Variation

The Audiolingual Method stresses the sentence pattern drilling or practice. Also, the language structure is always the core of the method, and thus the variation of the sentence patterns or structures are important for the learners to master the target language. Variation can be divided into three stages: substitution, conversion and expansion.

Substitution means one or several learned words or phrases are replaced by new ones belonging to the same syntactical function.

Conversion means changing the sentence structure or functional word in order to master more sentence patterns, mainly containing conversion between affirmative sentence and interrogative one, and between direct speech and indirect speech.

Expansion means to enlarge a sentence by adding some modifiers; thus, the extended sentence could express richer meaning and information, and in addition, it can help students know the functions of every part in the sentence.

(5) Selection

In this section, students are trained to select language materials they have learned, and apply them to a specific situation. For this aim, the techniques include: question and answer expanding exercises, retelling, creative talk, talking about something on a guided topic, learning to talk with the help of picture, talking and discussing a specific theme, or writing various kinds of narrative passages and so on. This section involves both speaking and writing. In other words, the basic skills are cultivated and strengthened.

三、教学原则与教学过程

1. 听说法的理论基础

听说法的理论基础主要包括语言学和心理学两个方面。

20 世纪 40 年代，美国结构主义语言学或称描写主义语言学得到了极大的普及和赞誉，代表人物是查尔斯、弗里斯和布龙菲尔德，他们的语言学理论成为听说法的理论基础。从结构主义语言学家的语言观来看，必须关注并强调语言结构。结构主义把语言看作由各个相互关联的成分按结构层次组成的一个表达意义的符号编码系统，这些关联的成分包括音位、语素、词、结构和句子类型。结构主义语言学的另一个重要观点是，语言的主要媒介是口语：语言即言语。此外，结构主义关于语言的科学分析方法也为听说法提供了方法论基础。

行为主义从心理学角度为听说法奠定了理论基础，它主张从刺激和反应、操作性条件反射和强化等方面进行语言学习，强调基于严格纠错的成功学习。

根据结构主义语言学和行为主义心理学的理论，美国普林斯顿大学教授莫尔登把听说法的理论基础总结为以下五点：

①语言是说出来的话，而不是写出来的文字；

②语言是母语者所说的话，而不是别人认为他们应该说的话；

③不同语言之间存在差异；

④语言是一套行为习惯；

⑤教授语言，而不是教有关语言的知识。

2. 听说法的教学原则

听说法的教学原则可以总结如下：

①听说领先。语言技能分为听、说、读、写四项。因为"语言是说出来的话，而不是写出来的文字"，所以听和说是首要的，应该放在第一位。

②反复操练。反复练习，养成习惯。也就是说，在教学中，反复练习和句型操练是必要的，这样的重复行为可以为掌握语言并形成语言能力奠定基础。

③教学以句型为中心。句子是进行言语交际的基本单位，句型应成为关注的焦点及教学的核心。

④在课堂教学中不使用母语。在听说法的课堂中，模仿起着重要的作用。为了给学习者提供一个纯粹的目的语语言环境，便于学生进行语言模仿和记忆，应该避免使用学习者的母语。

⑤对比语言结构，确定教学难点。通过学习者母语和目的语语言结构的比较，可以发现两种语言的差异，从而确定学习者的学习难点，以便在教学中突出难点。

⑥纠正错误，培养良好的语言习惯。当错误发生时，教师会给学生一个否定的反馈（即负强化），这样学生就不会重复错误，错误就可以避免。行为主义认为，语言学习即形成一种行为习惯。通过反复的正强化和负强化，可以学到正确的语言，并形成良好的语言习惯。

⑦充分利用现代化教育技术手段。20 世纪 50 年代，科学的发展和技术的革新为听说法提供了先进的教育技术手段。因此，听说法主张应采用磁带、语言实验室、MP3、视频等教学手段强化刺激。

3. 听说法的教学过程

布朗大学的特瓦德尔教授将听说法的教学步骤标准化为认知、模仿、重复、变换和选择五个阶段。

（1）认知

认知是听说法的第一步，即理解。学生通过聆听语言材料，跟随教师或磁带录音进行复述来学习，教师应充分利用语言结构（句型），通过复习学过的知识点来引入新的语言点，学生尽可能地将新旧知识进行联系，以便达到对新知识的认知和理解。

（2）模仿

模仿是行为主义中非常重要的一个概念，通过模仿母语的语音和语调，学生可以更接近母语者的发音。学生应该模仿教师用目的语朗读的新句型。由于模仿意味着操练和记忆，因此，通过听力练习来加深对模仿内容的印象是这个阶段的重点。

（3）重复

重复是形成习惯的关键。通过重复，记忆可以得到强化，在教师的语言强化下，语言的反应或习惯也会随之形成。学生通过不断重复所模仿和记忆的语言材料来达到掌握句型的目的。在这一阶段，教师将利用对话练习让学生进行重复和记忆，并同时强调正确的发音、重音、停顿和语调。

（4）变换

听说法强调句型操练，语言结构是该教学法的核心。因此，句型或语言结构的变换对学习者掌握目的语至关重要。句型变换可以分为替换、转换和扩展三个阶段。

替换是指一个或多个所学单词或短语被具有同一句法功能的新单词或新短语替换。

转换是指为掌握更多的句型而改变句子结构或功能词，主要包括肯定句与疑问句的转换、直接引语与间接引语的转换。

扩展是指通过增加一些修饰语来扩展句子，从而使扩展的句子能够表达更丰富的意义及信息。另外，这也有助于学生了解句子中各个部分的功能。

（5）选择

在这一阶段，教师将让学生选择学习过的语言材料并运用于特定的情景。具体的教学技巧有：拓展阅读后的问答练习、复述、自由谈话、谈论某一指定话题、看图说话、讨论某一特定主题，或编写各种叙述性段落等。这一阶段既涉及听说又涉及读写，也就是说，基本的语言技能都会得到培养和强化。

4 Conclusion

In sum, the Audiolingual Method which has a strong theoretical base in linguistics and psychology, is a linguistic or structure-based approach to language teaching. The elements of language, phonology, morphology, and syntax, are arranged according to their order of presentation or teaching. The four basic language skills are taught in order of listening, speaking, reading, and writing. Moreover, recognition and discrimination are followed by imitation, repetition, and memorization. Besides, the dialogues used for drilling sentence patterns also provide the means of contextualizing key structures and illustrate situations in which structures might be used as well as some cultural aspects of the target language. All of these principles and characteristics made the Audiolingual Method reliable, practical and systematic. Audiolingualism had great popularity and reputation in language teaching, reached its period of most widespread use in the 1960s in the United States.

Criticism of the Audiolingual Method came on two fronts. On the one hand, practitioners found that the practical results fell short of expectations. Students were often found to be unable to transfer skills acquired through Audiolingualism to real communication outside the classroom, and many found the experience of studying through Audiolingual procedures to be boring and unsatisfying. On the other hand, the theoretical foundations of Audiolingualism were attacked as being unsound in terms of both language theory and learning theory. The psychological base of the Audiolingual Method is Behaviorism, which is based on animal experiments, and thus in the Audiolingual method class, learners are compared to animals. Human beings have complicated and subtle cognitive mechanism, and pure Behaviorism cannot account for the complex learning activities, which is attacked by Cognitive Approach. While the most serious theoretical attack on Audiolingual beliefs resulted from changes in American linguistic theory in the 1960s. The MIT linguist Noam Chomsky rejected the Structuralist Approach to language description as well as the Behaviorist theory of language learning. Chomsky proposed his theory of Transformational Grammar that the fundamental properties of language derive from innate aspects of the mind and from how humans process experience through language. He stressed that sentences are not learned by imitation and repetition but "generated" from the learner's underlying "competence". Therefore, the most important Audiolingual paradigm, such as pattern practice, drilling, memorization, was called into question, because these teaching techniques might lead to language-like behaviors, but they were not resulting in competence.

四、小结

综上所述，听说法具有坚实的语言学和心理学理论基础，是一种以语言结构为纲的教学法。该教学法将语言学的音系学、形态学、句法学等研究领域的语言要素知识有序编排并进行教学。按照听、说、读、写的顺序教授四项基本的语言技能。在语言知识的识别和辨析的基础上开展一系列模仿、重复和记忆等教学活动。用于句型操练的对话既提供了关键句式的运用规则，描述了语言结构所使用的情境，又介绍了一些目的语文化方面的知识。这些原则和特点令听说法具有可靠性、实用性和系统性。因此，听说法在语言教学领域有着巨大的知名度和美誉度，其发展在20世纪60年代的美国达到了最鼎盛的时期。

对听说法的批评主要来自两个方面。一方面，听说法的实际效果不如预期的好。学生们发现通过听说法教学而获得的语言技能无法转化运用到课堂之外的实际交流中。还有许多人发现听说法的机械性操练过程十分枯燥，难以引起学习者的兴趣。另一方面，支撑听说法的语言学理论和学习理论的科学性也受到了抨击。听说法的心理学基础是行为主义，行为主义以动物实验为基础，因此在听说法的课堂教学中，学习者被视为动物来进行训练。认知学派认为人类有着复杂而微妙的认知机制，单纯的行为主义无法解释复杂的学习活动。然而，对听说法最严重的理论抨击来自20世纪60年代美国语言学理论的变革。麻省理工学院的语言学家诺姆·乔姆斯基否定了结构主义的语言描写方法和行为主义的语言学习理论。乔姆斯基提出的转换生成语法理论认为语言的基本属性来源于人类大脑固有的内在方面（语言习得机制）和人类在处理语言时所获得的外部经验。他强调句子不是通过模仿和重复学来的，而是通过学习者潜在的"语言能力"生成的。因此，诸如句型练习、机械操练、模仿记忆等听说法最典型的教学模式与方法都遭到了质疑，因为这些教学方法虽然可能会导致类似语言的行为，但绝不会形成语言能力。

○ Activities and Exercises

● Understanding and Thinking

1. "Pattern drill" is the most typical teaching technique of the Audiolingual Method. Please read the following points and talk about your understanding of the role and significance of pattern drills based on the theoretical basis of linguistics and psychology of the Audiolingual Method.

For Fries who is one of the representatives of the Audiolingual Method, grammar, or "structure," was the starting point. The structure of the language was identified with its basic sentence patterns and grammatical structures. The language was taught by systematic attention to pronunciation and by intensive oral drilling of its basic sentence patterns. Pattern practice was a basic classroom technique.

Hockett points out: "It is these basic patterns that constitute the learner's task. They require drill, drill, and more drill, and only enough vocabulary to make such drills possible."

Lado describes it: "In PATTERN PRACTICE ... the student is led to practice a pattern, changing some element of that pattern each time, so that normally he never repeats the same sentence twice. Furthermore, his attention is drawn to the changes, which are stimulated by pictures, oral substitutions, etc., and thus the PATTERN ITSELF THE SIGNIFICANT FRAMEWORK OF THE SENTENCE, rather than the particular sentence, is driven intensively into his habit reflexes."

2. Please discuss the roles of teachers and learners in the Audiolingual method class based on the teaching case and the following statements.

Learner's Roles

Learners are viewed as organisms that can be directed by skilled training techniques to produce correct responses. In accordance with behaviorist learning theory, teaching focuses on the external manifestations of learning rather than on the internal processes. Learners play a reactive role by responding to stimuli, and thus have little control over the content, pace, or style of learning. They are not encouraged to initiate interaction, because this may lead to mistakes. The fact that in the early stages learners do not always understand the meaning of what they are repeating is not perceived as a drawback, for by listening to the teacher, imitating accurately, and responding to and performing controlled tasks, they are learning a new form of verbal behavior.

Teacher's Roles

In Audiolingualism, as in Situational Language Teaching, the teacher's role is central and active; it is a teacher-dominated method. The teacher models the target language, controls the direction and pace of learning, and monitors and corrects the learners' performance. The teacher must keep the learners attentive by varying drills and tasks and choosing relevant situations to practice structures. Language learning is seen to result from active verbal interaction between the teacher and the learners. Failure to learn results only from the improper application of the method, for example, from the teacher not providing sufficient practice or from the learner not memorizing the essential patterns and structures; but the method itself is never to blame. Brooks argues that the teacher must be trained to do the following:

Introduce, sustain, and harmonize the learning of the four skills in this order: hearing, speaking, reading and writing.

Use — and not use — English in the language classroom.

Model the various types of language behavior that the student is to learn.

Teach spoken language in dialogue form.

Direct choral response by all or parts of the class.

Teach the use of structure through pattern practice.

Guide the student in choosing and learning vocabulary.

Show how words relate to meaning in the target language.

Get the individual student to talk.

Reward trials by the student in such a way that learning is reinforced.

Teach a short story and other literary forms.

Establish and maintain a cultural island.

Formalize on the first day the rules according to which the language class is to be conducted, and enforce them.

3. Dialogues and drills form the basis of Audiolingual classroom practices. Please refer to the following various kinds of drill[①] and pattern-practice exercises, choose a sentence pattern or grammar item, and design ten exercises.

(1) Repetition

The student repeats an utterance aloud as soon as he has heard it. He does this without looking at a printed text. The utterance must be brief enough to be retained by the ear. Sound is

---

① RICHARDS J C, RODGERS T S. 语言教学的流派 [M]. 2 版. 北京：外语教学与研究出版社，2008：60-62.

as important as form and order.

Example:

This is the seventh month. – This is the seventh month.

After a student has repeated an utterance, he may repeat it again and add a few words, then repeat that whole utterance and add more words.

Example:

I used to know him. – I used to know him.

I used to know him years ago. – I used to know him years ago when we were in school ...

(2) Inflection

One word in an utterance appears in another form when repeated.

Example:

I bought the ticket. – I bought the tickets.

He bought the candy. – She bought the candy.

I called the young man. – I called the young men ...

(3) Replacement

One word in an utterance is replaced by another.

Example:

He bought this house cheap. – He bought it cheap.

Helen left early. – She left early.

They gave their boss a watch. – They gave him a watch ...

(4) Restatement

The student rephrases an utterance and addresses it to someone else, according to instructions.

Example:

Tell him to wait for you. – Wait for me.

Ask her how old she is. – How old are you?

Ask John when he began. – John, when did you begin? ...

(5) Completion

The student hears an utterance that is complete except for one word, then repeats the utterance in completed form.

Example:

I'll go my way and you go ... – I'll go my way and you go yours.

We all have...own troubles. – We all have our own troubles ...

(6) Transposition

A change in word order is necessary when a word is added.

Examples:

I'm hungry. (so) – So am I.

I'll never do it again. (neither) – Neither will I ...

(7) Expansion

When a word is added it takes a certain place in the sequence.

Examples:

I know him. (hardly). – I hardly know him.

I know him. (well). – I know him well ...

(8) Contraction

A single word stands for a phrase or clause.

Examples:

Put your hand on the table. – Put your hand there.

They believe that the earth is flat. – They believe it ...

(9) Transformation

A sentence is transformed by being made negative or interrogative or through changes in tense, mood, voice, aspect, or modality.

Examples:

He knows my address.

He doesn't know my address.

Does he know my address?

He used to know my address.

If he had known my address.

(10) Integration

Two separate utterances are integrated into one.

Examples:

They must be honest. This is important. – It is important that they be honest.

I know that man. He is looking for you. – I know the man who is looking for you ...

(11) Rejoinder

The student makes an appropriate rejoinder to a given utterance. He is told in advance to respond in one of the following ways:

Be polite.

Answer the question.

Agree.

Agree emphatically.

Express surprise.

Express regret.

Disagree.

Disagree emphatically.

Question what is said.

Fail to understand.

Be polite.

Examples:

Thank you. – You're welcome.

May I take one? – Certainly.

Answer the question.

Examples:

What is your name? – My name is Smith.

Where did it happen? – In the middle of the street.

Agree.

Examples:

He's following us. – I think you're right.

This is good coffee. – It's very good ...

(12) Restoration

The student is given a sequence of words that have been culled from a sentence but still bear its basic meaning. He uses these words with a minimum of changes and additions to restore the sentence to its original form. He may be told whether the time is present, past, or future.

Examples:

students/waiting/bus – The students are waiting for the bus.

boys/build/house/tree – The boys built a house in a tree ...

● **Teaching Design**

1. Please study the following teaching procedures and teaching steps of a typical Audiolingual class intensively, choose a lesson, design the teaching details, and then make a teaching demonstration in group.

Teaching Steps of a Typical Audiolingual Class

① *Students first hear a model dialogue (either read by the teacher or on tape) containing the key structures that are the focus of the lesson. They repeat each line of the dialogue, individually and in chorus. The teacher pays attention to pronunciation, intonation, and fluency. Correction of mistakes of pronunciation or grammar is direct and immediate. The dialogue is memorized gradually, line by line. A line may be broken down into several phrases if necessary. The dialogue is read aloud in chorus, one half saying one speaker's part and the other half responding. The students do not consult their book throughout this phase.*

② *The dialogue is adapted to the students' interest or situation, through changing certain key words or phrases. This is acted out by the students.*

③ *Certain key structures from the dialogue are selected and used as the basis for pattern drills of different kinds. These are first practiced in chorus and then individually. Some grammatical explanation may be offered at this point, but this is kept to an absolute minimum.*

④ *The students may refer to their textbook, and follow-up reading, writing, or vocabulary activities based on the dialogue may be introduced. At the beginning level, writing is purely imitative and consists of little more than copying out sentences that have been practiced. As proficiency increases, students may write out variations of structural items they have practiced or write short compositions on given topics with the help of framing questions, which will guide their use of the language.*

⑤ *Follow-up activities may take place in the language laboratory, where further dialogue and drill work is carried out.*

Teaching Steps[①] **of a Typical Audiolingual Class**

In general, the Audiolingual Method have five teaching phases.

The first phase is recognition. It means that the students can understand what they listened. For example: "I am a worker. I drive a tractor. I am a tractor-driver. Mr. Wong drives a bus. Do you know what is he? He is a bus-driver." According to this example, the teacher told you a worker who drives a tractor can be called tractor-driver. Then the teacher asks you what a driver who drives a bus can be called. You should get the right answer. That is recognition, the model sentence can help the student to understand and make more sentences.

The second phase is imitation. It contains lots of steps, such as reading after a teacher, correcting the mistakes, asking and answering the questions and learning by heart. For example, your teacher made a sentence "His family is going to move." Then you imitated it and made a similar sentence "His family is very well," but you are wrong, because when the collective noun refers to the unit as a whole, the verb is singular. If it refers to the individual members of a unit, the verb is plural. You should remember this mistake and learn by heart.

The third phase is repetition. The students must imitate the given materials repeatedly and take some memorial exercises. The teacher should check if the students have understood and read the new sentence patterns correctly in order to ensure they can go to the next phase.

The fourth phase is variation. It asks students to use the sentences which they have already managed to make new sentences by changing some words or structures. For example: T: I will go with you to the cinema this afternoon. S: I will let him to go with you to the cinema tomorrow.

---

① 引自：李媛君. Brief Analysis of the Audio-Lingual Method English Teaching[J]. 商情，2011（3）：164-165.

Next type is conversion, such as the conversion of the meaning, the structure, the element of sentence. For example: change the active form into passive form, the declarative sentence into interrogative sentence. The last type is expansion. For example: using the figures of speech to make the sentence more vivid and powerful.

The fifth phase is selection. Select and use all you have learned in everyday life. Remember, you can't use the foreign language as a native speaker, but you can improve by practicing again and again, and you can begin with some simple sentences.

2. Please read the following teaching plan carefully, point out the inappropriate places according to the theory and principles of the Audiolingual Method, then revise and improve it.

Course Name: *My face*

Teaching Objectives: *Children aged 5–7 years old (elementary level of English)*

Teaching Language: *English*

Teaching Purpose: *Through learning English words and dialogues in textbooks, students can listen, recognize, read and speak English words related to people's faces, so that students can master simple sentence patterns and expressions.*

Teaching Emphases and Difficulties:

(1) Key Points

   A. word recognition

     Head, hair, eye, ear, mouth, nose, tooth, shoulder, knee, toe, foot.

   B. Key sentence structure

① *What have you got?   I have got...*

② *Have you got... ?   Yes, I have / No, I haven't*

(2) Difficult Points — Word Deformation and Sentence Expression

   Eye-eyes, ear-ears, shoulder-shoulders, knee-knees, toe-toes, foot-feet, tooth-teeth.

Teaching Process Design:

The teacher leads the students to recognize and read the words;

The teacher leads them to read the text; the students follow the text; the teacher corrects the words in time;

The students watch the dialogue video (with the textbook);

The students imitate the dialogue;

The students repeat the dialogue throgh role-play

The students do sentence transformation exercises;

The students choose the scene to narrate by themselves.

Teaching Duration: *2 hours.*

Teaching Contents:

The teacher leads the students to read the words and read the text (30 minutes);

Watch the video (10 minutes);

Imitate and repeat the dialogue (20 minutes);

Role-play (20 minutes);

Alternate exercises (25 minutes);

Class assignments (15 minutes).

Teaching Equipment: *multimedia video player, teacher's book, word cards.*

Training Contents:

① Spell the words in the textbook;

② Read dialogues:

  A: What have you got? / Have you got... ?

  B: ...

③ Imitate video dialogues and role-play.

Summary and Homework:

① Spell the word three times and copy the word two times;

② Read the dialogue twice;

③ Make up a dialogue by using the words and sentence patterns learned in class.

● **Further Reading**

A Brief Introduction of the Audiolingual Method①

The Audiolingual Method originated in America, lasting from 1959 to 1966. With a short history, it affects foreign language teaching greatly. The core of this method is mechanical drill. Nowadays, it is still used in the field of foreign language teaching and learning.

1. Origination of the Audiolingual Method

The origination of the Audiolingual Method was complex. First, it was once described by different words. Second, it emerged from various factors. Third, it lasted only 8 years in America. From 1967, it was criticized on theoretical and pragmatic grounds, which led to the decline of the Audiolingual Method.

(1) Various Names

The Audiolingual Method originated in America. Before the 1950s, it appeared under various names: oral approach, structural approach, linguistic method, pattern method, and army method, and Audiolingual Approach. The Audiolingual Method was proposed by Brooks. With

---

① WU L J. A Brief Introduction of the Audiolingual Method [J]. Overseas English, 2014(06): 66-68.

various names, the core of the Audiolingual Method is always the same from the beginning to the end, which will be explained later. According to various names and definitions, we can find some common points:

① It focused on oral fluency;

② Students paid much attention to practicing patterns in class;

③ It was related to structural linguistic;

④ The drill is a distinctive feature of the Audiolingual Method.

(2) Background

Before World War Ⅱ, the situation of foreign language teaching in American schools and colleges was terrible and backward. First, foreign language teaching was paid little attention in American schools and colleges. Few students learned foreign languages in schools. And the learning process lasted less than 3 years. Second, universities offered only 3–6 kinds of foreign languages for students. Third, the goal of foreign language teaching was to develop student's reading ability, ignoring oral fluency. The Coleman Report in 1929, recommending a reading-based approach, influenced considerably foreign language teaching in American schools and colleges. Fourth, the Grammar-Translation Method was still used widely in foreign language teaching. Teachers paid much attention to the translation and explaining grammar. In this case, it was a necessity of a reform in teaching methods.

The entry of the United States into World War Ⅱ also influenced the development of the Audiolingual Method. "To train a large number of interpreters, code-room assistants, and translators, the Army Specialized Training Program (ASTP) was established in 1942". In the ASTP, a new method, the Army Method, was adopted. There were four features of this method:

① The goal was oral proficiency;

② Teachers were foreigners, or native speakers;

③ There were 8–10 students in one class;

④ Students' courses were intensive.

"They studied 10 hours a day, 6 days a week. There were generally 15 hours of drills with native speakers and 20–30 hours of private study spread over two to three 6-week sessions". After World War Ⅱ, thousands of students entered the United States to study in universities. Before beginning their studies, they took part in various training to master English.

Generous financial support and political guides from the U.S. government also prompted the emergence of the Audiolingual Method. In 1957, the launching of the first Russian satellite shook the U.S. government. In this case, the National Defense Education Act (1958) came into being. According to the Act, "the U.S. government provided funds for the study and analysis of modern languages, for the development of teaching materials, and for the training of teachers". The Audiolingual Method was used widely in American schools and colleges.

The emergence of the Audiolingual Method was influenced by various factors: terrible situation in American schools and colleges before World War II, the army method during World War II, education reform and foreigners' English learning after World War II. According to Stern and Fries, informant method, the development of contrastive linguistics, and the new technology of the language laboratory also were factors contributing to the development of the Audiolingual Method.

(3) Decline

From 1967, two main reasons led to its decline. First, the theoretical foundations of the Audiolingual Method were criticized by Chomsky. For example, according to Chomsky, sentences are not learned by imitation and repetition but "generated" from the learner's underlying "competence". Chomsky also claimed that practice should involve meaningful languages. Students should be encouraged to use their creative ability for language learning. Second, the results were not so good. Students thought the study is boring and do not understand the meaning of what they are repeating in class. It was true that students performed well in classroom, but they were unable to speak and understand the language outside the classroom situation. In summary, in the early 1970s, the rapid changes in the theoretical positions and the slower development of practice led to the decline of the Audiolingual Method.

2. Theoretical Foundations of the Audiolingual Method

The theoretical foundations of the Audiolingual Method include two parts: theory of language and theory of learning. The theory of language is American Structural Linguistics and the theory of learning refers to Behaviorism.

(1) American Structural Linguistics

According to American Structural Linguistics, language is a system of structurally related elements for the coding of meaning. Before 1930s, language scholars focused on the grammar of Indo-European language, which was viewed as classical grammar. By the 1930s, some language scholars were interested in non-European language. For example, Bloomfield studied American Indian language and other non-European languages. In these experiences, Bloomfield and his colleagues used "informant method" in researches. A native speaker, the informant, provided phrases, vocabulary, and sentences for a linguist, the imitation. The linguist elicited the basic structure of the language from the informant. According to Richards and Rodgers, "Thus the students and the linguists were able to take part in guided conversation with the informant, and together they gradually learned how to speak the language, as well as to understand much of its basic grammar." They found that "language was viewed as a system of structurally related elements for the encoding of meaning, the elements being phonemes, morphemes, words, structures, and sentence types". Language is primarily what is spoken and only secondarily what is written. In the 1950s, the American Structural Linguistics was popular in the field of linguistic.

Pattern practice was a basic classroom technique. It is these basic patterns that constitute the learner's task. Hockett held that learners require drill, drill and more drill, and only enough vocabulary to make such drills possible. With teaching experience in University of Michigan, Fries and other linguists summarized the basic process of the Audiolingual Method and produced teaching materials. Nowadays, some basic principles still guide foreign language teaching in many countries.

(2) Behaviorism

In the mid-1950s, behaviorism established the psychology basis for the Audiolingual Method. Skinner, the famous neo-behaviorist, put forward the theory of operant conditioning. According to Skinner, language learning is a process of mechanical habit formation, depending on three crucial elements: stimulus, response and reinforcement. A stimulus elicits certain behavior, which is named a response. The key element is reinforcement. Chen and Liu claimed that the reinforcement not only marks the response being appropriate or inappropriate, but also, encourages the repetition of the response in the future. According to Richards and Rodgers, "To apply this theory to language learning is to identify the organism as the foreign language learner, the behavior as verbal behavior, the stimulus as what is taught or presented of the foreign language, the response as the learner's reaction to the stimulus, and the reinforcement as the extrinsic approval and praise of the teacher or fellow students or the intrinsic self-satisfaction of target language use."

According to Chen and Liu, behaviorists also put forward suggestions about reinforcement for teachers:

① To provide different kinds of reinforcement for different students. That is, paying attention to students' individual characters.

② To take students' age into account when teachers provide reinforcement.

③ To reinforce immediately. Skinner held that "The long-term goals in education, like wanting to be a doctor, have little effect upon the student at the moment. He may tell you that he really wants to an education, but he cannot write that term paper or read that text, and for a very good reason: nothing happens when he does. Something may happen a year or five years later, but that is too late." Therefore, immediate reinforcement was designed to encourage students' response.

④ At the beginning of foreign language learning, every appropriate response should be reinforced.

⑤ To ensure that the direction of the reinforcement is right.

3. Design of the Audiolingual Method

The theoretical foundations of the Audiolingual Method have direct and remarkable effect on its teaching objectives, teacher roles, learner roles, activities, procedures and so on. The following part introduces them in detail, including teaching principles and teaching procedures. Teaching objectives, teacher's roles, learner's roles, and activities will be introduced in the principles part.

(1) Principles

Principles of the Audiolingual Method were described by Brooks, Kirch, Zhang, and many other linguists. We can summarize them as the following:

① Foreign language learning is basically a process of mechanical habit formation. Through pattern drills, the verbal behavior can be learned.

② Speech has priority in foreign language learning and teaching. Language is speech. Speech is historically prior to writing in any culture where writing exists. Spoken language is acquired earlier than written language. The objective is oral fluency, especially the near-native pronunciation.

③ Dialogues and drills are basic audiolingual classroom practices. After a dialogue has been presented, specific grammatical patterns in the dialogue are selected. The focus of drills is these specific grammatical patterns. Brooks (1964) put forward 12 kinds of drills, including repetition, inflection, replacement, restatement, completion, transposition, expansion, contraction, transformation, integration, rejoinder and restoration.

④ To use the target language as much as possible. Kirch put forward a very simple rule about it: "use the foreign language (or the target language) exclusively, as long as there is adequate communication, but do not hesitate to make brief use of the native language to guarantee comprehension of essentials. This applies not only to dialogues, but also to grammar." If a teacher could explain it in target language, fine! Otherwise, a brief explanation in native language is OK.

⑤ Analogy and inductive approach were used in foreign language learning and teaching. Analogy provided a better foundation for learning than analysis. Wong and Patten claimed that if drills have been fully practiced, analogy will guide the learner along the right linguistic path, as it does in the mother tongue. Contrastive analysis is a distinctive feature of the Audiolingual Method.

⑥ Cultural aspects of native speakers were taught in teaching a foreign language, because the culture and language were related to each other.

⑦ It is a teacher-dominated method.

⑧ Teaching machines were used widely in audiolingual classroom, including Television, PowerPoint, video, tape and language laboratory. Tape recorders and audiovisual equipment often have central roles in an audiolingual course.

(2) Procedure

According to Richards and Rodgers, it also includes five steps:

① Students hear a model dialogue, which contains the key structures. Students memorize the dialogue line by line.

② The teacher changes certain keywords or phrases in the dialogue. This is acted out by students.

③ Key structures are selected from the dialogue. Students learn them through various kinds of drills. It is the most important step in this procedure.

④ Students learn reading and writing skills. Reading means that students read the dialogue loudly and writing refers to copying words, key structures, even the dialogue.

⑤ Students reinforce what have been learned in the language laboratory. There are still various descriptions, but the core is same: oral fluency and pattern drills.

4. Assessment of the Audiolingual Method

The Audiolingual Method made great contribution to the development of foreign language teaching methodology. First, Stern claimed that "It was among the first theories to recommend the development of a language teaching theory on declared linguistic and psychological principles." Second, it was used widely not only in the teaching of foreign languages in the United States, but also in the teaching of English as a second or foreign language all over the world. Third, contrastive analysis was used in class. What's more, it emphasized on pronunciation and syntactical progression. Teachers taught certain patterns directly, with inductive approach. While, there are some disadvantages: the pattern drills were boring and mechanical, ignoring students' creative ability; reading and writing skills were paid little attention; it was a teacher-dominated method, ignoring students' requirement and autonomy and so on.

5. Conclusion

The Audiolingual Method was popular in 1960s. Its theoretical foundations were American Structural Linguistics and Behaviorism. The main principles of the Audiolingual Method includes: paying attention to oral fluency, pattern drills, usage of teaching machines. Nowadays, it has some changes in certain respects. It is still used in schools and training program sometime. Thus, from a present-day perspective, it made great contribution to the development of language teaching methodology. Nowadays, we, teachers and linguists should be eclectic, absorbing the positive things in the Audiolingual Method and avoiding its shortcomings in teaching practice.

● **Knowledge Table**

Table 3-1　Summary of Characteristics of the Audiolingual Method

Key Points	The Adiolingual Method
Period	
Representatives	
Background	
Theory of Language	
Theory of Language Learning	
Objectives	
The Syllabus	
Types of Learning and Teaching Activities	
Teacher's Roles	
Learner's Roles	
The Role of Students' Native Language and Target Language	
The Role of Instructional Materials and Textbook	
Others	
Summary	

● **Mind Map**

Chapter 4　Total Physical Response

第 4 章　全身反应法

Contents

- Teaching Case of Total Physical Response
- Theoretical Basis of Total Physical Response
- Teaching Principles of Total Physical Response
- Teaching Procedures of Total Physical Response
- Comments on Total Physical Response
- Activities and Exercises

- 全身反应法教学示例
- 全身反应法的理论基础
- 全身反应法的教学原则
- 全身反应法的教学过程
- 对全身反应法的评价
- 活动与练习

O Wordle

1 Introduction

Total Physical Response (TPR) is a language teaching method developed by James Asher, a psychology professor at San Jose State University in the 1960s. As Richards and Rodgers say, motor activities are a means of language learning; TPR attempts to teach language through speech and physical activity at the same time.

TPR originates from the language acquisition process of infants. Let's take the communication between parents and their children for example. The father says, "Look at daddy. Look at daddy." The infant's face turns in the direction of the voice. Professor Asher calls this "a language-body conversation" because the parent speaks and the infant answers with a physical response such as looking, smiling, laughing, turning, walking, reaching, grasping, holding, sitting, running, so on and so forth. Since that time, for a certain period, usually a few months, the infant absorbs the language without being able to speak the language. But after this stage, the child is able to reproduce the language spontaneously. It is during that period that the internalization and codebreaking occurs.

Asher developed TPR as a result of his experiences observing young children learning their first languages. He made listening and responding with actions as the most important elements in language teaching and regarded the relationship between teachers and learners as the relationship between parents and their baby. Therefore, learners' role in TPR is to listen and perform what the teacher says, and they monitor and evaluate their own progress. They are encouraged to speak when they feel ready to speak. As a model and a director, the teacher takes on the role of the parent: providing opportunities for learning, giving prompts, setting patterns, playing games, and the learner then responds physically to the prompt. In giving feedback, the teacher responds positively to the correct answer, much in the way that a parent would. This reinforces the learning and encourages further steps.

Total Physical Response is often used alongside other methods and techniques. It is popular with beginners and with young learners, although it can be used with students of all levels and all age groups.

一、教学法概述

全身反应法（TPR）是美国圣约瑟州立大学心理学教授詹姆斯·阿舍在 20 世纪 60 年代提出的一种语言教学法。正如理查德和罗杰斯所说，运动是语言学习的手段，全身反应法就是一种试图通过将言语表达与身体动作相联系来教授语言的方法。

全身反应法源于婴儿的语言习得过程。以父母和孩子之间的交流为例。父亲说："看爸爸。看爸爸。"婴儿的脸便转向声音发出的方向。阿舍教授将其称为"语言 – 身体对话"，因为父母说话时，婴儿用身体反应进行回答，如看过来、微笑、大笑、转头、走、抓、拿、坐、跑，等等。从那时起，并在一定时期内，婴儿仅仅吸收内化所听到的语言而并不会说一句话。这一阶段通常持续几个月。过了这一阶段之后，幼儿便能够自发地进行语言表达了。正是在那个只听不说的阶段，婴儿将语言进行了内化和破译。

通过观察幼儿学习第一语言的经验，阿舍使全身反应法得到了发展。在该教学法中，听和用动作回应成为教学中最重要的元素，而师生关系也被视为父母与孩子的关系。因此，在全身反应法中，学习者的角色是倾听和执行教师所说的话，他们监控并评估自己的进步。当学习者在心理上、语言上都做好准备后，教师便鼓励他们进行表达。作为一个榜样和指导者，教师扮演着家长的角色，比如，为学习者提供语言学习的机会，给出提示，设置模式，进行游戏，然后学习者根据提示做出身体上的反应。教师对正确答案进行积极的反馈，以鼓励学习者的后续活动并强化学习效果，这与家长对孩子语言表达的反馈十分相似。

全身反应法通常与其他第二语言教学方法或技巧一起使用。它适用于各年龄段及各水平语言学习者，并尤其受到初级水平学习者及青少年学习者的欢迎。

2 Teaching Case[①]

The class is located in Sweden. It is a beginning class for 30 students of Grade 5. They study English three times a week.

It is the first class of the year, so after the teacher takes attendance, she introduces the method they will use to study English. She explains in Swedish: "You will be studying English in

---

① 　LARSEN-FREEMAN D, ANDERSON M. Techniques and Principles in Language Teaching [M]. Oxford: Oxford University Press, 2011: 104–107.

a way that is similar to the way you learned Swedish. You will not speak at first. Rather, you will just listen to me and do as I do. I will give you a command to do something in English, and you will do the actions along with me. I will need four volunteers to help me with the lesson."

Hands go up, and the teacher calls on four students to come to the front of the room and sit with her on chairs that are lined up facing the other students. She tells the other students to listen and to watch.

In English, the teacher says, "Stand up." As she says it, she stands up and she signals for the four volunteers to rise with her. They all stand up. "Sit down." she says, and they all sit. The teacher and the students stand up and sit down together several times according to the teacher's command; the students say nothing. The next time that they stand up together, the teacher issues a new command, "Turn around." The students follow the teacher's example and turn so that they are facing their chairs. "Turn around." the teacher says again and this time they turn to face the other students as before. "Sit down. Stand up. Turn around. Sit down." She says, "Walk." and they all begin walking towards the front row of the students' seats. "Stop. Jump. Stop. Turn around. Walk. Stop. Jump. Stop. Turn around. Sit down." The teacher gives the commands and they all perform the actions together. The teacher gives these commands again, changing their order and saying them quite quickly. "Stand up. Jump. Sit down. Stand up. Turn around. Jump. Stop. Turn around. Walk. Stop. Turn around. Walk. Jump. Turn around. Sit down."

Once again, the teacher gives the commands; this time, however, she remains seated. The four volunteers respond to her commands. "Stand up. Sit down. Walk. Stop. Jump. Turn around. Turn around. Walk. Turn around. Sit down." The students respond perfectly. Next, the teacher signals that she would like one of the volunteers to follow her commands alone. One student raises his hand and performs the actions the teacher commands.

Finally, the teacher approaches the other students who have been sitting observing her and their four classmates. "Stand up." she says and the class responds. "Sit down. Stand up. Jump. Stop. Sit down. Stand up. Turn around. Turn around. Jump. Sit down." Even though they have not done the actions before, the students are able to perform according to the teacher's commands.

The teacher is satisfied that the class has mastered these six commands. She begins to introduce some new ones. "Point to the door." She orders. She extends her right arm and right index finger in the direction of the door at the side of the classroom. The volunteers point with her. "Point to the desk." She points to her own big teacher's desk at the front of the room. "Point to the chair." She points to the chair behind her desk and the students follow.

"Stand up." The students stand up. "Point to the door." The students point. "Walk to the door." They walk together. "Touch the door." The students touch it with her. The teacher continues to command the students as follows: "Point to the desk. Walk to the desk. Touch the desk. Point to the door. Walk to the door. Touch the door. Point to the chair. Walk to the chair.

Touch the chair." She continues to perform the actions with the students, but changes the order of the commands. After practicing these new commands with the students several times, the teacher remains seated, and the four volunteers carry out the commands by themselves. Only once do the students seem confused, at which point the teacher repeats the command which has caused difficulty and performs the action with them.

Next, the teacher turns to the rest of the class and gives the following commands to the students sitting in the back row: "Stand up. Sit down. Stand up. Point to the desk. Point to the door. Walk to the door. Walk to the chair. Touch the chair. Walk. Stop. Jump. Walk. Turn around. Sit down." Although she varies the sequence of commands, the students do not seem to have any trouble following the order.

Next, the teacher turns to the four volunteers and says, "Stand up. Jump to the desk." The students have never heard this command before. They hesitate a second and then jump to the desk just as they have been told. Everyone laughs at this sight. "Touch the desk. Sit on the desk." Again, the teacher uses a novel command, one they have not practiced before. The teacher then issues two commands in the form of a compound sentence, "Point to the door, and walk to the door." Again, the group performs as it has been commanded.

As the last step of the lesson, the teacher writes the new commands on the board. Each time she writes a command, she acts it out. The students copy the sentences into their notebooks.

The class is over. No one except the teacher has spoken a word. However, a few weeks later, the students start to speak the new commands and some related sentences. The students in this class can direct other students and the teacher with the commands, such as: "Raise your hands. Show me your hands. Close your eyes. Put your hands behind you. Open your eyes. Shake hand with your neighbor. Raise your left foot."

二、教学示例

本示例中，全身反应法被应用于瑞典的一堂英语课程中。班里有 30 名五年级的学生，每周 3 次英语课。

这是本年度的第一次课，老师查完考勤后，便开始介绍他们将使用的英语学习方法。老师用瑞典语解释道："你们将使用与学习自己母语相同的方法学习英语。你们一开始可以不必说。你们只要听我说、跟我做就行。我会用英语告诉你们做什么，然后你们和我一起做动作。现在，我需要 4 名同学来协助我完成这项工作。"

学生们纷纷举起手来，老师找了 4 名学生，让他们到教室前面来，和她并排坐在椅子上，并面向其他学生。老师让其他学生认真听，仔细看。

老师一边用英语说"起立"，一边从椅子上站起来，她还示意旁边的 4 名学生也和她一起站起来。他们都起立以后，老师又说："请坐。"然后大家都坐下。随后，老师和学生们一起按照指令起立、坐下，反复进行了好几次，期间，学生们什么也没说。之后，大家一起站起来后，老师发出了一个新的指令："向后转。"学生们跟着老师的示范，都向后转身面向椅子。老师又说了一遍："向后转。"这次大家又转了回来，像之前一样面向其他学生。老师继续说着："坐下，起立，向后转，坐下。"之后，老师又说："向前走。"大家都开始朝其他学生座位的方向走去。"停，跳，停，向后转，向前走，停，跳，停，向后转，坐下。"老师发出指令，大家一起做动作。老师又继续发出指令，这次老师改变了指令的顺序，并且加快了语速。"起立，跳，坐下，起立，向后转，跳，停，向后转，走，停，向后转，走，跳，向后转，坐下。"

当老师再次发出指令时，她保持不动，不再示范，转而由4名学生来执行指令，即做动作。"起立，坐下，走，停，跳，向后转，向后转，走，向后转，坐下。"学生们出色地完成了指令。接下来，老师表示需要4名学生中的1名学生按照她的指令单独做动作。1名学生举起手来，并按照老师的要求完成了相关动作。

最后，老师走近那些一直坐着观察她和4名学生演示"起立"等动作的学生们，并发出指令："坐下，起立，跳，停，坐下，起立，向后转，向后转，跳，坐下。"那些观看动作的学生们虽然之前没做过这些动作，但他们也都能按照老师的指令完成动作。

全班学生都掌握了这6个指令，老师对此十分满意。接下来，她开始引入新的指令。老师伸出右臂，用右手食指指向教室一侧的门，说道："指门。"4名学生也跟着老师一起指。老师指着教室前面的讲台，说："指桌子。"然后，她又指向桌子后面的椅子，并说："指椅子。"4名学生继续像之前一样跟着老师做动作。

老师说："起立。"学生们便站起来。老师说："指门。"学生们便指向门。老师说："走到门口。"他们便一起走向门口。老师说："摸一下门。"学生们便和老师一样摸一下门。老师继续发出指令，与学生们一起演示动作，但这次她改变了指令的顺序："指桌子，走到桌子前，摸一下桌子，指门，走到门口，摸一下门，指椅子，走到椅子前，摸一下椅子。"在和学生们练习了几次这些新指令后，老师便坐在椅子上不做动作了，而由4名学生独自执行指令。此期间，学生们有一次表现出了困惑，老师便重复了一遍给学生造成困难的指令，并带着他们一起完成动作。

接下来，老师又转向班上其他同学，对坐在后排的学生发出指令："起立，坐下，起立，指桌子，指门，走到门口，走到椅子前，摸一下椅子，走，停，跳，走，向后转，坐下。"尽管老师随机改换指令，但学生们都十分顺利地按要求完成了相关动作。

之后，老师又转向四名学生，说："起立，跳到桌子上。"学生们以前从未听过这个命令。他们犹豫了片刻，然后便按指令跳到桌子上。在场的学生看到这一幕都大笑起来。老师又发出新奇的指令，仍然是他们以前从未练习过的指令："摸一下桌子，坐到桌子上。"然后，老师又以复句的形式发出两个命令："指门，然后走到门前。"4名学生依然按照指令做动作，并全部圆满完成。

作为本课的最后一个环节，老师在黑板上写下了新学的指令。她每写一个指令，就做一遍动作。学生们则把句子抄到本子上。

随后便下课了。除了老师之外没有人说过一句话。然而，几周后，学生们开始开口说这些新学的指令，并能说出一些与这些指令相关的句子。班里的学生可以用所学的指令来指挥其他学生和老师做动作，比如："举起手来，把手给我看，闭上眼睛，把手放在身后，睁开眼睛，和你的邻座握手，抬起左脚。"

3 Teaching Principles and Teaching Procedures

3.1 Theoretical Basis of TPR

As Asher states, "most of the grammatical structure of the target language and hundreds of vocabulary items can be learned from the skillful use of the imperative by the instructor." TPR reflects a grammar-based view of language and considers the verb in the imperative as the central linguistic motif around which language use and learning are organized.

Asher sees a stimulus-response view as providing the learning theory underlying language teaching pedagogy. TPR can also be linked to the "trace theory" of memory in psychology, which holds that the more often or the more intensively a memory connection is traced, the stronger the memory association will be and the more likely it will be recalled. Retracing can be done verbally and/or in association with motor activity. Combined tracing activities, such as verbal rehearsal accompanied by motor activity, hence increase the possibility of successful recall.

In addition, Asher outlined three main hypotheses about learning second languages that are embodied in the TPR method.

The first is that the brain is naturally predisposed to learning a language through listening. Specifically, Asher says that learners best internalize language when they respond with physical movement to language input. Asher hypothesizes that speech develops naturally and spontaneously after learners internalize the target language through input, and that it should not be forced. In Asher's own words, "A reasonable hypothesis is that the brain and the nervous system are biologically programmed to acquire language, either the first or the second in a particular sequence and in a particular mode. The sequence is listening before speaking and the mode is to synchronize language with the individual's body."

The second of Asher's hypotheses is that effective language learning must engage the right hemisphere of the brain. Physical movement is controlled primarily by the right hemisphere, and Asher sees the coupling of movement with language comprehension as the key to language acquisition. He says that left-hemisphere learning should be avoided, and that the left hemisphere needs a great deal of experience of right-hemisphere-based input before natural speech can occur.

Asher's third hypothesis is that language learning should not involve any stress, as stress and negative emotions inhibit the natural language-learning process. He regards the stressful nature of most language-teaching methods as one of their major weaknesses. Asher recommends that teachers focus on meaning and physical movement to avoid stress.

3.2 Teaching Principles of TPR

TPR tries to reach the goal of "physical action reaction, high-speed understanding, long-term retention, stress-free, and enjoyable for teachers as well as students." In a TPR course, comprehension is a means to the aim of the course, while the ultimate aim is to teach oral proficiency. The main principles of TPR are as follows:

① Listening comprehension is in the first place. Once a foundation in listening comprehension has been established, speech evolves naturally and effortlessly out of it.

② Listening should be accompanied by physical movement. Learners need stimulating actions that allow the body to act on language in order to improve their understanding ability.

③ Learners should be allowed to take part in activities after they are ready and have the requirements to speak the target language.

④ Teachers should make the students feel stress-free and successful. An important condition for successful language learning is the absence of stress. The key to stress-free learning is to focus on meaning interpreted through action, rather than on language forms studied in the abstract.

3.3 Teaching Procedures of TPR

The teaching process of TPR generally has the following steps:

First, the teacher introduces the teaching methods they will use in the lesson in his native language, and then makes demonstrations while giving instructions. The teacher gives instructions to individual students first, and then to the whole class.

Second, the teacher gives the instruction without acting, letting the whole class or individual student do the actions by themselves or by himself.

Third, the teacher combines the instructions given before and after, and makes demonstration actions at the same time; then the teacher gives instructions to the students.

Fourth, the teacher combines the instructions given before and after, but does not do demonstration actions. Let individual students do it, then let the whole class do it. Then the teacher changes the order of the instructions, and lets students respond.

Fifth, the teacher writes the instructions (short sentences) on the blackboard, no more than three at a time.

Sixth, encourage the students who can give instructions orally and let the teachers and other students do actions. After about 20 class hours, the teacher will have dialogue teaching, some short plays, games, slide shows and other classroom activities will be involved at that time.

三、教学原则与教学过程

1. 全身反应法的理论基础

正如阿舍所说，"大部分目的语语法结构和成千上万的目的语词汇，只需在教师的指导下熟练地使用祈使句就能学会"，由此可见，全身反应法是一种基于语法或结构的语言教学法，它以祈使句中的动词为核心要素，围绕这些动词来组织语言的学习与运用等活动。

阿舍认为刺激反应论的观点为全身反应法提供了学习理论方面的基础。另外，全身反应法与心理学中的"记忆痕迹理论"也关系密切。该理论认为，记忆联系被追踪的频率越高或强度越大，记忆关联就越强，被回忆的可能性也就越大。回忆可以口头完成，也可以通过肢体动作完成。结合对记忆关联痕迹的回忆，如伴随着肢体动作的言语复述，可以提高回忆的成功率与效率。

此外，在第二语言学习方面，阿舍还提出了三个假设。

阿舍的第一个假设是，大脑天生就倾向于通过听来学习语言。具体来讲就是学习者将语言内化的最佳方法是根据语言输入做出身体动作的反应。语言是学习者在将目的语输入进行内化后自然自发地发展起来的，而不是强迫灌输来的。用阿舍自己的话来说就是："一个合理的假设是，无论习得第一语言还是习得第二语言，人类的大脑和神经系统都遵循生物学上的一套既定机制，即都按照一个特定的顺序和模式进行。顺序就是先听后说，模式便是让语言与个人的身体动作同步进行。"

阿舍的第二个假设是，有效的语言学习必须与大脑的右半球发生联系。身体动作主要由大脑右半球控制，阿舍认为运动与语言理解的耦合是语言习得的关键。他说，语言习得应该避免基于大脑左半球进行，而应该在大脑右半球动作活动的基础上进行，当大脑右半球积累了足够量的学习动作输入后，大脑左半球的语言活动才被激活，言语行为才会自然产生。

阿舍的第三个假设是，语言学习不应该伴随任何压力，这是由于压力和负面情绪会抑制自然的语言学习过程。他认为大多数语言教学方法对学生产生的压力是它们的主要不足之一。因此，阿舍建议，教师应关注意义与身体动作的结合，以减轻并消除压力。

2. 全身反应法的教学原则

全身反应法试图达到"利用身体动作进行反应、快速理解、长期保持、零压力、师生心情愉悦"的目的。在运用全身反应法的课程中，理解是达到课程目标的手段，课程的最终目标是培养学习者的口语能力。全身反应法的主要教学原则是：

①听力理解是第一位的。听力理解一旦建立起来以后，在此基础上，语言表达就自然而然地生成了。

②倾听应该伴随着身体运动。通过全身动作的反应来训练理解能力，有利于学习者掌握目的语。

③在学习者已准备好并有了说目的语的需求后，再让他们开始参与语言表达活动。

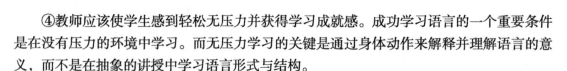

④教师应该使学生感到轻松无压力并获得学习成就感。成功学习语言的一个重要条件是在没有压力的环境中学习。而无压力学习的关键是通过身体动作来解释并理解语言的意义，而不是在抽象的讲授中学习语言形式与结构。

3. 全身反应法的教学过程

全身反应法的教学过程，一般有以下几个步骤：

第一，教师先用母语介绍本课要采用的教学方法，然后一边发出指令一边做动作进行示范。教师发指令先让个别学生做动作，再让全班学生做动作。

第二，教师只发指令，不做示范动作，让学生自己做。可以让学生集体做，也可以找个别学生单独做。

第三，教师将前后发出的指令结合起来，并同时做动作进行示范；然后发出指令让学生做。

第四，教师将前后发出的指令结合起来，但不做示范，先让个别学生做动作，再让全班做。随后，教师变换指令的顺序，并让学生做动作。

第五，教师把指令（短句子）写在黑板上，每次不超过3个。

第六，鼓励能说的学生发出指令，教师和其他学生听指令，做动作。大约在20课时后，教师再进行对话教学，并组织一些短剧、游戏、幻灯片展示等课堂活动。

4 Conclusion

Total Physical Response enjoyed some popularity in the 1970s and 1980s. It integrates vision, sense of hearing and organs, making learners do actions of speaking, acting, and thinking at the same time. It closely connects various daily life actions with language class, making the class vivid and active. By doing interesting actions with teachers and classmates, students' anxiety is relieved, the distance between teacher and students is shortened, a relaxing atmosphere is built up, and both teaching knowledge and developing emotions together make students learn willingly, like to learn, and keep the interest in learning. Besides, Asher stressed that TPR should be used in association with other methods and techniques. Therefore, the flexibility of TPR also provides great convenience for its widespread use.

While when using TPR teaching method, we should pay attention to the following points. Firstly, it is suitable for the beginning period of language study, since many of the actions and languages are very easy. So, it can't be used in teaching complex contents, unless combining with some other methods. Secondly, TPR teaching method contains a lot of games, role-plays, group competitions, etc. The students are more excited after doing the activities. It's difficult to control their feelings. Thus, teacher should build an effective class organization model to deal with this situation. Otherwise, the expected results will not be achieved even if much better teaching methods and plentiful teaching activities are applied.

四、小结

全身反应法在二十世纪七八十年代颇受欢迎。它集视觉、听觉、身体感觉于一体，让学习者在说话、表演、思考的同时做动作。它将日常生活中丰富多彩的行为活动与语言课堂紧密地联系在一起，使课堂生动、活跃。与老师和其他同学做有趣的动作，缓解了学生们的焦虑，拉近了师生之间的距离，营造了一种轻松的氛围。知识讲授与情感发展相辅相成，使学生愿意学习，喜欢学习，并持续保持学习兴趣。此外，阿舍强调，全身反应法应该与其他教学方法及教学技巧结合起来使用。因此，全身反应法的灵活性也为它的普及使用提供了很大的便利。

然而，在使用全身反应法时，也应注意到：首先，它更适合于在语言学习的初级阶段的学习者使用，这一学习阶段涉及的许多动作和言语表达都比较容易。而如果不和其他教学法结合起来使用，全身反应法较难用于复杂内容的教学。其次，全身反应法包含了大量的游戏、角色扮演、小组竞赛等活动内容，学生们在完成这类活动后会格外兴奋。这对教师如何在课堂中更好地控制和引导学生的情绪提出了挑战。因此，教师应建立起有效的班级组织模式来应对这种情况。否则，再好的教学方法、再丰富的教学活动也无法达到预期的效果。

○ Activities and Exercises

● Understanding and Thinking

1. Please read and combine the following background materials, and talk about your understanding of the origin relationship between these language teaching methods involved in the materials and the differences between TPR and other methods.

In the late nineteenth century, a Frenchman called Francois Gouin, having failed to learn German by traditional methods (including memorizing a dictionary), had a flash of insight on observing his young nephew recounting a visit to the local mill. The boy's story took the form of the description of a sequence of activities, inspiring Gouin to develop his "series method": Lessons consisted of series of actions that were simultaneously enacted and described. In addition, Gouin's observations of children's language learning suggested to him the need for an "incubation period" between listening and speaking. Not only was Gouin's approach a precursor of the Direct Method but his recognition of the need for a "silent period" also presaged the Natural Approach of Terrell and Krashen.

Gouin's influence was considerable, especially in the teaching of foreign languages in schools, and it persisted into the twentieth century. For Gouin, the key to language was the verb, and the structure that highlights verbs like nothing else is the imperative. Harold Palmer of the Oral Method developed this idea into what he called "imperative drill": "The teacher says 'get up', and makes the appropriate sign. The student has not understood the words but he does understand the sign and he gets up. The teacher says 'sit down' and the student obeys the gesture." Once students are trained to associate the command with the action, the gestures are withheld. And the commands increase in complexity — from "get up" to "take the fourth book from the side nearest the window, from the second shelf; open it at page 65 and point to the first word." For Palmer it was important that students remain silent during the performance of the actions.

It took another four decades before this technique was developed into a method in its own right, to be called Total Physical Response (TPR). It's perhaps significant that one of the early papers published on it by the method's architect, James Asher, was called "Children's first language as a model for second language learning". In that article, Asher argues that "not only is listening critical for the development of speaking, but children acquire listening skill in a particular way. For instance, there is an intimate relationship between language and the child's body." It is this intimate relationship that TPR seeks to exploit for second language learning.

2. A North American teacher, Dr Meece once told us a motto: "I hear, I forget; I see, I remember; I do, I understand." "Do" plays a very important role in English learning, and TPR is a kind of "Do" activity with fun and playfulness.

Please read the following materials, then combine the teaching principles of TPR with your own experience of learning a second language (eg. English), discuss the role and significance of "do" activities in language learning, and introduce the main teaching techniques used in TPR.

Using Performance in TPR.

Being active is students' nature; the teacher should make use of it and combine activities with teaching. In this way, the classroom become alive and students can take part in the teaching activities. This way also enables students to relax. With the help of the teacher's tips, students can use body language to convey their message. The teacher and students can follow some flash songs; do some games, which combine singing and action. The song of "Head and Shoulder, Knees and Toes" is a good example. The teacher and students are singing while touching their interrelated parts of body. After some practices, all the words are remembered by students. Using performance in the teaching, it amuses the students at once and arouses the students' desire to learn, and then students are relaxed. At the same time, performance can make the atmosphere of classroom active.

Using Competition in TPR.

Generally speaking, students have strong curiosity and ambition. Some competitive activities can improve students' learning motivation; especially some group competitions can greatly stimulate their enthusiasm for learning English. The teacher can take full advantage of the students' psychological characteristics and train students' language skills in the competition. In particular, during the reviewing lessons, the teacher can ask different group of students to sum up the knowledge they have learned. Then the teacher can summarize the students' answers. What is more, students can also name their groups, such as "tiger" group and "lion" group, "boys" group and "girls" group and so on. Competition makes students' enthusiasm higher, which makes the language learning more interesting.

Using Painting in TPR.

Have you ever thought of using the students' drawing skill to teach English? The teacher should allow students to draw some pictures when they are learning different words. The teacher should try his/her best to draw some pictures, which relate to the contents. The teacher can also ask students to draw together. For example, in teaching body parts, the teacher should ask students to draw the head, fingers, eyes, feet of a "monster." Some instructions are as follows. Draw a head. Draw three eyes. Draw two noses. For students, the one that can draw the most terrible monster is the best young painter. This method is good for students' understanding and memory of some words.

Using Actual Object in TPR.

One of the students' psychological characteristics is that students often focus on specific visual objects. The more specific the object is, the more intuitive the image is, the more interested the students will be. Therefore, the teacher should try to teach students some words, which are used, seen and heard by students in daily life. The teacher can bring some specific objects or certain pictures into classroom, so it can be easier for students to understand. For example, in teaching "We love animals," the teacher can imitate the shape and the sound of different animals, or bring some animals into classroom, such as cats or dogs. If the teacher can call for the students to imitate them, it would be better. When students learn the words "dog," "duck," and "panda," if the teacher can imitate their forms or their sounds, it may very funny for students. Students learn words in a relaxed environment and think of the animals and words, and then students can remember English words naturally.

3. Asher believes that foreign language instruction can and should be modeled on native language acquisition. What are some characteristics of his method that are similar to the way children acquire their native language?

● **Teaching Design**

1. Please study the characteristics of TPR intensively according to the following materials,

make the teaching details complete, and then make a teaching demonstration in groups.

Asher provides a lesson-by-lesson account of a course taught according to TPR principles, which serves as a source of information on the procedures used in the TPR classroom. The course was for adult immigrants and consisted of 159 hours of classroom instruction. The sixth class in the course proceeded in the following way:

Review. This was a fast-moving warm-up in which individual students were moved with commands such as:

Pablo, drive your car around Miako and honk your horn.

Jeffe, throw the red flower to Maria.

Maria, scream.

Rita, pick up the knife and spoon and put them in the cup.

Eduardo, take a drink of water and give the cup to Elaine.

New commands. *These verbs were introduced.*

wash	*your hands.*
	your face.
	your hair.
look for	*a towel.*
	the soap.
	a comb.
hold	*the book.*
	the cup.
	the soap.
comb	*your hair.*
	Maria's hair.
	Shirou's hair.
brush	*your teeth.*
	your pants.
	the table.

Other items introduced were:

Rectangle	*Draw a rectangle on the chalkboard.*
	Pick up a rectangle from the table and give it to me.
	Put the rectangle next to the square.
Triangle	*Pick up the triangle from the table and give it to me.*
	Catch the triangle and put it next to the rectangle.
Quickly	*Walk quickly to the door and hit it.*
	Quickly, run to the table and touch the square.

	Sit down quickly and laugh.
Slowly	Walk slowly to the window and jump.
	Slowly, stand up.
	Slowly walk to me and hit me on the arm.
Toothpaste	Look for the toothpaste.
	Throw the toothpaste to Wing.
	Wing, unscrew the top of the toothpaste.
Toothbrush	Take out your toothbrush.
	Brush your teeth.
	Put your toothbrush in your book.
Teeth	Touch your teeth.
	Show your teeth to Dolores.
	Dolores, point to Eduardo's teeth.
Soap	Look for the soap.
	Give the soap to Elaine.
	Elaine, put the soap in Ramiro's ear.
Towel	Put the towel on Juan's arm.
	Juan, put the towel on your head and laugh.
	Maria, wipe your hands on the towel.

Next, the instructor asked simple questions which the student could answer with a gesture such as pointing. Examples would be:

Where is the towel? (Eduardo, point to the towel!)

Where is the toothbrush? (Miako, point to the toothbrush!)

Where is Dolores?

Role reversal. *Students readily volunteered to utter commands that manipulated the behavior of the instructor and other students...*

Reading and writing. *The instructor wrote on the chalkboard each new vocabulary item and a sentence to illustrate the item. Then she spoke each item and acted out the sentence. The students listened as she read the material. Some copied the information in their notebooks.*

2. Please read the following teaching plan carefully, point out the inappropriate places according to the theory and principles of TPR, then revise and improve it.

Teaching Objectives: *Non-Chinese speaking students.*

Teaching Target: *Let students learn the pronunciation and meaning of the verb phrases taught and be able to practice simple sentence patterns.*

Teaching Content: *wash (hand, face); wipe (table, window); sweep (ground); drink (water,* *coffee); wear (clothing); comb (hair); read (book, newspaper); brush (teeth); eat (bread); walk; run; jump.*

Teaching Steps:

① *Start class, greet students in Chinese, and guide students to reply in Chinese.*

② *Teacher shows verb phrases on blackboard.*

③ *Teacher reads the phrase aloud while doing the action, and signals the students to follow along.*

④ *Group students and practice in turn. The teacher reads the phrase and students do the action. After the students have completed the action, the teacher repeats the action and gives a demonstration to the student who made mistakes.*

⑤ *Still do group practice. The teacher does actions and students read phrases. After the students finish reading, the teacher repeats it and gives a demonstration to the student who made mistakes.*

⑥ *Choose students randomly and do solo exercises. The teacher gives actions or voice instructions, and students read or do actions.*

⑦ *Do simple sentence pattern exercises, and do the same when reading sentences: I read the newspaper every afternoon. / Susan had bread and coffee for breakfast. / He is sweeping the floor and wiping the table today. / Mom got up and went to the bathroom to wash her face and brush her teeth.*

⑧ *Give students ten minutes to practice and make sentences freely, and the teacher gives guidance to each group.*

⑨ *Ask students to display in groups.*

⑩ *Assignment: Ask students to describe their morning life with the phrases they have learned today.*

● **Further Reading**

**Total Physical Response and Its Application
in Classroom English Teaching and Learning**[①]

1. General Application of TPR in Classroom Teaching

Since TPR originated from "parents-infant talking" process, in the classroom teaching, teacher would play the role of parents, and students would be the role of infants. The teaching process should be in a certain setting and the activity should be simple at first. Usually, teaching starts with basic commands (usually verbs). For instance, for the beginners, teacher tells the

---

① Chen M J. Total Physical Response and Its Application in Classroom English Teaching and Learning [J]. 魅力中国 . 2010（9）: 82-84.

students to stand up, sit down, or pick up something, etc. Teacher gives the commands as well as performing the actions and then repeats several times if necessary until the students grasp the meaning of the commands. In order to detect whether the students grasp the meaning of the commands or just simply remember the performance, the teacher may ask one of the students to give the commands and the rest perform following the commands the student gives out. Before that, the teacher can give students the scripts of the performance. There are two points worth noting: the first is that the commands must be simple and clear with performance. The second one is that the commands must be comprehensible, just as Krashen has mentioned in his *Input Hypothesis.*

To make TPR much more interesting, teachers can teach under a certain setting. For example, here is a setting.

It is time to get dressed.

① Go to the closet;

② Take your clothes out of the closet;

③ Put on your jeans;

④ Button up your shirt;

⑤ Put on your jeans;

⑥ Zip up your jeans;

⑦ Put a sock on each foot;

⑧ Put your sneakers on;

⑨ Tie your sneakers.

In order to explore the advantages and disadvantages of TPR approach, we did some experiments on it.

2. Exploring Advantages and Disadvantages of TPR

TPR, actually, has been widely applied in language teaching for a long time; however, it has also met some challenges. In order to know more about its advantages and disadvantages to find out the best way to improve Chinese student's communication skills, the following two teaching experiments are carried on.

(1) Experiment One

Before applying TPR in real classroom teaching, the author tried to apply TPR to graduate students. All the students are from different countries and speak different languages. That means their common language is English. In order to get real results, one of the rules is that "no English" in the class. All the students have a background in teaching English. The aim of this experiment is to explore the advantages and disadvantages of applying TPR through real practice by teachers themselves. Although they used to be English teachers, now they can experience the feelings of being TPR students. This role-changing experience may help them get to know TPR thoroughly and deeply.

Step One:

Students are divided into six groups. In each group, there are four people who must speak different languages. For example, in one group, there must not be two Japanese students or there must not be two or more students who know the same languages besides English because English is not allowed in all the groups.

Step Two:

In each group, select a student to perform as a teacher and the rest perform as students. The teacher will get a piece of paper which tells her or him what topic to teach. For example, one of them will teach the setting mentioned above — "It is time to get dressed" in his or her own mother language. That is to say, in one group, the Italian teacher will teach the German student, Chinese student and Indian student Italian language under the setting of "It is time to get dressed" through applying TPR. In this case, all the rest of the students are beginners in learning Italian.

Step Three:

In each group, students in turn teach the rest of students their mother language to experience TPR and summarize their opinions towards TPR.

According to this experiment, the author got feedbacks from all the participants about TPR as follows:

① This method pays attention to listening and speaking rather than writing and reading.

② Students can hardly grasp the utterance of a whole new language in a very short time but the steps of performance.

③ Based on behaviorism which requires repetition just like parrots.

④ This teaching method is good for active learners but not good for shy students.

⑤ You can't teach everything with it, and if used a lot, it would become repetitive.

⑥ It is an interesting teaching method which can draw students' attention and arouse their interest in learning a new language.

⑦ It is good to help students remember phrases or words.

⑧ It can be used in large or small classes. It doesn't really matter how many students you have; as long as you are prepared to take the lead, the students will follow.

⑨ It works well with mixed-ability classes. The physical actions get across the meaning effectively so that all the students are able to understand and use the target language.

⑩ It can hold the attention of students.

⑪ It may be very effective with teenagers and young learners.

(2) Experiment Two

Background information:

We work in Adult Basic Education in Morgantown, West Virginia, teaching English to nonnative speakers. All the students are from different countries, most of whom are from China, Japan, the Republic of Korea, Brazil and Africa. Most of them are new comers in America and they are beginners in English. In order to monitor their progress in learning English, they are tested before learning. Their test score is recorded. Because all of them are beginners and foreigners, their purpose of learning English is to communicate with each other in daily life, and be able to adapt to the environment quickly. What is more important is that they do not have to pass any designated examinations, that is to say, they have no pressure in studying the language. Their aim is just to listen and speak English. In that case, the author of this paper decided to try TPR on them. The aim of this experiment is to test the effectiveness of TPR teaching approach. It was conducted from September 1, 2009, to October 11, 2009. There are three participants altogether. They are chosen because they are beginners in English and they are of different ages with different mother languages. Most importantly, they have different motivations.

The first class is to tell them how to recognize American money. We have provided each of them one set of American money from a penny to one dollar. The teaching steps are as follows:

Step One:

Introduce one penny, one dime, one quarter, one nickel and one dollar to them three times.

Step Two:

The teacher asks the students to put one penny on the table.

Put one nickel on the table.

Put one nickel under one penny.

Put one dime on the table.

Put one dime on the nickel.

Put one dollar on the table.

Put all the coins on the ground...

After each command, the teacher would go around to check whether the students understand the command or not. If not, the teacher will repeat the command again until the student get the right coin.

Step Three:

After they are familiar with the coins, the teacher gives each student a script to read after the teacher. While reading, they are required to do the corresponding actions until they are familiar with the commands and the pronunciations.

Step Four:

Ask one of the volunteers to perform the role of teacher to repeat those commands and the rest of the students do actions following those commands. Then switch to another one in turn.

Step Five:

After all the activities, the teacher asks the students which is a dime, which is a penny, which is a nickel, and so on. The result is that all the students are familiar with coins.

Before each new class, the students are required to review what they have learned in the last class. Then, they can proceed into the next one.

Step Six:

Since they have English classes every Monday to Thursday from 9:00 am to 12:00 pm, they can learn four different settings per week. Sometimes, it is not easy to take everything to the classroom, so we try to use some cards with pictures instead. During the past few weeks, they have learned a lot in different settings. For instance, they have learned "money" "menu" "clothes" "food" and so on. Besides those nouns appear in those settings, they also learned some verbs.

After four weeks' training, the teacher retests them. This time, the test consists of three parts.

Part A Face-to-Face Interview:

The purpose of this interview is just to test whether the students have grasped required vocabulary the teacher has taught or not. In order to make the students relax, the teacher did not tell them this was a test.

The teacher showed the pictures to the students and asked students what they were. For instance, the teacher showed the students the picture of a sink and the students were expected to answer "This is a sink." In this test, students were tested at least 20 new words each and 99% of them could answer correctly without mistakes. Only one of them still had problems in pronunciations.

Part B Performance:

In order to make the students feel comfortable, they were not told this was a test. So, they just thought this was a role-playing game and got very excited.

Ask all the students to sit together and each of them got the chance to be the teacher to teach what they wanted to teach with new phrases and vocabulary without scripts. In this part, some students performed very well. For instance, one student asked the rest of the students to play a "pointing" game. In that game, she gave commands like "point your nose, clap your hands, touch your face, and so on." And we found that the rest of the students can follow, which means they can understand all the commands.

According to the observation, nearly everyone could achieve the goal of teaching, actually, except for the senior woman who came from China. She was not confident enough to perform and speak out.

Part C Effectiveness:

In order to know whether TPR teaching approach could improve students' reading abilities or not, we retested the students after 3 weeks' TPR teaching. After the retest, we made an investigation about the effectiveness of TPR approach by interviewing students. About 97% students admitted that with the help of this approach, they had benefited a lot in English learning, especially in listening and speaking. According to the test results of Part A and B, they had made great progress in communication. But they also had some problems. They said at first, without the script it is a little bit difficult for them to catch on the teacher's pronunciations. Although this approach helped, but it was not quite helpful for them to deal with paper-based tasks.

3. Conclusions and Discussions

From two experiments above, we can conclude that the advantages of TPR are as follows:

① It is a natural way for beginners to improve their listening and speaking abilities.

② Active and open-minded learners can benefit a lot from this teaching approach.

③ It can indeed expand students' vocabulary in a short time.

④ Students are concentrated on the teaching and have interest in learning in this way.

⑤ The physical actions get across the meaning effectively so that all the students are able to understand and use the target language.

However, the disadvantages are also obvious.

① It only focuses on vocabulary, speaking and listening and it cannot be applied to any situation to improve students' reading or writing abilities. That is to say, one can't teach everything with it.

② It is not so effective for senior people who are not confident enough.

③ It is difficult for beginners to follow the teacher's utterance and pronunciations without scripts.

Although the results of the two experiments indicate that TPR approach is effective in improving students' listening and speaking English, it should be noted that the test time period is not long enough. There is still a long way to go to find a better way to improve students' whole language proficiency, not only speaking, listening and vocabulary.

● **Knowledge Table**

Table 4-1　Summary of Characteristics of Total Physical Response

Key Points	Total Physical Response
Period	
Representatives	
Background	
Theory of Language	
Theory of Language Learning	
Objectives	
The Syllabus	
Types of Learning and Teaching Activities	
Teacher's Roles	
Learner's Roles	
The Role of Students' Native Language and Target Language	
The Role of Instructional Materials and Textbook	
Others	
Summary	

● **Mind Map**

Chapter 5　Community Language Learning

第 5 章　社团语言学习法

⭘ Contents

- ◆ Teaching Case of Community Language Learning
- ◆ Theoretical Basis and Core Elements of Community Language Learning
- ◆ Techniques of Community Language Learning
- ◆ Comments on Community Language Learning
- ◆ Activities and Exercises

- ◆ 社团语言学习法教学示例
- ◆ 社团语言学习法的理论基础及其核心要素
- ◆ 社团语言学习法的教学技巧
- ◆ 对社团语言学习法的评价
- ◆ 活动与练习

O Wordle

1 Introduction

Community Language Learning (CLL), also known as Counseling Learning, is a language teaching method developed in the 1960s and 1970s by Charles Curran, professor and consultant of psychology, University of Chicago. Curran studied adult learning for many years. He was also influenced by Carl Rogers' humanistic psychology, and he found that adults often feel threatened by a new learning situation. They are threatened by the change inherent in learning and by the fear that they will appear foolish. Curran believed that a way to deal with the fears of students is for teachers to consider their students as "whole persons" and become language counselors. In other words, in the process of this language teaching method which is based on the Counseling Approach, the teacher acts as a counselor and a paraphraser, while the learner is seen as a client and collaborator. Teachers consider not only their students' intellect, but they also have some understanding of the relationship among students' feelings, physical reactions, instinctive protective reactions, and the desire to learn.

The CLL emphasizes the sense of community in the learning groups, encourages interaction as a vehicle of learning, and prioritizes students' feelings and the recognition of struggles in language acquisition. There is no syllabus or textbook to follow, and it is the students themselves who determine the content of the lesson by means of meaningful conversations in which they discuss real messages. Notably, it incorporates translation, transcription, and recording techniques.

一、教学法概述

社团语言学习法（CLL），又称咨询法，是由美国芝加哥大学心理学教授和心理咨询专家查尔斯·柯伦在二十世纪六七十年代发展起来的一种语言教学法。柯伦研究成人学习多年。他也受到了卡尔·罗杰斯的人本主义心理学的影响，他发现成人在进入一个新的学习环境时通常会感到害怕。在经历固有知识变化的过程中，他们会感觉受到威胁，并害怕自己在学习过程中会显得很愚蠢。柯伦认为解决学生这种恐惧心理的方法是教师将学生视为"全人"，并成为语言咨询师。也就是说，在这种以心理咨询法为基础的语言教学过程中，教师扮演着咨询师和释义者的角色，而学习者则扮演着咨询者和合作者的角色。教师不仅要考虑学生的智力，还要了解学生的情感、身体反应、本能保护反应和求知欲之间的关系。

社团语言学习法强调学习群体中的集体意识，利用社团内成员的互动推进学习，并将关照学生的感受和关注学生在语言习得过程中所经历的心理挣扎作为首要任务。在社团语言学习中，没有教学大纲或教科书可供遵循，课程内容是由学生来决定的，以讨论真实信息、进行有意义的对话的形式进行。值得注意的是，它还融合了翻译、转录和记录技术。

2 Teaching Case[①]

The teaching case in CLL is from a class in a private language institute in Indonesia. Most of the students work during the day and come for language instruction in the evening. The class meets two evenings a week for two hours a session. This is the first class.

The students arrive and take their seats. The chairs are in a circle around a table that has a tape recorder on it. After greeting the students, the teacher introduces himself and has the students introduce themselves. In Indonesian, he tells the students what they will be doing that evening: They are going to have a conversation in English with his help. The conversation will be tape-recorded, and afterward, they will create a written form of the conversation — a transcript. He tells the class that the rest of the evening will be spent doing various activities with the language on the transcript. He then explains how the students are to have the conversation.

"Whenever one of you would like to say something, raise your hand and I will come behind you. I will not be a participant in the conversation except to help you say in English what you want to say. Say what you want to say in Indonesian; I will give you the English translation. I will give you the translation in phrases, or 'chunks.' Record only the chunks, one at a time. After the conversation, when we listen to the recording, your sentence will sound whole. Only your voices in English will be on the tape. Since this is your first English conversation, you may want to keep

---

① LARSEN-FREEMAN D, ANDERSON M. Techniques and Principles in Language Teaching [M]. Oxford: Oxford University Press, 2011: 86–90.

it simple. We have ten minutes for this activity."

No one speaks at first. Then a young woman raises her hand. The teacher walks to her chair. He stands behind her. "*Selamat sore,*" she says. The teacher translates, "Good...". After a little confusion with the switch on the microphone, she puts "Good" on the tape and turns the switch off. The teacher then gives "evening." and she tries to say "evening" into the microphone but only gets out "eve...". The teacher says again in a clear and warm voice, somewhat exaggerating the word, "Eve...ning." The woman tries again. She shows some signs of her discomfort with the experience, but she succeeds in putting the whole word "evening" onto the recording.

Another student raises his hand. The teacher walks to him and stands behind his chair. "*Selelamat sore,*" the second student says to the first student. "*Apckabar?*" he asks of a third. The teacher, already sensing that this student is a bit more secure, gives the entire translation, "Good evening." "Good evening," the student says, putting the phrase on the tape. "How are you?" the teacher continues. "How...," the student says into the microphone, then turns, obviously seeking help for the rest of the phrase. The teacher, realizing he needed to give smaller chunks, repeats each word separately. "How," repeats the teacher. "How," says the student into the microphone. "Are," repeats the teacher. "Are," the student says. "You," completes the teacher. "You," the student records.

The student to whom the question was directed raises his hand and the teacher stands behind him. "*Kabar baik. Terima kasih,*" he responds. "Fine," the teacher says. "Fine," the student records. "Thank you," the teacher completes. "Thank you," the student confidently puts on the tape.

A fourth student asks of another, "*Nama saudara siapa?*" The teacher steps behind her and says, "What's...your...name?" pausing after each word to give the student time to put her question successfully on the tape.

The other student replies, "*Nama saya Saleh.*" "My name is Saleh," the teacher says in English. "*Apa kabar?*" another student asks Saleh. "How are you?" the teacher translates. "*Saya tidak sehat,*" Saleh answers. "I am not well," the teacher translates. "*Mengapa?*" asks another student. "Why?" says the teacher. "*Sebab kepala saya pusing,*" Saleh replies. "Because I have a headache," translates the teacher. Each of these English utterances recorded in the manner of the earlier ones, the teacher trying to be sensitive to what size chunk each student can handle with confidence. The teacher then announces that they have five minutes left. During this time, the students ask questions like why someone is studying English, what someone does for a living, and what someone's hobbies are. In this conversation, each student around the table records some English utterances on the tape.

After the conversation ends, the teacher sits in the circle and asks the students to say in Indonesian how they feel about the experience. One student says that he does not remember any of the English he has just heard. The teacher accepts what he says and responds, "You have a concern that you haven't learned any English." The student says, "Yes." Another student says he, too, has not learned any English; he was just involved in the conversation. The teacher accepts this comment and replies, "Your attention was on the conversation, not on the English." Another student says that she does not mind the fact that she cannot remember any English; she has enjoyed the conversation. The teacher accepts her comment and reassures her and all the students that they will yet have an opportunity to learn the English words — that he does not expect them to remember the English phrases at this time. "Would anyone else like to say anything?" the teacher asks. Since there is silence, the teacher continues, "OK, then. Let's listen to your conversation. I will play the tape. Just listen to your voices in English." The students listen. "OK," the teacher says, "I am going to play the tape again and stop it at the end of each sentence. See if you can recall what you said, and say it again in Indonesian to be sure that everyone understands what was said. If you can't recall your own sentence, we can all help out." They have no trouble recalling what was said.

Next, the teacher asks them to move their chairs into a semicircle and to watch as he writes the conversation on the board. The teacher asks if anyone would like to operate the tape recorder and stop it at the end of each sentence. No one volunteers, so the teacher operates it himself. The teacher then writes line by line, numbering each English sentence. One student asks if he can copy the sentences. The teacher asks him to stay focused on the words being written up at this point and reassures him that there will be time for copying later, if not in this class session, then in the next.

The teacher writes all the English sentences. Before going back to put in the Indonesian equivalents, he quietly underlines the first English word and then pauses. He asks the students to give the Indonesian equivalents. Since no one volunteers the meaning, after a few seconds he writes the literal Indonesian translation. He continues this way until all the sentences are translated, leaving out any unnecessary repetition.

Next, the teacher tells the students to sit back and relax as he reads the transcript of the English conversation. He reads it three times, varying the instructions each time. The first time, students just listen. The next time, they close their eyes and listen. The last time, they silently mouth the words as the teacher reads the conversation.

For the next activity, the Human Computer, the students are told in a warm manner, "For the next five to ten minutes I am going to turn into a 'human computer' for you. You may use me to practice the pronunciation of any English word or phrase or entire sentence on the transcript. Raise your hand, and I'll come behind you. Then you say either the sentence number or the word you want to practice in English or Indonesian. As the computer, I am programmed to give back only correct English, so you will have to listen carefully to see if what you say matches what I am saying. You may repeat the word, phrase, or sentence as many times as you want. I will stop only when you stop. You control me; you turn the computer on and off."

A student raises his hand and says, "Thank you." He has trouble with the sound at the beginning of "thank." The teacher repeats the phrase after him and the student says it again. The teacher repeats it. Three more times, the student starts the computer by saying, "Thank you." After the teacher has said it for the third time, the student stops, which in turn stops the computer.

Another student raises his hand and says, "What do you do?" a question from the transcript. Again, the teacher moves behind the student and repeats the question the student has chosen to practice. The student works on this question several times just as the first student did. Several others practice saying some part of the transcript in a similar manner.

The teacher then asks the students to work in groups of three to create new sentences based upon the words and phrases of the transcript. Each group writes its sentences down. The teacher walks from group to group to help. The first group writes the sentence "Adik not work in a bank." The teacher gives the correct sentence to the group: "Adik does not work in a bank." The second group writes "What is my name?" "OK," says the teacher. After the teacher finishes helping the group, each group reads its sentences to the class. The teacher replays the tape two more times while the students listen.

Finally, the teacher tells the class they have 10 minutes left in the session. He asks them to talk in Indonesian about the experience they have had that evening, their English, and/or their learning process. As students respond, the teacher listens carefully and reflects back to the students in such a way that each feels he or she has been understood. Most of the students are positive about the experience, one student saying that it is the first time she has felt so comfortable in a beginning language class. "Now, I think I can learn English," she says.

For the next two classes, the teacher decides to have the students continue to work with the conversation they created. Some of the activities are as follows:

① The teacher selects the verb "be" from the transcript, and together he and the students conjugate it for person and number in the present tense. They do the same for the verb "do" and for the regular verb "work".

② The students work in small groups to make sentences with the new forms. They share the sentences they have created with the rest of the class.

③ Students take turns reading the transcript, one student reading the English and another reading the Indonesian. They have an opportunity to work on their English pronunciation again as well.

④ The teacher puts a picture of a person on the whiteboard, and the students ask questions of that person as if they have just met him.

⑤ The students reconstruct the conversation they have created.

⑥ They create a new dialogue using words they have learned to say during their conversation.

When they finish these activities, the class has another conversation, records and uses the new transcript as the basis for subsequent activities.

二、教学示例

本示例中，社团语言学习法应用于印度尼西亚一所私立语言学校的班级中。本班的大多数学生白天工作，晚上来上语言课。这个班每周 2 次课，每次 2 课时。以下是第一次课的教学情况。

学生们走进教室后就座。教室的椅子围成一圈，中间有一张桌子，桌子上摆了一台录音机。老师先和学生们打招呼，进行自我介绍，然后再让学生们各自介绍自己。随后，他用印尼语告诉学生们晚上的课程内容：他们将在老师的帮助下用英语进行一个对话。他们的对话将被录音，并形成书面材料，即一份对话抄本。老师告诉全班学生，形成抄本以后，剩下的时间将利用抄本上的对话进行各种各样的活动。随后，他开始向学生介绍如何开展对话。

"每当你们有想说的话时，就举手，我就会来到你们身后。我不会参与你们的对话，但我会帮助你们用英语表达你们想说的话。用印尼语告诉我你们想说的话之后，我会给你们翻译成英文短语或者'语块'。每次只录制一个语块。全部录制完成，再听录音时，就会听到一个完整的句子。录音机只会录下大家的英语发音。因为这是你们的第一个英语对话，你们可能会希望对话简单一点儿。所以咱们就用 10 分钟来进行这个活动。"

刚开始，没有学生说话。过了一会儿，有一位年轻的女士举起了手。老师走到她身后。那名女学生说："Selamat sore."老师翻译道："Good..."然后打开录音机的麦克风。那位女生在麦克风前略有迟疑，然后便发出了"Good"，这个音录在录音机上之后，录音机便关上了。老师接着给出"晚上"的发音，这个学生试着对着麦克风发出"evening"，但是却只发出了"eve..."的音。老师用清晰而亲切的声音又说了一遍"eve...ning"，这次的发音有些夸张，中间还拖长了音。学生又尝试发了一次音。虽然她对这段体验略显不适，但她还是成功地把"evening"这个音发出并录制到录音机中了。

之后，又有一名学生举起手来，老师便走到他身后。第二名学生对第一名学生说："Selelamat sore."然后对第三名学生说："Apckabar?"老师已经感受到这名学生已经有了安全感，所以就给出了一个完整的翻译："Good evening."学生说："Good evening"，并将这一短语录制到录音机上。然后老师继续说："How are you?"学生对着麦克风说："How..."，然后转身，显然是在寻求帮助。老师意识到学生需要切分成更小的"语块"，就把每个单词分别重复一遍。老师重复道："How"。学生对着麦克风说："How"。老师说："Are"。学生重复："Are"。老师说："You"。学生重复："You"。

被提问的那名学生举起了手，老师站在他后面。学生回答："Kabar baik. Terima

kasih."老师用英语说："Fine."学生也说："Fine."并录音。老师继续说："Thank you."学生自信地说出"Thank you."并录制到磁带上。

第四名学生提了另一个问题："Nama saudara siapa?"老师走到她后面，说："你叫……什么……名字？"说的时候，老师在每一个单词后停顿，以便给学生时间，让她把这句话成功地录到磁带上。

另一名学生回答说："Nama saya Saleh."老师用英语说："我叫萨利赫。"又有一名学生问萨利赫："Apa kabar?"老师翻译成英文："你好吗？"萨利赫回答说："Saya tidak sehat."老师翻译成英文："我不太好。"另一名学生问："Mengapa?"老师说："为什么？"萨利赫回答说："Sebab kepala saya pusing."老师翻译道："因为我头痛。"每一句英语对话都以同样的方式录入录音机，老师一直留心体会每名学生能从容复述"语块"的长度，并在翻译时做了恰当的切分。老师宣布对话时间还剩 5 分钟。在这段时间里，学生们问了一些问题，比如：你为什么学习英语；你从事什么工作；你的爱好是什么。在这段对话中，围坐在桌子四周的每名学生都在磁带上录下了一些英语句子。

谈话结束后，老师坐在圆圈中间，让学生们用印尼语说说他们对这次经历的感受。一名学生说他一点儿都不记得他刚才听到的英语了。老师表示理解，并说道："你担心你没有学到英语。"学生说："是的。"另一名学生说他也没有学到英语，他只是参与了谈话。老师接受了他们的评论，并回答说："你们的注意力集中在对话上，而不在英语上。"另一名学生说，她不介意自己没记住英语句子；她很喜欢这个对话。老师接受了她的评论，并向她和所有的学生保证，对于那些他们还没有学会的英语语句，他们之后还有机会学习。老师又问："还有人想说点儿什么吗？"大家都没再发言。于是，老师继续说："好的。那么接下来我们来听听你们的对话。我来放录音。你们听自己用英语说的话。"学生们听完后，老师说："好的。我要把录音再放一遍，在每句话的结尾停下来。看看你是否能回忆起你说的话，然后用印尼语再说一遍，以确保每个人都明白对话的意思。如果你记不起自己说过的话，我们会帮助你。"学生们都毫不费力地回忆起了刚才说过的话。

接下来，老师让他们把椅子围成半圆，老师在黑板上写对话。老师问是否有人愿意操作一下录音机，在每句话的结尾按下暂停。没有学生表示愿意，所以老师自己完成了操作。老师逐行书写英语句子，并给每个句子编号。一名学生问老师，是否要抄写句子。老师让他将注意力集中在所写的英语句子本身，并向他保证之后有时间抄写，如果这节课写不了，那么就在下节课上写。

老师用英语写出所有的句子。在翻译回印尼语之前，老师再次强调了一遍英语单词。他请学生翻译成印尼语，但没有学生自愿回答，所以几秒钟后，老师自己写出了相对应的直译句。他以这样的方式完成了所有英语句子的翻译，省去了不必要的重复。

接下来，老师朗读英语对话抄本，并让学生们坐回去放松一下。老师读了三遍，每次都有不同的要求。第一次，学生们只是听。第二次，学生们闭上眼睛听。最后一次，他们跟着老师配合口型默读这些对话。

下一个课堂活动是"人机互动"。老师亲切地告诉学生们："在接下来的 5 ~ 10 分钟里，我将变为你们的一台'人形计算机'。你们可以用我来练习对话抄本上任何一个英语单词、短语或整句的发音。举起你的手，我就来到你身后。你用英语或印尼语说出你想练习的句子或单词，或者说出它们的编号。作为'计算机'，我的程序是只给正确的英语，所以你必须仔细听，看看你说的是否与我说的相符。你可以任意重复一个单词、短语或句子，次数不限。你说我就说，你停我就停。你来控制'计算机'的开关。"

一名学生举起手，然后说："Thank you."他在"thank"这个词词头部分的发音上有点儿困难。老师随之重复了这个短语。然后，学生又说了一遍。老师又重复了一遍。学生说了三次，"计算机"也重复了三次。老师说完第三次之后，学生就停了下来，"计算机"也跟着停了下来。

另一名学生举起手，说："你是做什么工作的？"这是对话抄本上的一个问题。老师来到这名学生身后，重复了这名学生选择练习的问句。这名学生和第一名学生一样，练习了几遍这个问句的发音。其他学生用同样的方式，还练习了对话抄本上的其他句子。

然后老师让学生三人一组，根据对话抄本上的词语进行造句。每组都要将自己的句子写下来。老师一组一组地去巡视并提供帮助。第一组写道："阿迪克不工作在银行。"老师将这句话的正确句子告诉学生："阿迪克不在银行工作。"第二组写的是："我叫什么名字？"老师说："可以。"老师查看并辅助所有小组完成句子后，每个小组向全班学生朗读自己的句子。之后，老师重放了两遍录音让学生们听。

最后，老师告诉全班学生还有 10 分钟。他让学生们用印尼语谈谈这一晚的经历体验，比如：他们的英语，他们的学习过程。当学生做反馈时，老师仔细倾听，并以一种让每个人都感到自己被理解的方式向每名学生予以回应。大多数学生对这段经历持肯定态度。有一名学生说，这是她第一次在语言入门课上感到如此舒适。她说："现在我认为我可以学英语了。"

在接下来的两节课中，老师决定让学生继续练习他们所创造的对话。另外，还开展了一些活动：

①教师从对话抄本上选择系动词"be"，然后和学生一起用现在时态将人称、单复数与系动词 be 进行搭配。同样的方法，练习动词"do"和一般动词"work"。

②学生分组用新的形式进行造句，然后和班上其他学生分享他们创造的句子。

③学生轮流朗读对话抄本上的句子，一名学生读英语，另一名学生读印尼语。他们也有机会重新练习英语发音。

④教师在白板上放一张人物图片，学生们假设初次见到这个人，向这个人提问。

⑤学生将他们所创造的对话进行重新组合。

⑥使用之前在对话中所学的词语编写一个新的对话。

当他们完成这些活动后，学生们会开始另外一个对话，记录并使用新的对话抄本，并基于抄本开展后续语言活动。

3 Teaching Principles and Teaching Procedures

3.1 Five Stages of the Learning Process

The CLL compares the learning process to a person's growing process from a newborn baby to an adult. It vividly depicts the process of students' development from being totally dependent on teachers to being able to learn and use foreign languages independently. CLL divides this whole process into five stages. The first stage, stage of "Birth." Beginners are like babies who can't live without their mothers. They rely on teachers to communicate with each other. And feeling of security and belonging should be established at this stage. The second stage, stage of "Child." As the learner's ability improves, they achieve a measure of independence from the parent. At this stage, language learners acquire the most basic language knowledge and can speak the simplest words. The third stage, stage of "Separate Existence." The learners can speak independently. But they begin to resist, hate their dependence, and try to get rid of teachers. The fourth stage, stage of "Adolescence." The learners are becoming mature and able to use the language independently. They are secure enough to take criticism and be corrected. At this stage, they will spend more time working on improving style and knowledge of linguistic appropriateness. The last stage, stage of "Adult." The child becomes an adult. The learners have fully mastered the systematic language knowledge and the ability to use the language. They can independently carry out verbal communication activities without the help of teachers and become the knower finally.

Be paralleled by five stages of language learning and five stages of affective conflicts, interactions between learner and knower are characterized as dependent (Stage 1), self-assertive (Stage 2), resentful and indignant (Stage 3), tolerant (Stage 4), and independent (Stage 5).

3.2 Core Elements of Curran's Learning Philosophy

There are six core psychological elements of successful learning which is known as SARD[①] put forward by Curran:

S stands for security.

Unless learners feel secure, they will find it difficult to enter into a successful learning experience.

A stands for attention and aggression.

CLL recognizes that a loss of attention should be taken as an indication of the learner's lack

---

① RICHARDS J C, RODGERS T S. 语言教学的流派 [M]. 2 版 . 北京：外语教学与研究出版社，2008：92-93.

of involvement in learning, the implication being that variety in the choice of learner tasks will increase attention and therefore promote learning. Aggression applies to the way in which a child, having learned something, seeks an opportunity to show his or her strength by taking over and demonstrating what has been learned, using the new knowledge as a tool for self-assertion.

R stands for retention and reflection.

If the whole person is involved in the learning process, what is retained is internalized and becomes a part of the learner's new persona in the foreign language. Reflection is a consciously identified period of silence within the framework of the lesson for the student "to focus on the learning forces of the last hour, to assess his present stage of development, and to re-evaluate future goals."

D stands for discrimination.

When learners "have retained a body of material, they are ready to sort it out and see how one thing relates to another." This discrimination process becomes more refined and ultimately "enables the students to use the language for purposes of communication outside the classroom."

3.3 Techniques of Community Language Learning

CLL combines innovative learning tasks and activities with conventional ones. They include[①]:

(1) Translation

Learners form a small circle. A learner whispers a message or meaning he or she wants to express, the teacher translates it into (and may interpret it in) the target language, and the learner repeats the teacher's translation.

(2) Group Work

Learners may engage in various group tasks, such as small-group discussion of a topic, preparing a conversation, preparing a summary of a topic for presentation to another group, preparing a story that will be presented to the teacher and the rest of the class.

(3) Recording

Students record conversations in the target language.

(4) Transcription

Students transcribe utterances and conversations they have recorded for practice and analysis of linguistic forms.

(5) Analysis

Students analyze and study transcriptions of target language sentences in order to focus on particular lexical usage or on the application of particular grammar rules.

(6) Reflection and Observation

---

① RICHARDS J C, RODGERS T S. 语言教学的流派 [M]. 2 版 . 北京：外语教学与研究出版社，2008：92-93.

Learners reflect and report on their experience of the class, as a class or in groups. This usually consists of expressions of feelings — sense of one another, reactions to silence, concern for something to say, and so on.

(7) Listening

Students listen to a monologue by the teacher involving elements they might have elicited or overheard in class interactions.

(8) Free Conversation

Students engage in free conversation with the teacher or with other learners. This might include discussion of what they learned as well as feelings they had about how they learned.

三、教学原则与教学过程

1. 学习过程的五个阶段

社团语言学习法将语言学习过程比拟为一个人从新生婴儿到成人的成长过程，形象地描绘了学生从完全依赖教师到能完全独立学习和运用外语的发展过程。社团语言学习法把整个学习过程划分为五个阶段。第一个阶段为"诞生期"。初学者就像离不开母亲的婴儿，完全依赖教师来进行言语交际。这一时期将建立学习者的安全感和归属感。在第二阶段即"童年期"，随着学习者能力的提高，他们获得了脱离父母后的独立。此时的语言学习者获得了最基本的语言知识，能够说最简单的词语。到了第三阶段"叛逆期"，学习者可以独立说话了。学习者开始产生反抗情绪，憎恶自身的依赖性，并试图摆脱教师。在第四阶段"青春期"，学习者逐渐成熟起来，能够独立运用语言，并具有足够的安全感接受批评和纠正。此时，他们更多地需要增长有关如何得体运用语言的知识，并形成语言表达风格。最后一个阶段为"成年期"，孩子变为一个成人。学习者已完全掌握了系统的语言知识和语言运用能力，能不依靠教师的帮助而独立进行言语交际活动，最终成为语言的掌握者。

与语言学习五个阶段及情感冲突五个阶段相辅相成，学习者和语言掌握者（如教师）之间的互动关系也表现为五个阶段：依赖（阶段一）、自信（阶段二）、反抗（阶段三）、宽容（阶段四）和独立（阶段五）。

2. 柯伦学习观的核心四要素

柯伦提出 SARD 是成功学习的四个核心要素。

S 表示安全感。

学生只有感到安全，他们才能顺利地投入到成功的语言学习体验中去。

A 表示注意和进取。

社团语言学习法认为学习者注意力的丧失应被视为其缺乏学习参与性的迹象。那么，学习者任务选择的多样化将提升其注意力，从而促进学习。进取（原义为"侵略""攻击性"，此处表示学习者的积极态度）指如同儿童学习新知一般，当儿童在学习了一些新东西之后，通过吸收和掌握新知识，他们会寻求机会将新知识学以致用，以展现自己的力量，进行自我肯定。

R 表示记忆和反思。

如果一个人全身心都参与到学习过程中，那么学习并保留下来的内容就会被内化，成为学习者所掌握的外语知识的一部分。反思是学生在课程框架内一段有意识的沉默时段，以使学生"关注最后一个小时的学习力，评估自己目前的发展阶段，并重新评估未来的目标"。

D 表示辨微。

当学习者"记忆了大量的语言材料后，他们就可以整理出来，看看一个要素和另一个要素之间的异同"。这一辨微过程越来越精细，并最终"使学生能够将语言运用于课堂外的交流"。

3. 社团语言学习法的教学技巧

社团语言学习法既综合了其他传统的教学方法，又拥有自身独特的教学方法。这些方法包括：

（1）翻译

学生围坐成一个圆圈。一个学生小声说出他（她）想要表达的意思或者信息，教师将其翻译成目的语，学生重复教师所翻译的目的语。

（2）小组活动

学生将开展多种小组活动与任务，比如：就一个话题进行讨论；准备一段对话；在讨论一个话题之后准备一段总结发言；准备一个故事，讲给教师和其他小组听。

（3）录音

将学生所说的目的语用录音机录下来。

（4）誊写

学生将录音的句子与对话誊写下来，整理成文字，以便进行语言操练和语言结构形式分析。

（5）分析

学生分析并研究誊写下来的目的语句子，并特别关注词汇的特殊用法和某些语法规则。

（6）反思和观察

学习者进行课堂活动反思，并以班级或小组的形式向其他学生分享自己的学习感悟，一般是涉及情感的经历与体验——学生彼此间的感觉、沉默期的反应及对所说内容的关注等。

（7）聆听

教师用目的语进行朗诵，朗诵内容涉及他们在课堂互动中谈及或听到的对话、段落等，学生聆听。

（8）自由对话

学生与教师或其他学生进行自由交谈。内容既可以是他们对所学内容的讨论，也可以是他们的学习感受及学习过程。

4 Conclusion

CLL is one of the most well-known applications of humanistic learning in foreign language teaching and learning. Unlike approaches that force learners to memorize grammar patterns and rules without being able to cope with a conversation, the learning process in CLL is viewed as a unified, interpersonal experience. The learner is regarded as an identical member within a group rather than in isolation. The teacher is required to pay attention to students' personal needs and gain insight into their communicative intentions. The role of group work is to arouse students' attention to their peers by caring about each other's feelings and understanding each other's strengths and weaknesses, and form a united community. Members should interact and communicate. Meanwhile, teachers and students work together to facilitate learning by valuing each other.

However, CLL places unusual demands on language teachers. They must be highly proficient and sensitive to nuance in both L1 and L2. They must be familiar with and sympathetic to the role of counselors in psychological counseling. They must resist the pressure "to teach" in the traditional senses. The teacher must also be relatively nondirective and must be prepared to accept and even encourage the "adolescent" aggression of the learner as he or she strives for independence. The teacher must operate without conventional materials, depending on student topics to shape and motivate the class. Special training in CLL techniques is usually required.

Critics of Community Language Learning question the appropriateness of the counseling metaphor on which it is predicated. Questions also arise about whether teachers should attempt counseling without special training. Other concerns have been expressed regarding the lack of a syllabus, which makes objectives unclear and evaluation difficult to accomplish, and the focus on fluency rather than accuracy, which may lead to inadequate control of the grammatical system of the target language.

四、小结

社团语言学习法是人本主义学习理论在外语教学中最著名的应用之一。与那些让学习者脱离对话情境强行记忆语法形式与规则的教学法不同，社团语言学习法中的学习过程被视为一个完整、统一的人际互动经历。学习者是群体社团中的一名成员，而不是一个孤立的个体。教师应关注学生的个人需求并洞察学生的交际意图。而小组活动的作用则是通过关心彼此的感受，了解彼此的优势与不足，引起学生对同类人的关注，并形成一个团结的社团。社团成员应该在人际交往中进行互动交流。同时，教师和学生通过相互间的价值体现共同促进学习。

　　然而，社团语言学习法对语言教师提出了不寻常的要求。语言教师必须对母语和第二语言都深入了解、高度熟悉，并对两种语言之间的细微差别十分敏感。他们必须赞同并熟悉心理咨询师的角色与作用；必须抵制传统意义上"教书"的压力。教师们还必须相对不具有指导性，在学习者争取独立的过程中，必须准备好接受甚至鼓励"成长阶段"的不断进取（攻击性）。教师必须在没有传统材料的情况下，根据学生提出的主题，创建并激励课堂，实施语言教学。因此，社团语言学习法的教学技巧通常需要进行培训。

　　社团语言学习的批评者质疑将语言学习比作心理咨询是否具有恰当性。关于教师是否应该在没有特殊培训的情况下尝试进行咨询，也是该教学法存在的问题。另外，还有人提出社团语言学习法缺乏大纲，这将使教学目标不明确，教学评价难以完成。教学中关注流利性，而不是准确性，这也可能导致学生对目的语语法系统掌握不足。

○ Activities and Exercises

● Understanding and Thinking

1. Based on the following materials, state the significance and function of affective factors in language learning.

When I hear my voice, I just hate it ... It is not simply that my ears hate my mouth, or my mouth hates my eyes. The inner conflict inhabits my entire being. This makes me feel that my own "self" is falling apart. Now I have two "mes" inside myself. A "me" with whom I am familiar and with whom I feel connected ... The other "me" is a stranger.

Zhou Wu recalls the anxiety and loss of identity associated with migrating to Canada and discovering that his English, which seemed perfectly adequate at home in China, failed him in the Canadian context.

2. Curran says there are six elements of nondefensive learning: security, aggression, attention, reflection, retention, and discrimination (SAARRD). Please find some examples of these in the teaching case.

3. In CLL, the teaching syllabus emerges from the interaction between the learner's expressed communicative intentions and the teacher's reformulations of these into suitable target language utterances. Please state your opinion about the teaching materials and syllabus in language teaching.

● Teaching Design

1. Please study the sample lesson intensively, expand the teaching details, and then make a

teaching demonstration in groups.

Dieter Stroinigg presents a protocol of what a first day's CLL class covered, which is outlined here:

(1) Informal greetings and self-introductions were made.

(2) The teacher made a statement of the goals and guidelines for the course.

(3) A conversation in the foreign language took place.

① *A circle was formed so that everyone had visual contact with each other.*

② *One student initiated conversation with another student by giving a message in the L1 (English).*

③ *The instructor, standing behind the student, whispered a close equivalent of the message in the L2 (German).*

④ *The student then repeated the L2 message to its addressee and into the tape recorder as well.*

⑤ *Each student had a chance to compose and record a few messages.*

⑥ *The tape recorder was rewound and replayed at intervals.*

⑦ *Each student repeated the meaning in English of what he or she had said in the L2 and helped to refresh the memory of others.*

(4) Students then participated in a reflection period, in which they were asked to express their feelings about the previous experience with total frankness.

(5) From the materials just recorded the instructor chose sentences to write on the blackboard that highlighted elements of grammar, spelling, and peculiarities of capitalization in the L2.

(6) Students were encouraged to ask questions about any of the items above.

(7) Students were encouraged to copy sentences from the board with notes on meaning and usage. This became their "textbook" for home study.

2. Please read the following teaching plan carefully, point out the inappropriate places according to the theory and principles of CLL, and then revise and improve it.

Topics: *Learning English Fruits.*

Teaching Objectives and Requirements: *Make students familiar with the English name of fruits, and can master the relevant sentence type.*

Teaching Difficulties*: Accurate pronunciation, understanding the use of sentence patterns.*

Teaching Process:

① *The teacher uses English (the language of purpose) to make a simple hello, gives the students a comfortable, secure environment, then describes a relaxed scene, and introduces the teaching topic — fruits. (2 mins)*

② Student discussion. Students sit in a circle, use divergent thinking and make a free discussion in Chinese (mother tongue) according to the scene described by the teacher. Listen carefully to the speakers' pronunciation during the discussion. The teacher pays close attention to the students' discussion outside the circle. When they encounter words that students can't express in English, the teacher helps them in time and the students repeat. (7 mins)

③ Silence stage. The teacher stopped the discussion and gave the students time to think independently and sort out the content just discussed. (1 mins)

④ To teach contents. Through students' reflection, the teacher writes the words on the blackboard in English, leads to grammar points, and explains sentence patterns. Students are asked to follow and imitate the teacher's pronunciation individually or in groups. (5 mins)

⑤ The teacher encourages students to copy the contents on the blackboard into their notebooks, pay attention to the meaning of words and the usage of sentence patterns, and use them as teaching materials.

⑥ The teacher arranges homework in English.

⑦ The teacher summarizes the class contents in English, and the students evaluate the class or ask questions.

● **Further Reading**

Community Language Learning[①]

1. Introduction

This methodology is not based on the usual methods by which languages are taught. Rather, the approach is patterned upon counseling techniques and adapted to the peculiar anxiety and threat as well as the personal and language problems a person encounters in the learning of foreign languages. Consequently, the learner is not thought of as a student but as a client. The native instructors of the language are not considered teachers but, rather are trained in counseling skills adapted to their roles as language counselors.

The language-counseling relationship begins with the client's linguistic confusion and conflict. The aim of the language counselor's skill is first to communicate empathy for the client's threatened inadequate state and to aid him linguistically. Then slowly the teacher-counselor strives to enable him to arrive at his own increasingly independent language adequacy. This process is furthered by the language counselor's ability to establish a warm, understanding, and accepting relationship, thus becoming an "other-language self" for the client.

---

① AL-HUMAIDI M. Community Language Learning[EB/OL]. [2022–07–18]. https://idoc.pub/documents/community-language-learningpdf-9n0ky55wg34v.

2. Approach, Procedure and Objectives

Richards and Rogers explain five stages involved in using this method. They are as follows:

STAGE 1

The client is completely dependent on the language counselor.

① First, the client expresses only to the counselor and in English what he or she wishes to say to the group. Each group member overhears this English exchange but no other members of the group are involved in the interaction.

② The counselor then reflects these ideas back to the client in the foreign language in a warm, accepting tone, in simple language in phrases of five or six words.

③ The client turns to the group and presents his or her ideas in the foreign language. He or she has the counselor's aid if he mispronounces or hesitates on a word or phrase. This is the client's maximum security stage.

STAGE 2

① Same as above.

② The client turns and begins to speak the foreign language directly to the group.

③ The counselor aids only as the client hesitates or turns for help. These small independent steps are signs of positive confidence and hope.

STAGE 3

① The client speaks directly to the group in the foreign language. This presumes that the group has now acquired the ability to understand his simple phrases.

② Same as 3 above. This presumes the client's greater confidence, independence, and proportionate insight into the relationship of phrases, grammar, and ideas. Translation is given only when a group member desires it.

STAGE 4

① The client is now speaking freely and complexly in the foreign language. He or she presumes group's understanding.

② The counselor directly intervenes in grammatical error, mispronunciation, or where aid in complex expression is needed. The client is sufficiently secure to take correction.

STAGE 5

① Same as Stage 4.

② The counselor intervenes not only to offer correction but also to add idioms and more elegant constructions.

③ At this stage, the client can become the counselor to the group in stages 1, 2, and 3.

3. Points of Criticism

① A message/lesson/class is presented in this method in the native tongue and then again in the second language. The danger of this is that learners would be used to thinking in their first language and transferring their message to the second which might lead obviously to negative transfer of patterns and structures. Learners of a second language should be trained through the target language with no, or at least minimum, resort to the source language to avoid mother language interference.

② The focus of this method is on oral proficiency. Thus, its main aim is developing learners' proficiency of one of the four major skills of language which is speaking. With modifications, it may be used to teach writing, yet this is not sufficient in language teaching. Successful methods should take not only the full scope of language skills into account but also different language components.

③ The method is time-consuming as it requires each student to utter what he or she thinks of in the first language, the teacher's translation, repetition of the utterance collectively, recording, transcription and analysis. With limited language teaching classes, it could never work.

④ In this method, learning is not viewed as an individual accomplishment but as something that is achieved collaboratively. This does not take into account the difference between learners in terms of proficiency and language ability. The result would be having proficient students bored awaiting their counterparts to intake a certain aspect of language before moving on to another. This could only be avoided if the general level of students is similar or near similar.

⑤ It places unusual demands on language teachers. They must be highly proficient and sensitive to nuance in both L1 and L2; they must be familiar with and sympathetic to the role of counselors in psychological counseling; and they must resist the pressure to teach in the traditional sense.

⑥ The teacher must operate without conventional materials, depending on student topics to shape the class. This could lead to ignoring very important issues because they were not raised by students.

⑦ The focus is on fluency rather than accuracy.

4. Conclusion

Community Language Learning is the most responsive method in terms of its sensitivity to learner communicative intent. However, learners' intents may vary considerably and this would lead to contradicted needs and interests which would enlarge the scope of teaching and lead to disorganization. The appropriateness of the counseling metaphor is also criticized upon which it is predicated; there is no evidence that language learning in classrooms indeed parallels the processes that characterize psychological counseling. Nevertheless, certain application of this method could be applied in integration with other methods in an eclectic approach.

● **Knowledge Table**

Table 5-1   Summary of Characteristics of Community Language Learning

Key Points	Community Language Learning
Period	
Representatives	
Background	
Theory of Language	
Theory of Language Learning	
Objectives	
The Syllabus	
Types of Learning and Teaching Activities	
Teacher's Roles	
Learners' Roles	
The Role of Students' Native Language and Target Language	
The Role of Instructional Materials and Textbook	
Others	
Summary	

● **Mind Map**

Chapter 6　The Silent Way

第 6 章　沉默法

Contents

O Wordle

1 Introduction

The Silent Way is the name of a method of language teaching devised by Caleb Gattegno (1911–1988) in the late 1960s. Gattegno believed that learning is a process which we initiate by ourselves by mobilizing our inner resources (our perception, awareness, cognition, imagination, intuition, creativity, etc.) to meet the challenge at hand. Therefore, one of the basic principles of the Silent Way is that "Teaching should be subordinated to learning." In other words, to teach means to serve the learning process rather than to dominate it. In the Silent Way teaching class, the teacher should be silent as much as possible in the classroom, but the learner should be encouraged to produce as much language as possible. Elements of the Silent Way, particularly the use of color charts and the colored Cuisenaire rods, grew out of Gattegno's previous experience as an educational designer of reading and mathematics programs.

As Jack C. Richards points out, there are three learning hypotheses underlying Gattegno's work:

① Learning is facilitated if the learner discovers or creates rather than remembers and repeats what is to be learned.

② Learning is facilitated by accompanying (mediating) physical objects.

③ Learning is facilitated by problem solving involving the material to be learned.

Learning language can be seen as a problem-solving, creative, discovering activity, in which the learner is the main participant rather than a bench-bound listener. In the Silent Way teaching class, the teacher provides students with something like a puzzle, but they should work out this puzzle on their own with the little hints from the teacher. Through the help of some materials (physical objects) as Cuisenaire rods, charts and pointer, especially teacher's specific gestures and body language, the teacher leads the students to work out this puzzle, during which target language learning is also involved.

一、教学法概述

沉默法是加特诺于 20 世纪 60 年代末首创的一种第二语言教学法。加特诺认为学习是一个调动我们内在资源（包括个体的感知、意识、认知、想象、直觉、创造力等），自发地解决眼前挑战的活动。因此，沉默法的一个基本原则便是"教应该从属于学"，即教是为学习过程服务的，而不是支配学习过程的。在沉默法的课堂教学中，教师应在课堂上尽量少说话，而尽量鼓励学生多参与言语活动。该教学法的典型教学要素是使用彩色图表和彩色棒，这些教具来源于加特诺早期从事阅读和数学课程教学设计的经验。

正如杰克·C. 查理斯所指出的，加特诺的研究有三个基本的学习假设：

①学习者进行发现或创造活动比单纯记忆和重复所学知识更能促进学习。

②使用实物教具有助于学习。

③运用所学材料解决问题更能促进学习。

语言学习可以被看作解决问题式的活动，是一种创造性的、发现式的活动，在这种活动中，学习者是主要的参与者，而不是只会听课的"板凳生"。在沉默法的课堂中，教师给学生提出谜题，学生则需要根据教师的提示进行解题。在解答谜题的过程中，教师将通过一些材料（实物教具），如彩色棒、图表和指示棒，尤其是运用教师的手势及体态语进行引导，协助学生找出谜底，并在这一过程中学习并学会使用目的语。

2 Teaching Case[①]

This teaching Case is the first day of an English class in Brazil. There are 24 secondary school students in this class. The class meets for two hours a day, three days a week.

In this English course, the teacher first introduces the Silent Way in Portuguese. Then, the teacher walks to the front of the room, takes out a metal pointer and points to a chart taped to the wall. The chart has a black background and is covered with small rectangular blocks arranged in rows. Each block is in a different color. This is a sound-color chart. Each rectangle represents one English sound. There is a white horizontal line approximately halfway down the chart separating the upper rectangles, which represent vowel sounds, from those below the line, which represent consonant sounds.

---

① 　LARSEN-FREEMAN D, ANDERSON M. Techniques and Principles in Language Teaching [M]. Oxford: Oxford University Press, 2011:52–57.

Without saying anything, the teacher points to five different blocks of color above the line. There is silence. The teacher repeats the pattern, pointing to the same five blocks of color. Again, no one says anything. The third time the teacher does the pointing, he says /ɑ/ as he touches the first block. The teacher continues and taps the four other blocks of color with the pointer. As he does this, several students say /e/, /i/, /ɒ/, /u/. He begins with these vowels since they are the ones students will already know. (These five sounds are the simple vowels of Portuguese and every Brazilian schoolchild learns them in this order.)

The teacher points to the rectangle that represents /e/. He puts his two palms together, then spreads them apart to indicate that he wants the students to lengthen this vowel sound. By moving his pointer, he shows that there is a smooth gliding of the tongue necessary to change this Portuguese /e/ into the English diphthong /eɪ/. He works with the students until he is satisfied that their pronunciation of /eɪ/ closely approximates the English vowel. He works in the same way as /i: /, /əʊ/, and /u: /. Then the teacher hands the pointer to a girl in the front row. She comes to the front of the room and points to the white block in the top row. The class responds with /eɪ/. One by one, as she points to the next three blocks, the class responds correctly with /eɪ/, /i: /, /əʊ/. But she has trouble finding the last block of color and points to a block in the third row. A few students yell, "NO!" She tries another block in the same row; her classmates yell, "NO!" again. Finally, a boy from the front row says, "*À esquerda*" (Portuguese for "to the left"). As the girl moves the pointer one block to the left, the class shouts /u: /. The teacher signals for the girl to do the series again. This time she goes a bit more quickly and has no trouble finding the block for /u: /. The teacher signals to another student to replace the girl and points to the five blocks as the class responds. Then the teacher brings individuals to the front of the room, each one tapping out the sequence of the sounds as he says them. The teacher works with the students through gestures, and sometimes through instructions in Portuguese, to produce the English vowel sounds as accurately as possible. He does not say the sounds himself.

Apparently satisfied that the students can produce the five sounds accurately, the teacher next points to the five blocks in a different order. A few students hesitate, but most of the students seem able to connect the colored blocks with the correct sounds. The teacher varies the sequence several times and the students respond appropriately. The teacher then points to a boy sitting in the second row. The teacher moves to the chart and points to five colored blocks. Two of the blocks are above the line and are the /eɪ/ and /u: / they have already worked on. The three other blocks are below the line and are new to them. Two or three of the students yell, "Pedro!" which is the boy's name. The other students help him as he points to the colored blocks that represent the sounds of his name: /p/, /e/, /d/, /r/, /u/. Two or three other students do the same. In this way, the students have learned that English has a /p/, /d/, and /r/ and the location of these sounds on the sound-color chart. The students have a little problem with the pronunciation of the /r/, so the teacher works with them before moving on.

The teacher next points to a girl and taps out eight colored rectangles. In a chorus, the students say her name, "*Carolina*." and practice the girl's name as they did Pedro's. With this, the students have learned the colors that represent three other sounds: /k/, /l/, /n/. The teacher follows a similar procedure with a third student whose name is Gabriela. The students now know the location of /g/ and /b/ as well. The teacher has various students tap out the sounds for the names of their three classmates.

After quite a few students have tapped out the three names, the teacher takes the pointer and introduces a new activity. He asks eight students to sit with him around a big table in the front of the room as the rest of the class gathers behind them. The teacher puts a pile of blue, green, and pink wooden rods of varying lengths in the middle of the table. He points to one of the rods, then points to three rectangles of color on the sound-color chart. Some students attempt to say "Rod". They are able to do this since they have already been introduced to these sound-color combinations. The teacher points again to the blocks of color, and this time all of the students say, "Rod". The teacher then points to the block of color representing "a". He points to his mouth and shows the students that he is raising his jaw and closing his mouth, thus showing the students how to produce a new English sound by starting with a sound they already know. The students say something approximating /ə/, which is a new sound for them. The teacher follows this by pointing first to a new block of color, then quickly in succession to four blocks of color; the students chorus, "a rod." He turns to a different chart on the wall; this one has words on it in different colors. He points to the words "a" and "rod", and the students see that each letter is in the same color as the sound the letter signifies.

After pointing to "a" and "rod", the teacher sits down with the students at the table, saying nothing. Everyone is silent for a minute until one girl points to a rod and says, "A rod." The teacher hands the pointer and she goes first to the sound-color chart to tap out the sounds, and second to the word chart to point to the words "a" and "rod". Several other students follow this pattern.

Next, the teacher points to a particular rod and taps out "A blue rod." Then he points to the word "blue" on the word chart. A boy points to the rod and says, "A blue rod." He goes to the word chart and finds the three words of this phrase there. Other students do the same. The teacher introduces the word "green" similarly, with students tapping out the pattern after he is through.

The teacher then points to a pink rod and taps out /pɪnk/ on the chart. The /ɪ/ vowel is a new one for the students. It does not exist in Portuguese. The teacher points to the block of color which represents /i/ and he indicates through his gesture that the students are to shorten the glide and open their mouths a bit more to say this sound.

The first student who tries to say "a pink rod" has trouble with the pronunciation of "pink".

He looks to the teacher and the teacher gestures towards the other students. One of them says "pink" and the teacher accepts the pronunciation. The first student tries again and this time the teacher accepts what he says. Another student seems to have trouble with the phrase. Using a finger to represent each word of the phrase, the teacher shows her how the phrase is segmented. Then by tapping his second finger, the teacher indicates that her trouble is with the second word.

The teacher then mouths the vowel sound and, with gestures, shows the student that the vowel is shorter than what she is saying. She tries to shape her mouth as the teacher does and her pronunciation does improve a little, although it still does not appear to be as close to the target language sounds as some of the other students'. With the other students watching, he works with her a bit longer. The students practice saying and tapping out the three color words and the phrase, with the teacher listening attentively and occasionally intervening to help them to correct their pronunciation.

The teacher has another group of students take the places of the first eight at the table. The teacher turns to one of the students and says, "Take a green rod." The student doesn't respond; the teacher waits. Another student picks up a green rod and says the same sentence. Through gestures from the teacher, he understands that he should direct the command to another student. The second student performs the action and then says, "Take a blue rod", to a third student. He takes one. The other students then take turns issuing and complying with commands to take a rod of a certain color.

Next, the teacher puts several blue and green rods in the center of the table. He points to the blue rod and to one of the students, who responds, "Take a blue rod." The teacher then says "and" and points to the green rod. The same student says, "and take a green rod." The teacher indicates to the student that she should say the whole sentence and she says, "Take a blue rod and take a green rod." As the girl says each word, the teacher points to one of his fingers. When she says the second "take", he gestures that she should remove the "take" from the sentence. She tries again, "Take a blue rod and a green rod." which the teacher accepts. The students now practice forming and complying with commands with similar compound objects.

The teacher then points to the word chart and to one of the students, who taps out the sentences on the chart as the other students produce them. Later, students take turns tapping out the sentences of their choice on the word chart. Some students tap out simple commands and some students tap out commands with compound objects.

The students return to their desks. The teacher turns to the class and asks the class in Portuguese for their reactions to the lesson. One student replies that he has learned that language learning is not difficult. Another says that he is finding it difficult; he feels that he needs more practice associating the sounds and colors. A third student adds that she felt as if she were playing a game. A fourth student says he is feeling confused.

At this point the lesson ends. During the next few classes, the students will:

① Practice with their new sounds and learn to produce accurate intonation and stress patterns with the words and sentences.

② Learn more English words for colors and where any new sounds are located on the sound-color chart.

③ Learn to use the following items:

Give it to me/her/him/them

too

this/that/these/those

one/ones

the/a/an

put … here/there

is/are

his/her/my/your/their/our

④ Practice making sentences with many different combinations of these items.

⑤ Practice reading the sentences they have created on the wall charts.

⑥ Work with Fidel Charts, which are charts summarizing the spellings of all the different sounds in English.

⑦ Practice writing the sentences they have created.

二、教学示例

本示例中，沉默法被应用于巴西的一堂英语课中。班级中有 24 名中学生，该课程一周 3 次，每次 2 课时。

课上，老师首先用葡萄牙语介绍沉默教学法。然后，老师走到教室前面，拿出一根金属指示棒，指向贴在墙上的一张图表。这是一张音色对应表。图表背景为黑色，上面有一排排的小方块。每个方块的颜色不同。每个不同颜色的方块都代表英语中的一个发音。图上还有一条白色的水平线，水平线将音色对应表分为上下两个部分，上半部分是元音，下半部分是辅音。

老师指了指音色对应表上半部分中的五个不同色块，未发一言。此时教室中静寂无声。老师再次指示五个色块，重复刚才的行为，依旧没有说话。整个课堂也仍旧鸦雀无声。老师第三次进行指示时，他指着第一个色块，发出声音：/ɑ/。接着，老师继续用指示棒指示另外四个色块。随着老师的指示，有几个学生开始发音：/e/、/i/、/ɒ/、/u/。这些元音是学生们本已掌握的（这五个音是葡萄牙语的简单元音，每个巴西小学生都是按这个顺序学习的），因此，老师从这些元音开始进行教学。

老师指向表示 /e/ 的色块，将两只手掌合在一起，然后再分开，表示让学生们延长这个元音的发音。他通过移动指示棒指示学生活动自己的舌头，以便从这个葡萄牙语的 /e/ 发出英语的双元音 /eɪ/。老师通过以上方式指导学生进行发音练习，直至学生发出令人满意的接近英语元音 /eɪ/ 的音为止。之后，老师以相同的方式指导学生发出元音 /i: /、/əʊ/ 和 /u: /。然后，老师把指示棒交给坐在前排的一名女生。那名女生走到教室前，用指示棒指向音色对应表最上面一排的白色色块，其他学生进行发音 /eɪ/。随后，那名女生一个接一个地指示其他三个色块，学生们依次发音 /eɪ/、/i:/、/əʊ/，且发音正确。然后，那名女生在寻找最后一个元音色块时遇到了困难，她指向音色对应表第三排的一个色块。此时，有几个学生喊道："不对！"那名女生仍试着在第三排找，并指向了另一个色块，但是同学们又一次叫道："不对！"最后，坐在第一排的一名男生用葡萄牙语说："往左边（移动）。"女生将指示棒向左移动一个格子，全班便齐读 /u:/。老师示意那名女生再来一遍。在第二次进行指读时，这名女生的速度加快了，并且很顺利地指出了 /u:/。老师示意女生回到座位上，并让另外一名学生指示这五个元音，全班齐读。完成后，老师让每位学生都到教室前，按照老师教的顺序依次指示所学的元音。在这一过程中，老师通过手势，辅以葡萄牙语的引导，让学生尽可能准确地发出英语元音，而老师自己不进行发音示范。

当学生们能够发出令人满意的五个元音的准确发音后，老师打乱顺序进行点读。这时，一些学生有点儿迟疑，但大多数学生依然能够根据不同色块进行正确发音。老师随机点读，学生跟读发音。老师用指示棒指向坐在第二排的男生，然后回到音色对应表，并指向五个不同的色块。这五个发音中，其中两个色块位于音色对应表的上半部分，分别是他们已经学过的元音 /eɪ/ 和 /u:/。另外三个色块则位于音色对应表的下半部分，是没有学过的。这时，有两三名学生喊道："Pedro!""Pedro"是一名男生的名字。这名男生便在其他同学的帮助下指示出代表他名字发音的不同色块 /p/、/e/、/d/、/r/ 和 /u/。之后，又有两三名学生进行指示，全班朗读发音。通过这样的练习，学生们便掌握了英语中 /p/、/d/、/r/ 的发音及其在音色对应表中的位置。由于学生们在 /r/ 的发音上还有些困难，因此老师又花了一些时间指导学生进行练习。

随后，老师指向一名女生，然后又分别指向音色对应表上的八个不同色块。学生们齐声说出女生的名字"Carolina"。然后像之前练习 Pedro 的名字一样，全班练习 Carolina 这个名字的发音。由此，学生们又学会了三个色块 /k/、/l/、/n/ 的发音。老师通过相同的方法，练习了第三名学生的名字"Gabriela"的发音，让学生们学会了 /g/ 和 /b/ 的位置与发音。之后，老师让不同的学生在音色对应表中指出这三名学生名字的发音并加以练习巩固。

在很多学生都能指示出三名学生名字所代表的发音后，老师拿起指示棒，开展一项新的教学活动。老师让八名学生围坐在教室前面的一张大桌子旁，其他学生坐在他们后边。老师在桌子中间放了一些不同长度的木条，木条有三个颜色，分别是蓝色、绿色和粉色。老师指了指其中一根木条，然后指向音色对应表中的三个不同色块。由于学生们已经学会了利用音色对应表上的色块进行拼合，因此，一些学生便开始尝试发音"rod"。听到部分学生的发音后，老师再次指示不同色块，这时全班学生都发出"rod"的读音。老师又指示音色对应表中代表"a"的色块，然后，老师指向自己的嘴，向学生展示如何从一个他们已知的音发出一个新的英语发音，方式就是边抬起下巴，边合上嘴。学生们跟着老师的指示，发出了一个新的音，一个近似 /ə/ 的发音。随即，老师先指向一个新的色块，然后快速地依次指示四个色块，学生们齐声拼读："a rod"。老师转向墙上的另一张图表，这张图表上有很多不同颜色的单词。老师指向单词"a"和"rod"，学生们发现单词中每个字母的颜色与字母所表示的发音是相同的。

指示单词"a"和"rod"之后，老师便回到学生们的桌前坐下，不再说话。全班静默了一分钟。然后有一名女生指着一根木条说道："A rod.（一根木条。）"老师将指示棒交给她。她先走到音色对应表前，指示相应的色块，然后在词汇表中，指示单词"a"和"rod"。之后又有几名学生也进行了相同的课堂活动。

接下来，老师指着一根特殊的木条，在音色对应表中指示"A blue rod."的对应发音，然后在词汇表中指示单词"blue"。一名男生指着木条说："A blue rod.（一根蓝色木条。）"他走到词汇表前，在上面找到这个短语中的三个对应单词。然后其他学生也如此做。老师又以同样的方式向学生们介绍了单词"green"，学生们在他讲完后按照之前的方式找出了短语及相应的单词。

然后老师指向一根粉色的木条，在音色对应表中指示其发音 /pɪnk/。元音 /ɪ/ 对学生们来说是一个新的知识点，葡萄牙语中没有这个发音。老师指着代表 /ɪ/ 的色块，利用手势示意学生们缩短舌头滑行时间并在发音时将嘴张大一点儿，便可以发出这个新的元音了。

第一个尝试说"粉色木条"的学生在"粉色"的发音上遇到了困难。他看向老师寻求帮助，而老师用手势示意其他学生提供帮助。其中一名学生说出了"粉色"，老师认可了她的发音。之前那名学生再次尝试发音，老师也认可了他的发音。又有一名学生说不出整个短语，老师用一个手指来代表短语中的一个单词，并向她展示短语是如何切分的。然后老师指着第二根手指，示意那名学生，她的问题出在第二个单词上。

老师用口型示意单词中的元音的发音，利用手势告诉那名学生那个元音的发音应该比她的实际发音要短一些。那名学生模仿老师的口型，尝试发音，虽然这一次她的发音仍然像其他学生发的那样接近目的语的元音发音，但是也有了一些改善。老师在其他学生的注视下，对这名学生进行了较长时间的引导和纠正。学生们练习发音，并在音色对应表及词汇表中指示词的发音和短语所包含的单词，此期间老师认真倾听，并不时地进行干预，帮助学生们纠正发音。

老师让另一组学生代替前八名学生来到桌子前。老师转向其中一名学生，说道："拿一根绿色木条。"那名学生没有回应老师。老师便等着学生的回应。另一名学生拿起一根绿色木条，然后重复了一遍老师的句子。老师通过手势示意他向其他学生发出指令。第二名学生演示了第一名学生所说的动作，即拿起一根绿色木条，然后对第三名学生说："拿一根蓝色木条。"第三名学生也按照第二名学生的指令做了相应的动作。随后，其他学生开始进行接龙，轮流按照前一名学生说的做，并发出让下一名学生拿一根特定颜色木条的指令。

接下来，老师拿出一些蓝色和绿色木条放在桌子上，指了指蓝色木条，其中一名学生回答道："拿一根蓝色木条。"然后老师说："和"，并指了指绿色木条。刚才那名学生又说道："和拿一根绿色木条。"老师示意学生说整句，那名学生便说道："拿一根蓝色木条和拿一根绿色木条。"在那名女生说句子时，她每说一个单词，老师就掰一根手指。当女生说到第二个"拿"时，老师示意她去掉句子中的那个"拿"。女生又说了一遍，"拿一根蓝色木条和一根绿色木条。"这时老师认可了她的句子。随后，学生们开始模仿句子，练习发出指令和照着指令去做。

老师指向词汇表和其中一名学生，那名学生便在词汇表上指示其他学生所说句子的单词。随后，学生们轮流在词汇表中指示他们所选的句子，有的学生指示的是简单的指令句，有的学生指示的是复杂的指令句。

学生们回到自己的座位。老师面向全班学生，用葡萄牙语询问全班学生的上课感受。第一名学生说他觉得学习一门语言并不是那么难。第二名学生说他觉得很难，他觉得他需要更多的时间进行练习，把声音与颜色联系起来。第三名学生补充说她觉得这堂课好像是在做游戏。第四名学生说他还是觉得很困惑。

课程到此结束。在接下来的几节课中，学生们将进行以下活动：

①练习新的发音，运用所学词句，练习语调和重音。

②学习更多的英语颜色词，并掌握新发音在音色对应表中的位置。

③学习使用以下语言点：

把它给我 / 她 / 他 / 他们

也

这 / 那 / 这些 / 那些

一个 / 一些

定冠词 / 不定冠词

把……放在这儿 / 那儿

系动词

他的 / 她的 / 我的 / 你的 / 他们的 / 我们的

④练习用以上语言点造句。

⑤利用挂图（词汇表）造句，并进行朗读练习。

⑥学会使用音译表，音译表中包含了英语中所有不同发音的拼写方式。

⑦练习书写他们所造的句子。

3 Teaching Principles and Teaching Procedures

3.1 Teaching Principles of the Silent Way

Gattegno states that the processes of learning a second language are "radically different" from those involved in learning a first language and a successful second language approach will replace a "natural" approach by one that is very "artificial" and, for some purposes, strictly controlled. The "artificial approach" is based on the principle that successful learning involves commitment of the self to language acquisition through the use of silent awareness and then active trial. Silence is considered the best vehicle for learning, because in silence, students concentrate on the task to be accomplished and the potential means to its accomplishment. During this silence process, learners become "in awareness", then develop awareness proceeds from attention, production, self-correction, absorption, and acquire "inner criteria", which play a central role "in one's education throughout all of one's life".

According to these views, Gattegno proposed his following educational principles which he had developed to solve general problems in learning, and which he had previously applied to the teaching of mathematics and of spelling in the mother tongue.

① Teachers should concentrate on how students learn, not on how to teach;

② Imitation and drill are not the primary means by which students learn;

③ Learning consists of trial and error, deliberate experimentation, suspending judgement, and revising conclusions;

④ In learning, learners draw on everything that they already know, especially their native language;

⑤ The teacher must not interfere with the learning process.

These principles situate the Silent Way in the tradition of discovery learning, that regardes learning as a creative problem-solving activity.

3.2 Four Stages of Learning

The Silent Way teaching always applies to teaching beginning-level students oral or basic elements of target language more fluently with correct pronunciation and grammar. The ultimate aim is to make students know how to correctly use practical knowledge of grammar. The Silent Way adopts a basically structural syllabus, with lessons planned around grammatical items and related vocabulary. Gattegno mentions that there are four stages of learning in the class of Silent Way teaching method.

① To learn is to be confronted with the unknown. This is the stage that students become aware of the knowledge which they want to learn. The knowledge that they want to figure out is the unknown things. This kind of awareness is the first stage of the Silent Way class.

② The exploration of the unknown is done through awareness. When students want to learn something unknown, they might make a lot of mistakes in the process of understanding the new knowledge. This is the stage of Silent Way teaching that students learn the language by making mistakes.

③ The time to practice. In order to correct these mistakes students have made in the process of learning in Silent Way class, they need to keep practicing until they will not make the same mistake again.

④ The process of learning this unknown knowledge has been completed. That means what they have learned becomes automatic. After students finish this stage, they can learn something new.

In the Silent Way teaching class, students would produce a sentence and the teacher give them feedback on these sentences or sound combinations. The feedback includes the indication of where the mistake is. After several trails, students might find where the mistake is with the help of the teacher. Then they try again to produce some sentences of the target language to correct the mistakes they have made in the former trails. Then the teacher provides feedback again to the students, which helps tell them whether their sentences are appropriate. This kind of circle will repeat again and again until the students make the right sentences or utter the right sound of target language.

3.3 Teaching Techniques and Special Materials of the Silent Way

(1) Teacher's Silence

The Teacher's silence is the unique and the most important aspect of the Silent Way. Being silent moves the focus of the classroom from the teacher to the students, and can encourage cooperation among them. It also frees the teacher to observe the class. Silence can be used to help students correct their own errors. Teachers can remain silent when students make mistakes and give them time to self-correct. So the Silent Way asserts that the teacher can keep silent 90% of the time or more. The teacher uses nonverbal clues, such as gestures, charts, and manipulatives in order to make the students get across meanings, elicit and shape students' responses, test and monitor learners' interactions with each other, and complete his whole teaching silently. Just as Richards and Rodgers say: "The Silent Way teacher, like the complete dramatist, writes the script, chooses the props, sets the mood, models the action, designates the players, and is critic for the performance."

(2) Peer Correction

A Silent Way classroom also makes extensive use of peer correction. Students are encouraged to help their classmates when they have trouble with any particular feature of the language. This help should be made in a cooperative fashion, not a competitive one.

(3) Special Teaching Materials

The Silent Way makes use of specialized teaching materials: colored Cuisenaire rods, the sound-color chart, word charts, and Fidel charts.

The Cuisenaire rods are wooden, varying in length from 1 to 10 centimeters, and each length has a specific color. The rods are used to directly link words and structures with their meanings in the target language, thereby avoiding translation into the native language. They are used in a wide variety of situations in the classroom. At the beginning stages, they can be used to practice colors and numbers, and later they can be used for size comparisons, to represent people, build floor plans, constitute a road map, and in more complex grammar. For example, to teach prepositions, the teacher could use the statement "The blue rod is between the green one and the yellow one." They can also be used more abstractly, perhaps to represent a clock when students are learning about time.

The sound-color chart consists of blocks of color, with one color representing one sound in the language being learned. The teacher uses this chart to help teach pronunciation, make students understand the difference in pronunciation, and also help students learn word stress through tapping particular colors very hard. Later in the learning process, students can point to the chart themselves. The chart can help students perceive sounds that may not occur in their first language, and it also allows students to practice making these sounds without relying on mechanical repetition. It also provides an easily verifiable record of which sounds the students have mastered and which they have not, which can help their autonomy.

The word charts contain the functional vocabulary of the target language, and use the same color scheme as the sound-color chart. Each letter is colored in a way that indicates its pronunciation. The teacher can point to the chart to highlight the pronunciation of different words in sentences that the students are learning. There are twelve word charts in English, containing a total of around five hundred words.

The Fidel charts also use the same color-coding, and list the various ways that sounds can be spelled. For example, in English, the entry for the sound /eɪ/ contains the spellings "ay" "ea" "ei" "eigh" etc. All written in the same color. These can be used to help students associate sounds with their spelling.

Furthermore, there are wall pictures and books. Both types of materials are used to introduce certain extra-linguistic topics such as literature or cultural contexts. They are especially used in advanced classes to expand the typical rod- and chart-centered lessons. Finally, each teacher usually uses a metal pointer, which helps draw the students' attention away from the teacher and to the linguistic.

三、教学原则与教学过程

1. 沉默法的教学原则

加特诺指出：第二语言的学习过程与第一语言习得过程是"截然不同的"，成功的第二语言学习绝不是按"自然"的方法，而是采用"人为"的方法，是受到严格控制的。所谓"人为教学法"，其原则理念是认为成功的学习需要通过运用沉默意识和主动尝试来实现语言习得的自我投入。沉默被认为是学习的最佳方式，因为在沉默的过程中，学生可以专注于要完成的任务和完成任务的潜在手段。在这个沉默的过程中，学习者逐渐开启"自我意识"，然后通过关注语言、语言产出、自我纠正、吸收内化等意识活动进一步发展自我意识，并获得"内在图式"，"内在图式"在"一个人一生的教育中"起着核心作用。

基于以上观点，为解决学习中的普遍性问题，加特诺提出了沉默法的一些教学原则，这些教学原则他也曾应用于数学和学生母语拼写教学中。沉默法的教学原则具体如下：

①教师应该关注学生是如何学的，而非自己是如何教的；

②模仿和操练不是学生学习的主要手段；

③学习包括尝试和犯错，深入思考并尝试，暂停并进行判断，修正和总结；

④在学习中，学习者利用他们已经知道的一切，特别是他们的母语来建构并学习新知识；

⑤教师不得干预学习过程。

综合以上教学原则来看，沉默法的主要理论基础是布鲁纳的"发现学习"教育思想，认为学习是解决问题式的、创造和发现式的活动。

2. 沉默法的四个学习阶段

沉默法通常适用于教授初级阶段学生正确的语音和语法，以达到教授目的语基本语言要素及口语表达技能的目的。其最终目标是让学生知道如何正确运用语法知识进行语言实践。沉默法课程围绕语法项目和相关词汇展开，基本上采用了结构法的教学大纲。加特诺提出使用沉默法的课堂具有如下四个学习阶段。

①学习就是面对未知。在这一阶段，学生将开始意识到他们想要学习的知识。他们想要了解的知识是未知的事物。这种意识是沉默法学习过程的第一阶段。

②对未知的探索是通过意识来完成的。当学生想要学习一些未知的事物时，他们在理解新知识的过程中可能会犯很多错误。这是沉默法教学的第二个阶段，学生在这一阶段通过犯错来学习语言。

③实践练习。为了纠正在学习过程中所犯的错误，学生们需要不断地进行练习，直到不再犯同样的错误。

④完成对未知事物的学习。这意味着学生所学到的东西会变成自动的行为和意识。学生在完成这一阶段后，就掌握了新知识。

在沉默法的课堂教学中，学生每造一个句子，教师就会对这些句子的结构或发音组合给予反馈。反馈包括指出错误所在。经过几次尝试后，学生们可能会在教师的帮助下找到产生错误的地方。然后，他们会试着用目的语进行造句，纠正他们在前几次尝试中所犯的错误。同样，教师会再次向学生提供反馈，帮助他们判断自己的句子是否恰当。这种反馈与尝试一次次地循环往复，直到学生说出正确的句子或发出准确的目的语发音。

3. 沉默法的教学技巧与特殊教具

（1）教师的沉默

教师的沉默是沉默法最独特，也是最重要的特征之一。沉默将课堂的焦点从教师的讲授转移到学生自身的学习，并能够促进学生之间的沟通合作。沉默也使教师能够抽出时间进行课堂观察。沉默还可以帮助学生进行自我纠正，即当学生犯错时，教师依然保持沉默，给学生时间来进行自我纠正。沉默法提出教师可以在90%甚至更多的课堂时间中保持沉默。教师可以运用手势、图表、示意他人等非语言手段使学生理解意义，引导学生做出反应，测试、监控学生之间的互动，并最终以沉默的方式完成整个教学过程。正如理查德和罗杰斯所说："沉默法的教师就像一个操控全局的剧作家，他写剧本，选择道具，设定演员情绪，塑造演员的动作，挑选演员，并对表演进行评论。"

（2）同伴纠错

沉默法的课堂广泛使用同伴纠错的学习方式。教师鼓励学生在自己的同伴遇到个别语言问题时进行帮助。这种同伴间的互助并非以竞争方式，而是以合作方式进行的。

（3）特殊教具

沉默法在教学中会使用一些特殊教具，如彩色棒、音色对应表、词汇表和音译表等。

彩色棒是木制的，长度从 1 厘米到 10 厘米不等，每种长度的木棒都有特定的颜色。为了避免使用学习者的母语，教师用彩色棒直接指代目的语的意义和相关的单词及语言结构。它们可以在课堂中的各种情境中使用。在最初阶段，彩色棒可以用来练习颜色和数字，之后，它们也可以用以比较大小、代替人物、组建平面图、组成一幅路线图、指示更复杂的语法等。例如，教授介词时，教师可以用"蓝色棒在绿色棒和黄色棒之间"这样的句子进行介词意义和用法的教学。彩色棒还可用于更抽象的事物表达，比如：在学生学习与时间相关的表达时，用彩色棒代替时钟。

音色对应表由不同的色块组成，每一种颜色代表所学语言中的一个发音。教师利用这个图表进行语音教学，通过不同颜色使学生了解发音的不同，还可以通过重击某一个色块教学生练习词语的重音。在之后的学习过程中，学生们也可以自行指示图表。这张图表可以帮助学生感知并练习母语中没有的发音，也可以让学生在不依赖机械重复的情况下练习发音。它还为学生提供了一个检验所学的依据，学生可以对照图表查验哪些发音学会了，哪些发音没学会或还没有学，从而提高学生学习的自主性。

词汇表列出了目的语的功能性词汇，并在单词的颜色使用上与音色对应表的配色方案一致。每个字母的颜色都标示出了它的发音。教师可以在学生进行学习的过程中，利用指示词汇表的单词提示或强调所学句子中不同单词的发音。英语中有 12 张词汇表，合计约有 500 个单词。

音译表使用了与音色对应表、词汇表相同的发音配色方案，并列出了每个发音的各种拼写方式。例如，在英语中，/eɪ/ 这个发音的词条包含"ay""ea""ei""eigh"等拼写形式。同一发音的所有拼写形式在音译表中都使用了相同的颜色进行标识。音译表可以帮助学生把发音和拼写联系起来。

此外，还有贴在墙上的情景挂图和书籍资料。这两种类型的教具都可以辅助介绍一些语言本体知识以外的话题，如文学或文化背景知识。这些材料主要用于高级水平的课程中，以便对以彩色棒和图表为主要教学方式的课程进行补充和拓展。最后，每位教师通常都会使用一根金属指示棒，指示棒有助于把学生的注意力从教师身上转移到语言本身。

4 Conclusion

There are several features of the Silent Way that seem to have been imported from the Direct Method and other "natural" approaches, including the exclusive use of the target language, the symbolic use of aids to illustrate and elicit language items, and the strict rationing of the content to be learned, particularly vocabulary. The defining difference is the almost complete absence of teacher talk, including the question-answer sequences and corrective feedback so typical of most teaching. The silence of the teacher can leave more time for students to practice their language skills in class. Therefore, in the Silent Way teaching class, students are the center of the class and the key speakers. They are put into different groups in which they can practice their target language, correct others' mistakes, and evaluate what they have learned from the class. The potential of every student will be found through these learning trails and practices in groups. Besides, in the Silent Way teaching class, students would not be stuck in the burden of reciting the word or sentence structure and won't worry about making mistakes. As mistake is the virtue of learning a language, it is the key to successfully taking command of the target language. This method of teaching can make students motivated enough to be more creative and innovative in learning a new language.

The Silent Way teaching method is one of the most innovative ways of teaching as well as learning, but also "a seminal contribution to understanding the learning process at all ages". There are many unavoidable defects in the Silent Way teaching class. Language learning requires a long term memory of the words and gets to know the basic grammar through practices of using the target language. In the Silent Way teaching process, teachers will not push students to recite the basic knowledge as usual and only give a few examples for students to follow, which will cause a lot of trouble for students to be familiar with the unique language system. The big weakness of the Silent Way teaching method is that it could only be widely used in a small-sized class which allows each student to speak out the target language with the help of the teacher's body language or pointer. The process of Silent Way teaching is really slow to move on as teacher provides neither praise nor criticism for students in the very beginning, which pushes the students to work out the solutions on their own most of the time. For some teachers, they might not be capable of explaining any difficult grammar or sentence structures to students in the Silent Way teaching method. A simple grammar or sentence in target language will cost the teacher a long time to explain or prepare to present to students in class. The teaching with the help of rods and other physical materials requires the teacher to be very creative to involve each student in the class. It might cost time and money to support this kind of teaching class. This kind of teaching method can only be applied to an elementary level language class, as it is so hard to teach a high level language class in the Silent Way teaching method. As a matter of fact, in the teaching process, this method can't be widely applied to different level language classes.

四、小结

　　沉默法继承了直接法及其他（模仿母语习得过程的）"自然教学法"的特点，如使用目的语进行教学，采用辅助手段导入并解释语言项目，严格限定学习内容，尤其是词汇。与那些"自然教学法"显著不同的是，沉默法几乎完全避免教师语言，即使是大多数教学中的典型活动——问答和纠错环节，也要求教师沉默。教师的沉默给学生留出更多的时间进行课堂语言技能的练习。因此，在沉默法的课堂教学中，学生是学习的主体，是主要的发言人。学生们被分成不同的小组，在小组中，他们使用目的语进行练习，纠正其他学生的语言错误，评估自己的课堂所学。通过学习轨迹和小组练习，每位学生的潜能都会展现出来。另外，在运用沉默法进行学习时，学生不再承受死记硬背单词和句子结构的重负，也不必担心犯错误。因为语言学习依靠犯错，犯错是成功掌握目的语的关键。沉默法能够充分发挥学生的积极性，使其在学习一种新的语言时更具创造性和创新性。

　　沉默法是最具创新性的教学法之一，它对学习过程的理解对各时期的语言学习均产生了深远影响。沉默法在课堂教学中也存在许多无法避免的局限性。语言学习需要进行长期的词汇记忆，并通过使用目的语进行语言实践来掌握基本语法。而在沉默法的教学过程中，教师不会像往常一样强迫学生背诵基础知识，而是只举一些例子让学生学习，这使得学生很难熟悉并掌握一门独特的语言体系。更重要的是，沉默法只可能在小规模课堂中得到广泛应用。只有小班教学才能做到让每个学生都能借助教师的肢体语言或指示棒说出目的语。沉默法的教学进度相对较慢，教师在教学的初始阶段，既不表扬学生，也不批评学生，而将大多数教学时间用来促使学生自己去解决问题。对于一些教师来说，他们可能难以运用沉默的方式向学生解释较难的语法或句子结构。一个简单的目的语语法或句子可能会花费教师很长时间来解释或备课。在使用彩色棒和其他教具进行教学方面，教师也需要非常有创造力，以便使每个学生都参与到课堂中。采用沉默法教学还需要时间和经济支持。这种教学方法只适用于初级水平的语言课堂，而在高级语言课堂上采用沉默法是很难做到的。因此，这种方法并不能广泛应用于不同层次的语言课堂。

○ Activities and Exercises

● Understanding and Thinking

1. Based on the following materials, state the reasons for the teacher's silence in the Silent Way.

We may want to leave time in class for students to write in silence, to have a silent, private contact with the shape of a poem and its silent sounds, to listen in silence to the cadences of a student or to our own voice reading aloud, to follow silently the rhythm of a conversation played on tape, the episodic structure of a story well told. We may want to even foster silence as a way of letting the students reflect on what they are right now experiencing.

2. What does the sentence of Caleb Gattegno, "Stop teaching!" mean?

3. One of the mottos of the Silent Way is "The teacher works on the students; the students work on the language." What do you think this means?

● **Teaching Design**

1. Please read the sample lesson intensively, expand the teaching details, and then make a teaching demonstration in groups.

The language being taught is Thai, for which this is the first lesson.

① *Teacher empties rods onto the table.*

② *Teacher picks up two or three rods of different colors, and after each rod is picked up, says: [mai].*

③ *Teacher holds up one rod of any color and indicates to a student that a response is required. Student says: [mai]. If response is incorrect, teacher elicits response from another student, who then models for the first student.*

④ *Teacher next picks up a red rod and says: [mai sii daeng].*

⑤ *Teacher picks up a green rod and says: [mai sii khiaw].*

⑥ *Teacher picks up either a red or green rod and elicits response from student. If response is incorrect, procedure in step ③ is followed (student modeling).*

⑦ *Teacher introduces two or three other colors in the same manner.*

⑧ *Teacher shows any of the rods whose forms were taught previously and elicits student response. Correction technique is through student modeling, or the teacher may help student isolate error and self-correct.*

⑨ *When mastery is achieved, teacher puts one red rod in plain view and says: [mai sil daeng nung an].*

⑩ *Teacher then puts two red rods in plain view and says: [mai sii daeng song an].*

⑪ *Teacher places two green rods in view and says: [mai si khiaw song an].*

⑫ *Teacher holds up two rods of a different color and elicits student response.*

⑬ *Teacher introduces additional numbers, based on what the class can comfortably retain. Other colors might also be introduced.*

⑭ *Rods are put in a pile. Teacher indicates, through his or her own actions, that rods should be picked up, and the correct utterance made. All the students in the group pick up rods and make utterances. Peer-group correction is encouraged.*

⑮ *Teacher then says: [kep mai sii daeng song an].*

⑯ *Teacher indicates that a student should give the teacher the rods called for. Teacher asks other students in the class to give him or her the rods that he or she asks for. This is all done in the target language rough unambiguous actions on the part of the teacher.*

⑰ *Teacher now indicates that the students should give each other commands regarding the calling for of rods. Rods are put at the disposal of the class.*

⑱ *Experimentation is encouraged. Teacher speaks only to correct an incorrect utterance, if no peer-group correction is forthcoming.*

2. Please read the following teaching plan carefully, point out the inappropriate places according to the theory and teaching principles of the Silent Way, then revise and improve it.

Course Title: *What color is it?*

Teaching Objectives:

Through the content of this lesson, students will master the basic vocabulary and sentence patterns of colors, and be able to use them proficiently in daily conversations. At the same time, they will stimulate students' enthusiasm for English learning and students' interest.

Teaching Contents:

① *Teach new vocabulary in this lesson using color charts and Cuisenaire rods;*

② *Show the key sentence patterns of this lesson "What color is it?" "It's..." and demonstrate usage;*

③ *Practice in small groups and draw a small group display;*

④ *Summarize and arrange assignments.*

Teaching Focus and Difficulties:

(1) Teaching Focus

① *Learn to spell vocabulary about colors.*

② *Learn to use sentence patterns by Cuisenaire rods.*

(2) Teaching Difficulties

① *Master the pronunciation of related words with the aid of teaching materials.*

② *Use the learned sentence patterns in daily conversation.*

Teaching Process:

(1) Import

Introduce Teaching Tools.

Introduce students to the teaching chart for this lesson, and explain that everyone will find the pronunciation of certain letter combinations on the chart and read the words based on the pronunciation.

(2) Color Learning

① English words with blue, red, yellow, black, white and other basic colors.

Introduce new words, and tell the students how to pronounce some parts of the new words in the chart. Ask the students to try to read the words by themselves, and ask the students to read the words until a classmate reads the correct pronunciation. Encourage him and let other students repeat.

② Sentence Practice.

Learn the sentence pattern "What color is it? It's_____." Answer with the words you learned about color.

a. Put out the sentence pattern on the PPT; then the teacher and one student have a dialogue as a whole;

b. Ask the students to talk in pairs, and ask the students to demonstrate;

c. Ask other students to find out and correct the mistakes made during the conversation that they just demonstrated;

d. Ask students to compose a dialogue and display it in groups;

e. Ask other students to find out and correct the mistakes made during the conversation that they just demonstrated;

f. Encourage good performers. (Note: In the practice of color and sentence, the teacher does not read or correct mistakes, but only uses gestures to indicate right and wrong.)

(3) Homework Assignment

After class, you need to learn the pronunciation of orange, pink, purple and green in English according to the chart. Learn to use the sentence patterns taught in the class for dialogue, and each person uses the color words to learn a conversation. Make a show.

● **Further Reading**

The Silent Way Teaching Method[①]

1. Background

Tell me and I forget

Teach me and I remember

Involve me and I learn

—*Benjamin Franklin*

The Silent Way (SW), a method of language teaching introduced by Caleb Gattegno, an European educator, is well known for the use of colored wooden sticks called Cuisenaire rods and for his approach to the teaching of initial reading in which sounds are taught by colors. According

---

① JI H L, LI R, ZHANG Y H. The Silent Way Teaching Method [J]. Overseas English, 2011(11):139-141.

to Caleb Gattegno, one of the manifestations of subordinating teaching to learning is that "the teacher works on the student and the student works on the language".

The Silent Way derives its name from the fact that the teacher conducting a Silent Way class which is silent for most of the time. This silence means giving students the opportunity to fully exploit precious classroom time. The teacher's presence in the classroom is limited to providing a model of the language that the students are going to work on. The basic assumption is that the students will bring their potential and previous experience of learning their mother tongue to the foreign language classroom. The method is based on the premise that the teacher should be silent as much as possible and the learners should be encouraged to produce language as much as possible. The approach succeeds in enhancing learning because it is firmly based upon the subordination of teaching to learning. It can withstand the trials presented by the varying backgrounds, ages and temperaments of students because in this approach, teaching is guided at all times by the learning processes of the students.

The SW shares a great deal with other learning theories and educational philosophies. Gattegno states that learning is facilitated if the learners discover or create what is to be learned, and that learning is facilitated by accompanying physical objects and problem solving involving the material to be learned. The SW views learning as a problem-solving, creative, and discovering activities. We call it a problem-solving approach to learning. It is a methodology of teaching which has at its core the idea that the language, or indeed whatever is to be studied, should be approached by the learner as a puzzle to be worked out. By using tools such as Cuisenaire rods, a selection of specially prepared charts and a pointer, the teacher presents the puzzle to the learners. The learners work out the "puzzle" and ultimately learn the language involved in it.

The last line of Benjamin Franklin's famous quote about teaching and learning above can be said to lie at the heart of the Silent Way.

2. Approach: Theory of Language and Learning

As far as the presentation of language is concerned, the Silent Way adopts a highly structural approach, with language taught through sentences in a sequence based on grammatical complexity, described by some as a "building-block" approach. The structural patterns of the target language are presented by the teacher and the grammar "rules" of the language are learned inductively by the learners. Cuisenaire rods are often used to illustrate meaning. New items are added sparingly by the teacher and learners take these as far as they can in their communication until the need for the next new item becomes apparent. The teacher then provides this new item by modeling it very clearly just once. The learners are then left to use the new item and to incorporate it into their existing stock of language, again taking it as far as they can until the next item is needed and so on.

In the Silent Way class, learning takes place in four stages:

Stage 1: To learn is to be confronted with the unknown. We have to realize that there is an unknown to be explored. This realization takes place through an awareness, the basic awareness of the fact that there is an area to be explored.

Stage 2: The exploration of the unknown is done through awareness. Since it is unknown, we may, and usually do, make many mistakes. It is this stage that led many years ago to the recognition that we learn by trial and error.

Stage 3: The time to practice. Once an understanding of what is necessary in order to reach mastery has been reached, we require practice.

Stage 4: The sign that the learning process has finished is that what we have learned becomes automatic, leaving us free to go about our business of meeting a new unknown and learning something else.

In the Silent Way classroom, the subordination of teaching to learning can be implemented according to the following sequence of steps:

① Student experiments with the language. She or he produces a sentence, grammatical construction, or sound combination.

② Teacher gives feedback on the experiment by indicating the presence of a mistake or inadequacy. This feedback represents the teacher's own experiment or trial. Note that the feedback never involves the correction of the mistake, but only an indication of where the mistake is.

③ Student produces an additional experiment, trying to correct herself or himself, which provides feedback to the teacher.

④ Teacher deduces from the produced sentence whether her or his trial is appropriate or helpful.

⑤ The cycle continues until the student's utterance is adequate, correct and true.

3. Design

Based on the Silent Way, an English lesson plan among primary school students is carried out. The main points are as follows:

(1) Objectives

Give beginning-level students oral and aural facility in basic elements of the target language. The general goal set for language learning is near-native fluency in the target language, and correct pronunciation and mastery of the prosodic elements of the target language are emphasized. An immediate objective is to provide the learner with a basic practical knowledge of grammar.

(2) Syllabus

It adopts a basically structural syllabus, with lessons planned around grammatical items and related vocabulary. Language items are introduced according to their grammatical complexity, their relationship to what has been taught previously, and the ease with which items can be presented visually.

(3) Activities

① Responses to commands, questions, and visual cues constitute the basis for classroom activities.

② Using of charts, rods, and other aids to elicit learner responses.

(4) Learners' Roles

The learners are the prime cause for the class to work. They are expected to develop independence, autonomy, and responsibility. They need to make use of what they know, to free themselves of any obstacles that would interfere with giving their utmost attention to the learning task, and to actively engage in exploring the language.

(5) Teacher's Roles

The prominent writer in language teaching, Earl W. Stevick, has described the role of the teacher in the Silent Way as "Teach, test, get out of the way."

According to Richards and Rodgers, "In sum, the Silent Way teacher, like the complete dramatist, writes the script, chooses the props, sets the mood, models the action, designates the players, and is critic for the performance."

(6) Instructional Materials

① A sound/color wall chart (rectangle chart) made up of different colored rectangles in which each color represents a phoneme (sound) of the language, enabling learners to work on fine distinctions in the phonetics and prosody of the language studied, both on the level of production and of listening and recognition.

② Word wall charts on which the words are written with the same color code as the rectangle chart. These charts display the structural vocabulary of the language, about 500 words. The color code means that languages as different as Japanese and Russian, which use signs unfamiliar to the learner, can be immediately read and pronounced correctly.

③ Spelling charts (called the Fidel), which show all the possible spellings for each phoneme and which also use the same color code as the rectangle chart. The Fidel is particularly useful with languages like English and French, which have complex and irregular spellings.

④ Rods of different colors are used to create clear and visible situations that enable students to understand how a given concept is expressed in the language studied.

⑤ The Silent Way wall pictures representing everyday scenes. Very spare in style, these pictures encourage students to use their imagination to suggest interpretations. They are used to introduce common vocabulary and also to serve as a starting point for stories created by the students or to encourage discussion.

⑥ A pointer, with which the teacher or the learner can show a word or a sentence while maintaining the essential characteristic of language — its ephemeral nature. The pointer creates the dynamic of the language by introducing the element of time in relation to the different charts, which are in themselves, static. The use of the pointer is one of the ways in which the teacher calls on the learners to use their mental powers.

4. Procedure

A beginning or elementary lesson will start with working simultaneously on the basic elements of the language: the sounds and prosody of the language and on the construction of sentences. The materials described above will be frequently used. At first, the teacher will propose situations for the students to respond to, but very quickly the students themselves will invent new situations using the rods but also events in the classroom and their own lives.

In an advanced lesson, the students will be invited to talk to each other on any subject they wish. The lesson will be based on their mistakes — "the gifts of the student to the class" as Gattegno liked to call them. The teacher will not correct the mistakes, but help the students do so themselves by encouraging them to discuss the problem, and find other similar and/or contrasting examples. The materials described above may seldom or never be used but the students will be exploring the language in the same spirit.

5. The Major Characteristics of the Silent Way

As it is mentioned above, the Silent Way emphasizes students' involvement instead of teachers' explanation. It has the following characteristics:

① Teaching should be subordinated to learning.

② Learners are assumed to have developed their own inner criteria of correctness and are capable of correcting their own errors.

③ Learning is not primarily imitation or drill. However, in learning, the mind equips itself by its own working, trial and error, and deliberate experimentation, suspending judgment, and revising conclusions.

④ As it works, the mind draws on everything that has already been acquired, particularly its experience in learning the native language.

⑤ Students become familiar with new structures and recognize them through conceptualized use and practice.

⑥ Learning is facilitated if the learner discovers or creates rather than remembers and repeats what is to be learned.

⑦ Accompanying physical objects facilitates learning.

⑧ Learning is facilitated when problem solving involves the material to be learned.

⑨ Students may hear a given word only once. The teacher's strict avoidance of repetition forces alertness and concentration.

⑩ The teacher, as implied by the name of the approach, remains essentially silent. Therefore, the teacher silently monitors learners' interactions with each other. The teacher must stop trying to interfere and sidetrack that activity. When no peer group correction is forthcoming, the teacher speaks only to correct an incorrect utterance.

⑪ The teacher avoids translating words into the native language.

⑫ The material consists mainly of a set of colored rods, color-coded pronunciation and vocabulary wall charts, a pointer, and reading/writing exercises, all of which are used to elicit learners' response and to illustrate the relationships between sound and meaning in the target language.

⑬ The color rods provide physical foci for students' learning and also create memorable images to facilitate student recall. They are used to directly link words and structures with their meaning in the target language.

⑭ The rods vary in length, from one to ten centimeters, and each length has a specific color.

⑮ All teaching activities are done in the target language through unambiguous actions on the part of the teacher.

6. Criticism of the Silent Way

Caleb Gattegno's Silent Way is not only one of the most important and innovative for language teaching and learning, but also "a seminal contribution to understanding the learning process at all ages". However, it still has certain unavoidable defects, listed as follows:

① The apparent lack of real communication in the approach has been criticized, with some arguing that it is difficult to take the approach beyond the very basics of the language, with only highly motivated learners being able to generate real communication from the rigid structures illustrated by the rods. The fact that, for logistical reasons, it is limited to relatively small groups of learners, is also seen as a weakness.

② Learners do not work with authentic, culturally based materials or hear authentic native speech, at least in the early phases of instruction. Obviously, the SW does not set out to provide new immigrants the language they need to apply for a job or ask for a bus schedule by telephone, nor is it aimed at supplying this summer's tour group to Spain a repertoire of useful expressions for conceivable social encounters there. Compared with those of Competency-Based Language Training which aims to equip learners right up front with language that fits imagined social interchange scenarios, the SW with its at-first generic language seems irrelevant to any social purpose.

③ The whole learning process might be inefficient because the teacher offers neither praise nor criticism and does not allow questions or even recourse to the native language.

④ There is a large gap between the teacher and students because of the silence.

⑤ It is difficult to get the teaching tools, such as the colored rod. The teachers who are interested in the Silent Way have to buy the certain set of teaching tools from Educational Solutions Inc. in New York City.

● **Knowledge Table**

Table 6-1   Summary of Characteristics of the Silent Way

Key Points	The Silent Way
Period	
Representatives	
Background	
Theory of Language	
Theory of Language Learning	
Objectives	
The Syllabus	
Types of Learning and Teaching Activities	
Teacher's Roles	
Learners' Roles	
The Role of students' Native Language and Target Language	
The Role of Instructional Materials and Textbook	
Others	
Summary	

● **Mind Map**

Chapter 7 Suggestopedia

第 7 章 暗示法

○ **Contents**

- ◆ Teaching Case of Suggestopedia
- ◆ Teaching Principles of Suggestopedia
- ◆ Teaching Procedures of Suggestopedia
- ◆ Comments on Suggestopedia
- ◆ Activities and Exercises

- ◆ 暗示法教学示例
- ◆ 暗示法的教学原则
- ◆ 暗示法的教学过程
- ◆ 对暗示法的评价
- ◆ 活动与练习

○ Wordle

1 Introduction

Suggestopedia, also known as Desuggestopedia, is a method developed by the Bulgarian psychiatrist-educator Georgi Lozanov in the 1960s. Suggestopedia, which is a portmanteau of the words "suggestion" and "pedagogy," is a specific set of learning recommendations derived from Suggestology.

Lozanov asserts the reason for our inefficiency is that we set up psychological barriers to learning: We fear that we will be unable to perform, that we will be limited in our ability to learn, that we will fail. One result is that we do not use the full mental powers that we have. According to Lozanov and others, we may be using only five to ten percent of our mental capacity. In order to make better use of our reserved capacity, suggestology has been involved in second language learning by Lozanov to help students eliminate the feeling that they cannot be successful or the negative association they may have toward studying and, thus, to help them overcome the barriers to learning. Some Lozanov's view are: "The claims for suggestopedic learning are dramatic." "There is no sector of public life where suggestology would not be useful." "Memorization in learning by the suggestopedic method seems to be accelerated 25 times over that in learning by conventional methods."

One of the ways the learners' mental reserves are stimulated is through integration of the fine arts, such as music, art and drama. Lozanov also acknowledges ties in tradition to yoga and Soviet psychology. From raja-yoga, Lozanov has borrowed and modified techniques for altering states of consciousness and concentration, and the use of rhythmic breathing. From Soviet psychology, Lozanov has taken the notion that all students can be taught a given subject matter at the same level of skill. Thus, the most conspicuous characteristics of Suggestopedia are formed, which are the decoration, furniture, and arrangement of the classroom, the use of music, and the authoritative behavior of the teacher.

一、教学法概述

暗示法（Suggestopedia，又称 Desuggestopedia）是由保加利亚精神病医学家、心理学家、教育学家格奥尔基·洛扎诺夫于 20 世纪 60 年代创立的一种语言教学法。暗示法一词的英文是由"暗示"和"教育学"两个单词组合而成，暗示法是借鉴暗示学相关理论发展形成的一套独特的学习方法。

洛扎诺夫认为，人们在学习方面效率低下的原因是他们在学习中为自己设置了心理障碍：他们害怕自己表现不佳，担心自己学习能力有限，畏惧失败。在这些心理障碍的影响下，人们没能将自己所拥有的全部智能充分使用并展现出来。洛扎诺夫和有些学者认为，第二语言学习者真正用于学习的智能只占自身全部能力的 5% ~ 10%，而大部分精力则消耗在学习过程中产生的紧张和恐惧之中。为了更好地提升自身智能的利用率，激发潜在能力，帮助学生消除学习中的挫败感、无力感和消极思想，帮助他们克服学习障碍，洛扎诺夫将暗示法引入第二语言学习中。洛扎诺夫的观点有："暗示法的主张是引人瞩目的。""暗示法对社会生活方方面面的影响是无处不在的。""运用暗示法进行第二语言学习，记忆速度似乎比使用传统教学法高出 25 倍。"

激发学习者潜能的方法可以是将诸如音乐、美术及戏剧等艺术手段与语言教学结合起来。洛扎诺夫还将瑜伽和苏联心理学理论与传统的语言教学相关联。暗示法从王瑜伽[①]中借鉴并引用诸如提高意识、改善注意力、有节律地呼吸等训练技巧。从苏联心理学的观点出发，洛扎诺夫认为所有的学生都可以在同一技能水平上学习某一学科。基于这些理论，暗示法形成了自身的显著特征，即教室中物品的装饰、家具的摆放、环境的布置、音乐的使用以及教师的权威行为。

2 Teaching Case[②]

It is a university class in Egypt, where students on a beginning-level course are taught English using Suggestopedia. The class meets for two hours, three mornings a week.

When enter the classroom, you will find everything is bright and colorful. There are several posters on the walls. Most of them are travel posters with scenes from the United Kingdom; a

---

① 王瑜伽（Raja Yoga），意即犹如王者般地位崇高的瑜伽［薄伽梵歌称之为王学（Rajavidya）］。王瑜伽偏于意念和调息，是东方文明与灵性的哲学。其创始人是帕檀贾利 (Patanjali)，著有《瑜伽经》。他所总结的瑜伽八大分支，提供了瑜伽习练者纯洁身体和精神的实践步骤，常被称为"王者之道"。

② LARSEN-FREEMAN D, ANDERSON M. Techniques and Principles in Language Teaching [M]. Oxford: Oxford University Press, 2011: 71–75.

few, however, contain grammatical information. One has the conjugation of the verb "be" and the subject pronouns; another has the object and possessive pronouns. There is also a table with some rhythm instruments on it. Next to them are some hats, masks, and other props.

The teacher greets the students in Arabic and explains that they are about to begin a new and exciting experience in language learning. She says confidently, "You won't need to try to learn. It will just come naturally."

"First, you will all get to pick new names — English ones. It will be fun." she says. Besides, she tells them, they will need new identities (ones they can play with) to go along with this new experience. She shows the class a poster with different English names printed in color in the Roman alphabet. The students are familiar with the Roman alphabet from their earlier study of French. There are men's names in one column and women's names in another. She tells them that they are each to choose a name. She pronounces each name and has the students repeat the pronunciation. One by one, the students say which name they have chosen.

Next, she tells them that during the course they will create an imaginary biography about the life of their new identity. But for now, she says, they should just choose a profession to go with the new name. Using pantomime to help the students understand, the teacher acts out various occupations, such as pilot, singer, carpenter, and artist. The students choose what they want to be.

The teacher greets the students, using their new names and asks them a few yes/no questions in English about their new occupation. Through her actions, the students understand the meaning, and they reply yes or no. She then teaches the short English dialogue in which two people greet each other and inquire what each other does for a living. After practicing the dialogue with the group, they introduce themselves to the teacher. Then they play the rhythm instruments as they sing a name song.

Next, the teacher announces to the class that they will be beginning a new adventure. She distributes a 20-page handout. The handout contains a lengthy dialogue entitled "To want to is to be able to" which the teacher translates into Arabic. She has the students turn the page. On the right page are two columns of print: on the left one is the English dialogue; on the right, the Arabic translation. On the left page are some comments in Arabic about certain of the English vocabulary items and grammatical structures the students will encounter in the dialogue on the facing page. These items have been boldfaced in the dialogue. Throughout the 20 pages are reproductions of classical paintings.

Partly in Arabic, partly in English, and partly through pantomime, the teacher outlines the story in the dialogue. She also calls her students' attention to some of the comments regarding vocabulary and grammar on the left-hand pages. Then she tells them in Arabic that she is going to read the dialogue to them in English and that they should follow along as she reads. She will give them sufficient time to look at both English and Arabic. "Just enjoy." she concludes.

The teacher puts on some music — Mozart's Violin Concerto in A. After a couple of minutes, in a quiet voice she begins to read the text. Her reading appears to be molded by the music as she varies her intonation and keeps rhythm with the music. The students follow along with the voice of the teacher, who allows them enough time to read the translation of the dialogue in their native language silently. They are encouraged to highlight and take notes during the session. The teacher pauses from time to time to allow the students to listen to the music, and for two or three minutes at a time, the whole group stands and repeats after the teacher, joining their voices to the music.

Following this musical session, the students take a break. When they return from the break, they see that the teacher has hung a painting of a calming scene in nature at the front of the room. The teacher then explains that she will read the dialogue again. This time she suggests that the students put down their scripts and just listen. The second time she reads the dialogue, she appears to be speaking at a normal rate. She has changed the music to Handel's Water Music. She makes no attempt this time to match her voice to the music. With the end of the second reading, the class is over. There is no homework assigned; however, the teacher suggests that if the students want to do something, they could read over the dialogue once before they go to bed and once when they get up in the morning.

In the next class, after greeting the students and having them introduce themselves in their new identities once again, the teacher asks the students to take out their dialogue scripts. Next, the teacher pulls out a hat from a bag. She puts it on her head, points to herself, and names a character from the dialogue. She indicates that she wants someone else to wear the hat. A girl volunteers to do so. Three more hats are taken out of the teacher's bag and, with a great deal of playfulness, they are distributed. The teacher turns to the four students wearing hats and asks them to read a portion of the dialogue, imagining that they are the character whose hat they wear. When they finish their portion of dialogue, four different students get to wear the hats and continue reading the script. This group is asked to read it in a sad way. The next group of four read it in an angry way, and the last group of four in a cheerful way.

The teacher then asks for four new volunteers. She tells them that they are auditioning for a role in a Broadway play. They want very much to win the role. In order to impress the director of the play, they must read their lines very dramatically. The first group reads several pages of the dialogue in this manner, and the following groups do this as well.

Next, the teacher asks questions in English about the dialogue. She also asks students to give her the English translation of an Arabic sentence from the dialogue and vice versa. Sometimes she asks the students to repeat an English line after her; still other times, she addresses a question from the dialogue to an individual student.

Then she teaches the students a children's alphabet song containing English names and occupations, "A, my name is Alice, my husband's name is Alex. We live in Australia, and we sell apples. B, my name is Barbara, my husband's name is Bert. We live in Brazil, and we sell books." The students are laughing and clapping as they sing along.

After the song, the teacher has the students stand up and get in a circle. She takes out a medium-sized soft ball. She throws the ball to one student and, while she is throwing it, she asks him what his name is in English. He catches the ball as he says, "My name is Richard." She indicates that he is to throw the ball to another student while posing a question to him. Richard asks, "What you do?" The teacher corrects in a very soft voice saying "What do you do?" The student replies, "I am a conductor." The game continues on in this manner with the students posing questions to one another as they throw the ball. The second class is now over. Again, there is no homework assigned, other than to read over the dialogue if a student so wishes.

During the third class of the week, the students will continue to work with this dialogue. They will move away from reading it, however, and move toward using the new language in a creative way. They will play some competitive games, do role-plays and skits.

二、教学示例

本示例中，暗示法被应用于埃及一所大学的初级英语课堂中。这个班每周上 3 次课，都在早上上课，每次 2 课时。

当你走进教室，你会发现这个教室窗明几净，装饰丰富而多彩。墙上有一些挂图，其中大部分挂图是带有英国场景的旅游海报，还有一些是包含语法信息的挂图。一张挂图是系动词和主格代词的词语搭配图，另一张是包含宾语代词和所有格代词的词汇图。另外，教室里还有一张桌子，桌子上面放着一些打奏节拍的乐器。乐器旁边还有一些帽子、面具和其他道具。

老师用阿拉伯语和学生们打招呼，并告诉大家他们即将开始一个全新的、令人兴奋的语言学习体验。老师还自信地告诉学生："你们不需要刻苦努力。你们将自然而然地学会。"

老师接着说："首先，你们每一个人都会有一个新的英文名。这是一件非常有意思的事。"此外，她还告诉学生们，为了配合接下来的全新学习体验，他们还将拥有一个崭新的身份（用于角色扮演）。随后，老师拿出一张挂图展示给学生们看，挂图上印有很多英文名，英文名以罗马字母书写而成，颜色各异。学生们以前学过法语课，所以对罗马字母已经比较熟悉了。挂图的一列是男性的名字，另一列是女性的名字。老师告诉学生们每个人都要选一个名字。她逐一朗读挂图上的英文名，并让学生重复发音。然后学生们依次说出了他们选择的新名字。

随后，老师告诉学生们将在课程中利用新的身份生活，并创建一个虚拟人生。而现在，首先就要为这个新身份选择相匹配的职业。为帮助学生理解关于职业的生词的意思，老师通过表演的方式，演示了飞行员、歌手、木匠和艺术家等各种职业。学生们选择了他们想从事的职业。

　　然后，老师用学生的新名字与学生打招呼，并用英语问他们一些简单的有关新职业的问题。学生们通过老师的动作理解了她的意思，并且用"是"或"不是"进行了相应的回答。之后，老师教给学生们一个简短的英语对话，对话的内容是两个人打招呼并询问对方的职业。完成小组对话练习后，学生们向老师做了自我介绍。最后，他们用乐器拍打着节奏，唱了一首姓名歌。

　　接下来，老师宣布他们将开始新的探险。她给学生们分发了一份 20 页的讲义。讲义中有一段很长的对话，题为"想到就能做到"，老师已经把对话翻译成了阿拉伯语。她让学生们翻开讲义，讲义右侧分成了两栏，左边是英文对话，右边是阿拉伯语译文。讲义左侧印着右侧页对话中的某些英语词汇和语法结构的阿拉伯语注释。这些有注释的项目在右侧对话中都用黑体字进行了标注。讲义的每一页都配有古典绘画作品。

　　老师就对话中的故事内容进行了概述，有些用了阿拉伯语，有些用了英语，还有一些用的是动作演示。她还提醒学生们注意左侧关于词汇语法的注释。然后她用阿拉伯语告诉学生们，她将用英语给他们朗读这个对话，并让大家跟着她读。她会给大家足够的时间去阅读英语和阿拉伯语。最后，老师说："现在开始享受吧！"

　　老师在朗读对话的同时播放音乐——莫扎特的《A 大调小提琴协奏曲》。几分钟后，老师开始用一种安详的声音朗读对话。她的朗读伴着音乐音色的高低而变换语调，随着音乐的节奏而抑扬顿挫，朗读与乐曲水乳交融。学生们跟随着老师的朗读声，这让他们有足够的时间来安静地阅读对话的母语译文。老师鼓励学生们在这期间勾画重点并做记录。老师还时不时地停下来让学生们聆听音乐，全班学生每隔两三分钟便会全体起立，跟随老师一起重复，并享受音乐与朗读声的美妙融合。

　　这一环节结束后，学生们进行了短暂的休息。当学生们从课间休息回来时，他们看到老师在教室的前面挂了一幅自然风景画，其画面能使人沉静下来。老师解释说她会再朗读一遍对话。这一次她建议学生们把讲义合上不看，而只听老师朗读。老师的第二次朗读使用了正常的语速。她把音乐换成了亨德尔的《水上音乐乐曲》。这次朗读老师没有配合音乐的音色与节奏。在完成第二遍朗读后，本次课就结束了。老师没有布置家庭作业。但是，她建议学生们可以在晚上睡觉前和早上起床后朗读一遍对话。

　　第二节课上课后，老师先与学生们问好，让他们再次介绍一下自己的新身份，然后老师让学生们拿出他们的讲义。接着，老师从包里拿出一顶帽子。她把帽子戴到自己头上，指着自己，说出对话中一个角色的名字。她示意希望有人戴上这顶帽子。一名女生主动参与，戴上了这顶帽子。老师又从包里拿出三顶帽子，以一种滑稽的方式分发了帽子。老师面向这四名戴上帽子的学生，让他们分别读一部分对话，并让他们把自己想象成各自的帽子所代表的人物角色。这四名学生读完对话后，又有四名学生戴上帽子继续分角色朗读对话。而这次老师要求他们这一组以一种悲伤的语气进行朗读。而下一组的四名学生则要以愤怒的语气进行朗读。最后一组的四名学生以愉快的语气朗读。

　　随后，老师又找了四名学生，告诉他们：他们正在试演百老汇戏剧中的一个角色，他们非常想获胜并出演这个角色，为了给导演留下深刻的印象，他们必须以戏剧化的方式朗读台词。第一组以这种方式朗读了对话的前几页，后面的小组以同样的方式继续朗读后面的部分。

接下来，老师用英语就对话内容进行提问，并进行一些英、阿双语双向互译练习。她时而让学生们跟着她复述英语句子，时而就对话内容进行个别提问。

然后老师教学生们唱了一首包含英文名字和职业的字母儿歌："A，我叫爱丽丝，我丈夫叫亚历克斯，我们住在澳大利亚，我们以卖苹果为生。B，我叫芭芭拉，我丈夫叫伯特，我们住在巴西，我们以卖书为生。"学生们笑声不断，并一边拍手一边跟唱。

儿歌环节结束后，老师让学生们站起来围成一圈。老师拿出一个中等大小的软球，把球扔给一名学生，并在扔球的同时，问那名学生他的英文名字是什么。学生接住球的同时说："我叫理查德。"老师示意他把球扔给另一名学生，同时向另一名同学提出一个问题。理查德把球扔向另一名学生，并问："你做什么？"老师用很轻柔的声音纠正他的表达错误："你是做什么的？"另一名学生接住球并回答："我是一名指挥家。"游戏继续进行，学生们一边扔球，一边互相提问。第二节课便结束了。同样，这次课后仍然没有家庭作业，老师依旧表示，学生们如果愿意，可以读读对话。

在本周的第三节课上，学生们将继续练习这段对话。然而，他们将不再仅仅局限于朗读对话的活动，而是以创造性的方式来使用新语言。他们将玩一些竞赛类游戏，进行角色扮演和小品表演。

3 Teaching Principles and Teaching Procedures

3.1 Teaching Principles of Suggestopedia

There are seven major concepts of Suggestopedia according to Lozanov and Gatave as follows:

(1) Mental Reserve Capacities (MRC)

There is a general agreement among researchers that the human being uses 5%–10% of his/her brain capacity at the most. The primary objective is to tap into the MRC.

(2) Psychological "Set-Up"

The response to every stimulus is very complex, involving many unconscious processes which have become automatic responses. Only when a teacher is able to penetrate the set-up, engaging it in a way which allows it to be accepted and open to extensions and transformation, the real potential of a student begins to open up.

(3) Suggestion

There are two basic kinds of suggestion: direct and indirect. Direct suggestions are directed to conscious processes, i.e., what one says that can and will occur in the learning experience, suggestions which can be made in printed announcements, orally by the teacher, and/or by text materials. Direct suggestion is used sparingly, for it is most vulnerable to resistance from the set-up. Indirect suggestion is largely unconsciously perceived and is much greater in scope than direct suggestion.

(4) Anti-Suggestive Barriers

These anti-suggestive barriers are a filter between the environmental stimuli and the unconscious mental activity. They are inter-related and mutually reinforcing, and a positive suggestive effect can only be accomplished if these barriers are kept in mind. The overcoming of barriers means compliance with them; otherwise suggestions would be doomed to failure. It is clear that the suggestive process is always a combination of suggestion and desuggestion and is always at an unconscious or slightly conscious level.

(5) Means of Suggestion

① Authority: People remember best and are most influenced by information coming from an authoritative source. A positively suggestive authority is one of the most effective means which we as teachers can use, if we use it sensitively, wisely and purposefully. By indirect ways, the authority of the teacher can create an atmosphere of confidence and intuitive desire. Lozanov also puts forward a series of elements and practices that make students feel the authority of the school and teachers, such as the reputation of the school, the self-confidence of teachers, personal distance from students, acting ability, the highly positive attitude and the persistence of a certain teaching method.

② Infantilization: Infantilization in the process of education is a normal phenomenon connected with authority (prestige). Infantilization is also used to suggest a teacher-student relation like that of parent to child. In the child's role, the learner takes part in role playing, games, songs, and gymnastic exercises that help "the older student regain the self-confidence, spontaneity and receptivity of the child".

③ Intonation and Rhythm: Intonation is strongly connected with the rest of the suggestive elements. The intonation in music and speech is one of the basic expressive means, with formidable form creating influence and potential in many psycho-physiological directions. Specifically, varying the tone and rhythm of presented material helps both avoid boredom through monotony of repetition, and dramatize, emotionalize, and give meaning to linguistic material.

④ Concert Pseudo-Passivity: Both intonation and rhythm are coordinated with a musical background. The musical background helps induce a relaxed attitude, which Lozanov refers to as concert pseudo-passiveness. This state is felt to be optimal for learning, in which anxieties and tension are relieved and power of concentration for new material is raised. Therefore, Concert pseudo-passivity is regarded as the important moment in Suggestopedia.

(6) Successful Classroom Atmosphere

① Phycological: A nurturing, supportive atmosphere in which the student feels free to try out the new information, be inventive with it, make mistakes without being put down, and, in general, enjoy the learning experience.

② Education: The material should be presented in a structured fashion, combining the Big Picture, analysis and synthesis. Every moment should be a didactic experience even when the learning process is not that apparent.

③ Artistic: The classroom should not be cluttered with too many posters and unnecessary objects; otherwise the students don't see them. Good quality pictures should be displayed and changed every few days. Music can be played as the students enter the room, and during the breaks. Plants and flowers add to a pleasant atmosphere.

(7) Music

Music is regarded as a suggestion and relaxing medium. Lozanov researched a wide variety of means for presenting material to be learned which would facilitate the mentally relaxed, receptive state of mind he had found to be optimal for learning. Music proved to be the ideal medium, both for the purpose of creating a mentally relaxed state and for providing a vehicle for carrying the material to be learned in the open, receptive mind. Music can become a powerful facilitator of holistic full-brain learning. After conducting numerous controlled experiments using a wide variety of music, Lozanov concluded that the music of the Classical and Early Romantic periods was most effective for the first presentation of material to be learned.

3.2 Teaching Procedures of Suggestopedia

The objectives of Suggestopedia are to deliver advanced conversational proficiency quickly. A Suggestopedia course lasts 30 days and consists of ten units of study. Classes are held 4 hours a day, 6 days a week. The central focus of each unit is a dialogue consisting of 1,200 words or so, with an accompanying vocabulary list and grammatical commentary. The dialogues are graded by lexis and grammar.

A Suggestopedia class consists of a dozen students who are given new, target language names and biographies. They are seated in comfortable chairs in a softly-lit, tastefully decorated room. The teaching process is generally divided into three stages. Lessons begin with a review of the previous lesson, using standard oral practice techniques, including some kind of role play involving the spontaneous use of language. The second stage comprises the presentation and explanation of new material which takes the form of an extended written scenario with its accompanying L1 translation. The third stage is the one which most distinguishes Suggestopedia from other methods. It is called the séance or concert session, and aims to facilitate unconscious memorization of the new material. There are elaborate prescriptions as to how this must be done. Essentially, though having relaxed themselves doing breathing and other exercises, the learners listen to the text — and its translation — recited aloud to them by the teacher, to the accompaniment of Baroque music, whose soothing hypnotic rhythms, along with that of the teacher's carefully modulated voice, supposedly ensure maximum retention.

三、教学原则与教学过程

1. 暗示法的教学原则

根据洛扎诺夫和加塔夫所述，暗示法有 7 个主要原则理念。

（1）潜能（心理储备能力）

研究人员普遍认为人类最多仅使用了 5% ～ 10% 的大脑容量。因此，暗示法的主要教学目标是利用并开发学习者潜能。

（2）心理"防线"

人们对每一个刺激所产生的反应都是非常复杂的，其中很多自发性的反应行为都涉及无意识反应过程。只有当教师有能力渗透到学生心理"防线"之内，获得学生的接受与认同，参与学生心理的发展与变化，学生的真正潜能才能够显现出来。

（3）暗示

暗示分为两种：直接暗示和间接暗示。直接暗示是一个有意识的过程，比如描述出一个人在学习过程中能够或将会发生什么。这些直接暗示可以通过印制成册的说明、教师口头表述、文本资料等方式表现出来。直接暗示一般使用得很少，因为它最容易受到心理防线的阻碍。间接暗示在很大程度上是无意识的，且其影响范围远远超过直接暗示。

（4）反暗示障碍

反暗示障碍是环境刺激和无意识心理活动之间的一个过滤器。二者之间相互关联，相互促进。只有在心理上克服这些反暗示障碍，暗示才能产生积极的效果。顺应暗示就要克服障碍，否则暗示就注定失败。所以很显然，暗示的过程是一个暗示与解除暗示相互协调的过程，并总是处于无意识或稍有意识的心理状态。

（5）暗示的方式

①权威：人们往往容易记住权威人物或机构发布的信息。如果教师可以谨慎地、明智地、有针对性地使用教师权威，那么这将是一个最有效的暗示手段。教师权威可以间接地为学习者创造一种自信的、直觉的、强意愿的学习氛围。洛扎诺夫还提出了一系列帮助学校和教师在学生中建立、提升权威性的要素和做法，比如学校的声誉、教师的自信、与学生的人际关系、表演才能、积极的态度以及对某一教学法的执着等。

②稚化：教育过程中的（幼）稚化是一种与权威（威望）息息相关的正常现象。稚化也被用来表示师生之间建立如同父母与儿女的关系。如果让年龄较大的学习者参与角色扮演、做游戏、唱歌等儿童喜爱的活动，可以使其找回儿童所具有的那种自信心、自发性和接受能力。

③语调和节奏：语调与其他暗示成分紧密相连。音准音调是音乐和言语的基本表现手段之一，在许多心理、生理方面具有强大的、创造性的影响力和潜力。具体来讲，就是在呈现语言材料时，变换语调和说话节奏有助于避免因重复而产生的单调性，使语言材料戏剧化、感情化，并赋予语言材料新的含义。

④音乐拟被动性：洛扎诺夫提出的音乐拟被动性指统合教师语调、朗诵节奏及背景音乐而形成的音乐场景，在这样的音乐场景中，学习者身心放松，进入一个安宁、休憩的假消极状态。这种音乐场景下的学习环境和学习状态有利于消除学生的忧虑和紧张，提高学生对新材料的注意力，加速学生对新的语言材料的感受理解与吸收内化。这是暗示法中暗示的重要时刻。

（6）成功的课堂氛围

①心理上：在一种积极的、鼓励的课堂氛围中，学生可以自由地运用新信息，创造性地运用新知识，即使犯了错也不会受到批评或歧视，总之，在这样的氛围中，学习是一种享受的体验。

②教育性：教学素材应以结构化的方式呈现，应是宏观全局性的、分析性的和综合性的。即使学习过程并不那么明显，学习的每时每刻也应该是一种阐释性的经历。

③艺术性：教室里不能放太多的海报和不必要的东西，否则学生将视而不见。应该展示高质量的大挂图，并每隔几天进行更换。学生进入教室和休息间歇时可以播放音乐。教室里摆放花草可以增进舒适宜人的氛围。

（7）音乐

音乐被视为一种暗示手段，是放松的媒介。洛扎诺夫研究了各式各样呈现学习材料的方法，希望从这些方法中寻找到最有助于促进学习者放松精神，从心理上进入知识接收状态的方法。事实证明，音乐是一种理想的媒介，音乐既可以达到创造一种精神放松状态的目的，也可以完成作为一种学习载体的任务，使学习者能够在开放性的、接受性的身心状态下学习所需材料。音乐可以有力促进全脑整体学习。在使用各种各样的音乐进行了大量的对照实验之后，洛扎诺夫得出结论，古典和早期浪漫主义时期的音乐对学生学习首次接触的材料是最有效的。

2. 暗示法的教学过程

暗示法的教学目标是快速提高学习者的高级会话能力。使用暗示教学法的语言课程一般为期30天，学习内容由10个单元组成。每个星期学习6天，每天上课4小时。每个单元由1个核心对话构成，对话包含大约1200个词汇，并附有词汇表和语法注释。单元对话根据词汇和语法进行分级，并有序编排。

使用暗示法授课的语言班一般由12个学生组成，学生们在课程学习中将被赋予新的目的语姓名和身份背景。上课的教室灯光柔和、装饰雅致，学生们坐在舒适的椅子上进行学习。教学过程一般分为三个阶段。第一个阶段是复习前课内容，采用的方法与常见的口语练习一般无二，包括一些能促使学习者自主使用目的语的角色扮演练习。第二个阶段是对新材料的展示和解释，具体形式是以书面形式提供一个拓展场景，并配有学习者的母语翻译。第三个阶段是暗示法与其他语言教学法最大的区别所在，即"séance（降神）"，也称"音乐会"，其目的是促进学习者对新材料的无意识记忆。关于如何做到这一点，暗示法有详细的规定。从本质上说，学习者在巴洛克音乐的伴奏下听教师大声朗诵课文及其翻译，配合着音乐做呼吸和其他练习放松身心，加之巴洛克音乐舒缓的催眠节奏，以及教师精心调制的诵读语调与节律，据说能确保最大限度地调动潜意识记忆新的语言材料。

4 Conclusion

The notion that, simply by unlocking our unconscious minds, effortless learning capacities will result, has always had popular appeal. Lozanov's accomplishment was to provide a kind of solution to this "magical thinking", combining techniques from yoga meditation, hypnotherapy, and music therapy, so as to lull learners into an infantilized but highly receptive state in which any input they were exposed to would be unconsciously "absorbed". Practitioners of Suggestopedia attest that the method increases the speed of learning by as much as 25 times. Another frequently cited figure is the memorization of 1000 foreign language words in just an hour. Obviously, Suggestopedia attempts to address some of the challenges in language learning, such as the memory load, the psychological barriers, unconscious language acquisition, etc., and it indeed gets some achievements.

On the other hand, Suggestopedia has been called a "pseudo-science" by many critics. Because it depends, in a sense, on the trust that students develop towards the method. Earl Stevick assesses: "Virtually every element in a Suggestopedic course has, in addition to its overt effect, also a 'placebo' effect." Lozanov never admitted that Suggestopedia can be compared to a placebo. He argues, however, that placebos are indeed effective. Another point of criticism is brought forward by Baur who claims that the students only receive input by listening, reading and musical-emotional backing, while other important factors of language acquisition are being neglected. Furthermore, several other features of the method, like the "nonconscious" acquisition of language, or bringing the learner into a childlike state are questioned by critics. Therefore, it is not unreasonable to claim that "Suggestopedia lacks scientific backing and is based on pseudo-science."

四、小结

仅仅通过释放我们的潜意识便不费吹灰之力就能获得学习能力，这一观点一直具有普遍的吸引力。洛扎诺夫的成就便为这种"奇思妙想"提供了一种解决方案。暗示法这一解决方案结合了瑜伽冥想、催眠疗法和音乐疗法的技巧，使学习者进入一种稚化而又高度接受的状态，在这种状态下，学习者会将接触到的任何语言输入自然而然地"吸收内化"。暗示法的教学实践证明，该教学法可以将学习速度提高 25 倍。另一个经常被引用的数据则是在 1 小时内记住 1000 个外语单词。显然，暗示法试图解决语言学习中的一些挑战，比如记忆负荷、心理障碍、无意识语言习得等，并取得了一定的成果。

　　另外，批评家们称暗示法是一种"伪科学"。因为从某种意义上说，这种教学法的成功与否取决于学生对这种方法的信任度。厄尔·斯特维克对暗示法的评价是："实际上，暗示法中的每一个因素，除了其教学法本身所显现的效应外，还具有'安慰剂'的效用。"洛扎诺夫从未将暗示法比作语言教学的安慰剂，但他认为安慰剂确实有效。鲍尔从另一个角度也提出了批评的观点，他认为暗示法仅强调学生通过听、读和音乐情感支持获得语言输入，忽视了语言习得的其他重要因素。此外，该教学法的一些其他特点，如语言的"无意识"习得、将学习者带入儿童般的稚化状态，也受到了批评者的质疑。因此，称"暗示法缺乏科学依据，建立在伪科学之上"的观点也不无道理。

○ Activities and Exercises

● Understanding and Thinking

1. Please combine Hansen's and Earl Stevick's views, find out some teaching details which are designed for reducing learners' stress and learning anxiety, creating a comfortable and relaxed learning environment from our teaching case, and then analyse and illustrate the typical techniques of Suggestopedia.

Hansen stated that "Stress and anxiety tend to over-activate the left hemisphere and the sympathetic division of the autonomic nervous system, which reduces receptivity at the paraconscious level. With Lozanov's method, the mind must be soaring high and free."

Earl Stevick's assessment is: "Virtually every element in a Suggestopedic course has, in addition to its overt effect, also a 'placebo' effect."

2. Read the following materials and then talk about the roles of the teacher and the students in a Suggestopedia class.

Lozanov lists several expected teacher behaviors that contribute to these presentations.

① Show absolute confidence in the method.

② Display fastidious conduct in manners and dress.

③ Organize properly and strictly observe the initial stages of the teaching process — this includes choice and play of music, as well as punctuality.

④ Maintain a solemn attitude toward the session.

⑤ Give tests and respond tactfully to poor papers (if any).

⑥ Stress global rather than analytical attitudes toward material.

⑦ *Maintain a modest enthusiasm.*

3. Please read the following research conclusion of the actual effects between Suggestopedia and other language teaching methods by Kapitanova and Schukin in the Soviet Union (Table 7-1), and talk about the differences between the Suggestopedia Method and other language teaching methods in teaching principles and teaching procedures.

Table 7-1　The Actual Effect of Comparing Suggestopedia and Other Language Teaching Methods

Teaching Method	Number of Students	Total Vocabulary	Total Class Hours	Average Vocabulary for Each Lesson
Suggestopedia	10	2000	120	16.666
Audio-Visual Method	8–12	1500	270	5.555
Audiolingual Method	8–10	3500	700	5
Traditional Method	8–10	4500	840	5.357

● **Teaching Design**

1. Please study the characteristics of Suggestopedia intensively, according to the following materials about the teaching procedures of Suggestopedia, design the teaching details, and then make a teaching demonstration in groups.

Bancroft notes that the 4-hour language class has three distinct parts.

The first part we might call an oral review section. Previously learned material is used as the basis for discussion by the teacher and twelve students in the class. All participants sit in a circle in their specially designed chairs, and the discussion proceeds like a seminar. This session may involve what are called micro-studies and macro-studies. In micro-studies specific attention is given to grammar, vocabulary, and precise questions and answers. A question from a micro-study might be, "What should one do in a hotel room if the bathroom taps are not working?" In the macro-studies, emphasis is on role-playing and wider-ranging, innovative language constructions. "Describe to someone the Boyana church." (one of Bulgaria's most well-known medieval churches) would be an example of a request for information from the macro-studies.

In the second part of the class new material is presented and discussed. This consists of looking over a new dialogue and its native language translation and discussing any issues of grammar, vocabulary, or content that the teacher feels important or that students are curious about. Bancroft notes that this section is typically conducted in the target language, although student questions or comments will be in whatever language the student feels he or she can handle. Students are led to view the experience of dealing with the new material as interesting and undemanding of any special effort or anxiety. The teacher's attitude and authority are considered critical to preparing students for success in the learning to come. The pattern of learning and use is noted (i.e., fixation, reproduction, and new creative production), so that students will know what is expected.

The third part — the séance or concert session — is the one by which Suggestopedia is best known. Since this constitutes the heart of the method, we will quote Lozanov as to how this session proceeds.

At the beginning of the session, all conversation stops for a minute or two, and the teacher listens to the music coming from a tape-recorder. He waits and listens to several passages in order to enter into the mood of the music and then begins to read or recite the new text, his voice modulated in harmony with the musical phrases. The students follow the text in their textbooks where each lesson is translated into the mother tongue. Between the first and second part of the concert, there are several minutes of solemn silence. In some cases, even longer pauses can be given to permit the students to stir a little. Before the beginning of the second part of the concert, there are again several minutes of silence and some phrases of the music are heard again before the teacher begins to read the text. Now the students close their textbooks and listen to the teacher's reading. At the end, the students silently leave the room. They are not told to do any homework on the lesson they have just had except for reading it cursorily once before going to bed and again before getting up in the morning.

2. Please read the following teaching plan carefully, point out the inappropriate places according to the theory and teaching principles of Suggestopedia, then revise and improve it.

Students' Level: *Elementary English level students*

Topic of This Lesson: *"My favorite food"*

Teaching Place: *Pleasant and comfortable classroom environment with excellent hardware*

Teaching Objectives:

Through the explanation of the contents of this English teaching course, we can mobilize students' conscious activities and give full play to the positive role of unconscious activities, tap the potential of stimulating students' super conscious learning, and promote the unity of conscious and unconscious learning, so as to fully develop students' English potential. By creating comfortable situations to eliminate the psychological and spiritual pressure of students, students' imagination and super memory ability for English can be induced. Establish a natural and positive way of behavior, so as to force students to think about the English content of food to be expressed, rather than simply thinking about English as a language form, so as to achieve the purpose of encouraging students to use English independently and boldly, and to stimulate students' motivation to learn English, so as to improve the quality of English teaching.

Content of Courses:

The main content of this class is to teach students English words of food and let them learn how to use English in daily communication about food.

Teaching Key Points and Difficulties:

Teachers establish authority to make students feel and believe in the authority of teachers. With the melody and rhythm of the beautiful symphony, the teacher reads the text with vivid expression and strong emotion, while the students look at the text and follow the teacher quietly. This will help students consciously or unconsciously produce and improve their cognitive ability and memory ability, and unconsciously remember the English daily conversation materials related to food.

Teaching Methods:

① The required amount of language materials is several times more than that of the conventional foreign language teaching method courses.

② Mobilize the conscious activities of students, and take various means of suggestive art, give full play to the active activities of unconscious activities, and constantly tap and stimulate the potential of students' super conscious learning, so that students gradually learn to develop themselves.

③ By creating a relaxed, joyful, comfortable environment and warm and harmonious atmosphere to eliminate the tense psychological state caused by external mental pressure, students can naturally place themselves in the real situation of imagination, play a certain role in verbal communication, so as to promote the brain to move easily and freely, stimulate students' super memory ability, accelerate memory efficiency, and improve teaching quality.

④ Use Chinese translation in the teaching process.

⑤ Try to correct as few mistakes as possible in English speech communication, so as to build up the students' high self-confidence.

⑥ Set up a number of daily natural communication situations, and let the students apply the English language materials related to food to these ten typical natural situations and other new situations.

⑦ Integrate all the multiple factors of students into a whole organically, and the whole function is greater than the combination of parts.

Teaching Process:

(1) Pre-Program Stage

For the first time, students are familiar with English teaching materials about food. The teacher explains the new teaching materials concisely.

① The teacher says hello to the students in English and announces the beginning of class.

② Show your teaching level and ability, and establish the authority of rich teaching experience for students.

(2) Academic Stage

The teacher teaches about the main points and themes of food.

① *The teacher shows a picture with various foods, lets the students choose their favorite food, such as steak, hot pot, hamburger, etc., and shows the pictures of each food to make the students understand the food.*

② *The teacher sends each student an English material about daily food conversation, in which the English vocabulary and grammar structure will be marked in Chinese.*

③ *The teacher uses English, Chinese and body language to teach the dialogue, and reads the dialogue in English, so that the students have enough time to read the text.*

④ *The teacher plays passionate classical music and reads the dialogue aloud, changing the tone and rhythm with the music. The students read the dialogue silently and take notes.*

⑤ *The teacher pauses the music, and the students return to the classroom after a period of rest. They find that there are many elements and decorations of the restaurant in the classroom, which make the students feel interesting.*

⑥ *Read the dialogue again and ask the students to listen.*

⑦ *After reading at normal speed, the teacher plays deep and philosophical classical music. The class ends with the music.*

(3) Post-Program Stage

Make full use of all kinds of textbooks (including but not limited to reading, translating texts, songs, games, supplementary texts, retelling and conversations with specified themes) to make the activities active.

① *The teacher suggests that students read the dialogue text about food provided in class before going to bed or after getting up.*

② *In class the next day, the students should improve their understanding of the text by performing the dialogue.*

③ *Ask questions according to the dialogue content and translate them into Chinese and English.*

④ *The teacher beats the drum to spread the flowers, and the student will say the English name of his/her favorite food in English.*

Homework Assignments:

Do not assign homework, only suggest students to read the English dialogue texts provided in class before sleeping or after getting up.

● **Further Reading**

Suggestopedia, Yoga, and Its Application in Language Teaching[①]

① 陆小玲 . Suggestopedia, Yoga, and Its Application in Language Teaching [J]. 中外社科论坛 , 2010(1): 84–85.

Suggestopedia is one of the innovative methods of the 1970s. It is developed by the Bulgarian psychiatrist-educator Georgi Lozanov. As its name indicates, Suggestopedia derives from Suggestology, a science concerned with the systematic study of the nonrational and/or nonconscious influences that human beings are constantly responding to. Suggestopedia tries to use these influences and redirect them in order to optimize learning.

Suggestopedia has some ties with yoga and Soviet psychology. Lozanov has borrowed from yoga the techniques for alerting the state of consciousness and concentration and the use of rhythmic breathing. He also stresses the need for an optimal learning environment. Suggestopedia believes that attentiveness can be manipulated to optimize learning and recall; the unique potential of rhythm can energize and bring order and consequently relax learners.

Suggestopedia does not boast a theory of learning. It stresses lexical translation, rather than contextualization, and puts emphasis on memorization of vocabulary pairs, that is, a target language item and its native language translation. Materials used should be whole meaningful texts or lighthearted stories with emotional content, literary quality and interesting characters.

As far as learning theory is concerned, Suggestopedia claims the desuggestive-suggestive ritual placebo system, which can create a constant set-up to reserves through concentrative psycho-relaxation. Desuggestion refers to unloading the memory banks of unwanted or blocking memories, while suggestion involves loading the memory banks with desired and facilitating memories. Altogether six principal theoretical components are involved in the system. The first is authority. Since people remember best and are most influenced by information coming from an authoritative source, suggestopedia attempts to have students experience the learning environment and the teacher as having authority by establishing a ritual placebo system. The second component is infantilization, which means the students are encouraged to be as childlike as possible, for this helps them regain the self-confidence, spontaneity and receptivity of the child. The third component, double-planedness, means apart from direct instruction, students can learn from the environment. The other components are intonation, rhythm and concert pseudo-passiveness. The varied tone of the teacher helps avoid boredom of the students, and background music helps induce a relaxed attitude, which can in turn relieve anxiety and tension and at the same time raise the power of concentration. Actually, learning in a relaxed but focused state can lead to the best results.

Music plays a central role in Suggestopedia. The Baroque largo (sixty beats a minute) is chosen as the right kind of music for a Suggestopedia class. In such music, the body relaxes, the mind becomes alert, and the mind's efficiency is the highest.

The aim of this method is to deliver advanced conversational proficiency quickly. Mastery of vocabulary pairs is an important goal. The syllabus of Suggestopedia is unique. A course lasts 30 days and consists of 10 units. Each unit consists of a dialogue of 1200 words, a vocabulary list and some grammatical commentary. A variety of activities, including imitation, question and answer, role play and most important of all, listening, are conducted in the classroom. During these activities, students are expected to commit themselves to the class, give up mind-alerting substances and other distractions, encourage their own infantilization and give themselves over to classroom activities. To achieve a better result, they are even given a new name and a new identity in the target language. As for teachers, they are responsible for creating situations in which the students are most suggestible and present learning materials in a way most likely to encourage positive reception and retention by the students. They are expected to be good at acting, singing and psychotherapeutic techniques. Materials include direct support materials, i.e., text and tape, and indirect support ones, i.e., classroom fixtures and music.

The procedures for this method include: an oral review section, new material presentation and discussion session, and the séance or concert session. This method capitalizes on relaxed states of mind for maximum retention of material. It applies the study of suggestion to pedagogy and intends to help students eliminate the feeling that they can not be successful and thus help them overcome the psychological barriers that they bring with them. In a typical suggestopedia class, easy chairs, soft lighting and music constitute a relaxing learning environment in which students are as comfortable as possible. The decoration, furniture and arrangement of the classroom, the use of music, and the authoritative behavior of the teacher are the most distinctive features of Suggestopedia.

In fact, Suggestopedia has some obvious faults. One point is that it overstresses the role of memorization in language learning. Since one focus of its instruction is the memorization of vocabulary pairs, the issues of understanding and creative solutions of problems are somewhat neglected. Another problem is the practicality of using this method. Where music and comfortable chairs are not available, how can the teacher take advantage of this method? Anyway, teachers should extract the insightful and fruitful aspects of this method and adapt them to their own teaching situations.

● **Knowledge Table**

Table 7-2　Summary of Characteristics of Suggestopedia

Key Points	Suggestopedia
Period	
Representatives	
Background	
Theory of Language	
Theory of Language Learning	
Objectives	
The Syllabus	
Types of Learning and Teaching Activities	
Teacher's Roles	
Learner's Roles	
The Role of Students' Native Language and Target Language	
The Role of Instructional Materials and Textbook	
Others	
Summary	

● **Mind Map**

Chapter 8　Communicative Language Teaching

第8章　交际法

○ Contents

- ◆ Teaching Case of Communicative Language Teaching
- ◆ Background of Communicative Language Teaching
- ◆ Theoretical Basis of Communicative Language Teaching
- ◆ Teaching Principles of Communicative Language Teaching
- ◆ Teaching Procedures of Communicative Language Teaching
- ◆ Comments on and Significance of Communicative Language Teaching
- ◆ Activities and Exercises

- ◆ 交际法教学示例
- ◆ 交际法的产生背景
- ◆ 交际法的理论基础
- ◆ 交际法的教学原则
- ◆ 交际法的教学过程
- ◆ 交际法的重要意义及其评价
- ◆ 活动与练习

○ Wordle

1 Introduction

Communicative Language Teaching(CLT), also known as "Communicative Approach", was called "Functional Approach" or "Notional-Functional Approach" earlier. It is a kind of teaching approach which takes language functions and notions as the teaching syllabus and cultivates language communicative competence in a specific social context. Communicative Language Teaching was developed in the European Community countries in the 1970s, with its center in the United Kingdom. The emergence of Communicative Approach benefits from the diversification of language theory and the communication needs of Western European countries and its development is supported by the Council of Europe. The founder was British linguist D.A. Wilkins. The representative figures include British language educationists, such as L.G. Alexander, H.G. Widdowson, and J.A. Van EK of the Netherlands. And the most famous textbook of CLT is *Follow Me*.

The Communicative Approach is the result of people's in-depth study of language functions. It marks the beginning of a major paradigm shift within language teaching in the twentieth century, one whose ramifications continue to be felt all over the world today. After CLT was formed, various teaching methods focusing on communicative objectives and language functions have emerged, such as Content-Based Instruction and Task-Based Language Teaching. Although there are many discussions and debates about the theory and practice of Communicative Approach, and everyone has his own unique understanding about it, the "the Spirit of CLT" has been deeply rooted in the hearts of the people.

一、教学法概述

交际语言教学法又称"交际法"，早期也称为"功能法"或"功能-意念法"。该教学法以语言功能和意念项目为纲，目的在于培养在特定的社会语境下运用语言进行交际的能力。交际法兴起于 20 世纪 70 年代的欧洲共同体国家，其中心在英国。交际法的产生源于语言理论的多元化和西欧各国的语言交际需求，其发展得力于欧洲委员会的支持。交际法的创始人为英国语言学家威尔金斯，代表人物还有英国的语言教育家亚历山大、威多森，荷兰的范埃克等。《跟我学》是交际法最著名的代表教材。

交际法是人们深入研究语言功能所形成的成果，它标志着 20 世纪语言教学范式重大转变的开端，至今仍影响着世界各地的语言教学。交际法形成后，一大批如内容教学法、任务型教学法等新型教学法纷纷应运而生，这些教学法关注语言交际目的、重视语言功能教学。尽管围绕交际法的理论研究和教学实践仍有诸多探讨和争议，每个人都有自己的理解，但是交际法的理念早已深入人心。

2 Teaching Case[①]

The class in which a form of Communicative Language Teaching is conducted for adult immigrants to Canada. These twenty people have lived in Canada for two years and are at a high-intermediate level of English proficiency. They meet two evenings a week for two hours in each class.

The teacher greets the class and distributes a handout. There is writing on both sides. On one side is a copy of a sports column from a recent newspaper. The reporter is discussing the last World Cup competition. The teacher asks the students to read it and then to underline the predictions the reporter makes about the next World Cup. He gives them these directions in the target language. When the students have finished, they read what they have underlined. The teacher writes what they have found on the blackboard. Then he and the students discuss which predictions the reporter feels more certain about and which predictions he feels less certain about:

Malaysia is very likely to win the World Cup this year.

Italy can win if they play as well as they have lately.

France probably won't be a contender again.

England may have an outside chance.

Then he asks the students to look at the first sentence and to tell the class another way to express this same prediction. One student says, "Malaysia probably will win the World Cup."

---

① LARSEN-FREEMAN D, ANDERSON M. Techniques and Principles in Language Teaching[M]. Oxford: Oxford University Press, 2011: 116-119.

"Yes." says the teacher. "Any others?" No one responds. The teacher offers, "Malaysia is almost certain to win the World Cup." "What about the next?" he asks the class. One student replies, "It is possible that Italy will win the World Cup." Another student offers. "There's a possibility that Italy will win the World Cup." Each of the reporter's predictions is discussed in this manner. All the paraphrases the students suggest are evaluated by the teacher and the other students to make sure they convey the same degree of certainty as the reporter's original prediction.

Next, the teacher asks the students to turn to the other side of the handout. On it are all the sentences of the article that they have been working on. They are, however, out of order. For example, the first two sentences on this side of the handout are:

England may have an outside chance.

In the final analysis, the winning team may simply be the one with the most experience.

The first sentence was in the middle of the original sports column. The second was the last sentence of the original column. The teacher tells the students to unscramble the sentences, to put them in their proper order by numbering them. When they finish, the students compare what they have done with the original on the other side of the handout.

The teacher then asks the students if they agree with the reporter's predictions. He also asks them to get into pairs and to write their own prediction about who will be the next World Cup champion.

The teacher next announces that the students will be playing a game. He divides the class into small groups containing five people each. He hands each group a deck of thirteen cards. Each card has a picture of a piece of sports equipment. As the students identify the items, the teacher writes each name on the blackboard: basketball, soccer ball, volleyball, tennis racket, skis, ice skates, roller skates, football, baseball bat, golf clubs, bowling ball, badminton racket, and hockey stick.

The cards are shuffled and four of the students in a group are dealt three cards each. They do not show their cards to anyone else. The extra card is placed face down in the middle of the group. The fifth person in each group receives no cards. She is told that she should try to predict what it is that Dumduan (one of the students in the class) will be doing the following weekend. The fifth student is to make statements like, "Dumduan may go skiing this weekend." If one of the members of her group has a card showing skis, the group member would reply, for example, "Dumduan can't go skiing because I have her skis." If, on the other hand, no one has the picture of the skis, then the fifth student can make a strong statement about the likelihood of Dumduan going skiing. She can say, for example, "Dumduan will go skiing." She can check her prediction by turning over the card that was placed face down. If it is the picture of the skis, then she knows she is correct.

The students seem to really enjoy playing the game. They take turns so that each person has a chance to make the predictions about how a classmate will spend his or her time.

For the next activity, the teacher reads a number of predictions like the following.

By 2030, solar energy will replace the world's reliance on fossil fuels.

By 2050, people will be living on the moon.

The students are told to make statements about how probably they think the predictions are and why they believe so. They are also asked how they feel about the prediction. In discussing one of the predictions, a student says he does not think it is *like that a world government will be in place by the twenty-second century. The teacher and students ignore his error and the discussion continues.

Next, the teacher has the students divided into groups of three. Since there are twenty students, there are six groups of three students and one group of two. One member of each group is given a picture strip story. There are six pictures in a row on a piece of paper, but no words. The pictures tell a story. The student with the story shows the first picture to the other members of his group, while covering the remaining five pictures.

The other students try to predict what they think will happen in the second picture. The first student tells them whether they are correct or not. She then shows them the second picture and asks them to predict what the third picture will look like. After the entire series of pictures has been shown, the group gets a new strip story and they change roles, giving the first student an opportunity to work with a partner in making predictions.

For the final activity of the class, the students are told they will do a role-play. The teacher tells them that they are to be divided into groups of four. They are to imagine that they are all employees of the same company. One of them is the others' boss. They are having a meeting to discuss what will possibly occur as a result of their company merging with another company. Before they begin, they discuss some possibilities together. They decide that they can talk about topics such as whether or not some of the people in their company will lose their jobs, whether or not they will have to move, whether or not certain policies will change, whether or not they will earn more money. "Remember," reminds the teacher, "that one of you in each group is the boss. You should think about this relationship if, for example, he or she makes a prediction that you don't agree with."

For fifteen minutes, the students perform their role-play. The teacher moves from group to group to answer questions and offer any advice on what the groups can discuss. After it's over, the students have an opportunity to pose any questions. In this way, they elicit some relevant vocabulary words. They then discuss what language forms are appropriate in dealing with one's boss. "For example," the teacher explains, "what if you know that your boss doesn't think that the vacation policy will change, but you think it will. How will you state your prediction? You are more likely to say something like 'I think the vacation policy might change.' than 'The vacation policy will change.'""What if, however," the teacher says, "it is your colleague with whom you disagree and you are certain that you are right. How will you express your prediction then?" One student offers, "I know that the vacation policy will change." Another student says, "I am sure that the vacation policy will change." A third student says simply, "The vacation policy will change."

The class is almost over. The teacher uses the last few minutes to give the homework assignment. The students are to find out what they can about two political candidates running against each other in the upcoming election. The students are then to write their prediction of whom they think will win the election and why they think so. They will read these to their classmates at the start of the next class.

二、教学示例

本示例中，交际法应用于加拿大一所为成年移民开设的语言课程中。这个班级有 20 个成年人，他们已经在加拿大生活两年了，具备中等英语水平。他们每周上 2 次课，每次 2 课时，都在晚上上课。

老师向全班同学问好后分发讲义。讲义的两面都有文字。一面是一份最近报纸上的体育专栏，是记者对上一届世界杯比赛的评论报道。老师让学生们读报道，并画出记者对下一届世界杯进行预测的语言表述。老师发出教学指示时用的是目的语。学生们阅读完这篇报道后，老师让学生们把所画的句子读出来。老师则把他们朗读的句子写在黑板上。之后，老师和学生们一起讨论记者对哪些预测内容有把握，对哪些预测内容则不太确定：

马来西亚很有可能赢得今年的世界杯。

如果意大利保持住现在的巅峰状态，他们就能获胜。

也许法国不会再次成为竞争者。

英格兰可能还有机会。

之后，老师和同学生们一起看第一句话，并让学生们思考有没有其他说法可以表达相同的意思。一名学生说："马来西亚可能会赢得世界杯。""很好！"老师肯定了他的答案，继续问："还有其他的吗？"没有学生回答。老师给出了其他的例子："马来西亚几乎肯定会赢得世界杯。"老师接着问全班学生："下一个句子呢？还有其他的表述方式吗？"一名学生回答道："意大利有可能赢得世界杯。"另一名学生说："意大利有赢得世界杯的可能性。"师生一起将文章中每一个预测句依次讨论了一遍。每名学生提出的其他表述方式都会经过老师和其他学生的评定，以确保这些句子与记者最初所做预测的确定程度相同。

老师让学生们翻到讲义的另一面。上面正是他们刚刚一直在探讨的文章中的句子。只不过打乱了顺序。例如，讲义这面的前两句话是：

英格兰可能还有机会。

归根结底，获胜的队伍可能是最有经验的那一支。

　　第一句话原本在体育专栏的中间；第二句则是专栏中的最后一句话。老师让学生们读句子，并按正确的顺序对句子进行编号。学生们完成后，他们将自己的答案与原文进行比较，查验答案。

　　随后，老师问学生们是否同意记者预测的观点，还让学生两两结成一组，写下自己对于"谁将成为下一届世界杯冠军"这一话题的预测。

　　接着，老师宣布要玩一个游戏。老师将全班学生进行分组，5人1组。每1组都会拿到1副卡片，每副有13张。卡片上印有不同的体育器材。学生们辨认卡片上的体育器材，老师则在黑板上写下这些器材的名称：篮球、英式足球、排球、网球拍、滑雪板、冰刀鞋、旱冰鞋、橄榄球、棒球棒、高尔夫球杆、保龄球、羽毛球拍和曲棍球棒。

　　游戏开始。洗好牌（卡片）后，每组先出4名学生抽牌，每人分别获得3张牌，他们不能向别人展示自己的牌。多出的一张牌朝下扣在桌子中间。每组的第5个人没有牌，她要预测下个周末杜安（班级中的一个学生）要做什么。第5名学生会说："杜安这个周末可能去滑雪。"此时，如果她的小组成员中有一名成员手持一张滑雪板的牌，这名小组成员就要进行回应。比如："杜安这个周末不能去滑雪，因为她的滑雪板在我这儿。"相反，如果没有任何一名成员手中有滑雪板的牌，那么第5名学生便可以对"杜安去滑雪"的可能性做出更确定的推断，比如，她可以说："杜安这个周末要去滑雪。"随后，她可以翻开桌子中间那张牌，以验证自己的推测是否正确。如果牌上印的是滑雪板，即说明她的猜测是正确的。

　　学生们很喜欢这个游戏。大家轮流猜，这样每个人都有机会预测某个同学将如何度过他（她）的周末。

　　在下一个课堂活动中，老师朗读了一些预测句，例如：

　　到2030年，太阳能的应用将减轻世界对化石燃料（如煤或石油）的依赖。

　　到2050年，人类将生活在月球上。

　　学生们需要回答他们认为这些预言能够成真的可能性有多大，并给出推断的理由。他们还要说出自己对这一预测的看法。在讨论其中一个预言时，一个学生说：他不认为世界政府会很*喜欢（用词偏误）在22世纪建立起来。老师和其他学生都忽略了他的错误表述，讨论继续。

　　接下来，老师让学生们3个人1组。因为班里有20名学生，所以有6个组有3名学生，还有1组只有2名学生。每组的其中1名成员会拿到1张纸，纸上排列了6张图片，组成了一幅连环画，图片上没有任何文字。这些图片讲述了一个故事。讲故事的学生首先向小组其他成员展示第1张图片，同时盖住其余5张图片。

　　其他学生则预测第2幅图中会发生什么。讲故事的学生会告知他们的预测是否正确。然后给大家看第2张图片，再让大家预测第3张图片会是什么样子。在整套图片都展示出来以后，这个小组将得到另一个连环画故事。这次他们改换角色，让刚才负责预测的其中一名学生展示图片，而原先展示图片的学生则与另外一名学生合作，一起预测故事的发展。

　　这节课的最后一个活动是角色扮演。老师让学生们4个人一组。他们要把自己想象成在同一家公司工作的雇员，其中一名学生是其他人的老板。他们现在正在开会讨论他们的公司与另一家公司合并后可能发生的情况。在公司合并之前，他们一起讨论一些可能发生的事。他们自行商定谈论的话题，比如：可以讨论合并后公司里的一些人是否会失业，他们是否必须得搬家，公司现行的一些规定政策是否会改变，他们是否能赚更多的钱，等等。学生们在讨论前，老师提醒道："请记住，你们每个小组都有一个人是老板。如果他（她）做出了你不认同的推断，当你发言时，应该考虑到你们的这种关系。"

这个活动进行了 15 分钟。老师一组一组地倾听观摩，回答大家的问题，并为学生们就小组可以讨论的内容提供建议。活动结束后，老师留出一段时间让学生们进行提问。这一环节又引出了一些相关词汇。而后，他们开始讨论用什么样的语言形式与老板打交道是合适的。老师解释道："例如，如果你认为在公司合并后，原来的休假政策将会改变。但同时你也知道你的老板认为休假政策不会改变，在这样的情况下，你将如何陈述你的观点？可能你更应该说'我认为休假政策可能会改变'，而不是'休假政策会改变'。"老师接着提问："不过，如果和你意见相左的是你的同事，而你确信自己的观点是正确的，那么你该怎么表述呢？"一名学生提议说："我认为休假政策会改变。"另一名学生说道："我确信休假政策会改变。"第三名学生回答得更简洁："休假政策会改变。"

下课前，老师用最后几分钟布置了家庭作业。学生们要在即将到来的选举中找出两名互相竞争的政治候选人，并了解他们的相关情况；然后预测并写出他们认为谁会赢得选举，并陈述做出如此推断的依据是什么。他们将在下节课上课之初向其他同学展示自己的作业。

3 Teaching Principles and Teaching Procedures

3.1 Practical Background and Theoretical Basis of CLT

(1) Practical Background of CLT

With the increasing interdependence of European countries in the 1970s came the need for greater efforts to teach adults the major languages of the European Common Market. The Council of Europe, a regional organization for cultural and educational cooperation, sponsored international conferences on language teaching, published books about language teaching, and was active in promoting the formation of the International Association of Applied Linguistics. One of the milestones is that a British linguist, D.A. Wilkins proposed a functional or communicative definition of language that could serve as a basis for developing communicative syllabuses for language teaching. Wilkins's contribution was an analysis of the communicative meanings that a language learner needs to understand and express. He described two types of meanings: notional categories (concepts such as time, sequence, quantity, location, frequency) and categories of communicative function (requests, denials, offers, complaints). Wilkins later revised and expanded his 1972 document into a book titled *Notional Syllabuses*, which had a significant impact on the development of CLT and became the embryonic form of communicative approach syllabus.

Besides, the facts that students could produce sentences accurately in a lesson, but could not use them appropriately when genuinely communicating outside of the classroom, the views from different educational practitioners that language learning required a social context, and the learner-centered and experience-based view of second language teaching are allowed the wide acceptance of Communicative Approach.

(2) Language Theory of CLT

The Communicative Approach in language teaching starts from a theory of language as communication. Different from Chomsky's abstract linguistic competence, Hymes proposed that the goal of language teaching is to develop "communicative competence". Communicative competence was a definition of what a speaker needs to know in order to be communicatively competent in a speech community. In Hymes's view, a person who acquires communicative competence acquires both knowledge and ability for language use with respect to:

① whether (and to what degree) something is formally possible;

② whether (and to what degree) something is feasible by virtue of the means of implementation available;

③ whether (and to what degree) something is appropriate (adequate, happy, successful) in relation to a context in which it is used and evaluated;

④ whether (and to what degree) something is in fact done, actually performed, and what its doing entails.

Since then, a more pedagogically influential analysis of communicative competence is found in Canale and Swain, in which four dimensions of communicative competence are identified: grammatical competence, sociolinguistic competence, discourse competence, and strategic competence.

Halliday's theory of functional linguistics also provides a strong theoretical support for Communicative Approach. He describes seven basic functions that language performs for children learning their first language:

① the instrumental function: using language to get things;

② the regulatory function: using language to control the behavior of others;

③ the interactional function: using language to create interaction with others;

④ the personal function: using language to express personal feelings and meanings;

⑤ the heuristic function: using language to learn and to discover;

⑥ the imaginative function: using language to create a world of imagination;

⑦ the representational function: using language to communicate information.

Learning a second language was similarly viewed by proponents of CLT as acquiring the linguistic means to perform different kinds of functions.

At the level of language theory, CLT has a rich theoretical base. Some of the characteristics of this communicative view of language are as follows:

① Language is a system for the expression of meaning.

② The primary function of language is to allow interaction and communication.

③ The structure of language reflects its functional and communicative uses.

④ The primary units of language are not merely its grammatical and structural features, but categories of functional and communicative meaning as exemplified in discourse.

(3) Learning Theory of CLT

In contrast to the amount literature about communicative dimensions of language, little has been written about learning theory. The learning view of CLT advocates three principles which can be inferred from CLT practices. Frist is communication principle. Activities that involve real communication promote learning. Second is task principle. Activities in which language is used for carrying out meaningful tasks promote learning. Third is meaningfulness principle. Language that is meaningful to the learner supports the learning process. These principles address the conditions needed to promote second language learning, rather than the process of language acquisition.

3.2 Teaching Principles and Features of CLT

According to Jack C. Richards and Theodore S. Rodgers, Communicative Language Teaching is best considered an approach rather than a method. It refers to a diverse set of principles that reflect a communicative view of language and language learning and that can be used to support a wide variety of classroom procedures. These principles include:

– Learners learn a language through using it to communicate.

– Authentic and meaningful communication should be the goal of classroom activities.

– Fluency is an important dimension of communication.

– Communication involves the integration of different language skills.

– Learning is a process of creative construction and involves trial and error.

Specifically, the main features of CLT can be described from the major distinctive features of the Audiolingual Method and CLT by Finocchiaro and Brumfit (Table 8-1).

Table 8-1   The Major Distinctive Features of the Audiolingual Method and CLT

	the Audiolingual Method	Communicative Language Teaching
1	Attends to structure and form more than meaning.	Meaning is paramount.
2	Demands memorization of structure-based dialogues.	Dialogues, if used, center around communicative functions and are not normally memorized.
3	Language items are not necessarily contextualized.	Contextualization is a basic premise.

continued table

	the Audiolingual Method	Communicative Language Teaching
4	Language learning is learning structures, sounds, or words.	Language learning is learning to communicate.
5	Mastery, or "over-learning," is sought.	Effective communication is sought.
6	Drilling is a central technique.	Drilling may occur, but peripherally.
7	Native-speaker-like pronunciation is sought.	Comprehensible pronunciation is sought.
8	Grammatical explanation is avoided.	Any device that helps the learners is accepted — varying according to their age, interest, etc.
9	Communicative activities only come after a long process of rigid drills and exercises.	Attempts to communicate may be encouraged from the very beginning.
10	The use of the student's native language is forbidden.	Judicious use of native language is accepted where feasible.
11	Translation is forbidden at early levels.	Translation may be used where students need or benefit from it.
12	Reading and writing are deferred till speech is mastered.	Reading and writing can start from the first day, if desired.
13	The target linguistic system will be learned through the overt teaching of the patterns of the system.	The target linguistic system will be learned best through the process of struggling to communicate.
14	Linguistic competence is the desired goal.	Communicative competence is the desired goal (i.e., the ability to use the linguistic system effectively and appropriately).
15	Varieties of language are recognized but not emphasized.	Linguistic variation is a central concept in materials and methodology.
16	The sequence of units is determined solely by principles of linguistic complexity.	Sequencing is determined by any consideration of content, function, or meaning that maintains interest.
17	The teacher controls the learners and prevents them from doing anything that conflicts with the theory.	Teachers help learners in any way that motivates them to work with the language.
18	"Language is habit" so errors must be prevented at all costs.	Language is created by the individual, often through trial and error.
19	Accuracy, in terms of formal correctness, is a primary goal.	Fluency and acceptable language is the primary goal; accuracy is judged not in the abstract but in context.
20	Students are expected to interact with the language system, embodied in machines or controlled materials.	Students are expected to interact with other people, either in the flesh, through pair and group work, or in their writings.
21	The teacher is expected to specify the language that students are to use.	The teacher cannot know exactly what language the students will use.

continued table

	the Audiolingual Method	Communicative Language Teaching
22	Intrinsic motivation will spring from an interest in the structure of the language.	Intrinsic motivation will spring from an interest in what is being communicated by the language.

3.3 Thaching Procedures of CLT

Finocchiaro and Brumfit[①] offer a lesson outline for teaching the function "making a suggestion" for learners in the beginning level of a secondary school program.

① Presentation of a brief dialogue or several mini-dialogues, preceded by a motivation (relating the dialogue situation[s] to the learners' probable community experiences) and a discussion of the function and situation — people, roles, setting, topic, and the informality or formality of the language which the function and situation demand. (At beginning levels, where all the learners understand the same native language, the motivation can well be given in their native tongue.)

② Oral practice of each utterance of the dialogue segment to be presented that day (entire class repetition, half-class, groups, individuals) generally preceded by your model. If mini-dialogues are used, engage in similar practice.

③ Questions and answers based on the dialogue topic(s) and situation itself. (Inverted *wh* or *or* questions.)

④ Questions and answers related to the students' personal experiences but centered around the dialogue theme.

⑤ Study one of the basic communicative expressions in the dialogue or one of the structures which exemplify the function. You will wish to give several additional examples of the communicative use of the expression or structure with familiar vocabulary in unambiguous utterances or mini-dialogues (using pictures, simple real objects, or dramatization) to clarify the meaning of the expression or structure.

⑥ Learner discovery of generalizations or rules underlying the functional expression or structure. This should include at least four points: its oral and written forms (the elements of which it is composed, e.g., "How about + verb + ing?"); its position in the utterance; its formality or informality in the utterance; and in the case of a structure, its grammatical function and meaning.

⑦ Oral recognition, interpretative activities (two to five depending on the learning level, the language knowledge of the students, and related factors).

⑧ Oral production activities — proceeding from guided to freer communication activities.

① RICHARDS J C, RODGERS T S. 语言教学的流派 [M]. 2 版 . 北京：外语教学与研究出版社，2008：170–171.

⑨ Copying of the dialogues or mini-dialogues or modules if they are not in the class text.

⑩ Sampling of the written homework assignment, if given.

⑪ Evaluation of learning (oral only), e.g., "How would you ask your friend to _____? And how would you ask me to _____?"

The above procedures clearly have much in common with those observed in classes taught according to Audiolingual principles. Traditional procedures are not rejected but are reinterpreted and extended. In CLT's teaching procedures, each unit has an ostensibly functional focus, new teaching points are introduced with dialogues, followed by controlled practice of the main grammatical patterns. The teaching points are then contextualized through situational practice. This serves as an introduction to a freer practice activity, such as a role play or improvisation. As Littlewood points out that CLT classroom follows a sequence of activities in: "Pre-communicative activities which includes structural activities and quasi-communicative activities and Communicative activities which includes functional communication activities and social interaction activities." And the communicative activities are just one of the most distinctive and breakthrough features of CLT. Littlewood distinguishes between "functional communication activities" and "social interaction activities" as a major activity types in CLT(Figure 8-1). Functional communication activities include the task that learners could compare sets of pictures and note similarities and differences; could work out a likely sequences of events in a set of pictures; could discover missing features in a map or pictures. Social interaction activities include conversation and discussion sessions, dialogues and role plays, simulations, skits, improvisations, and debates. Role plays and simulations are very useful tools. It can be seen that communicative activities are often designed to focus on completing tasks that are mediated through language or involve negotiation of information and information sharing.

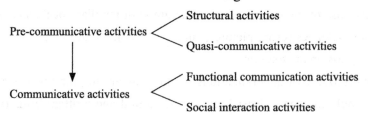

Figure 8-1   The Sequence of Activities in CLT Classroom

三、教学原则与教学过程

1. 交际法的实践背景与理论基础

（1）交际法的实践背景

20世纪70年代，随着欧洲国家之间相互依存关系的日益加深，迫切需要快速培养大量能掌握欧洲共同体国家主要语言的人才，解决欧洲各国间的语言沟通障碍。欧洲共同体委员会是一个区域性的文化和教育合作组织，该委员会主办了一系列语言教学领域的国际会议，出版了一些关于语言教学的书籍，并积极推动国际应用语言学协会的成立。其中一个里程碑事件便是英国语言学家威尔金斯提出了一个关于语言功能或语言交际的概念，这一概念成了交际法教学大纲制定的基础。威尔金斯的贡献就在于他指出了语言交际的意义，并分析了语言学习者在进行语言理解和表达时交际的重要意义。威尔金斯把意义分为两类：意念范畴（如时间、顺序、数量、位置、频率等概念）和交际功能范畴（如请求、拒绝、提议、抱怨等功能）。后来，威尔金斯又对 1972 年的观点进行了修改和扩充，形成了《意念大纲》。《意念大纲》对交际法的发展产生了重大影响并成为交际法教学大纲的雏形。

此外，语言教学也面临一个现实困境，即学生在课堂上可以准确地造句，但在课外却不能恰当地使用句子进行真正的语言交流。这使得不同教育工作者对语言学习形成了一些观点，如：语言学习需要社会语境，要以学习者为中心、以经验为基础，这些第二语言教学观都为交际法的产生和发展提供了背景条件。

（2）交际法的语言学理论基础

语言教学中的交际法是从"语言即交际"的理论出发的。与乔姆斯基提出的抽象的语言能力不同，海姆斯提出语言教学的目标是培养"交际能力"。交际能力指的是说话人为了能够在言语交流中拥有交际能力所需要掌握的知识及规则（即交际能力指的是不仅能使用语法规则来组成语法正确的句子，而且能在适当的场合、适当的时间恰当地使用语言）。在海姆斯看来，一个人获得了交际能力，同时也获得了语言运用方面的知识和能力。交际能力的四个重要参数如下：

①形式上是否（或者多大程度上）可能，即合法性；

②实际是否（或者多大程度上）可行，即适合性；

③实际使用和评估的上下文关系是否（或者多大程度上）合适，即得体性；

④实际上是否（或者多大程度上）已经实行，即实际操作性。

此后，卡纳莱和斯温又对交际能力进行了教学法层面的分析和阐述，认为交际能力应包含四个方面的能力：语法能力、社会语言能力、语篇能力和策略能力。

另外，韩礼德的功能语言学理论也为交际语言教学提供了理论支撑。他总结了儿童在其第一语言学习过程中，逐渐掌握的七种基本的语言功能：

①工具功能：用语言获取物品；

②控制功能：用语言控制他人行为；

③交流功能：用语言与周围的人进行交流互动；

④个体功能：用语言表达个人感情、好恶、意愿；

⑤启发功能：使用语言探索周围环境，发现并认识世界；

⑥想象功能：使用语言创造一个想象的世界；

⑦告知功能：使用语言向他人提供信息，与他人交换信息。

交际法学者认为，第二语言学习同样也是学习和掌握语言的各种功能。

总之，在语言理论层面，交际法有着坚实的理论基础。这种交际语言观的特点如下：

①语言是一个意义表达系统。

②语言的基本功能是互动和交际。

③语言结构反映其功能和交际用法。

④语言要素不仅包括语法结构，也包括体现在语篇中的功能和交际意义范畴。

（3）交际法的学习理论基础

与大量关于语言交际维度的理论相比，关于交际法学习理论的相关论述很少。从交际教学实践中可以总结出交际法的学习观，即倡导"交际性、任务性、意义性"三原则。第一是交际原则，即包含真实交际的课堂活动可以促进语言学习。第二是任务原则，即运用语言完成有意义任务的课堂活动可以促进语言学习。第三是意义原则，即对学习者有意义的活动有利于语言学习。这些原则都体现了促进第二语言学习所需的条件，而不是语言习得的过程。

2. 交际法的教学原则与主要特点

理查德和罗杰斯指出交际法应被视为一种教学理念，而非一种具体的教学方法。交际法反映了语言和语言学习的交际观，能够广泛应用于各类课堂教学过程中。这些教学原则包括：

①学习者通过使用语言进行交际而学会语言。

②开展真实而有意义的交际活动应作为课堂活动的目标。

③流利度是交际能力的一个重要指标。

④交际能力关系到听、说、读、写等不同语言能力的整合。

⑤语言学习是不断尝试和修正、创造性地建构知识的过程。

具体来说，交际法的教学原则和主要特征可以通过菲诺契阿罗和博拉姆菲特对听说法与交际法主要特征的对比来进行描述（表8-1）。

表8-1　交际法与听说法主要特征对比表

	听说法	交际法
1	关注语言结构和形式，而不是意义	关注语言的意义
2	要求记住基于结构的对话	围绕交际功能学习对话，对话通常不记忆
3	语言项目不一定需要语境	语境是一个基本前提
4	语言学习是学习结构、语音或词汇	语言学习要学习如何与人交流
5	寻求掌握或"过度学习"	寻求有效沟通
6	操练是一项核心教学技术	操练可以使用，但并非教学必需
7	语音要达到母语者的水平	发音使对方理解即可
8	避免语法解释	为帮助学习者理解，可以根据年龄、兴趣等不同因素选择任何方法
9	只有经过长时间的机械操练和练习后才能进行交际活动	可以从一开始就鼓励交际
10	禁止使用学生母语	在可行的情况下，允许明智地使用母语
11	初期禁止翻译	如果学生需要或能够从中受益，则可以使用翻译

续表

	听说法	交际法
12	掌握口语后再开始阅读和写作（听说领先，读写随后）	如果需要的话，阅读和写作可以从第一天开始（听说读写可以同时开始）
13	通过句型系统教授目的语语言系统	最好是通过沟通的过程学习目的语语言系统
14	以语言能力为培养目标	以交际能力为培养目标（即有效而恰当地使用语言系统的能力）
15	承认但不强调语言的多样性（不关注语言变体）	在教学材料和教学方法上，语言的多样性都是一个核心概念（关注语言变体）
16	教学单元的编排仅由语言复杂性决定	根据能保持学习兴趣的内容、功能或意义编排教学单元
17	教师控制学习者，阻止他们做任何违背教学理念的事情	教师通过任何方式帮助学习者，激励他们使用语言
18	"语言是习惯"，因此必须不惜一切代价防止错误产生	语言是由个人创造的，常常通过反复尝试和犯错学会
19	准确，即形式正确，是首要目标	语言的流利度和可接受性是首要目标；准确性不是抽象的判断，而是在上下文中判断
20	学生应与机械的或受控的语言材料进行互动	学生应通过双人或小组活动与他人互动，也可以与文本互动
21	教师应指定学生所使用的语言	教师不能确切地知道学生将使用什么语言
22	内在动机来自于对语言结构的兴趣	内在动机来自对语言所传达的内容的兴趣

3. 交际法的教学过程

菲诺契阿罗和博拉姆菲特描述了一个中学初级阶段语言课程的教学大纲，大纲所讲授的功能是"提出建议"，教学过程如下：

①引入并展示一个简短的对话或几个小对话，引出学习动机（联系对话情境与学习者可能有的社团经验，使之产生学习的兴趣和动机），并讨论对话所涉及的功能和情境——人物、角色、环境、话题以及表达该功能和情境所需使用的正式或非正式语言语体。（当学生处于语言学习的初级阶段，且所有学习者都拥有同一种母语的时候，也可以用他们的母语来描述，从而激发其学习动机。）

②学习者根据教师的语言示范，口头练习当天所呈现对话部分的每一个句子（采用全班、半个班、小组以及个人重复的方式）。如果使用短小的对话，则进行同类对话的练习。

③基于对话涉及的话题和情境进行问答练习（使用特殊疑问句或者选择疑问句进行问答）。

④围绕对话主题，联系学生个人经历，进行问答练习。

⑤学习对话中的一个交际功能的表达方式或一个表达语言功能的结构形式。教师（利用展示图片、展示简单的实物或动作演示及表演等方式）在明确的语境或小对话中使用学生熟悉的词汇进行交际表达，给学生尽可能多地举例，从而让学生明晰该语言表达或语言结构的意义、功能和用法。

⑥学习者归纳出功能性表达或语言结构背后的语言规则。所谓的语言规则至少应该包括四点：口语和书面形式（语言构成要素，例如，句型"How about + 动词 + ing？"）；句法位置；语体的正式或非正式性；如果是一个语言结构，还要了解它的语法功能和意义。

⑦认知性、理解性的口语表达练习（2 ~ 5次，可根据学生的学习程度与水平、语言知识及其他影响因素进行调整）。

⑧口语表达练习——从控制性练习到自由交流与表达活动。

⑨如果所学的对话没有相关文本或教材，要进行抄写记录。

⑩如果有书面作业，要对作业进行抽查或点评。

⑪进行（口头上的）学习评价：例如，"你会如何请你的朋友_____？你会怎么让我_____？"

前文列出的教学过程显然与听说法的授课过程有许多相似之处。应该说，在交际法中，传统的教学步骤并没有被否定遗弃，而是重新进行了解释和扩展。在交际法的教学过程中，每个教学单元都有一个功能焦点，通过对话引入新的教学项目，然后对主要语法结构进行控制性练习。之后通过情境练习将教学项目情境化。所谓的情境化就是将教学项目放在一个更自由的实践活动中去练习，如进行角色扮演或即兴表演。正如利特尔伍德指出的那样，交际法的课堂活动遵循一个活动序列，即"前交际活动和交际活动，前交际活动包括句型结构活动和准交际活动，交际活动包括功能交际活动和社会交际活动"。其中的交际活动便是交际法最鲜明且最具突破性的特点之一。利特尔伍德将交际法的主要交际活动类型分为"功能交际活动"和"社会交往活动"（图8-1）。功能交际活动包括：学习者比较一组图片并指出异同；能够在一组图片中找出可能的事件序列；能够发现并补全地图或图片中缺失的部分。社会交际活动包括交流与讨论、对话与角色扮演、模仿、表演小品、即兴表演和辩论。角色扮演和模仿都是既有用又有效的课堂活动。由此可见，交际法中的课堂活动通常被设计成交流任务，学生需要通过语言交流、意义协商和信息共享来完成。

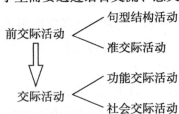

图 8-1　交际法课堂活动序列示意图

4 Conclusion

Communicative Language Teaching appeared at a time when language teaching in many parts of the world was ready for a paradigm shift. The Grammar-Translation Method and The Audiolingual Method were no longer felt to be appropriate methodologies. CLT appealed to those who sought a more humanistic approach to teaching, one in which the interactive processes of communication received priority. The rapid adoption and worldwide dissemination of the Communicative Approach also resulted from the fact that it quickly assumed the status of orthodoxy in British language teaching circles, receiving the sanction and support of leading applied linguists, language specialists, and publishers, as well as institutions such as the British Council. To a certain degree, as a positive, popular and widely acceptable approach around the world, Communicative Approach has already become the mainstream of language teaching and occupies a dominant position.

Today, CLT thus continues in its "classic" form. And it has influenced many other language teaching approaches and methods that subscribe to a similar philosophy of language teaching. For instance, some focus centrally on the input to the learning process. Content-Based Instruction stresses that the content or subject matter of teaching is of primary importance in teaching. Not only should the language input be authentic, but modes of learning should be authentic to the study of the subject as well. The Lexical Approach and Corpus-Based Learning Pedagogy start with a corpus of discourse relevant to learners' interests and needs and the goal of methodology is to engage learners directly with this material. Some teaching proposals focus more directly on instructional factors. Cooperative Language Learning, for example, which shares many of the characteristics of CLT, promotes learning through communication in pairs or small groups. Cooperative organization and activities are central to this approach. Task-Based Language Teaching advocates the importance of specially designed instructional tasks as the basis of learning. Other more recent proposals take learners and learning factors as the primary issues to address in teaching and learning. The Whole Language belongs to the humanistic tradition, which argues "Learner first, learning second." Learner engagement is a priority. Neurolinguistic Programming emerges from a therapeutic tradition in which individual growth and personal change are the focus, whereas Multiple Intelligences focuses on learner differences and how these can be accommodated in teaching. Outcome is another dimension of the process of communication and is central in Competency-Based Language Teaching. Outcomes are the starting point in program planning with this approach.

However, limitation also exists in CLT approach. Firstly, departing from grammar-based syllabus, communicative syllabus is going to another extreme. In ideal situations, such a syllabus may be the most conductive to the development of learners' communicative competence. However, its practicality is under question. It's impossible to make an exhaustive list of notions and functions. How to specify the notions and functions categories systematically and how to order them scientifically are still in the air.

Secondly, Communicative Approach sets the learners' communication ability as the classroom goal. In concrete teaching contexts, all teaching materials and classroom activities have to be elicited from the authentic situations and reflect communicative principles. Though it indeed motivates learners to communicate with target language, it does little help in learners' basic grammar ability, comprehensive understanding ability and all-round development. It is also too high for both the teaching materials and language teachers to achieve such a standard of real communication.

Thirdly, it seems that CLT means only listening and speaking practice without focus on reading and writing. The way that learners acquire the comprehensible input is through listening in the communicative interactions; accordingly, the comprehensible output they receive is by communicating and negotiating the meaning with participants. Such communicative interactions seem to neglect the reading and writing exercises. Carrell argues that reading and writing skills could not be acquired automatically by improving listening and speaking competence.

Another controversial issue is the adaptability of CLT. Based on research of CLT application to different countries such as India, South Africa, Pakistan and China, it is doubted that CLT can not be adapted to other language learning contexts in the world, due to different cultural expectations, country-specific educational policies, individual learning styles, learners' personal differences, and non-native teachers' language proficiencies.

Communication is the very reason why language exits. The ultimate aim of learning a language is for communication. The development of communication ability should be the essential role in language teaching methods. Just because of its strong emphasis on that, Communicative Approach has gained wider approval than the traditional methods in the world. Of course, it is not the "last word" for language teaching. Critically looking at it, we know Communicative Approach is not hundred percent perfect. But, we believe, based on this footstone, the research of modern language teaching methodology could go much further in the near future.

四、小结

交际法，其产生正是语法翻译法和听说法已不再被认为是最合适的语言教学方法之期，其出现恰逢世界许多国家和地区酝酿语言教学范式变革之时。它所提出的语言交流互动过程应处于语言教学的首要地位这个观点，正契合了那些寻求更优语言教学方法的人们的需求。因此，交际法迅速在英国语言教学界占据了正统的地位，并迅速在世界范围内广泛传播和使用，并得到了应用语言学家、语言学家、出版商以及诸如英国文化协会等机构的认可和支持。可以说，在一定程度上，交际法作为一种积极的、受欢迎的和被广泛接受的语言教学法，已经成了语言教学法的主流，并占据了统治地位。

交际法如今仍以其"经典"模式存留于世，并持续影响着众多其他语言教学理念和方法。这些新的教学理论和教学法都与交际法相同，共同遵循培养语言交际能力这一教学理念与目标。例如，有些教学理论关注学习过程的输入。内容教学法强调教学的内容或主题在教学中要处于首要地位，强调语言输入要来源于现实，是真实的语言材料，学习方式也应该是真实的，即要像学习学科课程内容那样学习语言。词汇法和基于语料库的教学法则从与学习者的兴趣和需求相关的语料库着手切入，以便使学习者更直接地接触这些真实的语言材料。有些教学理论更关注教学因素。例如，合作学习语言法。该教学法以组织学生合作及进行协作学习活动为教学核心，同时也具有交际法的许多特点，如通过双人或小组交流活动促进学习。再如任务型教学法，提倡以专门设计的教学任务为学习的基础。还有些新型教学法将学习者和学习因素作为教学中要解决的首要问题。如全语言法，这是一种基于人本主义传统的教学法，主张"学习者是第一位的，而学习是第二位的"，学习者的参与应放在首位。神经语言程序法源于一种心理治疗技术，关注学习者的个人成长与个体差异，而多元智能法则更关注学习者的个体差异以及如何在教学中因材施教。语言学习的产出是交际过程的另一个维度，学习成果正是能力导向型教学法的教学核心，是采用该教学法开展项目规划的初衷。

然而，交际法也存在局限性。

第一，交际法的功能大纲摆脱语法大纲，而走向了另一个极端。在理想情况下，这种功能意念大纲可能最有助于培养学生的交际能力。然而，其可行性却受到了质疑。把所有功能和意念无一遗漏地进行描写和列举是不可能的。如何科学系统地对功能和意念项目进行确定、分类、排序，至今尚未解决。

第二，交际法把学习者的交际能力作为课堂教学的目标。在具体的教学情境中，所有的教材、课堂活动都必须从真实的情境中引出，体现交际原则。虽然课堂教学的交际化确实能激发学习者使用目的语进行交流，但对学习者的基本语法能力、综合理解能力和全面发展帮助不大。而且无论是教材还是教师都难以达到这样的真实交际标准。

第三，交际法的运用似乎意味着只进行听说练习，而不注重读写训练。学习者获得可理解性输入的途径是在交际互动中通过倾听获得的，而他们获得的可理解输出是通过与参与者进行有意义的交流和协商获得的。这种交流互动仅仅通过听和说，似乎忽视了阅读和写作练习。卡雷尔认为，阅读和写作技能无法通过提高听说能力而自动获得。

另一个有争议的问题是交际法的适用性。基于交际法在不同国家，如印度、南非、巴基斯坦和中国适用性的研究，结果表明：由于文化期望不同、国家教育政策差异、学习者学习风格等个体差异以及非母语教师的语言能力不均衡等因素，交际法在世界其他语言学习环境中的适应性还有待商榷。

总之，沟通交流是语言存在的根本原因。语言学习最终是为了交流。交际能力的培养在语言教学中已成为至关重要的一环。正是基于这个原因，交际法才能在世界范围内得到比传统语言教学法更广泛的认可。当然，这并不是语言教学这一学科发展的终点。批判性地来看，交际法并不是百分之百完美的。但是，我们相信基于交际法的贡献，现代语言教学方法论的研究在不久的将来定会有更深远的发展。

○ Activities and Exercises

● Understanding and Thinking

1. Please read the following materials, talk about your understanding of the statement "Communicative Language Teaching (CLT) marks the beginning of a major paradigm shift within language teaching in the twentieth century, one whose ramifications continue to be felt today." and the significance of Communicative Approach in language teaching.

(1) Meaning vs. Structure and Form

As is well known, many traditional language teaching approaches used various more or less repetitive drills to teach languages and meaning was generally neglected in favour of the processes of practice and "over learning". Within CLT, meaning is given far more importance than grammar, structure and form, which are the language elements emphasized by traditional structural or grammar translation language teaching methods. Although grammar rules can make speakers produce well-structured sentences, this does not mean that all sentences made according to pure structural rules make sense to others, for example, "I can see you later." This sentence is structurally correct but native speakers do not use it when they want to express "See you later." Again, sometimes learners who have been taught solely by older language courses cannot decode sentences properly. What we aim for when we are talking with others is to make them understand the meaning we wish to deliver. If we fail in this, the "talk" produced will lose communicative value and the speech we produced will become nonsense. A good example which helps demonstrate this point is the sentence "The policeman is crossing the road." which may have several meanings. Swan has used this as an example in his article as well: Four burglars are busy with one house. One of them, who is on watch, says "The policeman is crossing the road." to others then disappears. However, only the one who has learned English language from a communicatively oriented language class considers it as a warning and runs away. Unfortunately, the other two burglars who are from a structural syllabus are caught by the policeman because they cannot decode the meaning properly in that situation.

In real life, in some situations we cannot comprehend the speech used in its full context by only paying attention to the grammar or structure that we have learned from traditional teaching methods. This is particularly a problem with sarcastic or ironic speech. Here is part of one dialogue between C, the writer herself, who is a non-native speaker and trained within the Grammar Translation teaching tradition and M who is an English native speaker and artist:

C: There is a popular saying "If you want to die early you should marry a writer or artist."

because writers and artists are moody and good at torturing others.

M: That sounds great to me!

If we understand the sentence said by M only from the aspects of rules of grammar and structure, we may think that M is abnormal and likes to build his pleasure on the basis of others' pain. Learners needs to be aware that there is not an exactly one-to-one fit between the form of a sentence and the meaning that a speaker wants to express in a specific context.

(2) Fluency and "Acceptable" vs. Accuracy and "Nativelike"

Language teaching is being regarded as based on the premise that language is for communication. That is, language is seen as a social tool for speakers to communicate with each other, to make meaning in certain social contexts and to exchange information and meaning with someone else, either orally or in writing. CLT approaches support this belief, and take fluency and acceptable language as the main goals of language teaching. However, traditional language teaching methods, such as Structural teaching or the Grammar-Translation Method, require speakers to use fine-tuned language during speech or error-free sentences during writing. No one disputes the fact that finely structured sentences should be used in writing or very formal speech. However, in relation to spoken languages, native speakers do not always use well-structured sentences. In addition, there is often little time to think about the structures and details of grammar during real life conversation. What is more, there is no need to pursue structure and grammar at the cost of fluency, which can spoil the natural flow of communication.

In relation to pronunciation, the Audiolingual Method requires a "native-speaker-like" pronunciation while CLT simply aims for comprehensible or understandable pronunciation. Here, we can take English as an example. Nowadays, English has become a "global language" and is spoken for all kinds of purposes. We all know that certain linguists think there is a Critical Period and that after this period it is very difficult for second or foreign language learners to acquire native-like pronunciation. This may or may not be the case, but such concerns involve placing emphasis upon features of language use that are not central to practical communication. World English use today includes countries in which English might be a primary language, an additional language and an international language. Each area, province or country has a different accent and even different forms of English (e.g., Indian English) but this does not really affect our communication in English. As long as we can speak fluently and can express our opinions clearly, comprehensible pronunciation is acceptable.

2. *Follow Me* is the typical textbook of CLT published by BBC in the late 1970s. Please read the catalogue of the textbook, compare the differences between structural syllabus and functional-notional syllabus, and then talk about your understanding of the significance and the role of language functions in language teaching.

Lesson 1 What's your name?

Lesson 2 How are you?

Lesson 3 Can you help me?

Lesson 4 Left, right, straight ahead.

Lesson 5 Where are they?

Lesson 6 What's the time?

Lesson 7 What's this? What's that?

Lesson 8 I like it very much.

Lesson 9 Have you got any wine?

Lesson 10 What are they doing?

Lesson 11 Can I have you name, please?

Lesson 12 What does she look like?

Lesson 13 No smoking.

Lesson 14 It's on the first floor.

Lesson 15 Where's he gone?

Lesson 16 Going away.

Lesson 17 Buying things.

Lesson 18 Why do you like it?

Lesson 19 What do you need?

Lesson 20 I sometimes work late.

Lesson 21 Welcome to Britain.

Lesson 22 Who's that?

Lesson 23 What would you like to do?

Lesson 24 How can we get there?

Lesson 25 Where is it?

Lesson 26 What's the date today?

Lesson 27 Whose is it?

Lesson 28 I enjoy it.

Lesson 29 How many and how much?

Lesson 30 What have you done?

3. Read the following materials, choose any topics you are interested in, and design 3–5 communicative activities of CLT.

The most obvious characteristic of CLT is that almost everything that is done is done with a communicative intent. Students use the language a great deal through communicative activities such as games, role-plays, and problem-solving tasks. Activities that are truly communicative, according to Morrow, have three features in common: information gap, choice, and feedback.

An information gap exists when one person in an exchange knows something the other person does not know. If we both know today is Tuesday and I ask you, "What is today?" and you answer, "Tuesday." Our exchange is not really communicative. In communication, the speaker has a choice of what she will say and how she will say it. If the exercise is tightly controlled so that students can only say something in one way, the speaker has no choice and the exchange, therefore, is not communicative. In a chain drill, for example, if a student must reply to her neighbor's question in the same way as her neighbor replied to someone else's question, then she has no choice of form and content, and real communication does not occur.

True communication is purposeful. A speaker can thus evaluate whether or not his purpose has been achieved based upon the information he receives from his listener. If the listener does not have an opportunity to provide the speaker with such feedback, then the exchange is not really communicative. Forming questions through a transformation drill may be a worthwhile activity, but it is not in keeping with CLT since a speaker will receive no response from a listener, so is unable to assess whether her question has been understood or not.

Another characteristic of CLT is the use of authentic materials. It is considered desirable to give students an opportunity to develop strategies for understanding language as it is actually used.

Finally, we noted that activities in CLT are often carried out by students in small groups. Small numbers of students interacting are favored in order to maximize time allotted to each student for communicating.

4. Read the following materials, talk about your understanding of the characteristics of CLT, and use teaching examples to illustrate.

Johnson and Johnson identify five core characteristics that underlie current applications of communicative methodology.

① Appropriateness: Language use reflects the situations of its use and must be appropriate to that situation depending on the setting, the roles of the participants, and the purpose of the communication, for example. Thus learners may need to be able to use formal as well as casual styles of speaking.

② Message focus: Learners need to be able to create and understand messages, that is, real meanings. Hence the focus is on information sharing and information transfer in CLT activities.

③ Psycholinguistic processing: CLT activities seek to engage learners in the use of cognitive and other processes that are important factors in second language acquisition.

④ Risk taking: Learners are encouraged to make guesses and learn from their errors. By going beyond what they have been taught, they are encouraged to employ a variety of communication strategies.

⑤ *Free practice: CLT encourages the use of "holistic practice" involving the simultaneous use of a variety of subskills, rather than practicing individual skills one piece at a time.*

5. In the sight of the following materials, talk about the differences between functional syllabus and grammatical syllabus.

The grammatical and situational approaches are essentially answers to different questions. The former is an answer to the question how. How do speakers of Language X express themselves? The latter is a response to the questions when. or where. When and where will the learner need the target language? There is, however, a more fundamental question to be asked, the answer to which may provide an alternative to grammatical or situational organizations of language teaching, while allowing important grammatical and situational considerations to continue to operate. The question is the question what. What are the notions that the learner will expect to be able to express through the target language? It should be possible to establish what kind of thing a learner is likely to want to communicate. The restriction on the language needs of different categories of learner is then not a function of the situations in which they will find themselves, but of the notions they need to express. One can envisage planning the linguistic content according to the semantic demands of the learner. While there are, no doubt, some features of what may be communicated that are so general that no language learner can avoid acquiring the means to express them, others may be limited to people who will use the language only in certain fields. In this way the association of certain communication needs and certain physical situations is seen to be coincidental and those needs that cannot be related to situation can be handled just as easily as those that can. Furthermore, although there is no one-to-one relationship between grammatical structure and the notions they express, we should be able to take advantage of grammatical generalizations wherever these provide important ways of meeting a particular communication need.

The Categories of a Notional Syllabus

① *Time.*

● *Point of time*

● *Duration*

● *Time relations*

● *Frequency*

● *Sequence*

● *Age*

② *Quantity.*

● *Grammatical number*

- *Numerals*
- *Quantifiers*

③ *Space.*

- *Dimensions*
- *Location*
- *Motion*

④ *Matter.*

Reference to the physical world is principally a matter of deciding the semantic fields within which the learner will operate. A notional analysis is less valuable than an analysis in terms of situation and/or subject-matter.

⑤ *Case.*

- *Agentive*
- *Objective*
- *Dative*
- *Instrumental*
- *Locative*
- *Factitive*
- *Benefactive*

⑥ *Deixis.*

- *Person*
- *Time (see above)*
- *Place*
- *Anaphora*

⑦ *Modality — i.e., utterances in which the truth value of the propositional content is modified in some way.*

- *Certainty*
- *Necessity*
- *Conviction*
- *Volition*
- *Obligation incurred*
- *Obligation imposed*
- *Tolerance*

⑧ *Moral evaluation and discipline — i.e, utterances involving assessment and judgement.*

- *Judgement*
- *Release*
- *Approval*

- *Disapproval*

⑨ *Suasion — i.e., utterances designed to influence the behaviour of others.*

- *Suasion*

- *Prediction*

⑩ *Argument — i.e., categories relating to the exchange of information and views.*

- *Information asserted and sought*

- *Agreement*

- *Disagreement*

- *Denial*

- *Concession*

⑪ *Rational enquiry and exposition — i.e., categories relating to the rational organization of thought and speech.*

e. g, Implication, hypothesis, verification, conclusion, condition result, explanation, definition, cause, etc.

⑫ *Personal emotions — i.e., expression of personal reactions to events.*

- *Positive*

- *Negative*

⑬ *Emotional relations — i.e., expression of response to events usually involving interlocutor.*

- *Greeting*

- *Sympathy*

- *Gratitude*

- *Flattery*

- *Hostility*

⑭ *Interpersonal relations — i.e., selection of forms appropriate to relationship of participants in the event.*

- *Status (formality)*

- *Politeness*

● **Teaching Design**

1. Please study the characteristics of CLT intensively, find out the function or the topic of the following teaching design, supplement and enlarge more other details, and then make a teaching demonstration in groups.

The teacher gives the students two role-cards each group and asks them to make a pair work. Students who play role A and role B get different information.

Student A	Student B
You meet B in the street.	*You meet A in the street.*
A: Greet B.	*A:*
B:	*B: Greet A.*
A: Ask B where he is going.	*A:*
B:	*B: Say you are going for a walk.*
A: Suggest somewhere to go together.	*A:*
B:	*B: Reject A's suggestion.*
A: Accept B's suggestion.	*　Make a different suggestion.*
B:	*A:*
	B: Express pleasure.

After finishing the pair work, students are asked to show their dialogues to others. Then the teacher summarizes and supplements the expression of "giving suggestions" in English.

> give suggestions
> ◎ *Perhaps we would...*
> ◎ *Let's...*
> ◎ *Why not...?*
> ◎ *If I were you, I'd...*
> ◎ *Don't you think it's a good idea to...?*
> ◎ *I think we should...*

Next, the teacher shows a piece of recording material. Before showing, he explains that the material is selected from a psychological counseling program called "Give me your hand" from the broadcasting station. The teacher asks the students to pay attention to what problems Xiao Ming had encountered when he wrote to the broadcasting station for help (He is an introverted and not very gregarious student. The purpose of his letter is to hope that the broadcasting station can give him some tips, pointers and suggestions on making friends). Then, the teacher asks the whole class to discuss Xiao Ming's problems and give him some suggestions on making friends. The teacher divides the students into groups of four. Like the previous activities, each student receives an instruction card, which specified their roles and tasks in the group activities.

> *Student A:*
>
> *You've recently had a sleeping problem: you either find it hard to go to sleep at night or sleep too much. You are going to talk about your problem with your group members and ask for some advice or suggestions.*

> *Student B & C:*
>
> *After listening to Student A talking about his/her problem, you are going to give him/her some advice or suggestions. Please use the sentence patterns of giving suggestions you've learned.*

> *Student D:*
>
> *Your job is to take down what the other three students have said in the group work and report to the whole class the advice and suggestions you've given to Student A. You are expected to use the sentence patterns of giving suggestions.*

Then, the teacher creates a situation to let students use the functional sentence patterns in a more real social context. The second activity is that the school recently received a donation of 100,000 yuan. The teach divides the students into four groups, playing the role of principal, teacher, student and parent respectively, and giving suggestions on how to use the 100,000 yuan. Students should try to use the expressions of suggestions in English.

When students participate in the above two activities, the teacher moves from group to group in the classroom to help each group understand the intention of the activities, give guidance when necessary, and sometimes participate in the activities. When each group reports or shows the results of the activities, the teacher listens carefully and seldom interrupts. However, when they encounter difficulties, he gives verbal guidance and help. After the students' speech, the teacher evaluates the performance of each group, especially makes a detailed comment and summary on how to give suggestions on the core content of the lesson.

Finally, the teacher gives homework assignment to the students and asks them to write back to Xiao Ming or any other student in the class as the editor of the radio program "Give me your hand" giving suggestions on how to solve their problems in study or life, and "broadcast" the reply content in the next class.

2. Please read the following teaching plan carefully, point out the inappropriate places according to the theory and teaching principles of CLT, and then revise and improve it.

Text:

Part I

Kyle: Hey, Beth, would you like to try the new restaurant on Green Street?

Beth: Sounds great! Let me wrap up what I was doing.

Kyle: There is no need to rush. We've got enough time.

Beth: Thank you for stopping by. I hate eating alone.

Kyle: My pleasure. I didn't really feel like cooking today.

Beth: Trying on new things once in a while isn't too bad, right?

Kyle: Of course it isn't.

Beth: I'm done. Let's go.

Part II

Kyle: Good evening. Do you have ang places available?

Waiter: Yes sir. I guess you need a table for two, am I right?

Kyle: Yes, thank you very much.

Waiter: This way, please.

Kyle: May I have the menu?

Beth: What do you want, Kyle? They have many kinds of food.

Kyle: Yeah…Oh, I want Combo number one and…an iced latte. What about you?

Beth: Well, I'd like two spicy chicken wings and an apple pie.

Waiter: Is that everything?

Beth: I'd like a decaf coffee.

Waiter: OK, got it.

Kyle: May I have the check, please?

Waiter: 15 dollars in total.

Kyle: It's on me.

Beth: Kyle, don't do that. Let's just go Dutch.

Key Sentences:

- *I would like a iced latte.*
- *Would you like any room for cream?*
- *I would like a coffee with cream and sugar.*
- *Are you sure you don't want to try an espresso?*

Teaching Content Analysis:

The theme of the two dialogues is "to eat at a restaurant." Two dialogues will be seen at the beginning of the classroom in the form of pictures and text, combined with some of the relevant food expressions the class has learned. This lesson includes:

- *Sentence pattern: I would like something.*
- *Gradually complex expressions about "coffee": lattes, ice-filled lattes, creamy coffee with sugar, decaf, espresso.*
- *Two common colloquial expressions: "It's on me" and "go Dutch".*
- *Common expressions of communication with waiters in restaurant scenarios: Do you still have empty seats? / I want a (two) table(s) / Can I (have the menu/bill) / How much is it?*

After teaching the above sentence patterns and content, play a TV series "Friends" clips, so that students experience the relevant situation in the local tone and expression.

Students Analysis:

The course is aimed at a ten-day short-term English express course for overseas travellers, aged between 25 and 35, with two to three thousand English vocabulary and a certain degree of grammar knowledge but particularly poor communication skills. There are a total of nine students.

Teaching Objectives:

Knowledge and competence: Avoid the situation of "dumb English" when students go to restaurants during the trip; Master the sentence patterns and words mentioned in the teaching content of this lesson.

Emotion and value: Cultivate students' polite manner and know how to express their gratitude to the waiter.

Teaching Focus:

Teaching focus is on sentence patterns, such as "I'd like sth." and "May I have the check/menu?" These two sentence patterns in the restaurant situational communication are essential and very common.

Teaching Difficulties:

Expressions about coffee: "lattes" "lattes with ice" "espresso" "coffee with sugar and cream" and so on. These words are not very widely used, basically only in restaurants and coffee shops and when chatting, and not everyone uses them.

Teaching Preparation:

PPTs, some pictures of restaurant scenarios and physical pictures of related words.

Duration of Teaching:

60 minutes.

Teaching Procedures:

Class begins.

Teacher: "Good morning! Let's review what we have learned last lesson!"

The teacher picks some students to say the words such as hamburger, chicken wings, apple pie, coke, sandwich, etc., by using pictures.

Teacher shows the teaching content and reads for the class.

Teacher: "Let's practice these two conversations. Start with the first paragraph. I need three students to play the waiter, Kyle and Beth, respectively."

Three students start practicing the conversation, after one exercise, the other group starts the exercise, and the last group starts the exercise to make sure that each student has done it.

Teacher: "OK, now I'm going to play the waiter, and two students play Beth and Kyle."

Students start practicing again until each student practiced with a different role from the first exercise.

Teacher: "I believe that we all have mastered the conversation. Now let's learn a little new knowledge. Now I'm going to play the customer; who's going to play the waiter?"

A student plays the waiter.

The student asked: "What would you like to eat?"

Teacher: "I'd like a cup of latte. / I'd like a cup of iced latte. / I'd like a decaf. / I'd like a cup of espresso. / I'd like a cup of Italian espresso with sugar and cream."

Teacher puts out the words of latte, iced latte, decaf, Italian espresso, coffee with sugar and cream, introduces them to the students, and shows physical pictures at the same time.

Teacher: "All right class, we are now to learn some common expressions about coffee. Follow me, and read aloud. Now let's practice with the sentence we have just read!"

The teacher plays the waiter, and the students play customers.

Teacher: "What would you like to eat?"

Student: "I'd like a cup of latte."

Student: "I'd like a cup of iced latte."

Student: "I'd like a cup of espresso."

Students: "..."

Teacher: "OK, now we use the sentence patterns and words we have just learned to carry out new exercises according to the grouping just now!"

Students practice the dialogue freely.

Teacher shows a picture of a restaurant, and says: "Now imagine that we are going to have dinner in this restaurant. Please make a new dialogue with your partners."

Teacher acts as a waiter and guides students to make new conversations, and ensures that every student has a chance to participate in the context practice.

Teacher: "OK, now the practice is over. I'll take the picture off. Now you set the scene, and use the knowledge we learned today and before to make a bold and interesting conversation!"

Students set the scene and begin the conversation.

Teacher: "OK, now let's review the knowledge points we learned today."

Teacher points to the knowledge points, students read.

Teacher: "Finally, let's watch the clips of the TV series Friends *and experience how native speakers express themselves."*

Play and watch video.

Teacher: "OK, today's class is over! Everybody's great today!"

Homework Assignments:

Consolidate and practice the situational dialogue you have learned, and actively think about some of the necessary expressions that you will encounter as a traveler, and give feedback to the teacher, so as to avoid any omission in the course design.

● **Further Reading**

Communicative Language Teaching

1. A Historical Perspective on the Communicative Approach

Until the latter part of the 20th century, the theoretical foundations of language education were firmly anchored in behavioral psychology and structuralism, which held that learning mainly took place through a process of repetition and habit forming. Language teaching was typically divided into four skill categories, including the active skills of speaking and writing, as well as the passive skills of listening and reading; and foreign language lessons often centered on rehearsing a fixed repertoire of grammatical patterns and vocabulary items until they could be reproduced easily and precisely, with a low tolerance for error. However, Richards points out that because the focus of learning was primarily confined to accuracy of production, rather than meaningful interaction, individuals taught according to this approach frequently experienced considerable difficulty in real-life communicative encounters.

Noted linguist and social theorist Noam Chomsky criticizes this aspect of language instruction, arguing that:

Linguistic theory is concerned primarily with an ideal speaker-listener, in a completely homogeneous speech community, who knows its language perfectly and is unaffected by such grammatically irrelevant conditions as memory limitations, distractions, shits of attention and interest, and errors (random or characteristic) in applying his knowledge of the language in actual performance. This criticism of the traditional view of language learning as a sterile, intellectual exercise, rather than as a practical undertaking resulting in skills that may be applied in real-life situations, was echoed by scholars such as Habermas, Hymes, and Savignon, who based their understanding of language on the psycholinguistic and socio-cultural perspectives that meaning is generated through a collaborative process of "expression, negotiation and interpretation" between interlocutors. Hymes, in particular, stresses the need for language learners to develop communicative competence, which suggests that successful communication requires "knowing when and how to say what to whom"; in his view, knowledge of grammatical structures and vocabulary was not sufficient to enable communication on a functional level.

Hymes' ideas were supported by an evolving understanding of how communication occurs. Research on language and communication revealed that the so-called "passive" language learning skills — reading and listening — in fact require active engagement on the part of the learner; as a result, these skills were re-conceptualized as receptive activities, while the skills of speaking and writing were reclassified as productive. Furthermore, it was recognized that communication consists not only of production (message-sending) and reception (message-receiving), but negotiation of meaning, or collaboration between senders and receivers. Added to the dramatic shit in the international social and political climate of the late 1960s and early 1970s, along with the expansion of global English, this changing viewpoint brought recognition of the need to reframe our conception of language education from that of teaching a language to teaching students how to use the language.

2. Principles of Communicative Language Teaching

Unlike many of the other instructional techniques covered in this book, Communicative Language Teaching (CLT) does not constitute a method in itself. Rather, CLT is a set of principles framing an overarching approach to language teaching which may be carried out according to a variety of different methods [some of these, including Content-Based Instruction (CBI) and Task-Based Language Teaching (TBLT) will be dealt with in separate chapters later on]. These principles have been summarized by Berns as follows:

① Language teaching is based on a view of language as communication. That is, language is seen as a social tool that speakers use to make meaning; speakers communicate about something to someone for some purpose, either orally or in writing.

② Diversity is recognized and accepted as part of language development and use in second language learners and users, as it is with first language users.

③ A learner's competence is considered in relative, not in absolute, terms.

④ More than one variety of a language is recognized as a viable model for learning and teaching.

⑤ Culture is recognized as instrumental in shaping speakers' communicative competence, in both their first and subsequent languages.

⑥ No single methodology or fixed set of techniques is prescribed.

⑦ Language use is recognized as serving ideational, interpersonal and textual functions and is related to the development of learners' competence in each.

⑧ It is essential that learners be engaged in doing things with language — that is, that they use language for a variety of purposes in all phases of learning.

Because the Communicative Approach does not comprise a standardized framework for teaching, curriculum design is largely up to individual institutions and the language instructors who teach according to these principles. However, regardless of the specific techniques employed, any teaching methods that can be classified as truly communicative share these assumptions.

3. Instructional Practices in Communicative Language Teaching

As Richards and Rodgers stress, communicative learning activities are those which promote learning through communication itself; therefore, the range of instructional practices that may be employed in CLT is bounded only by the creativity of curriculum designers and classroom instructors in developing authentic communicative tasks. Breen describes these as structured activities which "have the overall purpose of facilitating language learning — from the simple and brief exercise type, to more complex and lengthy activities such as problem solving or decision making."

(1) Designing Communicative Tasks

Nunan enumerates six basic elements that should be taken into account in designing communicative tasks, including: ① learning goals; ② linguistic input; ③ classroom activities; ④ the role of the teacher; ⑤ the role of the students; and ⑥ the setting in which the activity is situated.

① Learning Goals

According to Nunan's understanding, learning goals of a communicative exercise denote the range of outcomes that are expected as a result of carrying out a specified learning task. In terms of communicative language learning, these goals entail "establishing and maintaining relationships"; exchanging information; carrying out daily tasks; and obtaining and utilizing information from a variety of sources (such as the Internet, television, newspapers, public announcements, research materials, and so on).

② Linguistic Input

The input of a communicative task refers to any type of information source on which the exercise is centered. For instance, depending on the learning objective and the needs of the students, a teacher might design an activity framed around a newspaper article, a class schedule, a recipe, a feature film, a schematic of a computer circuit, or a map.

③ Glassroom Activities

Learning activities in a communicative context are drawn from the relevant input in order to develop competencies such interactional ability in real-life settings, skills building, or fluency and accuracy in communication. These should be designed to mirror authentic communicative scenarios as closely as possible, and "methods and materials should concentrate on the message, not the medium". Özsevik and Richards suggest the use of information-gap and problem-solving exercises, dialogues, role-play, debates on familiar issues, oral presentations, and other activities which prompt learners to make communicative use of the target language; in doing so, they develop the skills that they will need to use the language in unrehearsed, real-life situations.

④ The Role of the Teacher

The teacher's role in implementing a communicative learning exercise is somewhat malleable in comparison with other, more instructor-oriented approaches to language learning. In traditional language classrooms, the instructor is generally the dominant figure; the focus of the class is on the teacher, and students may assume a passive role as they receive direct instruction. In the communicative classrooms, on the other hand, the focus is on interaction between students. Richards and Rodgers emphasize the teacher's role in this setting as that of a "needs analyst" who is responsible for "determining and responding to learner language needs" within a specific learning context. In this case, the teacher serves mainly as a facilitator, designing activities that are geared toward communication and monitoring students' progress, as well as stepping in as necessary to resolve breakdowns in communication. Beyond this, the instructor may take on the role of a participant in a given exercise, or even act as a co-learner herself, as students express themselves during the course of a communicative task. When errors occur, the instructor may note them without comment so as not to disrupt the law of the activity, instead addressing the issues that appear to cause difficulties at a later time. As Richards and Rodgers suggest, teachers who lack specialized training may find classroom development to be challenging in such a learning environment, as they strive to find a balance between providing structures and the learning process while still maintaining a natural law of communication.

⑤ The Role of the Students

Within the framework of a communicative approach, students are the focal point of classroom activity, assuming primary responsibility for their own learning. As it is assumed that using a language is the most effective way to learn it, students are encouraged to work together to negotiate meaning in order to accomplish a given communicative task; thus, learning activities are highly interactive and may take place in smaller groups or with an entire class. In this context, learners are responsible for choosing which forms of the language they use to convey their messages, rather than following a prescribed lexis.

⑥ Setting

Finally, Nunan notes the significance of the setting in which communicative learning takes place. While the classroom is the most typical venue for language learning, communicative tasks may also be carried out in venues as diverse as occupational settings, online instruction or in the community at large; therefore, activity designers should consider the specific requirements of the learning context in developing learning tasks.

(2) The Role of the Target Language

Because the goal of language learning in a communicative context is, by definition, developing the ability to communicate in the target language, nearly everything is done with this in mind, as it is essential to make it clear to students that the language is not only a subject to be mastered, but a means for real interactions. Accordingly, not only learning tasks, but classroom management and direct instruction are carried out in the target language whenever practicable, with teachers turning to the students' native language only when required to ensure comprehension. Activities are focused on authentic use of the target language, utilizing "games, role-plays and problem-solving tasks", to approximate real-life situations in which the language may be used. In addition, the use of teaching materials — restaurant menus, greeting cards, music videos, comic strips, TV episodes, concert tickets, newspaper articles and travel guides — that showcase authentic functions of the language underscores its communicative nature and helps students develop the skills they need to interact in real-life situations.

(3) The Role of the Native Language

Unlike some modern approaches to language instruction, such as the Direct Method, the use of the students' mother tongue is not prohibited in CLT. However, in order to emphasize the communicative aspect of the target language, use of the mother tongue should be kept to a minimum and used only as needed for issues such as classroom management or giving complex instructions that are beyond the students' level of proficiency in the target language.

(4) Where Do Grammar, Fluency and Accuracy Fit in

As Nunan relates, in the earlier days of CLT, there was a tendency among certain linguists to de-emphasize the teaching of grammar and other aspects of form; this idea was based on the belief that learners would acquire this knowledge naturally through the process of learning how to use the language. However, the current thinking on this issue is that effective communication cannot take place without attention to the rules of grammar, punctuation, sentence structure, pronunciation, and other more formalized aspects of the language; and therefore, teaching these elements is seen as a necessary component of CLT, as discussed later on in the section concerning learner outcomes in CLT.

(5) Feedback, Evaluation and Assessment

A final consideration in designing and carrying out communicative activities concerns the need to provide meaningful feedback for students, as well as to evaluate their progress. In terms of feedback, as mentioned earlier in the chapter, offering verbal corrections during the course of a communicative activity may constitute a disruption, as well as creating anxiety among learners; therefore, error correction should be administered with discretion. However, in this respect, Larson-Freeman and Anderson point out that feedback may occur as a natural result of a communicative activity, since learners are able to determine whether or not their communication attempts have been successful based on the responses they receive from their instructor and classmates. Concerning the evaluation and assessment of learners in a communicative context, Richards and Savignon point to current trends in language education which favor holistic evaluation of learner progress based on the results of in-class presentations, writing portfolios, recorded interactions, and other types of projects. On the other hand, Savignon cautions that in many educational contexts, teachers have little leeway in choosing a more qualitative approach to assessment, as testing and evaluation are carried out according to nationalized standards.

4. Considerations in Implementing CLT in an EFL Context

In spite of ongoing debate concerning the most effective means of implementing CLT, the Communicative Approach to language teaching has become increasingly popular in the field of English language education, not only in areas where it is as taught as a second language, but in countries where English is not the primary means of communication and opportunities to use the language in real-life interactions are limited. As Wenjie explains, CLT is often regarded in such contexts as a progressive, and therefore preferred, approach to foreign language teaching; however, Widdowson reasons that the notion of creating authentic communicative scenarios in a foreign language setting is, in essence, a contradiction. As he argues, the target language as it is used in the EFL classroom "cannot be authentic because the classroom cannot provide the contextual conditions for it to be authenticated by learners." In his view, CLT constitutes, at most, a sort of dress rehearsal, where learners have the opportunity to try out the language, engaging with and internalizing its semantic forms before putting it to use in real-life interactions.

In this respect, Özsevik also points out that in an EFL context such as Turkey, where learning English is an academic requirement rather than a means for survival, students are frequently under-motivated. Their interest in learning the language may only extend to passing standardized tests such as university entrance exams; therefore, they are more likely to resist attempts to encourage them to interact in English and to develop their communicative skills. Furthermore, the mismatch between the principles of the communicative approach and the current national assessment methods, not to mention the content of standardized teaching materials, often lead to problems with implementation on a practical level.

In addition to these issues, Richards and Rodgers maintain that students who are accustomed to a more traditional, teacher-fronted approach to language instruction may resist the need to become active partners in the learning process. Under these circumstances, İnceçay contends that, as demonstrated by researchers such as Harley and Swain and Spada, combining communicative exercises with conventional, form-focused learning tasks may be the most effective means for building communicative competence in the English language.

5. Learner Outcomes in CLT – What the Research Says

It seems logical that if the ultimate goal of studying a language is communication, then teaching according to a communicative approach should produce the desired results. However, in determining the effectiveness of a particular instructional method, real-life evidence concerning learner outcomes must be considered in addition to theoretical arguments. Accordingly, multiple studies have been carried out to evaluate the effects of CLT on learner success. Researchers around the world have viewed the issue from a variety of perspectives, considering the impact of CLT on skills such as oral fluency, accuracy, comprehension and overall proficiency. Some of the major findings concerning each of these aspects of communicative competence are summarized below.

◎ Chang: In a comparative study of Chinese EFL students, it was found that learners taught by the standard Grammar-Translation Method performed better in an assessment of grammar skills than an experimental group taught via CLT.

◎ Genesee: Observation of students in a French language immersion program revealed that communicative language teaching allowed learners to develop near-native proficiency in comprehension.

◎ Guo and Chang: In an experimental study carried out with fifth-grade EFL students, learners in a CLT course outperformed those taught via a form-based approach in an evaluation of their communicative competence.

◎ Harley and Swain: Students in a French language immersion program who were taught via the Communicative Approach that emphasized meaning over form did not develop accuracy in skills-based tasks to the same extent as peers who received instruction in form and function in addition to communicative skills.

◎ Ma: An experimental study conducted with non-English major Chinese EFL students demonstrated that learners taught through CLT scored significantly higher on listening comprehension tests than peers who were taught via a traditional, grammar-based method.

◎ Savignon: Learners who participated in a communicative component of French as a foreign language course performed better in both communicative assessments and linguistic tasks than peers who received instruction through the Audiolingual Method.

◎ Spada: An observational study on learner outcomes in three separate CLT classrooms revealed that overall learner success depended in large part on the approach of the individual instructor in implementing CLT.

◎ Spada: In a review of classroom and laboratory research on CLT instruction, it was concluded that integrating form-focused instruction and communicative exercises, rather than relying on CLT alone, tends to have a positive effect on learner outcomes.

◎ Spada and Lightbown: Francophone students in an intensive, content-based EFL course focused on communication showed significantly greater oral fluency than their peers who were taught via traditional methods emphasizing the rules of grammar and structure; however, they tended to make frequent grammatical errors when speaking.

◎ Spangler: In a comparative study with students of Spanish as a foreign language, it was demonstrated that learners taught by a CLT approach underperformed with respect to oral fluency in relation to their peers who received instruction through a TPTRS (Teaching Proficiency Through Reading and Storytelling) approach.

◎ Thuy: A comparative study of Vietnamese EFL students revealed that CLT-based instruction resulted in significantly greater oral fluency than conventional, grammar-oriented language teaching.

An examination of the research outlined above makes it clear that, on the whole, communicative language teaching has had positive results in terms of comprehension, oral fluency and overall communicative competence. However, in terms of grammar and other structural aspects of language, results have been mixed, with some learners showing no significant difference, or even underperforming, with respect to their peers who were taught using other approaches; while in other cases, the students taught by CLT performed significantly better than their peers in terms of form-based as well as communicative tasks.

● **Knowledge Table**

Table 8-2　Summary of Characteristics of Communicative Language Teaching

Key Points	The Communicative Language Teaching
Period	
Representatives	
Background	
Theory of Language	
Theory of Language Learning	
Objectives	
The Syllabus	
Types of learning and Teaching Activities	
Teacher's Roles	
Learner's Roles	
The Role of Students' Native Language and Target anguage	
The Role of Instructional Materials and Textbook	
Others	
Summary	

● **Mind Map**

Chapter 9 Content-Based Instruction

第 9 章 内容教学法

O **Contents**

- ◆ Teaching Cases of Content-Based Instruction
- ◆ Developing Background of Content-Based Instruction
- ◆ Contemporary Models of Content-Based Instruction
- ◆ Features of Content-Based Instruction
- ◆ Teaching Procedures and Teaching Techniques of Content-Based Instruction
- ◆ Comments on Content-Based Instruction
- ◆ Activities and Exercises

- ◆ 内容教学法教学示例
- ◆ 内容教学法的发展背景
- ◆ 内容教学法的当代模式
- ◆ 内容教学法的主要特点
- ◆ 内容教学法的教学过程与教学技巧
- ◆ 对内容教学法的评价
- ◆ 活动与练习

○ **Wordle**

1 Introduction

The CBI, which is called "Content-Based Instruction," emphasizes that language teaching should integrate the topic content and language learning closely, and finally achieves the dual purpose: learning the topic content and improving language ability.

The earliest CBI concept can be traced back to 389 A.D., proposed by Saint Augustine: "Language learning needs to focus on meaningful content learning." Since the 1980s, schools in the United States and Canada have been widely used. In the same period, the European Union proposed "Content and Language Integrated Learning (CLIL)", which was called "the best way to make progress in foreign languages".

So far, although the basic theoretical ideas of different advocates are the same, there are still some differences in the specific implementation measures. Several representative definitions of CBI at present include:

① The CBI is a comprehensive teaching of special content related to language teaching objectives. It teaches both special content and second language skills. It generally regards the target language as a tool for learning thematic content, not as a direct object of learning.

② The CBI is an approach of language teaching. It combines topics and tasks related to other topics with a second language.

③ The CBI means to completely integrate language learning and content learning. It represents a significant change to the traditional foreign language pedagogy. The traditional teaching method regards direct learning of language as the center of teaching, while the center of

CBI is to learn language and acquire language ability through thematic study.

④ The CBI refers to an approach of second language teaching, which organizes teaching around the content or information students want to obtain, rather than around linguistics or other forms of syllabus.

一、教学法概述

内容教学法（CBI），全称为"基于内容的教学法"，强调语言教学应该把专题内容与语言学习有机地、紧密地结合起来，最终达到既学习了专题内容又真正提高了语言能力的双重目的。

内容教学法最早可追溯到公元 389 年。圣·奥古斯丁提出："语言学习需要注重有意义的内容学习。"20 世纪 80 年代起，内容教学法在美国、加拿大多地学校被广泛运用。同时期，欧盟提出了"内容语言融合学习（CLIL）"，这一教育理念被称为是"在外语方面获得进步的最佳方法 [1]"。

发展至今，尽管不同倡导者的基本理论主张相同，但是具体的实施措施还是存在一定程度上的差异。目前学界对内容教学法的几个有代表性的定义 [2] 包括：

①内容教学法是对跟语言教学目标有关的特殊内容的综合教学，它同时教授专题内容和第二语言技能。整体而言，内容教学法把目的语看作学习专题内容的工具，而不是学习的直接对象。

②内容教学法是一种语言教学的方式，它把与其他专题有关的话题和任务跟第二语言结合在一起教学。

③内容教学法的意思是把语言学习和内容学习完全结合在一起，它代表了对传统外语教学法的显著改变。传统教学法把对语言的直接学习作为教学的中心，而内容教学法的中心是通过专题内容来学习语言并获得语言能力。

④内容教学法指第二语言教学的一种方式，它围绕学生要获得的内容或信息来组织教学，而不是围绕语言学或其他形式的大纲来组织教学。

2 Teaching Cases

● Case I[3]

A sixth-grade class in an international school in Beijing is studying both geography and English through Content-Based Instruction. Most of the students are Chinese speakers, but there

---

① 武和平，武海霞. 外语教学方法与流派 [M]. 北京：外语教学与研究出版社，2014：134.

② 曹贤文. 内容教学法在对外汉语教学中的运用 [J]. 云南师范大学学报，2005（1）：7-11.

③ LARSEN-FREEMAN D, ANDERSON M. Techniques and Principles in Language Teaching [M]. Oxford: Oxford University Press, 2011: 134-136.

are several native speakers of Japanese and a few Korean.

The teacher asks the students in English what a globe is. A few call out "world." Some make a circle with their arms. Others are silent. The teacher then reaches under her desk and takes out a globe. She puts the globe on her desk and asks the students what they know about it.

They call out answers enthusiastically as she records their answers on the blackboard. When they have trouble explaining a concept, the teacher supplies the missing language. Next, she distributes a handout that she has prepared based on a video, "Understanding Globes." The top section on the handout is entitled "Some Vocabulary to Know." Listed are some key geographical terms used in the video. The teacher asks the students to listen as she reads the ten words: "degree" "distance" "equator" "globe" "hemisphere" "imaginary" "latitude" "longitude" "model" "parallel".

Below this list is a modified cloze passage. The teacher tells the students to read the passage. They should fill in the blanks in the passage with the new vocabulary where they are able to do so. After they are finished, she shows them the video. As they watch the video, they fill in the remaining blanks with a certain degree of the vocabulary that the teacher has read aloud.

The passage begins:

> A _____ is a three-dimensional _____ of the earth. Points of interest are located on a globe by using a system of _____ lines. For instance, the equator is an imaginary line that divides the earth in half. Lines that are parallel to the equator are called lines of _____ . Latitude is used to measure _____ on the earth north and south of the equator …

After the video is over, the students pair up to check their answers.

Next, the teacher calls attention to a particular verb pattern in the cloze passage: "are located" "are called" "is used" etc. She tells students that these are examples of the present passive, which they will be studying in this lesson and later in the week. She explains that the passive is used to "defocus" the agent or doer of an action. In fact, in descriptions of the sort that they have just read, the agent of the action is not mentioned at all because the agent is not relevant.

The teacher then explains how latitude and longitude can be used to locate any place in the world. She gives them several examples. She has the students use latitude and longitude coordinates to locate cities in other countries. By stating "This city is located at latitude 60° north and longitude 11° east." the teacher integrates the present passive and the content focus at the same time. Hands go up. She calls on one girl to come to the front of the room to find the city. She correctly points to Oslo, Norway on the globe. The teacher provides a number of other examples.

Later, the students play a guessing game. In small groups, they think of the names of five cities. They then locate the city on the globe and write down the latitude and longitude coordinates. Later, they read the coordinates out loud and see if the other students can guess the name of the city. The first group says: "This city is located at latitude 5° north and longitude 74° west." After several misses by their classmates, group 4 gets the correct answer: "Bogotá." Group 4 then give the others new coordinates: "This city is located at 34° south latitude and 151° east longitude." The answer: "Sydney!"

For homework, the students are given a description of Australia and a graphic organizer to help them organize and recall the new information. They have to read the description and label the major cities and points of interest on the map.

AUSTRALIA

Australia is the 6th largest country in the world. With an area of 7,692,000 sq km, it has a relatively small population of around 22.5 million people. Its largest city is Sydney, home of the famous Opera House and Harbour Bridge and is located on the east coast to the north-east of the capital city, Canberra. Other major cities include Melbourne, in the south, and Perth, which is situated on the west coast, over 3,500 km from the capital.

Australia's highest peak, Mount Kosciuszko, is relatively small at 2,228 metres and is situated in Kosciuszko National Park. Australia has many national parks including Kakadu, the largest national park in Australia, which covers almost 2,000 sq km, and Karijini, which features spectacular waterfalls and gorges. Other places of interest include Alice Springs, in the heart of the Australian outback and situated in the centre of the country. To the south-west of Alice Springs is Uluru (Ayers Rock), a huge sandstone rock and an Aboriginal sacred site situated in the Uluru-Kara Tjuta National Park.

There are many other famous attractions. Situated off the north-east coast, visitors can marvel at the Great Barrier Reef — the world's largest coral reef. Further south, beach lovers may wish to visit The Gold Coast, a 70 km stretch of golden sand running along Australia's east coast.

● **Case II**[①]

Two classes in the fourth grade of the Chinese Language and Culture Department of a Chinese university conducted a teaching activity with the content of "Idioms related to Xiang Yu and Liu Bang."

Section 1

In the introduction of the course, the teacher gives a brief introduction to the historical background of the peasant uprising in the late Qin Dynasty — Chen Sheng and Wu Guang's uprising.

The teacher plays the story video of the idiom "*Qu er dai zhi*". Students retell the story and the teacher asks questions based on the content of the story to deepen their impressions.

---

① 来源于网络，略有删改。

Combined with Liu Bang's answer "*Da zhang fu dang ru shi ye*", the teacher ask students to discuss: "Think of Xiang Yu and Liu Bang as one of your friends, whose answer do you prefer, and who do you appreciate more? Why? How do you think they are different?"

The teacher explains the meaning and specific use of idioms, example sentences, etc.

The teacher shows the story video of the idiom "*Po fu chen zhou*", and asks students to understand the meaning of the story. Then, the teacher ask questions about the content: "Why did Xiang Yu ask the soldiers to destroy the pot and ship? What do you think of his approach? If it were you, would you do it? Talk about your understanding of Xiang Yu's character from this story."

The teacher summarizes the use of idioms (grammar, context, example sentences), etc.

With the main content of "*Xiang zhuang wu jian, yi zai Pei gong*", the teacher broadcasts a video of the story of the Hongmen Banquet and asks questions about the main idea of the story.

Group discussion:

Why did Xiang Yu not follow Fan Zeng's suggestion and get rid of Liu Bang?

Fan Zeng is so angry, why? Why is the Hongmen Banquet a turning point?

Evaluate the character's characteristics of Xiang Yu, Fan Zeng, Zhang Liang, Fan Kuai, and Liu Bang in one sentence.

Section 2

The teacher broadcasts the video of "*Si mian Chu ge*" to guide students to experience the strong tragedy atmosphere on all sides:

A very powerful hero suddenly fell into a dilemma, unable to see hope in front of him, and hometown songs suddenly sounded around him. In such an atmosphere, not only the external failure, but also the experience of the character's state of mind at that time, the inability to return to the end of the road, the feeling of the vicissitudes of the past, and the feeling of the failure and success.

The teacher broadcasts the video materials related to "*Ba wang bie ji*" to let students know about the other side of Xiang Yu:

At this time, Xiang Yu was no longer the hero, but showed the other side of his tenderness. His affection for Yu Ji, Yu Ji's indispensability to him, also made the love classics.

The focus here is to lead students to appreciate their love stories and experience their tragic atmosphere. Ask students to discuss:

Why did Yu Ji commit suicide?

What new understanding do you have for Xiang Yu?

What do you think of Xiang Yu?

Extension: It is recommended that students watch the classic movie *Farewell My Concubine* after class.

The teacher teaches the idiom "*Wuyan jian Jiangdong fulao*." This is Xiang Yu's suicide, the final result of the tragic hero.

Contact Li Qingzhao to write Xiang Yu's poem "*Sheng dang zuo ren jie, si yi wei gui xiong. Zhijin si Xiang Yu, buken guo Jiangdong.*" Think and discuss:

Why did Xiang Yu refuse to cross Jiangdong?

If you were Xiang Yu, would you choose to endure it, in order to make a comeback someday, or would you rather die in glory than live in dishonor?

Explore different cultural values and the impact of the characters' personality on their final outcome.

二、教学示例

● 教学示例一

本示例中，北京一所国际学校的六年级学生正在通过内容教学法来学习地理和英语。大多数学生的母语是汉语，也有以日语、韩语为母语的学生。

老师用英语问学生什么是"globe"。少数学生说是"world"，一些学生用手臂围成一个圈，其他学生沉默。老师从书桌下面拿出一个地球仪。她把地球仪放在桌子上，问学生对此物有何了解。

学生们踊跃作答，老师在黑板上记录答案。当学生难以解释一个概念时，老师会提供相关词汇。接下来，老师分发她根据视频《了解世界》整理的讲义。讲义最上面的部分名为"你需要知道的词"，列出的是视频中使用的一些关键地理术语。老师让学生听她读这十个词："度""距离""赤道""地球仪""半球""虚构""纬度""经度""模型""平行"。

下面是一段完形填空。老师告诉学生们阅读后，他们应该可以用新词填空。学生填完后，老师向他们展示视频。观看视频时，学生可以把没有填上的地方，用老师读过的词汇补上。

完形填空的段落是这样的：

> 一个＿＿＿＿＿是一个三维的地球＿＿＿＿＿。要找到我们研究的地方，要使用地球仪上的＿＿＿＿＿线。比方说，赤道是一条虚构的线，把地球分成了两半。和赤道平行的线叫作＿＿＿＿＿。纬度是用于测量赤道南、北部的＿＿＿＿＿的……

视频结束后，学生们两两一组互相检查答案。

随后，老师提醒学生注意段落中重要的动词结构模式："位于""叫作""用于"等。她告诉学生，这些都是被动结构，本课及本周后续课程将学习这些内容。她解释说，被动结构是用来使动作的行为主体"散焦"的。他们刚刚阅读的那段描述中，因为动作的主体不明显，所以根本没有提到。

接着，老师解释了如何使用纬度和经度来定位世界上任何一个地方。她给了学生几个例子。学生使用经纬度坐标来定位其他国家／地区的城市。老师说："这座城市位于北纬

60°，东经11°。"这样就将当前的被动结构和内容结合到了一起。学生们举起手来，老师将一个女孩叫到前面寻找城市，她正确地指向了地球仪上的挪威奥斯陆。老师又提供了很多其他例子。

随后，学生们玩猜谜游戏。老师将学生分成若干小组，每个小组要想出五个城市的名称，在地球仪上定位城市并写下纬度和经度坐标。接着，他们大声朗读坐标，看看其他学生能否猜出城市的名称。第一组说："这个城市位于北纬5°，西经74°。"在同学们答错几次之后，第四组说出了正确答案："波哥大。"然后，第四组给其他人新的坐标："这个城市位于南纬34°和东经151°。"答案是："悉尼！"

布置作业时，老师提供了一段描写澳大利亚的文字和一个图形提示题，以帮助他们组织、回忆新信息。他们必须阅读文字并在地图上标记主要城市和感兴趣的地方。

澳大利亚

澳大利亚是世界第六大国家。面积为769.2万平方公里，人口相对较少，约为2250万人。澳大利亚最大的城市是悉尼，这里是著名的歌剧院和海港大桥的所在地，位于首都堪培拉东北部的东海岸。其他主要城市包括南部的墨尔本和西海岸的珀斯，距离首都超过3500千米。

澳大利亚的最高峰，是海拔2228米的科斯修斯科山，位于科斯修斯科国家公园。澳大利亚有许多国家公园，包括占地近2000平方千米的澳大利亚最大的国家公园卡卡杜，以及拥有壮观的瀑布和峡谷的卡瑞吉尼。其他景点包括澳大利亚内陆中部的爱丽丝泉。爱丽丝泉的西南面是乌鲁鲁（艾尔斯岩石），它是一块巨大的砂岩岩石，位于乌鲁鲁－卡拉·丘塔国家公园中，是一个土著人圣地。

还有许多其他著名景点。游客在东北沿海可以欣赏世界最大的珊瑚礁——大堡礁。再往南，海滩爱好者不妨去黄金海岸，黄金海岸沿澳大利亚东海岸绵延70千米。

● 教学示例二

中国一所大学的中国语言文化专业四年级的两个班进行了内容为"项羽和刘邦的相关成语"的教学活动。

第一课时

课程引入部分，老师对秦末农民起义——陈胜吴广起义的历史背景做了简单介绍。

老师播放成语"取而代之"的故事视频。学生复述故事大意，老师根据故事内容提问，加深学生印象。然后，老师让学生们结合刘邦的回答"大丈夫当如是也"，讨论："把项羽和刘邦想象成你的朋友，你更倾向于谁的回答，更欣赏谁？为什么？你认为他们有什么不同？"

老师解释成语意义及其具体运用的例句等。

老师播放成语"破釜沉舟"的故事视频，让学生了解故事大意。然后，老师就内容进行提问："项羽为什么让将士们砸破锅，毁掉船？你认为他的做法怎么样？如果是你，你会这样做吗？说一说通过这个故事，你对项羽的性格有什么了解。"

老师总结成语用法（语法、语境、例句）等。

老师以"项庄舞剑，意在沛公"为主要内容，播放鸿门宴故事视频，就故事大意进行提问。

小组讨论：

项羽为什么没有听从范增的建议，把刘邦除掉？

为什么范增如此生气？鸿门宴为什么是一个转折点？

分别用一句话评价项羽、范增、张良、樊哙、刘邦的性格特点。

第二课时

老师播放"四面楚歌"的视频，引导学生感受四面楚歌强烈的悲剧氛围：

一个非常强势的英雄突然陷入困局，眼前看不到希望，而四周突然响起家乡的歌谣，在这样的氛围下，不仅仅是外在的失败，更重要的是体会此时人物的心境，那种兽困笼中、无力回天的穷途末路之感，那种今非昔比、功败垂成的沧桑之感。

老师播放"霸王别姬"相关视频材料，让学生对项羽的另一面有所认识：

此时的项羽不再是那个力拔山兮气盖世的豪迈英雄，骄傲自负，有着征服天下的雄心，而是展现出了其铁汉柔情的一面。他对虞姬的深情，虞姬对他的不离不弃，也让二者的爱情成为经典。

这里的重点是带领学生欣赏他们的爱情故事，体会其悲剧氛围。让学生讨论：

虞姬为什么要自杀？

你对项羽有了什么新的认识？

你怎么看待项羽这个人物？

扩展：推荐学生课下观看经典电影《霸王别姬》。

老师教授成语"无颜见江东父老"——这是项羽的自杀，悲剧英雄的最后结局。

联系李清照写项羽的诗词"生当作人杰，死亦为鬼雄。至今思项羽，不肯过江东。"让学生思考讨论：

项羽为什么不肯过江东？

如果你是项羽，你会选择隐忍，以图有朝一日东山再起，还是宁为玉碎，不为瓦全？

探讨不同的文化价值观，以及各人物性格对其最后结局的影响。

3 Teaching Principles and Teaching Procedures

3.1 Developing Background and Theory Base

Although Content-Based Instruction (CBI) was proposed by Saint Augustine in early times, it became more popular from the 1960s, since CBI took the principles of Communicative

Language Teaching. Depending on different initiatives, CBI included at least 3 models[①]:

(1) Language across the Curriculum

It was a model for native language education conducted by Britain, America, and Singapore. They encouraged "Every teacher, an English teacher" and recommended all subjects to focus on reading and writing. Besides, the teaching materials were produced that integrated subject matter and language teaching goals.

(2) Immersion Education

It was a model for foreign language education for native language speakers in regular schools. The pioneer immersion program was developed in Canada in the 1960s to provide English-speaking students with the opportunity to learn French. Besides high proficiency in foreign language, positive attitude towards the people who speak the foreign language and towards their culture (s), the students' goals also included gaining designated skills and knowledge in the content areas of the curriculum, as well as commensurate English language skills.

(3) Immigrant On-Arrival Programs

It was a model for newly arrived immigrants in a country need for social survival, such as shopping, finding a job/accommodation and so forth. Australia was the first attempt to integrate notional, functional, grammatical, and lexical specifications built around particular themes and situations.

Gradually, Programs for Students with Limited English Proficiency (SLEP), English as a Second Language (ESL), Language for Specific Purposes (LSP) (such as EAP — English for Academic Purposes) and various programs have aroused more attention nowadays, aiming at getting limited language proficient learners as rapidly as possible for entry into mainstream courses in schools.

In short, CBI has enjoyed a fruitful popularity both in regular schools and programs in many different settings, covering all ages.

3.2 Features

CBI took root from Second Language Acquisition, Cooperative Learning, Cognitive Learning and many other theories. Leaver and Stryker pointed CBI in its purest form should have four characteristics:[②]

(1) Subject Matter Core

The fundamental organization of the curriculum should be derived from the subject matter, rather than from forms, functions, or situations. Communicative competence will be acquired

---

① RICHARDS J C, RODGERS T S. Approaches and Methods in Language Teaching[M]. 2nd ed. Cambridge University Press, 2001: 205-207.

② LEAVER B, STRYKER S B. Content-Based Instruction for Foreign Language Classrooms[J]. Foreign Language Annals, 1989, 2 (3), 269-275.

during the process of mastering content information on specific topics, such as social studies, culture, business, history, political systems, international affairs, economics, etc.

(2) Use of Authentic Texts

The core material (texts, video tapes, audio recordings, visual aids, etc.) should be selected primarily (but not exclusively) from those produced for native speakers of the language. The learning activities should be both expository and experiential in nature and focus on conveying real messages and accomplishing specific tasks.

(3) Learning of New Information

Students should use the foreign language to learn new information and to evaluate that information, based on knowledge of their own culture (C1) and their own emerging cultural literacy in the second culture (C2).

(4) Appropriate to the Specific Needs of Students

The topics, content, materials, and learning activities should correspond to the cognitive and affective needs of the students and should be appropriate to the proficiency level of the class.

3.3 Contemporary Models of Content-Based Instruction

The principles of CBI can be applied to the design of courses for learners at any level of language learning, mainly including Theme-Based Language Instruction, Sheltered Content Instruction and Adjunct Language Instruction. They form a continuum.

(1) Theme-Based Language Instruction

This refers to a language course in which the syllabus is organized around themes or topics. The language syllabus is subordinated to the more general theme. Language analysis and practice evolve out of the topics that form the framework for the course. A topic might be introduced through a reading, audio or video material, followed by written assignments integrating information from several different sources. Most of the materials used will typically be teacher-generated and the topic treated will cross all skills.

(2) Sheltered Content Instruction

This refers to content courses taught in the second language by a content area specialist, to a group of the ESL learners who have been grouped together for this purpose. Since the ESL students are not in a class together with native speakers, the instructor will be required to present the content in a way which is comprehensible to second language learners and in the process use language and tasks at an appropriate level of difficulty. Typically, the instructor will choose texts of a suitable difficulty level for the learners and adjust course requirements to accommodate the learners' language capacities.

(3) Adjunct Language Instruction

In this model, students are enrolled in two linked courses, one a content course and one a language course, with both courses sharing the same content base and complementing each other in terms of mutually coordinated assignments. Such a program requires a large amount of coordination to ensure that the two curriculums are interlocking and this may require modifications to both courses.

Brinton, Snow and Wesche summarize the above features in the Table 9-1:

Table 9-1　Main Features of Contemporary Models of Content-Based Instruction

	Theme-Based	Sheltered	Adjunct
Primary Purpose(s)	Help students develop L2 competence within specific topic areas	Help students master content material	Help students master content material. Introduce students to L2 academic discourse and develop transferable academic skills
Instructional Format	ESL course	Content course	Linked content and ESL courses
Instructional Responsibilities	Language instructor responsible for language and content instruction	Content instructor responsible for content instruction, incidental language learning	Content instructor responsible for content instruction; Language instructor responsible for language instruction
Student Population	Nonnative speakers	Nonnative speakers	Nonnative and native speakers integrated for content instruction; Nonnative speakers separated for language instruction
Curriculum	Topic-based curriculum units integrate all four skills	Content course syllabus. Study skills may be; integrated into content syllabus	Curriculum objectives coordinated between content and language staffs; Treatment of general language skills in addition to content-specific language skills
Focus of Evaluation	Language skills and functions	Content mastery	Content mastery (in content class); Language skills and functions (in language class)
Teacher Training	Language teachers need training in curriculum/ syllabus design and materials development	Content teachers need awareness of second language development	Language and content teachers need training in curriculum and syllabus design and in materials development; Training should focus on curriculum coordination and team teaching

3.4 Teaching Procedures

Since Content-Based Instruction refers to an approach rather than a method, no specific techniques or activities are associated with it. At the level of teaching procedures, teaching materials and activities are selected according to the extent to which they match the type of program it is. Stryker and Leaver describe a typical sequence of classroom procedures in a Content-Based lesson. The lesson is a Spanish lesson built around the viewing of the film *El Norte*.[①]

Preliminary Preparation: Students read reference materials regarding U.S. immigration laws as well as an extract from Octavio Paz's *El Laberinto de la Soledad*.

① Linguistic analysis: Discussion of grammar and vocabulary based on students' analysis of oral presentations done the day before.

② Preparation for the film: Activities previewing vocabulary in the film, including a vocabulary worksheet.

③ Viewing a segment of the film.

④ Discussion of the film: The teacher leads a discussion of the film.

⑤ Discussion of the reading.

⑥ Videotaped interview: Students see a short interview in which immigration matters are discussed.

⑦ Discussion: A discussion of immigration reform.

⑧ Preparation of articles: Students are given time to read related articles and prepare a class presentation.

⑨ Presentation of articles: Students make presentations, which may be taped so that they can later listen for self-correction.

⑩ Wrap-up discussion.

3.5 Teaching Techniques[②]

(1) Dictogloss

In a dictogloss, students listen twice to a short talk or a reading on appropriate content. The first time through, students listen for the main idea, and then the second time they listen for details. Next, students write down what they have remembered from the talk or reading. Some teachers have their students take notes while listening. The students then use their notes to reformulate what has been read. Students get practice in note-taking in this way. Next, they work with a partner or in a small group to construct together the best version of what they have heard. What they write is shared with the whole class for a peer-editing session. Through these processes, students become familiar with the organization of a variety of texts within a content area.

---

① RICHARDS J C, RODGERS T S. Approaches and Methods in Language Teaching[M]. Cambridge University Press, 2001: 219.

② LARSEN-FREEMAN D, ANDERSON M. Techniques and Principles in Language Teaching[M]. Oxford: Oxford University Press, 2011: 152-153.

(2) Graphic Organizers

Graphic organizers are visual displays that help students organize and remember new information. They involve drawing or writing down ideas and making connections. They combine words and phrases, symbols, and arrows to map knowledge. They include diagrams, tables, columns, and webs. Through the use of graphic organizers, students can understand text organization, which helps them learn to read academic texts and to complete academic tasks, such as writing a summary of what they have read. A key rationale for the use of graphic organizers in CBI is that they facilitate recall of cognitively demanding content, enabling students to process the content material at a deeper level and then be able to use it for language practice.

(3) Language Experience Approach

Students take turns dictating a story about their life experiences to the teacher who writes it down in the target language. Each student then practices reading his or her story with the teacher's assistance. The Language Experience Approach applies the principles of the Whole Language: The text is about content that is significant to the students; it is collaboratively produced; it is whole; and since it is the student's story, the link between text and meaning is facilitated.

(4) Process Writing

Traditionally, when teachers teach writing, they assign topics for students to write on; perhaps they do a bit of brainstorming about the topic during a pre-writing phase, and then have students write about the topic without interruption. Subsequently, teachers collect and evaluate what students have written. Such instruction is very "product-oriented"; there is no involvement of the teacher in the act or "process" of writing. In process writing, on the other hand, students may initially brainstorm ideas about a topic and begin writing, but then they have repeated conferences with the teacher and the other students, during which they receive feedback on their writing up to that point, make revisions, based on the feedback they receive, and carry on writing. In this way, students learn to view their writing as someone else's reading and to improve both the expression of meaning and the form of their writing as they draft and redraft. Process writing shifts the emphasis in teaching writing from evaluation to revision.

(5) Dialogue Journals

Another way to work on literacy skills is to have students keep dialogue journals. The particular way that journals are used varies, but it essentially involves students writing in their journals in class or for homework regularly, perhaps after each class or once a week. There may be a particular focus for the writing, such as the students' expressing their feelings toward how and what they are learning, or the writing focus could be on anything that the student wishes to communicate to the teacher. Usually it is the teacher who "dialogues" with the student, i.e., is the audience for the journal. The teacher reads the student's journal entry and writes a response to it, but does not correct its form.

三、教学原则与教学过程

1. 发展沿革与理论基础

尽管基于内容的教学法是圣·奥古斯丁早期提出的，但是直至 20 世纪 60 年代，它才变得越来越流行。内容教学法采用了交际法的教学原则，根据不同的项目，内容教学法至少包括以下三种模式：

（1）全科语言教学

这是一种在英国、美国和新加坡等地进行母语教学的模式。全科语言教学的理念是"每位老师都是英语老师"，并建议所有科目都将重点放在阅读和写作上。此外，还编写了将主题和语言教学目标结合在一起的教材。

（2）沉浸式教学

这是一种在正规学校中，对母语者进行外语教育的一种模式。沉浸式教学始于 20 世纪 60 年代的加拿大，其目的在于为说英语的学生提供学习法语的机会。学生的学习目标包括：较高的外语水平；对说外语的人及外来文化具有积极态度；在课程内容领域获得指定的技能和知识；相称的英语技能。

（3）移民入境计划

这是一个针对新移民的语言学习模式。新移民在一个国家需要生存，如购物、找工作、住宿，等等。澳大利亚是第一个尝试此种模式的国家，即围绕特定主题和情境，整合并构建概念、功能、语法以及词汇规范。

如今，面向"英语水平有限的学生"（SLEP），以及服务英语作为第二语言（ESL）、专门用途语言（LSP）（例如 EAP——学术英语）的教学项目和各种语言项目引起了广泛关注。这些项目旨在让对语言不太熟练的学习者尽快适应学校的主流课程。

简而言之，内容教学法在学校以及许多项目中都取得了丰硕的成果，适应各个年龄段的学习者。

2. 教学法特点

内容教学法的产生基于第二语言习得、合作学习、认知学习等理论。里弗和斯特赖克指出，内容教学法本身应具有四个特征：

（1）以主题为核心

课程的基本组织应围绕主题，而非形式、功能或情境。学生通过掌握社会、文化、商业、历史、政治制度、国际事务、经济学等特定领域的主题内容信息，获得交际能力。

（2）使用真实文本

教学核心材料（文本、视频、音频、视觉辅助材料等）应主要（但不仅限于）从为母语人士制作的材料中选择。学习活动本身应该是说明性的和体验性的，并且应着重传达真实的信息并完成特定的任务。

（3）学习新信息

学生应基于自己的文化背景（C1）以及已了解的第二种文化（C2）中的文化元素，用外语学习新信息并评估该信息。

（4）适合学生的特殊需求

主题、内容、材料和学习活动应与学生的认知和情感需求相对应，并应与班级的水平相适应。

3. 内容教学法的当代模式

内容教学法的原则可以应用于任何语言学习水平的课程设计，主要包括主题模式、保护模式和附加模式。它们结合在一起可以形成一个连续体。

（1）主题模式

语言课程大纲基于主题或话题展开。语言课程大纲从属于更广泛的主题。语言分析和实践从组成课程框架的主题中衍化而来。主题可以通过阅读、音频或视频材料来引入，随后进行书面任务，这项任务将整合不同来源的信息。教学材料由教师整理统合，聚焦于一个主题，并覆盖所有技能。

（2）保护模式

在这种模式中，第二语言（英语作为第二语言）学习者出于学习某一特殊内容主题而组成班级，由内容教学专家用第二语言（目的语）向学习者讲授课程。由于英语非母语的学习者不会与母语为英语的学生一起上课，教师将以二语学习者可以理解的方式呈现内容，并在此过程中使用难度适当的语言，布置水平相当的任务。教师通常会为学习者选择难度适当的文本，并调整课程要求以适应学习者的语言能力。

（3）附加模式

这种模式下，学生将参与两门课程，一门为内容课程，一门为语言课程。两门课程在内容上一致，在任务上相互补充。这种模式需要大量的商议协调，以确保两门课程有效衔接，这可能涉及对两门课程的修订。

布林顿、斯诺和威斯契总结了上述特点（表 9-1）：

表 9-1　内容教学法当代模式的主要特征表

	主题模式	保护模式	附加模式
首要目的	帮助学生发展特定主题领域的第二语言能力	帮助学生掌握内容材料	帮助学生掌握内容材料；向学生介绍第二语言学术领域语篇，发展可迁移的学术技能
教学形式	英语作为第二语言课程	内容课程	统合内容课程与英语作为第二语言的课程
教师责任	语言教师负责语言和内容教学	内容教师负责内容教学，附带语言学习	内容教师负责内容教学；语言教师负责语言教学
学生来源	非母语者	非母语者	内容教学中，非母语者与母语者共同上课；语言教学中，非母语者单独成班

续表

	主题模式	保护模式	附加模式
课程设置	整合了四项技能的主题课程	内容课程大纲 学习技巧可以整合到课程内容中	课程目标在内容和语言之间进行协调；除特定内容的语言技能外，还兼顾一般语言技能
评估焦点	语言技能和语言功能	掌握内容	掌握内容（在内容教学中）；语言技能和语言功能（在语言教学中）
教师培训	语言教师需要进行课程和教学大纲设计以及材料开发方面的培训	内容教师需要具有第二语言教学的意识	语言和内容的教师需要进行课程和教学大纲设计以及材料开发方面的培训；培训应注重课程协调和团队教学

4. 教学过程

内容教学法是一种教学路径，而非具体方法，因此没有特定的技术或活动与之关联。就过程而言，要根据内容与课程类型的匹配程度来选择教材和活动。里弗和斯特赖克在内容教学法示例中描述了课堂过程的典型顺序。该课程是一门围绕电影《北方》展开的西班牙语课程。

初步准备：学生阅读有关美国移民法的参考资料，以及奥克塔维奥·帕斯的诗歌《孤独的迷宫》摘录。

①语言分析：基于学生前一天对口头报告的分析，对语法和词汇进行讨论。

②准备电影：预览将会在电影中出现的词汇，完成一张词汇任务表。

③观看电影片段。

④有关电影的讨论：老师主持有关电影的讨论。

⑤有关阅读材料的讨论。

⑥观看访谈录像：学生看一个简短的采访，该采访讨论了移民问题。

⑦讨论：关于移民改革的讨论。

⑧汇报准备：留出时间让学生阅读相关文章并准备课堂展示。

⑨汇报展示：学生进行报告，录制报告内容以便日后回看进行自我更正。

⑩总结讨论。

5. 教学技巧

（1）合作听写

在一次合作听写中，学生听两遍材料，材料可以是一段简短的演讲或一篇内容合适的文章。第一遍，学生主要听取材料大意；第二遍学生主要听取细节。接下来，学生写下记住的内容。一些教师会让学生边听材料边做笔记。随后，学生可以使用他们的笔记重新整理内容。学生可以通过这种方式完成练习。接下来，他们通过与伙伴或小组合作的方式，共同完善他们听到的最佳版本。学生编写的内容将与全班同学共享，进行学生互评。这些过程将使学生熟悉特定内容领域文本组织的不同方式。

（2）图谱化组织

图谱化组织指通过内容可视化帮助学生组织并记住新信息。学生绘制或写下想法，并在想法间建立联系，结合单词和短语、符号和箭头来构建知识地图，包括图、表、层级框架和网络等。运用图谱化组织，学生能够深入了解文本的组织结构，有助于他们阅读学术文章并完成学术任务，例如撰写所读内容的摘要。在内容教学法中使用这一方法的一个重要性在于，它会帮助学生回忆较难理解的内容，使学生能够更深入地处理内容材料，然后将其用于语言练习。

（3）语言体验法

学生轮流给教师讲故事，讲述他们的生活经历，并用目的语写下来。然后，每个学生都在教师的帮助下练习阅读他（她）的故事。语言体验法遵循全语言法的原则：文本是对学生有意义的内容，是经过协作产生的，它具有整体性，并且由于这些文本是学生的故事，因此文本和意义之间的联系得到了促进。

（4）过程写作法

教师教授写作时，往往会给学生分配写作主题。也许学生们在预写阶段已就该主题进行了一些头脑风暴，然后让学生一口气写下有关该主题的内容。随后，教师收集并评估学生所写的内容。这种指导是"以产出为导向"的，教师没有参与写作这一行为或写作的"过程"。不过，在过程写作法的模式下，学生可能会首先就某个主题进行头脑风暴并开始写作，但随后他们将与教师和其他学生反复交谈，他们将在这一过程中收到对自己写作内容的反馈，并对文章进行修改，再根据反馈意见继续写作。这种方式会使学生把自己的写作内容视为他人的阅读材料，并在起草和重新修订时优化自己的表达方式和写作形式。过程写作将教学的重点从评估转移到了修改。

（5）对话日记

提高写作能力的一种方法是让学生记录对话日记。记录的形式可以各不相同，但本质上都是让学生定期在课堂上或作为家庭作业来进行记录，可以是在每堂课后记录，也可以每周记录一次作为作业记录。在写不同的对话日记时，可能会有不同的侧重点，例如：学生可以表达对学习方式和学习内容的感受，或者其他希望与教师交流的任何内容。通常是由教师与学生进行"对话"，也就是说，教师成为该"对话日记"的读者。教师会阅读学生的对话日记并对一些对话条目做出回应，但不会更正其形式。

4 Conclusion

Since the 1980s, CBI aims to organically combine language learning with subject knowledge learning as well as cognitive improvement. During its development, it has undergone different changes and developments. The main difference lies in whether the focus of the teaching objectives is language ability or subject knowledge. When teachers choose content teaching methods, they should have a strong sense of purpose and clarify the difficulties of teaching. They can choose different teaching modes according to different purposes, and they can also break the boundaries between the modes to make flexible choices according to the teaching objects, teaching goals and teaching situations.

CBI provides another way to make language learning more interesting and motivating. Students can use the language to fulfill a real purpose, which can make students both more independent and confident. Students can also develop a much wider knowledge of the world through CBI which can feed back into improving and supporting their general educational needs. Taking information from different sources, reevaluating and restructuring that information can help students develop very valuable thinking skills that can then be transferred to other subjects. The inclusion of a group work element can also help students develop their collaborative skills, which can have great social value.

On the other hand, still, "CBI isn't explicitly focused on language learning. Some students may feel confused or may even feel that they aren't improving their language skills."[①] Besides, it's also important that a school system should involve CBI in the total syllabus design or in modular form. Although CBI has some successful cases, it still remains much, however, to be explored and understood. As Snow said, researches and experimentations with innovative techniques and approaches should continue — "all in the name of exploiting the Content-Based setting for its rich resources that improve our understanding of second/foreign language teaching and learning."[②]

四、小结

自 20 世纪 80 年代以来，内容教学法旨在有机结合语言学习与学科知识学习，注重提高学生的认知能力。在其发展过程中，改变和革新不可避免，主要分歧点在于教学目标的重点是语言能力还是学科知识。教师选用内容教学法时，要有较强的目标意识，明确教学重难点，可以根据不同的教学目的选择不同的教学模式，也可根据教学对象、教学目标和教学情境的不同，打破模式间界限，进行灵活选择。

内容教学法无疑提供了一种让语言学习更加有趣并激发学生学习动力的方法。学生可以通过使用语言在真实场景中实现交际目的，这样会使学生更加独立、更加自信。学生还可以从接受内容教学的过程中获得更广泛的知识，起到教育效果。从不同来源获取信息、重新评估和整合信息也可以帮助学生提升思维能力，并且迁移至其他学科的学习中。小组合作的方式也会帮助学生提高协作能力，具有很高的社会价值。

① BAO Z M, HU S S. Content-Based Instruction in Foreign Language Learning [J]. Zhouyi Research, 2014 (5): 1-2.

② SNOW M A. Trends and Issues in Content-Based instruction [J]. Annual Review of Applied Linguistics, 1998: 18.

但是，"内容教学法没有明确地专注于语言学习，有些学生可能会感到困惑，甚至可能会感到他们没有提高自身的语言技能。"此外，学校还需要在整个课程大纲中（或以模块形式出现）有机纳入内容教学法课程内容。尽管内容教学法已有一些成功案例，不过仍有许多值得进一步探索的地方。正如斯诺所说，运用新技术和新方法的研究和实验应当继续下去——"一切都是为了充分利用内容教学法提供的丰富资源，这些资源可以增进我们对第二语言/外语教学的理解。"

○ Activities and Exercises

● Understanding and Thinking

1. Based on the following materials, state the similarities and differences between language focused course and content focused course.

Material 1

An English lesson in a Grade 3 classroom in the U.S.: Nearly all the students come from Hispanic background. Some speak mostly English at home; others speak Spanish as their home language. All students have had about half their schooling in English and half in Spanish since kindergarten. Teacher A sees the students for about 30 minutes a week, for a lesson that is focused on reading and writing in English.

Teacher A: I want you to tell me about your spring break. Tell me in a complete sentence what you did on your spring break. First, I'll tell you what I did. On my spring break, I visited my sister in California.

Student 1: On my spring break, I went to New York.

Teacher A: Did you go with your parents?

Student 1: No, with my grandma.

Student 2: On my spring break, I went to the park.

Teacher A: The weather was great, wasn't it? Did you ride your bike?

Student 2: Yes.

Student 3: On my spring break, I played with my friends.

Teacher A: Nice.

Student 4: On my spring break, I went to the hospital to see my aunt.

Teacher A: Was she sick?

Student 4: She was in an accident.

Teacher A: Is she all right?

Student 4: Yes, she went home now.

Teacher A: Good.

Student 5: On my spring break, I have a sleepover with my friends.

Teacher A: You had a sleepover? At your house?

Student 5: Yes.

Teacher A: Who did something really exciting?

Student 6: I go to Disney World.

Teacher A: On my spring break, I...

Student 6: I went to Disney World.

Teacher A: That is exciting.

Material 2

A mathematics lesson with the same Grade 3 students: Teacher B is with the students for most of every school day in alternate weeks, teaching all subjects in Spanish. Another teacher is with the students every other week, teaching all subjects in English. The lesson in Material 2 was taught in Spanish and is translated here.

Teacher B does a brief review of multiplication. Students quickly and accurately provide the answers as she writes examples such as 3×2 and 4×2 on the board. Then she writes $3 \times 4 \times 2$ on the board.

Teacher B: Who knows how to do this one? Can we multiply three numbers?

Several Students: You can't do that.

Teacher B: Why not?

Sandra: You have to multiply two numbers.

Teacher B: Are you sure? Who thinks you can do this? Hector, do you want to try?

Hector: [comes to the board and writes $3 \times 4 = 12$ and $4 \times 2 = 8$]

Teacher B: What do you think, class? Is that how you do it? Who has another idea? Natalie.

Natalie: [comes to the board and writes $3 \times 4 = 12$ and then stops]

Teacher B: What do you think she should do next?

Students: Multiply by 2.

2. Based on the following materials, talk about your understanding of Content-Based Instruction and illustrate what should be paid attention to when implementing CBI in class.

Material 1

An example of objectives in CBI comes from the Theme-Based Intensive Language Course (ILC) at the Free University of Berlin. Four objectives were identified for its yearlong, multi-theme program. These objectives were linguistic, strategic, and cultural. Objectives were:

① *To activate and develop existing English language skills.*

② *To acquire learning skills and strategies that could be applied in future language development opportunities.*

③ *To develop general academic skills applicable to university studies in all subject areas.*

④ *To broaden students' understanding of English-speaking peoples.*

Material 2

Stryker and Leaver suggests the following essential skills for any CBI instructor:

① *Varying the format of classroom instruction.*

② *Using group work and team-building techniques.*

③ *Organizing jigsaw reading arrangements.*

④ *Defining the background knowledge and language skills required for student success.*

⑤ *Helping students develop coping strategies.*

⑥ *Using process approaches to writing.*

⑦ *Using appropriate error correction techniques.*

⑧ *Developing and maintaining high levels of student esteem.*

3. With reference to the following materials, discuss the principles and characteristics of selecting teaching contents and resources in CBI class.

Material 1

According to Brinton et al., the following points concerning text selection for Content-Based courses should be noted:

Content authenticity; task authenticity; interest level; difficulty level; accessibility; availability; packaging; textual aids; supporting materials; flexibility; source.

Material 2

On the other hand, in the organization of the Intensive Language Course at the Free University of Berlin consists of a sequence of modules spread over the academic year. The topical themes of the modules are:

① *Television.*

② *Religious Persuasion.*

③ *Advertising.*

④ *Drugs.*

⑤ *Britain and the Race Question.*

⑥ *Native Americans.*

⑦ *Modern Architecture.*

⑧ *Microchip Technology.*

⑨ *Ecology.*

⑩ *Alternative Energy.*

⑪ *Nuclear Energy.*

⑫ *Dracula in Myth, Novel, and Films.*
⑬ *Professional Ethics.*

● **Teaching Design**

1. Please study the characteristics of CBI intensively, choose one material below, design the teaching details, and then make a teaching demonstration in groups.

Material 1

Procedure[①]

There were two pre-courses ahead, a content component and an ESOL component. The content part was an undergraduate literature course entitled Human Rights in Literature and Art. The class, which was composed of 150 native speakers, met three times a week: two 1-hour lectures with the course professor, and a 1-hour discussion session with teaching assistants in six smaller groups. The texts used in this course were novels, dramas, and films.

The following texts were used during the 8-week period of the Pre-course:
● *Monsieur Toussaint, a play by Edouard Glissant.*
● *The Communist Manifesto, by Karl Marx.*
● *Vindication of the Rights of Women, by Mary Wollstonecraft.*
● *The Subjection of Women, by John Stuart Mill.*
● *My Bondage/My Freedom, by Frederick Douglas.*
● *Anthills of the Savannah, by Chinua Achebe.*
● *I Will Fight No More Forever (a film).*
● *Incident at Oglala — The Leonard Peltier Story (a film).*

The ESOL component of the Precourse was an advanced English for Academic Purposes course offered in the Center for English as a Second Language (CESL) at the University of Arizona in Spring Session II, 1994. In the class there were thirteen ESOL students from six countries: five came from Kazakhstan, two from the United Arab Emirates, three from Korea, and one each from Saudi Arabia, Jordan, and Japan. The class met 5 days a week for a total of 7 hours. Instruction in this course was based completely on the content materials in the literature course.

Material 2[②]

The following is the teaching plan of this reading named A Night the Earth Didn't Sleep.

(1) Teaching Objectives

① *Knowledge and ability objective: Students can use new words and phrases that appear*

---

① HESS N, GHAWI M. English for academic purposes: Teacher development in a demanding arena [J]. English for Specific Purposes, 1997, 16(1): 15-26.
② 秦瑶. 内容教学法在高中英语阅读教学中的应用研究 [D]. 开封：河南大学，2019.

in this unit to make new sentences. What's more, students can understand the causes and signs of the earthquake, the damage caused by the earthquake, the emergency measures during the earthquake, and the rescue after the earthquake.

② Process and method objective: Through the guidance of the teacher, students learn some reading skills. Different teaching activities can help improve their abilities to work with others in groups.

③ Emotional and value objective: To make students understand the scientific common sense of the cause of earthquakes, strengthen the literacy of natural sciences, and stimulate enthusiasm for science. In addition, let the students know what a correct attitude towards a disaster is and what they should do in a disaster for themselves and for the other people.

(2) Teaching Aids: Multi-media, a Computer, and Pictures

(3) Teaching Procedures

Step I Pre-reading

Activity 1. Presentation. Before this class, students are asked to collect the relevant materials about earthquake in the group and make a class presentation in the form of drama and speech. Therefore, at the beginning of this class, two groups are asked to display the information related to this topic "earthquake". Group 1: Mini-play. Students in this group give the situation performance at the time of the earthquake. Group 2: Speech. Students in this group give the speech to introduce the reasons for the earthquake. After the presentation of each group. The teacher gives an evaluation. The purpose of this design is to make students actively explore the content to be learned before the class, and stimulate students' curiosity.

Activity 2. Lead-in. Let students watch a video about earthquake. After their watching, the teacher tries to guide the students to find out the characteristics of the earthquake. Then students are asked to think about this question: What should we do if the earthquake strikes? In the process of students' answering, the teacher can give an evaluation and provides some supplementary explanation timely. The purpose of this design is to inspire students' background knowledge and guide students to prepare for the learning of this reading essay.

Step II Skimming and Scanning

Activity 1. According to the title of the article A Night the Earth Didn't Sleep, *the teacher asks students to think about why the title should be named in this way. Then students are given five minutes to quickly browse the text. After their fast reading, students are encouraged to find out the main idea of this article and explain the meaning of the title.*

Activity 2. The students read the article quickly again. Then they are asked to divide the content of this article into three parts, and summarize the meaning of each part.

Step III Detailed Reading

Activity 1. Students are asked to read this article carefully. Then the teacher writes down some questions on the blackboard for students to answer. Students in different groups have a competition by getting scores in a limited time. They can discuss these questions in groups and the winners can get a little gift from the teacher. The questions about the passage A Night the Earth Didn't Sleep *are as follows: What are the predictions of an earthquake? Why is the Tangshan Earthquake causing such a large casualty? How is the rescue work carried out after the earthquake? If you lived in that era, how would you help the people in Tangshan?*

Activity 2. There is a debate for students in different groups. Two groups are chosen to have a debate according to their own understanding. The teacher presents the question. What are the decisive factors that helped Tangshan recover from the earthquake, help from the other people or the spirit of the Tangshan people? Students can express their true feelings justifiably.

Step IV Post-reading

The teacher presents an extracurricular reading essay on the multimedia. Then students read this news excerpted from the Global Times on August 9th, 2017. With the help of the teacher, students try to have a general idea about how to write news report after reading.

Step V Homework

Task 1. The reading materials in this unit mention that many children have lost their parents in the earthquake and the People's Liberation Army struggle to save people regardless of their own safety. The teacher makes students choose one aspect to write a news report about the earthquake.

Task 2. Read the article Earthquakes Around the Pacific *and combine the Tangshan Earthquake learned in this lesson to create a poster about earthquake.*

Material 3①

Topics are the subunits of content which explore more specific aspects of the theme. They are selected to complement student interests, content resources, teacher preferences, and larger curricular objectives. In general, topics should be organized to generate maximum coherence for the theme unit and to provide opportunities to explore both content and language. A given theme, unit will evolve differently depending on the specific topics selected for exploration.

2. Please revise or fulfill the following teaching plan in details according to the theory and teaching principles of CBI.

In a unit on fast food, it might consist of the following:

① A prereading exercise matching product ingredient listed on the labels with the product type.

---

① STOLLER F L, GRABE W. A Six-T's Approach to Content-Based Instruction[M]. New York: Longman, 1997:174-192.

② *A reading taken from the food section of a local newspaper describing how selected pizzerias compare with one another.*

③ *A longer reading (from the core ESL text) analyzing the fast-food phenomenon as a reflection of societal change.*

Table 9-2　Different Sets of Topics Which Can Define a Theme Unit

Theme	One Set of Sample Topics	Another Set of Sample Topics
Insects	a. Insects which are helpful b. Insects which are harmful c. Insects which eat other insects d. Insects which eat vegetatio	a. Ants b. Bees c. Caterpillars
Solar system	a. Humans in space b. Technology in space c. Research in space d. Pluto	a. Earth b. Venus c. Mercury
Demography	Impact of population on a. air b. water c. natural resources	Population trends a. in developing countries b. in developed countries c. and their impact on the environment

④ *A song satirizing the fast-food craze.*

⑤ *An off-air radio broadcast discussing eating out at a local fast-food outlet.*

⑥ *A film presenting a foreigner's impression of the local cuisine.*

⑦ *A video describing the clientele of several local fast-food chains and analyzing their respective advertising strategies.*

● **Further Reading**

Content-Based Instruction in Tertiary Education in China[1]

Content-Based Instruction (CBI) is a pedagogical approach in which language classes are integrated with students' content subject(s). The approach has enjoyed increasing popularity since the 1980s. The term CBI has gained wide acceptance in education institutions in the United States. In the United Kingdom as well as other European countries, however, CLIL (Content Language Integrated Learning) seems more popular. Since most CBI courses take place in academic settings and aim at both language acquisition and academic success, the approach inevitably shares some common ground with English for Academic Purposes (EAP) as a subset of

① 都建颖 , 布鲁 . Content-Based Instruction in Tertiary Education in China[J]. 英语研究 , 2008, 6(1): 1-7.

English for Specific Purposes (ESP). Although the term CBI remains new in China, the approach itself has great potential among Chinese students as EFL learners. It is the aim of this thesis to evaluate the effectiveness of CBI in tertiary education in China, where the non-English-major students learn English as a compulsory course alongside a content subject that relates closely to their future career.

1. The Effectiveness of CBI Depends on Appropriate Use of the Approach

There are many successful examples on CBI in the Chinese colleges and universities. However, the approach itself does not guarantee success. An effective CBI program depends heavily on the teachers' appropriate use of the approach, which is closely related to the teachers' understanding of CBI. It is the purpose of this section to reintroduce the concept of CBI as well as its application.

(1) The Evolutionary Side of CBI

There are many forms of content and language integration including L2 content teaching and ESP (English for specific purposes) or EAP (English for academic purposes) in academic settings. However, CBI differentiates itself from these approaches due to the following features:

① CBI is not L2 content teaching although the L2 content text is used in the class.

② Content teaching refers to the content classes where the target language is the only medium of teaching. This approach is similar to the immersion program, where content mastery is the only purpose of instruction. The students are expected to acquire the language as the byproduct of the approach. However, the immersion students might be "submerged" if their language and content background is not matched with the language and the content introduced in the classes.

Although there is a certain amount of L2 use in CBI classes to introduce some content-area information, CBI is different from L2-medium content teaching. First of all, the students have full L1 access to the content area information. In the Chinese market, it is more convenient for the teachers and the students to get L1 content materials than those written in L2. Most content courses are taught in L1 as the mother tongue shared by the teachers and the students. Secondly, the students' content study is not the only focus of the CBI classes. The use of L2 content text in CBI may lead to an in-depth understanding of some content-related concepts and information.

Sometimes, however, the students' content-area language skills may carry more weight in the CBI curriculum. Both the language and the content can be at the center of different stages of a CBI program.

③ CBI is not EAP although explicit language teaching may take place in the approach.

The EAP approach aims to develop the students' language skills in order to support their study or research in the content area. An EAP curriculum is composed of linguistic features and register or discourse analysis in the academic field. The aviation English course for colleges and universities in China, for example, follows a framework in which an aviation English course should include corpus study of the language and register and/or discourse analysis in the field.

④ CBI is not bilingual education although both L1 and L2 are used in the approach.

Since both L1 and L2 (i.e., English in the Chinese context) are used in the CBI classes, there is a misunderstanding that CBI is bilingual education. The purpose of bilingual education is to develop the students' L1 and L2 knowledge and help them to be bilingual and bicultural. Although some CBI students may achieve a bilingual state, bilingualism is not the aim of the CBI teachers' use of L2 or L1 + L2. It is not unusual in CBI and the EAP classes that the students try to find the L1 equivalents of the L2 items, while the teachers are focusing on the L2 as the target language. Instead of bilingualism and biculturalism, the CBI approach aims at the students' development in content, L2 and cognitive skills.

It can be seen from the above mentioned three features that the evolutionary side of CBI lies in its concurrent focus on the language and the content. The term "Content-Based Language Teaching", which is sometimes named as "Content-Based Instruction" (CBI), is rejected by researchers like Davison and Williams. They suggest that "language and content integration" is more appropriate a term to describe the range from contextualized language teaching and language-conscious content teaching.

Davison and Williams' term seems safer than CBI. However, contextualized language teaching and language-conscious content teaching are not always two different approaches. Although the former focuses on the language and the latter places more emphasis on the content knowledge, the weight of language and content varies in the classes during the same CBI program. That is, the teachers changed the focus of teaching and other pedagogical activities according to the students' needs.

(2) The Link Between CBI and Other Approaches: the Traditional Side of CBI

CBI as an evolutionary approach does not indicate its isolation from other traditional approaches. On the contrary, an effective CBI program depends heavily on appropriate use of those approaches.

In the Chinese context, most students receive L2 skills through grammar-translation approach before they enter the further or higher educational settings. This English language teaching method in traditional Chinese school settings include introducing grammatical items, practicing the usage of words and expressions and sentence level translation. The method is believed to be effective in helping the students understand and memorize the text. The use of traditional language approaches in CBI can also be found in CLIL (Content Language Integrated Learning) programs in many ESL settings including France and Germany. It may take time for the students to accommodate to CBI as a new approach. However, the effectiveness of the grammar-translation approach in introducing linguistic rules indicates that the CBI teachers do not need to avoid explicit language teaching through the traditional approaches.

The evolutionary side of CBI is reflected by its concurrent focus on language, content and the students' cognitive abilities. However, this aim is hardly achievable through activities in the CBI classes. According to Van Lier, "language development occurs between lessons rather than during lessons". Task-Based Language Teaching provides an effective way or balancing what is done in the classroom and what is done outside the classroom. In this sense, tasks in the CBI approach should satisfy the criteria proposed by Skehan.

— Meaning is primary.

— There is a goal which needs to be worked towards.

— The activity is outcome-evaluated.

— There is a real-world relationship.

and, as far as Van Lier's argument is concerned.

— There is a reasonable gap between the classroom knowledge and abilities required for the fulfillment of the task.

Content-related tasks, as well as the student homework, provide opportunities for the students to practice language and content knowledge that is introduced in the CBI classes. The process of completing the tasks also helps the students develop their cognitive skills. They need to decide what kind of information to use and how to attain the information. Before presenting the self-collected information, the students experience a process of information analyzing and synthesizing.

In brief, Task-Based Language Teaching can be used by the teachers to improve the efficiency and effectiveness of the CBI classes. These tasks are either language- or content-oriented. The teacher can decide the difficulty of the tasks according to the students' language and content background. The popularity of Task-Based Language Teaching in CBI is also reflected by CLIL teachers in European countries, as reported by Wolff.

A growing number of CLIL/MLAC teachers are also trying to introduce project work, independent learning, and learning strategies into classroom pedagogy. They have realised that there is a great pedagogical potential in a CLIL learning environment. Although in general these teachers base their teaching on written materials from various sources, they also have their pupils work on these materials more independently in small groups by giving them tasks to solve and by encouraging them to use other materials at their disposal. These materials can be language materials (dictionaries, grammars) but also content subject materials (authentic materials from other sources, for example reviews, text-books, the Internet).

2. The Effectiveness of CBI on Students' Content, Language and Cognitive Development

Most Chinese students claim that they want to learn English and are aware of the significance of a high level of English language proficiency. Traditional language classes do not seem to fully develop the students' language abilities, and the students are blamed by both the teachers and themselves for not making enough effort. It is the purpose of this section to illustrate the difference that CBI has made in students' language, content and cognitive development through emphasis on the quality of exposure-language, student participation in CBI tasks and activities, and the development of the learner autonomy.

(1) The Quality of the Exposure-Language

The quality of the exposure-language may be important in second language acquisition. In China as an EFL context, however, the students do not normally have a rich L2 environment. Most of their exposure-language comes from the L2 classes. To most students, the teaching in traditional language classes is more likely "gardening in a gale": The teachers plant "tender seedlings" of the target language in the class, which are blown away as soon as the students go out into the corridor and the playground. In this sense, the amount of language exposure can hardly be fruitful without the students forcing themselves to regularly recall what has been introduced in the L2 classes.

The exposure-language in the CBI classes may be not as rich as that in the general language classes. However, the students have received better quality of the exposure-language in the CBI classes. In Van Lier's words, "the learner can make sense of it, is receptive to it, and makes an effort to process it."

The CBI teachers provide the students with some L2 content texts as the course materials. Compared with the L2 materials provided in the general language classes, these texts seem boring since there are no pictures, graphs and audio-visual materials as the supplementary resources. However, the content-related CBI materials are usable to the students since, in Van Lier's words, the learners can make sense of the exposure-language by relating it to their content background. Meanwhile, the students are receptive to the language since they find what they are learning is useful and bear realistic meaning to their future profession.

Consequently, the students are willing to make an effort to process the language knowledge in and outside of the CBI classes. The students' effort is proved by their extra time investment in the CBI program.

(2) Enhanced Engagement

The usable and useful exposure-language provided in the CBI classes motivates the students to use it in the legal context. It raises the students' spirit of exploration. Guided by the tasks issued in the classes, the students practise the language items and explore the content knowledge. This is a significant process in which the students develop their content and cognitive abilities.

Being interested in the usable language skills and curious about how to use them, the students are engaged in a variety of content-related tasks. In order to fulfill the tasks, they need to fill the gap between the known and the unknown information. It is the students' responsibility to figure out what is known, what they need to know, where and how to find the information, and what to do after finding it.

(3) Autonomous Learning

Choice and responsibility are the two central features of learner autonomy. In a CBI program, the teachers provide the exposure-language and decide the feature of the tasks (i.e., language- or content-oriented). Being responsible for the accomplishment of the tasks, the students choose what they need from what is offered by the teacher. They also decide what else to add in order to fulfill the tasks.

Individuality is emphasized in the program. The teachers pushed the students to complete the tasks. Meanwhile, they encourage the students to pay attention to how others fulfill the tasks and to finish them in their own way. In brief, the CBI program provides opportunities for the students to practice, evaluate and maybe discover learning strategies and thus make their study more energy-efficient.

3. Teacher Development Required by CBI

The CBI experience in many academic settings in China, including the teachers' different attitude towards CBI as well as their different degree of participation in the program, indicates that a successful CBI program is not possible without the teachers' development in their educational attitude and professional abilities. The following conclusions are, however, should not be viewed as CBI-specific.

Students are responsible for their own study, but the teacher should be capable of and willing to provide assistance.

In the CBI progam, the students are encouraged to take care of their study by selecting materials and solving content- or language-related problems in their own ways. The teachers often let the students decide the coverage of their homework.

The students' responsibility for their own study, however, does not relive the teachers of their role as assistants in the students' overall development. While providing the students with academic information and advice for effective learning, the teachers should also reflect on their academic and pedagogic capability and attitude. They need to invest some interest in the new approaches and keep an open mind to criticism of the approaches they have applied in the classroom. Self-improvement is critical although it can be challenging in most cases.

Authentic materials need to be used in the classes, but it is the teachers' responsibility to authenticate the materials.

A significant role of the CBI teachers is to authenticate the materials. Materials used in the CBI classes are regarded as authentic not only because these materials are written in L2. The students' needs and their educational background are taken into account when the teachers select the materials. The students are also encouraged to seek materials from various resources.

It is on the basis of precise need analysis that the teachers select the CBI materials. However, it takes more for the teachers to authenticate them. Need analysis enables the teachers to know what the students need to learn, while authentication addresses the students' genuine belief that they are doing what they need or want to do. Authenticity is, as stated by Van Lier, "the result and the origin of awareness and autonomy."

The CBI approach contains motivational factors, but the effectiveness of these factors depends on how motivating the teacher is.

The CBI approach aims to enhance the students' motivation in language learning by involving meaningful content materials in language classes. However, the teachers' effort is needed to motivate the students: an approach can be motivational but the students might not be motivated. In other words, motivational and motivating are two different concepts. The former is related to choosing appropriate teaching method and materials, and the latter values the appropriate application of the method and materials.

According to Deci et al., "intrinsically motivated behaviors are engaged in for their own sake — for the pleasure and satisfaction derived from their performance." By contrast, extrinsically motivated behaviors are related to the outer world reward and self-evaluation of the behaviors which is affected by a variety of external factors. Based on the understanding of the interdependence of the intrinsic and extrinsic motivation, the teachers should strive to make the in-class activities enjoyable for the students. At the same time, they should also make the students realize that learning is not always fun. Effort is demanded for any type of studying, especially in academic settings.

The integration of language and content teaching in China can be traced back to the 1860s. With the efforts of government officials, the integrative approach aiming at studying abroad for a limited number of students was proved successful. However, this educational reform vanished with the political failure of its government advocates. A new wave of language and content integration started in China in the 1980s. CBI in China is still at its initial stage. Theoretically, CBI is mixed with other language approaches including bilingual education and English language for specific purposes. Practically, critical issues such as teaching materials, teachers' development and teaching models are subject to further research and practice.

EIGHT APPROACHES TO CONTENT-BASED INSTRUCTION[①]

One of the best-known approaches to CBI is one we label the Center for Applied Linguistics (CAL) approach. For a number of years, CAL has been being carried out broad-based research on CBI and training K-12 teachers in content-area instruction to make learning tasks more

---

① STOLLER F L, GRABE W A Six-T's Approach to Content-Based Instruction [M]. New York: Longman, 1997 (5): 174–192.

manageable for language-minority students. CAL's efforts have focused on (1) how to integrate the teaching of content and language, (2) how the language used in particular academic content areas may create comprehension problems — not due to the content but to the language itself, and (3) how to assess students' knowledge of language and subject matter. Based on CAL's activities across the United States, and its analysis of language demands in different content areas, many instructional recommendations, teaching techniques, and assessment tools have been developed to achieve CBI objectives.

A second well-known set of approaches to CBI follows from discussions of English for Academic Purposes (EAP) instruction at North American universities. This work is best represented by studies reported in Adamson, Brinton, Snow, Wesche, Met, and Genesee. They suggest that Content-Based EAP instruction may follow one of three prototype models: sheltered instruction, adjunct instruction, and theme-based instruction. In the two former models of instruction (sheltered and adjunct), content is relatively predetermined; in the latter case (theme-based), content is selected by the language teacher (and/or students). Extensions of this framework — from strictly EAP contexts to other instructional contexts — have also been explored.

A third approach, sometimes overlapping with the second one, is that of university-level foreign language CBI. There are two distinct contexts for this general approach. The first involves foreign language instruction that is organized around cultural, geographic, historical, political, and literary themes. For example, in North America, students might attend a university language course defined by a curriculum that is centered on content themes related to the countries in which the language is spoken. The second context involves instruction in non-language courses (e.g., philosophy, history, anthropology, political science) that makes extensive use of informational resources in a foreign language or in content courses taught in a foreign language. The latter two contexts have, at times, made use of sheltered and adjunct formats to combine language and content.

A fourth distinguishable approach is that developed by Mohan. In this approach to K-12 language and content instruction, learning centers around the use of discoursal knowledge structures to convey content information. The key to the approach is the assertion that all content information is organized according to six basic types of knowledge structures: description, sequence, choice, classification, principles, and evaluation. The first three types of knowledge structures (description, sequence, and choice) represent more specific ways to organize information; the latter three (classification, principles, and evaluation) represent more general patterns for organizing knowledge, allowing for generalization and theorizing. Regardless of the persuasiveness of Mohan's overall theory of knowledge structures, the approach provides a pedagogical framework for combining content and language instruction, as well as for helping students develop higher order thinking skills. This approach provides teachers with a natural forum for introducing detailed content information while also helping students see the discourse patterns that support and organize many types of content knowledge. It is assumed that the identification of underlying knowledge structures in one topic area, signaled in various ways through the language used, will transfer to other content areas, thereby providing students with skills for future classroom settings. Mohan and Tang emphasize the importance of using graphic representations to reveal textual knowledge structures and to help students develop competence in academic discourse. The coordination of language and content learning resulting from this approach to CBI reinforces knowledge structures and teaches related language functions and forms.

A fifth approach to CBI is that of researchers in Australia who propose a Genre-Based Approach to K-12 literacy instruction with a content emphasis. Based on Halliday's functional theory of language use, this approach proposes that language forms and language uses serve communicative functions; these functions are reflected in basic instructional genres which students can recognize and then use for their own learning purposes. In this respect, the Genre-Based Approach is similar to the Canadian approach presented by Mohan.

A sixth approach is that of language immersion programs in K-12 contexts in North America. In these instructional contexts, content which is normally taught to first language students is taught to students in their second language. Extensive research documents the relative success of this approach. However, little attention has been given to how to teach content in a way that is appropriate for L2 learners, and little discussion is reported of ways that instruction is specifically designed to focus on and enhance language learning.

A seventh approach is the Cognitive Academic Language Learning Approach, or CALLA. Initially developed for L2 students in North American secondary education contexts, this approach combines emphases on language development, content-area instruction, and explicit strategy training. Its goal is to prepare language minority students to handle advanced academic skills and content knowledge in mainstream classrooms. In CALLA lessons, content drives decisions about academic language objectives and the types of learning strategies that are appropriate. Just as Mohan's model reinforces the importance of graphic organizers, the CALLA approach relies heavily on scaffolding, that is, "the provision of extensive instructional supports when concepts and skills are being first introduced and the gradual removal of supports when students begin to develop greater proficiency, skills, or knowledge".

An eighth approach combining language and content instruction is a version of whole language instruction explored by Enright and McCloskey and others in elementary school contexts. In this approach, instruction centers on thematic units or theme cycles which integrate language-skills instruction and content information from social studies, natural science, arts, math, and so on. The emphasis is on purposeful language use to communicate personally important and motivating content. Thematic units are developed by brainstorming possible topics within a theme, transitioning between topics to provide thematic coherence, and developing a culminating task to complete the cycle.

An examination of these eight approaches to CBI leads us to believe that there is, in fact, much more overlap among them than the preceding classificatory discussion would indicate. These approaches (and perhaps a few others) share a number of common features which any good CBI program would want to incorporate and which we have tried to incorporate into our Six-T's Approach. In general, these approaches promote student involvement in content learning, provide opportunities for student negotiation of language and content tasks, allow for cooperative learning, focus on the development of discourse-based abilities, and use content materials that should motivate students.

● **Knowledge Table**

Table 9-3　Summary of Characteristics of Content-Based Instruction

Key Points	Content-Based Instruction
Period	
Representatives	
Background	
Theory of Language	
Theory of Language Learning	
Objectives	
The Syllabus	
Types of Learning and Teaching Activities	
Teacher's Roles	
Learner's Roles	
The Role of Students' Native Language and Target Language	
The Role of Instructional Materials and Textbook	
Others	
Summary	

● **Mind Map**

Chapter 10　Task-Based Language Teaching

第 10 章　任务型教学法

Contents

- Teaching Cases of Task-Based Language Teaching
- Definitions of Task
- Classifications of Tasks
- Teaching Principles of Task-Based Language Teaching
- Teaching Procedures of Task-Based Language Teaching
- Comments on Task-Based Language Teaching
- Activities and Exercises

- 任务型教学法教学示例
- 任务的定义
- 任务的类型
- 任务型教学法的教学原则
- 任务型教学法的教学过程
- 对任务型教学法的评价
- 活动与练习

○ Wordle

1 Introduction

Task-Based Language Teaching (TBLT) is a language teaching method that emphasizes "learning by doing" and is the development of Communicative Language Teaching (CLT). It emerged in the 1980s. It was formally proposed by the British Indian linguist N.S. Prabhu who represented by the strong version of CLT in 1983, and gradually matured in the 1990s. In the late 1990s, it was also called "the age of tasks". The prototype of the Task-Based Language Teaching is the "Bangalore Project" guided and implemented by N.S. Prabhu in the Bangalore region of southern India. The characteristics of the "Bangalore Project" emphasize "learning by doing" using task syllabus instead of a list of grammatical patterns, classroom teaching is mainly organized activities, and activities are presented in the form of tasks. Other important specialists who had great influence on the production and development of Task-Based Language Teaching are H. Douglas Brown, Jane Willis, David Nunan and Rod Ellis.

Regarding the definition of Task-Based Language Teaching, scholars have put forward different views. With the continuous development of knowledge, the definition of Task-Based Language Teaching is also deepened. In general, the teaching method advocates that in teaching activities, teachers need to design targeted and operable communicative tasks around specific communicative goals and language projects. In the process of performing these tasks, students should use the target language and use various forms of language activities such as expression, inquiry, communication, negotiation, interpretation, coordination, etc., to achieve the purpose of learning and mastering specific language projects. With the increasing attention of scholars in the field of language teaching research on Task-Based Language Teaching, it has become the most influential school of language teaching in the past two decades.

The two theoretic sources of Task-Based Language Teaching are the development of Communicative Approach and the research results of second language acquisition. Specifically, the formation of the Task-Based teaching model is mainly influenced by the input hypothesis, the interactive hypothesis and the output hypothesis. At the same time, Task-Based Language Teaching also reflects the constructivist view of learning and cognition. It emphasizes language output, content, interaction and meaning construction in interaction. The above situations all reflect that Task-Based Language Teaching has a diverse theoretical foundation.

一、教学法概述

任务型教学法（TBLT），是一种强调"在做中学"的语言教学方法，是交际语言教学的发展。它兴起于20世纪80年代，由强式交际法代表学者，英籍印度语言学家普拉布于1983年正式提出，后于20世纪90年代逐步趋于成熟，20世纪90年代后期，也被称为"任务时代"。任务型教学法的雏形源自普拉布在印度南部班加罗尔地区指导并实施的"班加罗尔项目"。"班加罗尔项目"的特点即强调"在做中学"，采用任务大纲代替语法大纲，课堂教学以组织活动为主，活动又以任务的形式来呈现。对任务型教学法的产生及发展具有重要影响的人物还有道格拉斯·布朗、简·威利斯、大卫·纽南及罗德·埃利斯等。

关于何谓任务型教学法，学者们提出了不同的观点，随着认识的不断深入，对任务型教学法的定义也在不断深入。总的来说，该教学法主张在教学活动中，教师需围绕特定的交际目的和语言项目，设计有针对性的、可操作性强的交际任务，学生在执行任务的过程中，使用目的语，运用表达、问询、沟通、交涉、解释、协调等多种语言活动形式，以达到学习和掌握具体语言项目的目的。由于语言教学研究领域学者很关注任务型教学法，近20年来任务型教学法也成了最有影响的语言教学流派。

任务型教学法的两大理论来源分别是交际法的发展以及第二语言习得研究成果。具体来说，基于任务的教学模式的形成，主要受到了输入假说、互动假说和输出假说三个第二语言习得研究假说的影响。同时，任务型教学法还反映了建构主义的学习观和认知观，它强调语言输出，重视内容，强调互动过程中的意义建构。以上种种都反映出任务型教学法具有多元理论基础。

2 Teaching Cases

● **Case I**[①]

This is an eighth grade English class, and the teacher uses Task-Based Language Teaching. All the students in the class sit in four groups according to the teacher's pre-class arrangement and language level. Those who are closer to the podium are students with lower levels, and those who are farther from the podium are students with higher levels.

During the class, the teacher first assigns the students the task to be completed in this lesson: Purchasing food and beverages for a class picnic, and make budget plans.

Subsequently, the teacher shows the students several pictures related to the task, guides the students to speak the English words marked on these pictures, and asks several students to classify these pictures according to the three categories of Food, Drinks and Fruit, and then pastes on the blackboard. After completing this step, the teacher leads the students to read these words aloud.

Next, the teacher distributes the materials, instruction cards and task lists required to complete the tasks to each group. The task material is a supermarket advertising leaflet printed with pictures and unit prices of various foods and beverages. The content of the materials received by students of different levels is slightly different. For example, the supermarket advertising leaflet obtained by the lower level group contains not only the pictures and unit price, but also the English words of these foods and drinks. At the same time, the language prompts on the instruction card obtained by the lower level group are also more detailed.

The activity instruction card contains activity content and language prompts:

Work in groups of six. Tell your group members what food you would like to buy for the class picnic.
Remember:
Eat more healthy food.
Eat more fruit.
Don't eat too much sweet food.
Don't eat too much fatty food.
Don't spend too much money on any individual item.

You can use the following sentence patterns:
· Let's buy _____.
· I like _____, because it's/they're tasty/delicious/yummy...
· Why not have more _____?
· That's a good idea. I like _____, too.
· I don't like _____, because they're/it's too sweet/salty.
· How much is a piece (package, box) of _____?

---

①　武和平，武海霞. 外语教学方法与流派 [M]. 北京：外语教学与研究出版社，2014：106–108.

The task list is a form that students need to fill out after completing the task:

Table 10-1　Form of Task List

Food/Drinks/Fruit	Quantity	Price
Chicken wings	2 packets	54 dollars

After arranging the tasks, the teacher and a group of students demonstrate how to complete the tasks.

T: I'd like to buy some chicken wings. They are yummy. We are going to buy five packets of deep-fried chicken wings.

S1: I like chicken wings, too.

S2: But they are junk food.

T: Do you think they're junk food? Then let's buy fewer. We are going to buy two packets of deep-fried chicken wings.

After the demonstration, each group starts a discussion to complete the task of purchasing picnic food. In the course of student discussions, the teacher has been walking around in the classroom, carefully listening to the speeches of students in all groups, guiding and encouraging students to try to communicate by using the target language. If necessary, the teacher will also participate in the discussion of a group to help students organize the language, so as to encourage them to express their ideas in the target language.

Teacher pays attention to observe that when all groups are about to complete the task, let each group select representatives, report their completed task list, and show the results of their tasks to the whole class. Students from different groups discuss how to report, what to say and how to say. Some people suggest that it should be written first. Students discuss the word, sentence structure and seek advice from the teacher.

Finally, the teacher guides the class to evaluate the completion of the tasks of each group from the dimensions of language quality, budget control and the richness of purchased foods.

● **Case II**[①]

TASK: Miss Wang has just graduated to work. This is her first business trip. Please give her some suggestions on business trips.

---

① 史中慧. 任务型教学法与高职英语课堂实践 [M]. 北京：中国财富出版社，2019：111-113.

Pre-Task

① Brainstorm and encourage everyone to open their minds.

② Record the suggestions related to the materials on the blackboard.

● Keep a Packed Bag.

● Choose Regional Airports.

● Book Direct Flights.

● Select Your Seat.

● Program Your GPS Unit.

Task-Cycle

Listen to practical travel suggestions and complete the form.

① Urge everyone to focus on listening materials.

② Complete the form (Table 10-2).

Table 10-2   Task List of Travel Suggestions

Tips on business travel	Details
Keep a Packed Bag	Get in the habit of repacking your carry-on bag (1) with fresh clothing and essentials when you return from being on the trip.
	It will save your time for an early morning flight and all you have to do is to (2) reach for a bag and go.
Choose Regional Airports	Fly out of smaller airports.
	Security lines and the check-in process are often (3) easier and quicker at smaller or regional airports.
	Be sure to (4) consider all of your options before booking.
Book Direct Flights	Take direct flights (5) to and from your destination, which often means savings beyond just your time.
	(6) Avoid overnight stays, which will save on potential hotel, car and meal expenses.
Select Your Seat	Book the seat near the front of the plane whenever possible.
	Check your seat assignment as you (7) check in online, and make changes if it's available further to the front.
	(8) Hop off the plane quickly and avoid throngs of amateur travelers in the aisles, which will save time.
Program Your GPS Unit	(9) Program the addresses for all of the stops you'll be making on your trip into the "favorites" section of your GPS unit.
	It will eliminate the need to fumble with maps or ask for and (10) look up directions on the road.

Post-Task

① Ask students to display their suggestions in groups.

② Provide correct answers.

③ Please extend the discussion: In addition to the above suggestions, what are the necessary preparations before traveling?

二、教学示例

教学示例 1

任务型教学法被应用于一堂八年级的英语课上。全班同学按照老师的课前安排，依据语言水平的高低，围坐成四个小组。离讲台较近的是水平较低的学生，离讲台较远的是水平较高的学生。

上课时，老师首先给学生布置了本节课要完成的任务：为班级郊游野餐采购食品和饮料，制定采购预算。

随后，老师向学生展示了几幅与本次任务相关的图片，引导学生说出这些图片上所标注的英文单词，并让几位学生按照食物、饮料和水果三大类对这些图片进行分类，然后贴到黑板上。完成这一步骤后，老师带领学生朗读这些单词。

接下来，老师给每个小组发放完成任务所需的材料、指令卡和任务单。任务材料是一张超市广告宣传单，印有各种食品和饮料的实物图片及单价。不同水平组的学生拿到的材料内容略有不同。例如，水平较低的小组拿到的超市广告宣传单上不仅有实物图片和单价，还有这些食物和饮料的英文单词。同时，水平较低的小组所拿到的活动指令卡上的语言提示也更加详细。

活动指令卡上为活动内容及语言提示：

每六人一组。告诉你的小组成员你想为班级野餐活动购买什么食物。

注意：

多吃健康食品。

多吃水果。

不要吃太多甜食。

不要吃太多高脂肪食物。

不要在任何单个物品上花费太多钱。

你可以使用以下句型：

· 咱们买_____吧。

· 我喜欢_____，因为它 / 它们很美味 / 好吃 / 鲜美……

· 为什么不多买些_____?

· 真是个好主意。我也喜欢_____。

· 我不喜欢_____，因为它们 / 它太甜了 / 太咸了。

· 一块（包、盒）_____多少钱?

任务单是学生在完成任务后需要填写的表格：

表 10-1　任务单

食物 / 饮料 / 水果	数量	价格
鸡翅	2 包	54 美元

布置完任务后，老师和其中一组学生示范如何完成任务。

老师：我想买一些鸡翅，鸡翅很好吃，我们要买五包炸鸡翅。

学生 1：我也喜欢吃鸡翅。

学生 2：但是鸡翅是垃圾食品。

老师：你们认为是垃圾食品吗？那就少买点儿吧。咱们买两包炸鸡翅吧。

示范结束后，各个小组展开讨论，以完成野餐食品采购这一任务。在学生讨论过程中，老师一直在教室里四处巡视，仔细倾听各组学生的发言，引导、鼓励学生尝试使用目的语进行交际。如有必要，老师也会参与到某一小组的讨论中，帮助学生组织语言，促使他们用目的语表达自己的想法。

老师需要注意观察。当所有小组即将完成任务时，让每个小组选派代表，汇报他们填好的任务单，并向全班展示他们的任务成果。各组学生一起讨论如何汇报，说什么、怎么说，有人提议先写出来，大家讨论"如何用词，如何组织句子结构"，并征求老师的意见。

最后老师引导全班学生从语言质量、预算控制以及采购食品的丰富性等维度对各个小组的任务完成情况进行评价。

教学示例 2

任务：王小姐刚刚毕业参加工作，这是她第一次出差，请给她提供一些关于出差的建议。

任务前阶段

①头脑风暴，鼓励大家打开思路。

②把与材料有关的建议记录在黑板上。

● 整理行李。

● 选择当地机场。

● 预订直航。

● 选座。

● 编辑导航系统。

任务中阶段

听取实用的出行建议并填写表格。

①督促学生专注于听力材料。

②完成表格填写（表10-2）。

表 10-2　出行任务单

商务旅行提示	细节
整理行李	当旅途归来时，请养成打包（1）干净衣物和必需品的习惯
	清晨的航班可以帮助你节省时间，你只需要（2）拿上行李出发
选择当地机场	从较小的机场出发
	在较小的或当地的机场，安检和登机手续通常（3）更加简单和快捷
	预订前请务必（4）考虑所有情况
预订直航	搭乘直达航班（5）往返目的地，这通常意味着你节省的不仅仅是时间
	（6）避免过夜航班，这样可以节省潜在的酒店、用车和餐饮费用
选座	尽可能预订靠近飞机前部的座位
	（7）在线办理登机手续时请核查你的座位位置，如果允许更改，请尽量换成更靠前的座位
	快速（8）下飞机，避免在通道上与其他旅行者拥挤在一起，这样可以节省时间
编辑导航系统	将旅途中要经过的所有站点的（9）地址录入 GPS 系统的"收藏夹"里
	这样就减少了搜寻地图和在旅途中问路及（10）查找方向的需求

任务后阶段

①请学生以小组为单位展示他们提出的建议。

②提供正确答案。

③请大家进行延伸讨论：除了以上所建议的内容，出差前还需要做哪些准备？

3 Teaching Principles and Teaching Procedures

3.1 Definitions of Task

If we want to fully and accurately understand the Task-Based Language Teaching, we should first understand what a task is. Regarding the definitions of task, many scholars have interpreted them from different angles. Long, Nunan, Richards, Crook, Prabhu, Willis, Skehan, Lee, and Ellis all put forward different definitions. Among them, Ellis's views are the most representative and most accepted by the public. Here we sort out the task definition according to the time of the proposed:

Long points out that the task is one thing which can be done for yourself or for others. At the same time, this thing can be done at will, or it can be done to achieve a certain purpose. Such things can be dressing children, booking air tickets, writing letters, helping people cross the street, etc. In other words, a task can be a variety of things in people's lives, whether it is work or leisure, or something in between.

Richards, Platt, and Weber believe that a task is a behavior or activity that processes language or understands the results of language, and it can also be said to be a reaction, such as doing things according to the teacher's instructions, drawing maps based on recordings, etc.

Crook, on the basis of Long's definition of "mission is a thing or an activity" stresses that the mandate is often an important part of the education curriculum, and a particular purpose or activity that can lead to the teaching material.

Prabhu defines a task as an activity, which requires the learner to think based on the information obtained and ultimately obtain a result. At the same time, this process should allow teachers to monitor.

Breen believes that a task refers to a series of overall work plans aimed at promoting language learning. It can be a simple and short exercise or a longer and more complex activity. For example, teamwork solves problems, simulates activities, and decides on problems.

Nunan points out that a task is a communicative activity, in which learners use language to obtain and express meaning in order to achieve a certain purpose.

Willis proposes that the task is the activity of learners using the target language in order to achieve communicative purposes.

Skehan still defines a task as activities, but it emphasizes the meaning of activities and the close connection between activities and the objective world. At the same time, he also proposes that this task needs to have a result, and through this result, the completion of the task can be evaluated.

Lee defines tasks from two levels. One is that the task is a classroom activity or practice; the other is that the task is a language learning.

Bygate, Skehan, and Swain believe that a task is an activity. During the activity, learners are required to use language to achieve a certain purpose and emphasize the expression of meaning.

Ellis believes that a task is a work plan, which requires learning to process language from objective reality in order to obtain a result that can assess whether the task conveys correct or appropriate content.

In summary, there is no consensus definition, but it is certain that a comprehensive and accurate understanding of the definitions of task is helpful for teachers to master the concept of Task-Based pedagogy, and helps teachers design task activities accurately.

3.2 Classifications of Tasks

Different scholars have different classified tasks from different perspectives. The earliest one to classify tasks was the linguist N.S. Prabhu who implemented the "Bangalore Project". He divided the central tasks of the classroom into three categories:

① Information-gap activity: This type of task can be said to be an activity that encodes or decodes language, which involves transferring given information from one person to another, from one form to another, or from one place to another. An example is pair work in which the text materials or diagrams distributed by the teacher to the two students are incomplete, and the two students can only know the entire content of the materials by communicating, that is, passing the known information to each other.

② Reasoning-gap activity: The learner needs to reason and deduce the given information. In this process, the learner derives new information from the information conveyed. For example, the teacher gives the learner a map (provides the given information), and asks the student to find the best route to a specified location (derive new information).

③ Opinion-gap activity: This type of task includes identifying and expressing personal preferences, feelings, or attitudes under certain circumstances. For example, when interviewing students' views on the school, this interview task includes an opinion-gap activity, because the students who undertake the interview do not know the views of others on the school. If they want to understand it comprehensively and accurately, they must communicate in language.

Terasa Pica, Ruth Kanagy and Joseph Falodun classify tasks according to the type of interaction that occurs in task accomplishment and give the following classifications:[①]

① Jigsaw tasks: These involve learners combining different pieces of information to form a whole (e.g., three individuals or groups may have three different parts of a story and have to piece the story together).

② Information-gap tasks: One student or group of students has one set of information and another student or group has a complementary set of information. They must negotiate and find out what the other student's or group's information is in order to complete an activity.

③ Problem-solving tasks: Students are given a problem and a set of information. They must arrive at a solution to the problem. There is generally a single resolution of the outcome.

④ Decision-making tasks: Students are given a problem for which there are a number of possible outcomes and they must choose one through negotiation and discussion.

⑤ Opinion-exchange tasks: Learners engage in discussion and exchange of ideas. They do not need to reach agreement.

3.3 Teaching Principles of Task-Based Language Teaching

① Principle of emphasizing meaning: The task must first have practical significance. This is the biggest difference between the task and other exercises, and it is also the key to the difference between the Task-Based Language Teaching and the traditional teaching method.

----

① PICA T, KANAGY R, FALODUN J. Choosing and using communicative tasks for second language instruction [M]//CROOKES G, GASS S M. Tasks and language learning: integrating theory & Practice. Clevedon: Multilingual Matters. 1993: 9–34.

② Principle of authenticity: The design of the task should be connected with the real world and life experience, especially with the actual life of the learner, so that they can experience and master the target language in a natural and real situation.

③ Principle of clear purpose: The completion of teaching tasks must have a clear goal. If there is no clear goal, then the Task-Based Language Teaching is incomplete and irregular. Therefore, the entire classroom activity should be carried out around this goal. In other words, the goal is the direction of the entire learning task.

④ Principle of testability: The results of classroom tasks should be able to be tested. Through the test and evaluation of task results, students can discover the strengths of others and their weaknesses to further improve their language communication skills.

⑤ Principle of subsidiarity: Teachers and teaching materials should provide necessary help for learners to complete tasks, make adequate preparations before implementing tasks, give necessary help in the implementation of tasks, and help conclude, summarize, reflect and improve after completing tasks.

⑥ Principle of "learning by doing": In task-based classes, teachers should pay attention to students' operations on tasks, guide students to actively participate in task activities, and encourage students to learn language while using language.

3.4 Teaching Procedures of Task-Based Language Teaching

In 1996, British linguist Jane Willis published the book *A Framework for Task-Based Learning*. In this book Willis discusses the three stages[①] of Task-Based Language Teaching, namely: the pre-task stage, the task-cycle stage and the language focus stage. This procedure is accepted and used by most researchers and teachers.

(1) Pre-Task: Introduction to Topic and Task

– T (teacher) helps Ss (Students) understand the theme and objectives of the task, for example, brainstorming ideas with the class, using pictures, mime, or personal experience to introduce the topic.

– Ss may do a pre-task, for example, topic-based odd-word-out games.

– T may highlight useful words and phrases, but would not pre-teach new structures.

– Ss can be given preparation time to think about how to do the task.

– Ss can hear a recording of a parallel task being done (so long as this does not give away the solution to the problem).

– If the task is based on a text, Ss read part of it.

---

① RICHARDS J C, RODGERS T S. 语言教学的流派 [M]. 2 版 . 北京：外语教学与研究出版社，2008：238-240.

(2) The Task Cycle

① Task

– The task is done by Ss (in pairs or groups) and gives Ss a chance to use whatever language they already have to express themselves and say whatever they want to say. This may be in response to reading a text or hearing a recording.

– T walks round and monitors, encouraging in a supportive way everyone's attempts at communication in the target language.

– T helps Ss to formulate what they want to say, but will not intervene to correct errors of form.

– The emphasis is on spontaneous, exploratory talk and confidence building, within the privacy of the small group.

– Success in achieving the goals of the task helps Ss' motivation.

② Planning

– Planning prepares for the next stage, when Ss are asked to report briefly to the whole class how they did the task and what the outcome was.

– Ss draft and rehearse what they want to say or write.

– T goes round to advise students on language, suggesting phrases and helping Ss to polish and correct their language.

– If the reports are in writing, T can encourage peer editing and use of dictionaries.

– The emphasis is on clarity, organization, and accuracy, as appropriate for a public presentation.

– Individual students often take this chance to ask questions about specific language items.

③ Report

– T asks some pairs to report briefly to the whole class so everyone can compare findings, or begin a survey. (NB: There must be a purpose for others to listen.) Sometimes only one or two groups report in full; others comment and add extra points. The class may take notes.

– T chairs, comments on the content of their reports, rephrases perhaps, but gives no overt public correction.

④ Post-Task Listening

– Ss listen to a recording of fluent speakers doing the same task, and compare the ways in which they did the task themselves.

(3) The Language Focus

① Analysis

– T sets some language-focused tasks, based on the texts students have read or on the transcripts of the recordings they have heard.

– Examples include the following:

- Find words and phrases related to the title of the topic or text.
- Read the transcript, find words ending in "s" or "'s" and say what the "s" means.
- Find all the verbs in the simple past form. Say which refer to past time and which do not.
- Underline and classify the questions in the transcript.

– T starts Ss off, then Ss continue, often in pairs.

– T goes round to help; Ss can ask individual questions.

– In plenary, T then reviews the analysis, possibly writing relevant language up on the board in list form; Ss may make notes.

② Practice

– T conducts practice activities as needed, based on the language analysis work already on the board, or using examples from the text or transcript.

– Practice activities can include:

- Choral repetition of the phrases identified and classified.
- Memory challenge games based on partially erased examples or using lists already on blackboard for progressive deletion.
- Sentence completion (set by one team for another).
- Matching the past-tense verbs (jumbled) with the subject or objects they had in the text.
- Kim's game① (in teams) with new words and phrases.
- Dictionary reference words from the text or transcript.

三、教学原则与教学过程

1. 任务的定义

若想全面且准确地理解任务型教学法，首先应了解何为任务。关于任务的定义，诸多学者从不同角度出发，对其进行了相关阐释。朗、纽南、理查德、克鲁克、普拉布、威利斯、斯凯恩、李和埃利斯都提出了不同的定义，其中埃利斯的观点最具代表性，也最被大众所接受。下面我们按照定义提出的时间先后进行梳理：

朗提出，任务就是一件事情，这件事情可以是为自己做的，也可以是为其他人做的。同时，这件事情可以是随意做的，也可以是为了达到某种目的而做的。这样的事情可以是给孩子穿衣服、预订机票、写信、帮人过马路等。换言之，任务可以是人们生活中各种各样的事情，无论是工作方面还是休闲娱乐方面，或是介于二者之间的事情。

理查德、普拉特、韦伯认为，任务是一种处理语言或理解语言结果的行为或活动，也可以说是一种反应，如按照教师的指令做事，根据录音画地图，等等。

---

① 　Kim's game: The name of the game comes from Joseph Rudyard Kipling's story *Kim* where the character Kim plays this game as part of his training as a spy. Now in the classroom teaching process, it is a kind of memory exercise and it is a good way of developing students' memory skills and concentration.

克鲁克在朗的定义"任务是一件事情或一个活动"的基础上，强调任务通常是教育课程的重要组成部分，是具有特定目的或可引出教学素材的活动。

普拉布将任务定义为一种活动，它要求学习者根据所获取的信息进行思考，并最终获得一个结果。同时，这一过程应允许教师进行监控。

布林认为，任务是指一系列旨在促进语言学习的总体工作计划，它可以是简单而简短的练习，也可以是较长且较为复杂的活动。例如，小组合作解决问题、模拟活动和问题决策。

纽南指出，任务是一种交际活动，在活动中，学习者为了达到某种特定目的，使用语言去理解和表达意义。

威利斯提出，任务是学习者为了达到交际目的而使用目的语的活动。

斯凯恩依然将任务定义为活动，但更加强调活动中的意义以及活动与客观世界的紧密联系。同时，他也提出，这个任务需要有一个结果，且通过这个结果可以对该项任务的完成情况进行评估。

李从两个层面定义了任务，一是任务是一个课堂活动或练习；二是任务是一种语言学习活动。

比盖特、斯凯恩、斯温认为任务是一种活动，在活动过程中要求学习者使用语言达到某个目的，且强调意义的表达。

埃利斯认为，任务是一项工作计划，需要从客观现实中学习处理语言，从而获得一个结果，这个结果可以评估任务，传达正确而恰当的内容。

综上所述，任务的定义并不是一定的，但可以肯定的是，全面且准确地理解任务的定义有利于教师掌握任务型教学法的概念，且有助于教师精准地设计任务活动。

2. 任务的类型

不同学者从多种角度出发，对任务进行了不同的分类。最早对任务进行分类的是"班加罗尔项目"的实施者——语言学家普拉布。他将课堂的中心任务分成了三类：

① 信息差任务：这一类任务可以说是一种对语言编码或解码的活动，涉及将给定信息从一个人转述给另一个人，从一种形式转换为另一种形式，或从一个地方转移到另一个地方。如双人活动，教师分发给两名学生的教学材料或图表均是不完整的，两名学生只有通过沟通，即互相传递已知信息，才能知晓材料的全部内容。

② 推理差任务：学习者需要对给定信息进行推理、演绎，在此过程中学习者从所传达的信息中推导出新信息。如教师给学生一张地图（提供给定信息），要求学生找出到某一个指定地点的最优路线（推导新信息）。

③ 观点差任务：这一类任务包括在特定情况下，识别和表达个人喜好、感觉或态度等。如采访学生们对学校的看法，这个采访任务中包含了一个观点差任务，因为承担采访任务的学生并不知道他人对学校的看法，要想全面、准确地了解，就必须用语言进行沟通。

特雷莎·皮卡，露丝·卡纳吉和约瑟夫·法杜尔根据任务在完成过程中所发生的交互类型，对任务进行了如下分类：

① 拼图任务：此类任务要求学习者将不同的信息组合成一个整体（例如，三名学生

或一组学生可能获得了一个故事的三个不同部分，他们必须将这个故事拼凑在一起，形成一个完整的故事）。

② 信息差任务：一名学生或一组学生有一组信息，而另一名学生或另一组学生有一组补充性信息。他们必须协商并获得对方的信息，才能完成这个活动。

③ 解决问题型任务：给学生一个问题和一组信息，他们必须找到解决问题的办法，而且这个问题往往只有一个解决方案。

④ 决策型任务：给学生一个具有多种可能性结果的问题，他们必须通过协商和讨论来最终确定一个解决方案。

⑤ 观点交换型任务：学习者参与讨论和思想交流活动。但在这一过程中，他们无须达成一致观点。

3. 任务型教学法的教学原则

①强调意义原则：任务首先要有实际意义，这也是任务与其他练习的最大区别，也是任务型教学法区别于传统教学法的关键。

②真实性原则：任务的设计应与真实世界和生活经验相联系，特别是应与学习者的实际生活结合起来，使其在一种自然、真实的情境中体会、掌握目的语。

③ 目标明确原则：教学任务要有一个明确的目标。如果没有明确的目标，那么任务型教学是不完整的，也是不规范的。因此整个课堂活动都应该围绕这一目标来进行。换言之，目标是整个学习任务的努力方向。

④成果可检验性原则：课堂任务的成果应是可以被检验的。通过对任务成果的检验、评估，学生可以发现他人长处和自身短处，以进一步增强自己的语言交际能力。

⑤辅助性原则：是指教师和教学材料应为学习者完成任务提供必要的帮助，在实施任务之前做好充分的铺垫和准备工作，在实施任务中给予必要的帮助，在完成任务后帮助归纳、总结、反思、提高。

⑥"在做中学"原则：在任务型课堂中，教师应关注学生对任务的操作，引导学生积极参与到任务活动中，鼓励学生在使用语言的过程中学习语言。

4. 任务型教学法的教学过程

1996 年，英国语言学家简·威利斯发表《任务型学习框架》一书，在该书中威利斯讨论了任务型教学法的三个阶段，即任务前阶段、任务环阶段和语言焦点阶段。这一观点为大多数研究者和教师所接受并运用。

（1）任务前阶段：介绍任务主题及内容

——教师帮助学生了解任务主题及目标，例如，和全班学生一起进行头脑风暴，使用图片，以哑剧或个人经验的分享来介绍主题。

——学生可以做一个前期任务，例如，基于任务主题的"找不同"游戏。

——教师可以强调有用的单词和短语，但不能提前讲授新的句法结构。

——给学生准备的时间用以思考如何完成任务。

——学生可以听到正在完成的任务的录音（但要确保这样做不能帮助他们解决问题）。

——如果任务是基于某教学材料设计的，学生可以读取部分材料。

（2）任务环阶段

①任务

——学生执行任务（双人形式或者小组形式），并且给学生机会，让他们运用任何可以表达自己意思的语言，说出他们想说的话。学生所说的话可以是对教学材料或教学音频的反馈。

——教师四处走动并进行观察，支持并鼓励所有学生尝试使用目的语进行交流。

——教师帮助学生规划想表达的内容，但不对语言形式上的错误进行干预。

——重点是在小组范围内进行自发的、探索性的讨论，并建立信心。

——任务目标的成功实现有助于激发学生的学习动机。

②计划

——计划阶段是对下一阶段的准备环节，在下一阶段学生需要向全班同学简要汇报他们是如何完成任务的以及任务的结果。

——学生起草并练习他们想说或想写的内容。

——教师巡视，为学生提供关于使用语言和短语的建议，并帮助学生完善和纠正语言。

——如果任务报告是以书面形式呈现的，教师可以鼓励学生自行撰写并使用字典。

——重点在于报告的清晰度、组织性和准确性，以确保报告适合公开展示。

——个别学生经常在此环节对特定语言点提出问题。

③报告

——教师要求几组学生向全班同学作简要汇报，以便班级中的每个人比较调查结果，或者着手准备本组调查。（特别注意：其他学生必须明确倾听目的。）有的时候，只需一到两个小组进行完整的任务报告即可，其他学生可以发表评论或表达观点。教师可以要求全班学生做笔记。

——教师负责对报告发表评论，也可以对报告内容进行改写，但是不要公开修改。

④任务后聆听

——学生聆听完成相同任务的出色汇报者的报告录音，并与自己的任务报告进行比较。

（3）语言焦点阶段

①分析

——教师根据学生阅读的教学材料或听过的录音材料，设置一些语言相关任务。

——相关任务包括以下内容：

- 查找与主题或教学材料相关的单词和短语。
- 阅读录音材料，找到以"s"或"'s"结尾的单词，并说出"s"的含义。
- 查找所有一般过去式的动词，说说哪些是表明过去的，哪些不是。
- 在录音材料中对问题进行画线和分类。

——教师开始讲解时学生应停止讨论，随后学生可两人一组继续讨论。

——教师在班级内巡视，帮助各组学生；此时学生可根据个人情况向教师提问。

——在全体讨论时，教师对内容进行回顾分析，可以用列表形式在黑板上写下相关语言点；学生可以做笔记。

②训练

——教师基于黑板上已有的语言分析板书，或使用教学材料及录音材料中的示例，根据学生需要开展练习活动。

——练习活动可以包括：

- 反复齐读已讲授或分类的短语。
- 记忆挑战游戏。即基于教学材料或黑板上的板书，擦除相关内容后，让学生回忆补全。
- 完成句子（由一组给另一组设定）。
- 将教学材料中所涉及的过去式动词（乱序）与主语或宾语进行匹配。
- 组织"金的游戏"①（以小组为单位进行），游戏中应包含新词和新短语。
- 用字典查询教学材料或录音材料中的词。

4 Conclusion

Task-Based Language Teaching is based on the Communicative Language Teaching. It promotes the advanced teaching concepts of "student-centered" and "learning by doing," subverting the traditional top-down teaching method. By guiding students to complete various tasks, it can effectively stimulate students' interest in learning and cultivate students' ability to communicate in a comprehensive way. Due to the wide range of task activities, the large amount of information, and the complicated procedures for completing tasks, it helps to broaden the knowledge of students, cultivate their ability to think independently, communicate with each other, and solve problems, which is conducive to the overall development of students.

Task-Based Language Teaching also has some limitations. It emphasizes the viewpoint of "focusing on the learning process, not focusing on the learning results," which distracts the students' attention from language learning and practice, and affects the students' language learning effect. In addition, the Task-Based Language Teaching blindly requires students to use the target language flexibly when completing tasks, without considering the students' basis of vocabulary and sentence structure, which leads to the students' unfounded language foundation, thereby increasing the frustration of the students. Finally, the Task-Based Language Teaching puts extremely high requirements on teachers' classroom teaching ability and classroom management ability. If it is difficult to meet this requirement, the classroom teaching effect will be poor.

---

① 金的游戏：游戏的名称来自约瑟夫·鲁德亚德·吉卜林（Joseph Rudyard Kipling）的故事《金》，故事中的角色金将这个游戏作为他间谍训练的一部分。现在在课堂教学过程中，这个游戏是一种记忆练习，是发展学生记忆能力和注意力的一种好方法。

四、小结

任务型教学法由交际法发展而来，它倡导"以学生为中心"和"在做中学"的先进教学理念，颠覆了传统的自上而下的教学方式。该教学法通过引导学生完成多样性任务，有效地激发学生的学习兴趣，培养学生综合运用语言进行交际的能力。由于任务活动内容涉及范围较广，信息量较大，完成任务的步骤较为复杂，因此，这更有助于拓宽学生知识面，培养学生独立思考、人际交往、解决问题的能力，有利于学生的全面发展。

任务型教学法也存在一些局限性。它强调的"注重学习过程，而不注重学习结果"的这一观点，分散了学生对语言学习和练习的关注度，反而影响了学生的语言学习效果。另外，任务型教学法在未考虑学生词汇、句型结构掌握情况的基础上，一味要求学生在完成任务时灵活运用目的语，导致学生语言基础不扎实，加重了学生的挫败感。最后，任务型教学法对教师的课堂教学能力和课堂管理能力提出了极高要求。如果教师难以具备相应的能力，课堂教学效果也会大打折扣。

○ Activities and Exercises

● Understanding and Thinking

1. Read the following materials and try to analyze the role of teachers in different task stages in the process of Task-Based classroom teaching, and talk about the role and position of teachers in TBLT.

(1) Leader and Organizer of Discussion

Most task sequences begin with a teacher-led discussion. You may then choose to move into group/pair work. But in most cases it is possible to conduct the whole task sequence in teacher-led form.

(2) Manager of Group/Pair Work

The teacher needs to be able to organize this kind of work to get the best out of students. It is important to make sure that learners are absolutely clear about what is expected of them before they move into groups. It is also important to monitor groups carefully to make sure that they are on track. If things do seem to be going wrong, you should not be afraid to suspend group work and sort out problems before continuing.

(3) Facilitator

You need to find a balance between setting a task which provides the right kind of challenge, and making sure that learners can manage the task.

544

(4) Motivator

It is very important to give learners all the encouragement you can. There are two basic ways of doing this. First you should be as positive as you reasonably can be in the feedback you give learners. The second important way to enhance motivation is to highlight progress.

(5) Language Knower and Adviser

This involves helping learners with meanings. You should join in learners' discourse as an equal participant, but one who has greater language knowledge and experience.

(6) Language Teacher

There are, however, stages at which you do adopt the traditional teacher role, explaining, demonstrating, and eliciting appropriate language forms. In a task-based approach this focus on form normally comes at the end of a task sequence. It is an important role, and also a difficult one which demands careful thought and preparation.

2. Based on the following two views of Skehan, do you think that tasks and exercises can be completely separated in actual teaching? What is the connection and difference between the two?

Skehan points out that the task needs to have the following elements: ① Expressing meaning is the primary purpose; ② The learner needs to solve a communication problem; ③ What the learner does must be related to certain activities in real life; ④ The completion of the task is the most important (how to complete and the completion of the situation is secondary); ⑤ The evaluation of activities should be based on the results.

In addition, Skehan believes that language learning in the following classroom activities cannot generally be counted as a task in Task-Based Language Teaching:

① Sentence pattern conversion exercises, such as turning active sentences into passive ones.

② Q&A exercises between students and teachers.

③ Sentence pattern replacement exercises based on prompts.

④ Students first learn a dialogue, and then do similar dialogue exercises in pairs.

⑤ Students first listen to an interview recording, and then do similar interview exercises in pairs.

⑥ Summarize the grammar rules according to the language materials prepared in advance.

3. Task-Based Language Teaching requires students to use the target language to complete a variety of tasks on their own or in small groups to achieve the purpose of classroom teaching. At this time, the difficulty of the task designed by the teacher is crucial, which affects the degree of completion of the classroom task and the final teaching effect of the task-based classroom. Read the materials given below, select the teaching theme in groups, design tasks of different difficulty, and display the teaching.

One of the problems we need to tackle is the question of grading tasks. Skehan offers a list of variables for assessing the difficulty of tasks. The list is too extensive to be included here, but it includes features such as:

Cognitive familiarity of topic and its predictability. Some topics, such as the family, will be well-known to learners, something they talk about frequently in their first language. Other topics, such as "volcanoes" might be new to them. They may even need to do some research before being able to handle a topic like this. The "Busy day" task would rate highly in terms of familiarity; since learners are talking about their own experience, it is clearly something well-known to them.

Cognitive processing: the amount of computation. How much work do language users have to do in preparing their message, or how much intellectual effort is required in understanding a message? A text about a volcano which simply recounts an anecdotal experience would be much lighter in terms of cognitive processing than a text which explains how an eruption occurs. The "Busy day" task is not intellectually demanding, so there is little in the way of computation once the events of the day have been recalled.

Communicative stress: time limits and time pressure. A task is much easier if learners have time to think about it before they begin to tackle it. The amount of communicative stress can be controlled. If, for example, learners are asked to prepare the topic for homework, there will be no time pressure, but if they are suddenly asked to produce a narrative spontaneously this will be much more difficult.

Code complexity: linguistic complexity and variety. To some extent code complexity will be determined by the learners themselves. They may be very ambitious in their chosen story, or they may choose something less demanding. We can, however, impose more demands on linguistic complexity. If, for example, learners were asked to talk about their most embarrassing experience, this would probably be lexically more demanding. It would also require more in the way of organization and evaluation of events, which again would make more linguistic demands.

● **Teaching Design**

1. According to the following curriculum outline[①], in accordance with the operating procedures of Task-Based Language Teaching, expand the teaching details, and conduct teaching demonstration in groups.

Class and Course Background

Intermediate/upper intermediate multi-lingual learners, mixed level, mixed ability, ages from 16 upwards. Part-time class, two two-hour lessons a week.

Course Theme: sea journeys.

---

① WILLIS J. A Framework for Task-Based Learning [M]. Addison Wesley Longman Limited, 1996: 159–160.

Starting Lesson

(1) Announce New Topic

Give overview of work for next two weeks (In this session, you can discuss various aspects of journeys by boat with students, or you can ask students to make preparations after class).

(2) Pre-Task

Aim: To introduce topic of sea journeys, and give class exposure to topic-related talk, to activate and highlight useful words and phrases.

① Talk about pictures experience of topic.

② Brainstorm with class on words and phrases.

③ Announce recording of a sea journey story. (Play recording two or three times. Guide students to pay attention to the words and phrases in the recording.)

(3) Task-Cycle

① Task

Students do task in twos, then combine with another pair to re-tell their stories and compare their experiences.

② Planning

Each group of four selects two stories to present to the class.

③ Report

Pick four or five pairs to tell their stories.

(4) Language Focus Analysis and Practice

① Guide students to pay attention to language forms in various ways.

② Guide students to focus on language features in various ways.

③ Assign homework. (NB: Homework should be closely related to the tasks in this lesson, and reflect the characteristics of the Task-Based Language Teaching.)

2. Please read the following teaching plan carefully, point out the inappropriate places according to the theory and principles of Task-Based Language Teaching, then revise and improve it.

Course Type: *Elementary Spoken Chinese.*

Teaching Objectives: *12 Chinese students with zero basics at Juntendo University in Japan.*

Teaching Content:

Words: *38 (Master the usage of key new words: time, from...to, bar, poor, big day before, etc.)*

Phrase: *What day, day of the week, what time, when.*

Text: 3

Teaching Points and Difficulties:

① Master and use key phrases and structures: What day, day of the week, what time, when.

② *Master the common sentence patterns of expression and inquiry time.*

③ *Be able to sort out the differences between "两"and "二."*

Teaching Steps:

(1) Pre-Task

Table 10-3   Pre-Task Teaching Links, Steps and Corresponding Instructions

Teaching Links	Teaching Steps	Design Description
Teaching Preparation	*At the beginning of the course, the teacher and students exchange greetings briefly, and the teacher inspect the attendance of students based on student registration numbers.*	*The course begins. Warm up and review.*
Review	*The teacher checks the mastery of the texts and vocabulary of the previous lesson, and reviews the topic of the previous lesson by displaying maps and questions and answers.*	*Awaken students' memory of the learning content of the previous lesson, and pave the way for learning new content.*
Task Import	*Explain to the students the communicative task of this lesson: "Let's play together on weekends." Each group will discuss according to the scenes on the cards distributed by the teacher (Narita, climbing, eating cereal rice, Disneyland, roller coaster, watching fireworks, etc.), and decide the time of the assembly and the detailed itinerary of the day. After the discussion, each group will send a student as a representative to report the design plan of the group.*	*Clarifying tasks before learning a new lesson allows students to master new knowledge more quickly when learning new words and sentences.*
Vocabulary and Text Teaching	*The teacher reads and explains the new words. The students follow and imitate the pronunciation. After repeating it several times, let the students randomly read the words until they can read the new words independently.* *The teacher uses a self-made dial to make students familiar with and practice the expression of time points, and at the same time let them master "half, a moment, poor" and other expressions of time.* *The teacher and students have communicative dialogues, such as: When do you get up/class/ sleep. Let the students fill in the blanks and report according to their own real situation.* *The teacher reads and explains the text, encourages students to imitate reading, and interprets keywords and sentences.*	*The teaching of new words and texts should clarify the meaning of new words and texts as much as possible, and calibrate the pronunciation for students.* *Relatively uncommon and special words and sentences should be explained and taught by the teacher in a targeted manner to assist students in their learning and make them understand their specific context and usage in daily applications.*

continued

Teaching Links	Teaching Steps	Design Description
Exercise	*The teacher designed two exercises: "Look at the picture and say a sentence" and "Tell about your timetable", and give some tips to guide students to give full play to their subjective initiative and say the sentence "who + when + what".*	*Through the practice of mechanical exercises, students can better grasp the new words and expressions, and lay the foundation for the implementation of the next task.*

(2) Task-Cycle

First, 12 students are divided into 3 groups, each group has 3 to 4 students, and a team leader is selected to coordinate the development of the organization's tasks.

Secondly, organize group discussions to prepare for the classroom presentation of the plan.

If students need to use unstudied new words, they can ask the teacher or other students for help. The team leader is responsible for coordinating and recording the discussion. Teachers should go back and forth to monitor students' discussions, such as whether the target language is used during the discussion, whether the task is performed, whether the discussion is active, etc., as well as answer students' questions, record the performance of students, and pay attention to controlling time.

In the end, each group takes turns to show the task of "Let's play together on the weekend" and submits the corresponding schedule (the format is "date + time + place + event").

After the task report is completed, the evaluation of the task is completed. The evaluation consists of three parts: self-evaluation, students' mutual evaluation and teacher's comment.

(3) The Language Focus

The teacher collects the schedule of each group and asks questions based on the contents shown in the tables of each group.

Homework:

Review the vocabulary and text of this lesson and practice diligently.

Complete the after-class exercises.

Preview new class.

Finally, the teacher guides the students to reflect on the task in light of the evaluation results, and puts forward relevant suggestions.

● **Further Reading**

A Brief Introduction of Task-Based Language Teaching (TBLT)[①]

1. Introduction

For the past decade, Task-Based Language Teaching (TBLT) has got the attention of second language acquisition experts, course developers, and language teachers all over the world. Since the first biennial International Conference on Task-Based Language Teaching was held at the University of Leuven in Belgium in 2005, a lot of articles on how TBLT can promote language learning have been published. However, much of the research on TBLT has been conducted in western and American countries. Furthermore, TBLT has been regarded as vehicles to introduce other language phenomena, such as interaction, negotiation of meaning, processing of input, to enhance second language acquisition. Much less research on tasks used as the basic units for the organization of teaching activities in language classrooms has been carried out. Last but not least, the importance of reading abilities in a second language has been focusedon. Therefore, the purpose of this article is to briefly introduce Task-Based Language Teaching (TBLT), analyze the possibility to be implemented in an English reading course for Chinese college students.

2. Task-Based Language Teaching

Task-Based Language Teaching, also known as Task-Based Instruction (TBI) or Task-Based Language Learning, is a modern language teaching approach for second language learners. It started in the 1970s when scholars argued that language instruction should teach both grammar and meaning. Willis believes that TBLT originates from Communicative Language Teaching (CLT), because TBLT bears some common principles with CLT.

(1) What Is Task-Based Language Teaching

N.S. Prabhu, who carried out the Bangalore Communicational Teaching Project in India for about five years, has been widely regarded as one of the first proponents for Task-Based Language Teaching. He offers the definition of task as "an activity which required learners to arrive at an outcome from given information through some process of thought and which allowed teachers to control and regulate that process".

Nowadays, TBLT involves testing and curriculum design as well as research and teaching in SLA. Different people define task in various ways. Long gives a non-technical and non-linguistic definition to task as "a piece of work undertaken for oneself or for others, freely or for some reward." Skehan concludes some features of a task, such as "meaning is primary" and "task completion has some priority". In Ellis's opinion, a task is a work-plan that requires the

---

① 欧亚美. A Brief Introduction of Task-Based Language Teaching (TBLT) [J]. Overseas English. 2014 (1): 90–92.

learners to process language pragmatically in order to achieve an outcome that can be evaluated in terms of whether the correct or appropriate propositional content has been conveyed. To end this, it requires them to give primary attention to meaning and to make use of their own linguistic resources. A task is intended to result in language use that bears resemblance, direct or indirect, to the way language is used in the real world.

Samuda and Bygate made some modification to Ellis's definition and put their own definition of task as "a holistic activity which engages language use in order to achieve some nonlinguistic outcome while meeting a linguistic challenge, with the overall aim of promoting language learning, through process or product or both".

Although these definitions are expressed in different ways. They all put emphasis on the learners focusing on meaning instead of grammatical form through communicative language use.

(2) The Rationale for TBLT

Although TBLT is considered to share some features with CLT and even have originated from that, it has its own rationales and approaches toward language instruction.

① The Theory of Language for TBLT

TBLT evolved as a branch of communicative language teaching. It shares some common points with CLT in terms of the nature of language. Hymes draws attention to the need for communicative competence. Brown takes communicative competence as some kind of competence which enables people to convey and interpret messages and to negotiate meanings interpersonally. Halliday views language as a system of meaning instead of a group of words. Austin suggests the use of language and idioms to arrive at some communicative goals, such as to persuade, to entertain or to make a suggestion.

The emergence of TBLT indicates that language in the classroom is "truly communicative rather than pseudo-communicative". The language can be transferred to real world activities and "is best accomplished by doing some of these activities in the classroom", language is basically a means of making meaning.

② The Theory of Language Learning for TBLT

TBLT has its psychological origin, with which tasks are regarded as a tool to stimulate learners to engage in negotiation. Platt and Brooks suggest that task engagement is a turning point in foreign language development. Other theories such as Long's Interaction Hypothesis, Swan's Output Hypothesis and Skehan's Cognitive Approach agree with the principles of Task-Based Language Teaching partly. Long advocates that tasks stimulate learners to use a wide range of strategies to negotiate meaning. Swan believes that interactive language tasks can produce outputs to provide learners with opportunities for contextualized, meaningful language use.

Task-Based Language Teaching has its social-cultural origin. The social-cultural theory indicates that language acquisition can be realized and maximized through interaction with other people in the society. Just as Richards and Rogers say that approaches are at the level of theoretical principles. While theory can not be separated from the practice, as theory can not provide the teaching activities and techniques. Thus in the next part links between theory and practice will be presented.

③ The Roles of Teachers for TBLT

Several different roles are assumed for teachers in different teaching approaches and contexts. Kennedy believes "Teachers, like other learners, interpret new content through their existing understandings and modify and reinterpret new ideas on the basis of what they already know or believe." In terms of course-developing, Graves holds the opinion that "A teacher develops a course in ways that reflect her experience and the values and priorities that are products of her experience as well as the prevailing wisdom around her."

Teachers play a key role in Task-Based Language Teaching, though the role in TBLT differs from that in other more linguistic or structure-oriented approaches. Avermaet et al conclude the teachers' role in Task-Based Language Teaching into two points: ① motivating the language learners; ② supporting language learners.

In my understanding, the roles of teachers in a task-based context can be

● Chairperson of the classroom;
● Facilitator of the learning process;
● Task designer;
● Supervisor of the reporting of the task;
● Suggestion provider.

④ The Roles of Learners for TBLT

One feature of learner's role in a TBLT classroom is learner-centred, which has been shared with other traditional approaches, such as CLT. While there are some differences. The most remarkable feature distinguishing TBLT from the other approaches is that the information about learners will be taken into consideration at all the curriculum processing stages and will be involved in the decision on the content selection, methodology and evaluation.

In my opinion, learners in a TBLT context present the following three roles:

● Active participants.
● Willing co-operators.
● Good meaning-negotiators.

Skehan proposes five mayor principles for the implementation of TBLT, although his cognitive approach to TBLT taking learners as an individual information processor has always been criticized.

⑤ The Role of Materials: Task-Based Materials

As TBLT is not only a communication in the classroom, but also out of classroom and requires true communication, the materials needed in TBLT are more than the textbooks and related materials usually used in the classroom. The materials can be magazines, newspapers, CDS, the TV programs, the radio broadcast, the work sheets, the Internet, including all kinds of social networks.

3. Limitations and Difficulties of TBLT

Prabhu suggests there is no best method because it all depends and there is some truth to every method. Some methods are more suitable or appropriate than others in a particular context.

It can not be denied that TBLT has a lot of advantages. ① TBLT puts an emphasis on practice for the purpose of real-world communication. ② It is suitable for a wider range of learners. ③ In the TBLT Classroom, learners have much more freedom from language exposure. ④ Learners are the center of the classroom. ⑤ Authentic texts are to be used in the learning situation. ⑥ With the access to different kinds of materials, learners will get more fun as well as language acquisition from the TBLT process.

Although with all of the above merits. TBLT has been criticized by a lot of researchers and educators. Skehan admits that TBLT is more likely to be with adults, generally at middle proficiency levels, and mostly with English as the target language. Swan suggests TBLT can only be implemented in the classroom for those learners whose receptive language knowledge is wider than their productive language knowledge. There are claims that TBLT might negatively affect young learners, development in other aspects if they are overburdened with learning a foreign language and performing tasks.

Practically, TBLT requires a higher degree of creativity for the teacher. As TBLT is learner-centred, interactions between learners are required a lot, and thus higher and better cooperation between learners is needed. Furthermore, learners are supposed to achieve fluency at the price of accuracy.

4. Conclusion

In this article, Task-Based Language Teaching has been introduced to an English reading course in a Chinese university, then the author presented the rationale behind TBLT, analyzed the suitability and the difficulties in implementing this method on the basis of the context, and thus presented a mixed and effective approach suitable for Chinese college students to promote their English reading skills and meet their other language learning needs.

● **Knowledge Table**

Table 10-4   Summary of Characteristics of Task-Based Language Teaching

Key Points	Task-Based Language Teaching
Period	
Representatives	
Background	
Theory of Language	
Theory of Language Learning	
Objectives	
The Syllabus	
Types of Learning and Teaching Activities	
Teacher's Roles	
Learner's Roles	
The Role of Students' Native Language and Target Language	
The Role of Instructional Materials and Textbook	
Others	
Summary	

● **Mind Map**

Chapter 11   Reviews and Conclusions

第 11 章   复习与总结

O Contents

- A Brief History of Second Language Teaching
- The Post-Method Era and Language Teaching Methods
- Comparison and Analysis of Different Methods and Approaches
- The Development Trend of Second Language Teaching
- Activities and Exercises
- Further Reading

- 语言教学作为一门学科的历史发展概况
- 后方法时代与语言教学法
- 语言教学法对比分析
- 第二语言教学法的发展趋势
- 活动与练习
- 拓展阅读

1 A Brief History of Second Language Teaching[①]

The history of foreign language teaching can be traced back to the ancient Roman when Latin was taught as a second language. Unfortunately, it is very difficult to present here a complete picture of the historical development of foreign language teaching because of its poor documentation. So we will only cover the recent history of more than two hundred years. To facilitate our research and discussion, this part will only briefly sort out the historical development of foreign language teaching and quote the division based on the book *Foreign Language Teaching Methods* by Professor Baimei Shu etc. In her book, the short history of foreign language teaching was divided into four periods according to the main trends, events and important figures in those periods.

1.1 The Reform Movement

By the end of the 18th century, nearly all the European languages had been studied as foreign languages in schools. The principal aim of foreign language teaching at that time was to help learners acquire a reading knowledge of the target languages. To satisfy the requirements of group teaching in schools, the Grammar-Translation Method was devised and developed. For the next scores of years, the Grammar-Translation Method dominated foreign language teaching. Although there were individual endeavours to reform foreign language teaching in those years, none of them was successful in shaking the position of the Grammar-Translation Method. However, they had helped pave the way for the Reform Movement. Then, in the second half of the 19th century, as communications among the European countries became more and more frequent, people were not satisfied with a mere reading knowledge of foreign languages. They wanted to be able to talk in a foreign language and they became more and more interested in reforming the teaching methods.

In 1882, Wilhelm Viëtor published a pamphlet entitled *Language Teaching Must Start Afresh!* and a movement of reform started all of a sudden. The principles of the movement were the primacy of speech, the centrality of the connected text as the kernel of the teaching-learning process, and the absolute priority of an oral methodology in the classroom. A lot of scholars as well as ordinary teachers were involved in the movement, the influence of which was felt everywhere in Europe and in some other countries in the world. The movement lasted more than ten years and made remarkable achievements: an applied linguistic approach to language teaching began to take shape with the publication of Henry Sweet's *The Practical Study of Languages* in

---

① 舒白梅，陈佑林. 外语教学法 [M]. 北京：高等教育出版社，1999(8)：28–33.

1899; a lot of books, pamphlets and reports were published; new professional organizations such as the International Phonetic Association were set up; experiments on new teaching methods were carried out; and school systems and administrative policies were affected. In 1904, Jespersen published his book *How to Teach a Foreign Language*, which presented a good summary of the movement's practical implications for the language teachers.

1.2 Modern Language Teaching and Research

Foreign language teaching in this period as a whole had little to be proud of. Theories and practices of the period were usually the target of criticism and condemnation. However, the teaching of English as a second/foreign language in Britain made great progress during this period. It became an autonomous profession and produced a number of world-famous scholars. Daniel Jones was the first one that helped make a profession the teaching of English as a second/ foreign language and became well-known in the world because of his research on the profession. In the spring of 1907, he began to offer lectures on the phonetics of French at the University of London and then in 1908 he started to give lectures on the phonetics of English. In the following year, courses for overseas students of English were offered. The program was so successful that soon after other courses had to be included. During these years, he wrote a number of works on English phonetics: *The Pronunciation of English* (1909), *A Phonetic Dictionary of the English Language* (1913), *English Pronouncing Dictionary* (1917), and *Outline of English Phonetics* (1918).

Harold Palmer was another well-known scholar who had made great contributions to the profession of English teaching. He taught English as a second/foreign language for eight years at the University of London and then for seven years in Japan. He tried out the Oral Method in his teaching and did his research on the English vocabulary in his spare time. He published a lot of books in these years, ranging from books on methods of language teaching, textbooks, to simplified readers.

Other important figures of this period include Michael West who, together with Palmer, published a lot of books, such as simplified English readers, grammar books and dictionaries; Lawrence Faucett who started the first training course for teachers of English as a foreign language in 1932; C.E. Eckersley who published a set of course books called *Essential English for Foreign Students*.

1.3 Structural Language Teaching

We label this period of foreign language teaching as structural because a new approach, which took American structuralism and behaviourism as its theoretical basis, was born at the beginning of the period, rose into its peak of fame in the 1950s, and declined at the end of the period. During the war years, a lot of American structuralists such as Leonard Bloomfield and C.C. Fries began to take an active part in the wartime language programs. They applied theories and ideas of behaviorism and structuralism systematically to foreign language teaching and devised a new approach called Audiolingual Method, and introduced it into their language teaching programs. After World War, the new approach was met with enthusiasm in America and then elsewhere in the world. It enjoyed extreme popularity in the 1950s. Unfortunately, towards the end of the 1950s, a new baby called transformational generative linguistics was born and started a war soon after its birth against the theoretical foundation of the Audiolingual Method — behaviorism and structuralism. It attacked the foundation violently and forcefully from every angle and finally brought it down successfully from its dominant position at the end of the period.

Another important feature of this period is that foreign language teaching itself became a science of its own. Although London University began to offer a course for teachers of English as a foreign language, it was in this period that applied linguistics was admitted into universities as a subject.

In this period, quite a number of centres for applied linguistics were founded. For instance, the Foundation of the English Language Institute was set up at the University of Michigan in 1941; the School of Applied Linguistics was founded at Edinburgh University in 1957; and the Center for Applied Linguistics was set up in Washington, D.C. in 1959. These centers not only offered advanced training programs for teachers of foreign languages, but also did research on the subject. Apart from the centers, this period also saw the appearance of professional journals such as *English Language Teaching Journal* (1946), *Language Learning: A Journal of Applied Linguistics* (1948), and the founding of professional organizations such as the International Association of Applied Linguistics (1964), and TESOL Association (1966).

Still another important feature of the period is that a lot of academic works on applied linguistics were published. Among the authors were well-known figures like L. Bloomfield, B. Bloch, G.L. Trager, T. Anderson, C.E. Osgood, R. Lado, N. Brooks, M.A.K. Halliday, P. Strevens, and W. Rivers, to name just a few. They published their findings and research on the subject and many of the works have become classics in this field and are still widely read by students of applied linguistics as well as teachers of foreign languages.

1.4 Communicative Language Teaching

At the end of the1950s, Chomsky's transformational generative linguistics started a revolution in the linguistics world. And then at the end of the 1960s, Cognitive Psychology came into being and began to make its impact felt in the world. Inspired by the new approaches in linguistics and psychology, people began to look at things from different angles. The consequence of this is that new disciplines seem to appear from day to day. Applied linguists and language teachers are no exceptions. They began to study foreign language teaching from different perspectives and new trends and ideas appeared so quickly that it is difficult for people to digest them. The main aspects are as follows:

(1) Communicative Language Teaching

This is probably the main trend dominating the language teaching profession today. The appearance of functional linguistics, as a new approach to linguistic study, and new disciplines like sociolinguistics and pragmatics enabled people to look at foreign language teaching from a different angle and induced people to take a functional attitude to the teaching of foreign languages. As a matter of fact, the word communication has come into fashion and our teaching is sure to sound outdated if it is not labelled with the word.

(2) New Theories of Second Language Acquisition

Influenced by Chomsky's hypothesis of Language Acquisition Device (LAD) and Cognitive Psychology, people became more and more interested in the mental process of human beings. In the 1970s, linguists, psychologists and applied linguists did serious research into the language acquisition process and a lot of theories were proposed. Most of the theories of second language acquisition made their first appearance in the 1970s.

(3) New Methods of Language Teaching

Though Communicative Language Teaching is the main trend in this period, this does not mean that people have ceased to find new methods for the teaching of foreign languages. Actually, people have never stopped searching for new efficient ways of language teaching. The appearance of the new methods and practices we discussed in this book is clear evidence of this endeavor.

(4) New Approaches to Language Syllabus

When some applied linguists were busy searching for the best way to teach languages, some other applied linguists began to turn their attention to the ways of organizing the teaching content. They got new ideas from the new disciplines and tried them in experiments. The notional syllabus designed by a group of scholars from different countries is just one example of this trend.

(5) Exploration of Human Relations

Language teaching involves teachers and students. The relations between teachers and students, and the relations among the students themselves must have some impact on the result of learning. People begin to make investigate into the problem of relations in the classroom in this period, hoping that the most optimal relations could be found.

一、语言教学作为一门学科的历史发展概况

外语教学的历史可以追溯到古罗马时期拉丁语作为第二语言的教学。但遗憾的是，由于文献资料缺失，我们很难完整地描述外语教学的发展历史。因此，我们仅介绍二百多年

来的近代发展史。为了便于研究和讨论，本部分仅对外语教学的历史发展做简要的梳理。对外语教学发展阶段的划分，我们引用舒白梅教授等专家在《外语教学法》一书中所做的论述，即根据该时期外语教学的主要事件、重要人物和发展趋势将外语教学近代发展划分为四个时期。

1. 改革运动时期

到 18 世纪末，几乎所有的欧洲语言都已在学校里作为外语开设课程并进行教学。当时外语教学的主要目是帮助学习者掌握目的语的阅读知识和技能。为了满足学校班级教学的需要，语法翻译法应运而生，迅速发展。在接下来的几十年里，语法翻译法在外语教学中一直占据着主导地位。期间，虽然也有一些改革外语教学法的努力和尝试，但都未能成功撼动语法翻译法的统治地位。然而，这些教学改革尝试却为随后的语言教学改革运动铺平了道路。到了 19 世纪下半叶，随着欧洲国家之间交流的日益频繁，人们不再仅仅满足于利用外语进行阅读。他们更希望能用外语进行交流，因此，对语言教学领域的改革呼之欲出。

1882 年，威廉·维耶托出版了一本小册子，名为《语言教学必须重新开始！》，一场改革运动随之而来。这场语言教学改革运动的原则是口语要放在语言教学的首要地位，要以有上下文语境的文本作为教学过程的核心，以及口语教学方法在课堂上的绝对优先地位。许多学者和一线教师都参与了这场改革运动，该运动的影响在欧洲和世界很多国家都随处可见。这场运动持续了十多年，取得了令人瞩目的成就：1899 年亨利·韦斯特的《语言实践研究》一书的出版，使语言教学中的应用语言学方法初具雏形；出版了大量的书籍、小册子和研究报告；成立了国际语音协会等新的专业组织；人们开始创新教学方法并开展教学应用实践；进一步影响了学校的教育制度和政策。1904 年，杰斯珀森出版了《如何教外语》一书，该书将语言教学改革运动对语言教师的实际意义和影响进行了充分的梳理与总结。

2. 现代语言教学与研究时期

外语教学作为一门学科在这一时期的发展相对缓慢，成就不大。在这一时期，无论是教学理论还是教学实践通常都成了受批评、受谴责的对象。然而，也就在这一时期，在英国，英语作为第二语言/外语的教学取得了长足的发展。语言教师成为一个独立自主的职业，继而产生了一大批世界著名的学者。丹尼尔·琼斯是推动英语作为第二语言/外语教学成为一个专门职业的第一人，他也因对这一职业的研究而闻名于世。1907 年春，他开始在伦敦大学讲授法语语音，然后在 1908 年开始讲授英语语音。在接下来的一年里，他为外国学生开设英语课程。这一教学项目进行得非常成功，因此，之后又相继开设了其他课程。在那些年里，琼斯撰写了许多关于英语语音的著作：《英语发音》（1909）、《英语语音词典》（1913）、《英语发音词典》（1917）、《英语语音概要》（1918）。

哈罗德·帕默是另一位对英语教学事业做出重大贡献的著名学者。他在伦敦大学教授英语作为第二语言/外语的课程，历时 8 年，之后又在日本教了 7 年英语。他在教学中实践口语法，并利用业余时间对英语词汇进行了深入研究。期间，他出版了许多书籍，包括语言教学法相关著作、教科书（教材）及简易读本等。

这一时期的其他重要人物还有迈克尔·韦斯特，他和帕默一起出版了许多书籍，如一些英语简明读本、语法书和词典等；劳伦斯·福塞特于 1932 年开办了第一个英语作为外语的教师培训课程；埃克斯利出版了一套教材，名为《外国学生英语要略》。

3. 语言教学结构法时期

这一时期的外语教学称之为结构主义时期。在这一时期之初诞生了一种以美国结构主义和行为主义为理论基础的全新的外语教学法，这一教学法在 20 世纪 50 年代达到鼎盛，并在这一时期末逐渐衰落。在战争年代，许多美国结构主义者如伦纳德·布龙菲尔德和里弗斯都开始积极参与战时语言培训项目。他们把行为主义和结构主义的理论与思想系统地运用到外语教学中，设计了一种新型教学法，即听说法，并将其引入他们参与的语言教学项目之中。第二次世界大战结束后，这种新型教学法先在美国，继而在世界各地受到热烈追捧，并在 20 世纪 50 年代盛极一时。然而，到了 50 年代末，一个全新的语言学理论——转换生成语法诞生了，它诞生不久就引发了一场"战争"，它抨击听说法的理论基础——行为主义和结构主义，从各个角度有力地、激烈地冲击着听说法的语言学和心理学基础，并最终成功地将听说法从当时的统治地位上拉下来。

这一时期的另一个重要特征是外语教学本身成了一门独立的科学。虽然伦敦大学早已为教师开设对外英语这门课程，但应用语言学作为大学的一门学科专业，则是在这一时期开始的。

这一时期，众多应用语言学研究中心相继成立。例如，1941 年英语语言研究所在密歇根大学建立；1957 年应用语言学学院在爱丁堡大学成立；1959 年应用语言学研究中心在华盛顿成立。这些研究中心不仅为外语教师提供高级培训项目，而且还在这一领域开展科学研究。除了研究中心以外，这一时期还出现了一些专业学术期刊，如《英语教学杂志》（1946）、《语言学习：应用语言学杂志》（1948）。国际应用语言学协会（1964）和英语作为第二语言教学协会（1966）等学术组织也先后成立。

这一时期的另一个重要特点还有一大批应用语言学学术著作先后出版。这些著作的作者不乏一些著名的专家学者，如布龙菲尔德、布洛克、特雷格、安德森、奥斯古德、拉多、布鲁克斯、韩礼德、斯特雷文斯和里弗斯等等。他们发表了自己的研究及相关成果，许多成果已成为这一领域的经典著作，至今仍被应用语言学界的学生和外语教师广泛研读。

4. 交际语言教学时期

20 世纪 50 年代末，乔姆斯基的转换生成语言学在语言学界掀起了一场革命。20 世纪 60 年代末，认知心理学诞生并开始在世界范围内产生影响。受语言学和心理学新理论新方法的启发，人们开始从不同的角度观察事物。其结果便是不同的学术观点如雨后春笋般涌现。应用语言学家和语言教师也不例外。他们开始从不同的角度研究外语教学，新的观点和前沿发展日新月异，使人们应接不暇。主要是以下几个方面：

（1）交际法

交际法可能是当今语言教学的主流趋势。功能语言学作为一种全新的语言学研究理论，它的产生以及社会语言学、语用学等新兴学科领域的出现，都促使人们从不同的视角看待外语教学，并促使人们对外语教学采取功能主义的态度。事实上，"交流"这个词已经广泛流行于世，因此，语言教学如果不加上"交流 / 交际"这一标签，便一定会老旧过时。

（2）第二语言习得新理论

受乔姆斯基语言习得机制假说和认知心理学的影响，人们越来越关注人类的心理过程。20 世纪 70 年代，语言学家、心理学家和应用语言学家对语言习得过程进行了深入研究，提出了许多理论假说。大部分第二语言习得理论和假说都是在 20 世纪 70 年代首次出现的。

（3）语言教学新方法

虽然交际法成为这一时期的主流教学法，但这并不意味着人们已经停止探寻新的外语教学方法。事实上，人们一直在寻找新的、更有效的语言教学法。我们在本书中讨论的新方法的产生及其教学实践探索就是这一努力探寻的有力证据。

（4）语言教学大纲新探索

当一些应用语言学家忙于寻找最佳的语言教学法时，另一些应用语言学家则开始将注意力转向教学内容的组织方式。他们在新理论的兴起中受到启发，产生了新的想法，并在教学中加以尝试。来自不同国家的学者共同关注并设计的意念大纲便是这一发展趋势的典型例证。

（5）人际关系探微

语言教学活动涉及教师和学生双方。师生关系、生生关系必然会对学习效果产生一定的影响。在这一时期，人们开始对课堂中的人际关系问题展开研究，希望能找到最理想的人际关系。

2 The Post-Method Era and Language Teaching Methods

The heyday of methods, according to Richards and Rogers, was the 1950s to 1980s, when correct use of a particular method or approach was thought to yield better results than using another method. Indeed, this coincided with a time when education in general was preoccupied with finding the best method (e.g., New Math of the 1960s or Whole Language of the 1980s). The idea was that the best method would improve the quality of instruction if teachers just adhered to the classroom techniques and activities associated with it. Yet the notion of methods came under criticism in the 1990s for other reasons, and a number of limitations implicit in the notion of all-purpose methods were raised. By the end of the twentieth century, mainstream language teaching no longer regarded methods as the key factor in accounting for success or failure in language teaching. Some spoke of the death of methods and approaches and the term "Post-Methods Era" was sometimes used. In the Post-Method Era, do language teachers need to learn approaches and methods of language teaching?

In fact, approaches and methods have played a central role in the development of our profession, and it will continue to be useful for teachers and students to become familiar with the major teaching approaches and methods proposed for second and foreign language teaching. Mainstream approaches and methods draw on a large amount of collective experience and practice from which much can be learned. Approaches and methods can therefore be usefully studied and selectively mastered in order: ① to learn how to use different approaches and methods and understand when they might be useful; ② to understand some of the issues and controversies that characterize the history of language teaching; ③ to participate in language learning experiences based on different approaches and methods as a basis for reflection and comparison; ④ to be aware of the rich set of activity resources available to the imaginative teacher; ⑤ to appreciate how theory and practice can be linked from a variety of different perspectives.[①]

Language teachers are expected to use approaches and methods flexibly and creatively based on their own judgment and experience. But in the process of growing up as new teachers, in their early stages of teaching, it will be easier for them to a specific method to teach language, because an approach or a predetermined method, with its associated activities, principles, and techniques, can provide them with the confidence that they will need to face learners and it can provide techniques and strategies for presenting lessons. As new teachers gain experience and knowledge, they will begin to develop an individual approach or personal method of teaching, one that draws on an established approach or method but that also uniquely reflects the teachers' individual beliefs, values, principles, and experiences. And when they teach a language, they will add, modify, and adjust the approach or method to the realities of the classroom. While in developing a personal approach to teaching, the teacher may draw on different core principles at different times, depending on the type of class he or she is teaching (e.g., children or adults, beginners, or advanced learners) and make his or her personal instructional plans. These core principles which are developed through the comprehensive analysis of various teaching approaches and methods in the history of language teaching can provide the source for teacher's plans and instructional decisions. Bailey summarizes and proposes the core principles as follows:[②]

- Engage all learners in the lesson.
- Make learners, and not the teacher, the focus of the lesson.
- Provide maximum opportunities for student participation.
- Develop learner responsibility.
- Be tolerant of learners' mistakes.
- Develop learners' confidence.

---

① RICHARDS J C, RODGERS T S. 语言教学的流派 [M]. 2 版 . 北京：外语教学与研究出版社，2008：250.

② BAILEY K. The best-laid plans: Teachers' in-class decisions to depart from their lesson plans [M]. In K. Bailey and D. Nunan, Voices from the Language Classroom. New York: Cambridge University Press, 1996: 15–40.

- Teach learning strategies.
- Respond to learners' difficulties and build on them.
- Use a maximum amount of student-to-student activities.
- Promote cooperation among learners.
- Practice both accuracy and fluency.
- Address learners' needs and interests.

Experience with different approaches and methods can provide teachers with an initial practical knowledge base in teaching and can also be used to explore and develop teacher's own beliefs, principles, and practices. Therefore, even in the post-method era, to know the approaches or methods of language teaching, including the background of their emergence, the theoretical basis, characteristics, teaching principles, and their procedures is very important for language teachers.

二、后方法时代与语言教学法

理查德和罗杰斯认为，方法的全盛时期是 20 世纪 50 年代至 80 年代，当时人们认为正确使用某一特定的教学法会比使用另一种方法产生更好的教学效果。事实上，这与整个教育界都在专注于寻找最好的方法的时代背景（例如，20 世纪 60 年代的新数学教学法或 80 年代的全语言法）相契合。当时的观点是，最好的教学法如果由教师带入课堂，并配置相应的教学技巧与课堂活动，将有效提高教学质量。然而，由于一些原因，方法的概念在 20 世纪 90 年代受到了批评，隐藏在通用方法概念下的局限性逐渐显现出来。到了 20 世纪末，语言教学界的主流思想已不再把教学法作为衡量语言教学成败的关键因素。有些人提出方法已消亡，方法时代已过去，并时而提及"后方法时代"这一说法。那么，在后方法时代，语言教师是否还需要学习语言教学法呢？

事实上，教学法在我们的专业发展中起到了核心作用，它有助于教师和师范生熟悉并掌握第二语言教学和外语教学的主要理论与方法。而那些主流的教学理论和教学法都曾借鉴了大量的集体经验，拥有丰富的教学实践，从中我们可以学到很多。因此，对教学理论和教学法进行有益的研究及选择性地掌握，我们便能够：①掌握如何使用不同的教学法，并了解这些教学法用在何时何处更有效；②了解语言教学历史上曾产生的一些问题和争论；③参与并体验使用不同教学法开展的语言学习，并进行教学反思与对比；④为富于想象力的教师展示并提供多种丰富的活动资源；⑤从不同的角度理解理论和实践是如何联系在一起的。

语言教师应根据自己的经验和判断，灵活地、创造性地运用教学理论与方法。但是对于正处于成长阶段的新手教师来说，在他们从事教学的早期阶段，选择并使用一种特定的教学法来教授语言，会使他们的教学更容易上手。因为一种教学法或成型的教学模式，一般都配有相应的课堂活动、教学原则及教学技巧，这可以为新手教师在面对学习者进行教学时带来更多便捷与自信，也可以为他们在课程设计和组织教学等方面提供相应的教学策略与技巧。随着新手教师教学知识的丰富和教学经验的积累，他们能够逐渐形成个人的个性化教学方法与技巧，这种个性化的教学方法既借鉴了已成型的教学理论与方法，又体现了教师自身独特的教学理念、价值、原则和实践经验。当他们教授一门语言时，他们会根据课堂的实际情况增加、修改和调整教学方法。在个性化教学方法形成和发展的过程中，教师可以根据所教授课程的类型（例如，儿童或成人、初学者或高级水平学习者），在不同时期借鉴核心教学原则，制订自己的个性化教学设计方案。这些核心教学原则是通过对语言教学历史上各种不同的教学理念与教学法的综合分析发展而来，可以为教师的教学设计与教学决策提供参考依据。贝利总结并提出了以下核心原则：

- 让所有学习者都参与到课堂中来。
- 让学习者而不是教师成为课堂的焦点。
- 最大限度地为学习者提供参与或实践的机会。
- 培养学习者的责任感。
- 容忍学习者犯错。
- 增强学习者的自信心。
- 教授学习策略。
- 正视学习者的学习困难，并帮助学习者克服困难，再接再厉。
- 最大限度地组织并利用生生互动。
- 促进学习者之间的交流合作。
- 既训练准确性，也训练流利度。
- 满足学习者的学习需求和学习兴趣。

不同的教学理念与方法可以为教师提供扎实的教学理论知识与实践基础，也可以辅助教师探索并形成自身个性化的教学理念、原则和实践。因此，即使在后方法时代，作为一名语言教师，了解并掌握语言教学理论与教学法，包括各教学法的产生背景、理论基础、特点、教学原则及教学过程，都是非常重要的。

3 Comparison and Analysis of Different Methods and Approaches

The emergence of language teaching approaches dates back from the early nineteenth century. In that century, teach linguists of western European countries proposed the Grammar-Translation Method to teach dead languages, such as Greek and Roman. Individuals learned these languages through translation of classic literature. The nature of the Grammar-Translation Method made it to center on the written form mainly, paying little attention to the oral form. While with the increasing exchanges between European countries, foreign language learning, especially oral ability, has been put on the agenda. Linguists and applied linguists began to pay attention to and search for more effective ways of teaching foreign or second languages. Thus, as an improvement over the Grammar-Translation Method, the Direct Method was enthusiastically embraced in the early part of the twentieth century. During the period of World War II, the U.S. government decided to supply its troops with staff fluent in different languages and requested American universities to prepare foreign language programs for the military, resulting in the setup of the Army Specialized Training Program (ASTP) in 1942. The Audiolingual Method stood out in this training program and had great influence in the academic community of the U.S. The Method was soon dominant in foreign or second languages teaching and was thought to provide a way forward, incorporating the latest insights from the sciences of linguistics and psychology. When Noam Chomsky challenged the view that language was a set of patterns acquired through habit formation, its influence began to wane. Following its decline, the field entered into a period of great methodological diversity in the 1970s, a period in which a number of "innovation methods" emerged, such as the Silent Way, Community Language Learning, Total Physical Response, and Suggestopedia.

Interest in developing students' communicative competence reunified the field in the 1980s. It was David A. Wilkins who made one of the first contributions to Communicative Language Teaching (CLT) with his notional syllabus and its focus on linguistic function. CLT became mainstream language teaching on both sides of the Atlantic and continues to be considered the most plausible basis for language teaching today. Under the language teaching methodology basis recommended by CLT, the research perspective of second language teaching began to shift from looking for the "best teaching method" and "how to teach a language" to focusing on the learners' learning process and "how to learn a language". Innovation in the language teaching field in the late 1980s and 1990s has been stimulated by a special concern for the language learning process. New methods propose that language learning is best served when students are interacting — completing a task or learning content or resolving real-life issues — where linguistic structures are not taught one by one, but where attention to linguistic form is given as necessary.

By the 2000s, it seems that changes in the language teaching field have been made in response to the influence from outside the field — the continuing development of technology. The modern distance education based on network, Computer-Assisted Learning, the Flipped Classroom, MOOC, SPOC, and STEAM, etc., are all innovations in pedagogy and language teaching by using advanced educational and internet technology.

From the historical development of language teaching approaches and methods, we can see that language teaching as a discipline is developing stronger from scratch. Each language teaching approach or method has been proposed considering the constraints of former approaches and as a response to the needs of the society of each time. And each of these methods has made important contributions to second or foreign language teaching and learning.

In the philosophy of language teaching, Richards and Rodgers proposed the framework to compare particular methods and approaches in language teaching, which is three levels and nine elements. The three levels are approach, design and procedure. Approach refers to theories about the nature of language and language learning that serve as the source of practices and principles in language teaching. Design is the level of method analysis in which we consider: ① what the objectives of a method are; ② how language content is selected and organized within the method, that is, the syllabus model the method incorporates; ③ the types of learning tasks and teaching activities the method advocates; ④ the roles of learners; ⑤ the roles of teachers; and ⑥ the role of instructional materials. Procedure is the level at which we describe how a method realizes its approach and design in classroom behavior. This encompasses the actual moment-to-moment techniques, practices, and behaviors that operate in teaching a language according to a particular method. According to this framework, table 11-1 has been compiled to summarize and compare the differences between each method or approach from the above two levels: approach and design. (Because procedure is a kind of detailed and practical level and was introduced in the front chapters, this chapter will not mention it anymore.)

Table 11-1　A Comparison of Different Language Teaching Methods in the Levels of Approach and Design

	Theory of Language	Theory of Learning	Teaching Objectives	Syllabus	Activity Types	Learner's Roles	Teacher's Roles	Roles of Materials
The Grammar-Translation Method	Literary language is considered superior to spoken language. "The first language is maintained as the reference system in the acquisition of the second language."	Language learning is viewed as consisting of little more than memorizing rules and facts in order to understand and manipulate the morphology and syntax of the foreign language.	To read literature written by a language. To benefit from the mental discipline and intellectual development that result from foreign language study.	The text is extracted from literary works. The syllabus was followed for the sequencing of grammar points throughout a text, and there was an attempt to teach grammar in an organized and systematic way.	Traditional classroom activities, such as translation, reading comprehension questions, memorization, making sentences, fill-in-the-blanks exercise and composition.	The learner's role is very traditional. Learners should do what their teacher asks them to do.	The teacher is the authority in the classroom.	The textbooks come from the classic literature. It is the classic model of language and the basis for teachers' teaching and students' learning.
Situational Language Teaching The (Direct Method)	Language is a set of structures, related to situations.	Memorization and habit formation.	To teach a practical command of the four basic skills. Automatic, accurate control of basic sentence patterns. Oral before written mastery.	A list of structures and vocabulary graded according to grammatical difficulty.	Repetition, substitution drills; avoid translation and grammatical explanation; learners should never be allowed to make a mistake.	To listen and repeat, respond to questions and commands. Learners have no control over content, later allowed to initiate statements and ask questions.	Acts as a model in presenting structures; orchestrates drill practice; corrects errors, tests progress.	Relies on textbooks and visual aids. Textbooks contain tightly organized structurally graded lessons.
The Audiolingual Method	Language is a system of rule-governed structures hierarchically arranged.	Habit formation. Skills are learned more effectively if oral precedes written. Analogy not analysis.	Control of the structures of sound, form and order mastery over symbols of the language. Goal is native-speaker mastery.	Graded syllabus of phonology, morphology and syntax. Contrastive analysis.	Dialogues and drills, repetition and memorization, pattern practice.	Organisms that can be directed by skilled training techniques to produce correct responses.	Teacher-dominated. Central and active teacher provides modes, controls direction and pace.	Primarily teacher oriented. Tapes, visuals and language laboratory are often used.

continued table

	Theory of Language	Theory of Learning	Teaching Objectives	Syllabus	Activity Types	Learner's Roles	Teacher's Roles	Roles of Materials
Total Physical Response	Basically a structuralist, grammar-based view of language.	L2 learning is the same as L1 learning. Comprehension before production is "imprinted" through carrying out commands (right brain functioning). Reduction of stress.	To teach oral proficiency to produce learners who can communicate uninhibitedly and intelligibly with native speakers.	Sentence-based syllabus with grammatical and lexical criteria being primary, but focus on meaning not form.	Imperative drills to elicit physical actions.	Listener and performer. Little influence over the content of learning.	Active and direct role as "the director of a stage play" with students as actors.	No basic text. Materials and media have an important role later. Initially voice, action and gestures are sufficient.
The Silent Way	Each language is composed of elements that give it a unique rhythm and spirit. Functional vocabulary and core structure are a key to the spirit of the language.	Processes of learning a second language are fundamentally different from L1 learning. L2 learning is an intellectual, cognitive process. Surrender to the music of the language, silent awareness then active trial.	Near-native fluency, correct pronunciation, basic practical knowledge of the grammar of the L2. Learners learn how to learn a language.	Basically structural lessons planned around grammatical items and related vocabulary. Items are introduced according to their grammatical complexity.	Learners response to commands, questions and visual cues. Activities encourage and shape oral responses without grammatical explanation or modelling by teacher.	Learning is a process of personal growth. Learners are responsible for their own learning and must develop independence, autonomy, and responsibility.	Teachers must ① teach, ② test and ③ get out of the way. Remain impassive. Resist temptation to model, remodel, assist, direct exhort.	Unique materials: coloured rods, colour-coded pronunciation, and vocabulary charts.
Community Language Learning	Language is more than a system for communication. It involves the whole person, culture, educational developmental, communicative processes.	Learning involves the whole person. It is a social process of growth from childlike dependence to self-direction and independence.	No specific objectives. Near native mastery is the goal.	No set syllabus. Course progression is topic-based. Learners provide the topics. Syllabus emerges from learners' intention and the teacher's reformulations.	Combination of innovative and conventional. Translation, group work, recording, transcription, reflection and observation, listening, free conversation.	Learners are members of a community. Learning is not viewed as an individual accomplishment, but something that is achieved collaboratively.	Counselling/parental analogy. Teacher provides a safe environment in which students can learn and grow.	No textbook, which would inhibit growth. Materials are developed as course progresses.

continued table

	Theory of Language	Theory of Learning	Teaching Objectives	Syllabus	Activity Types	Learner's Roles	Teacher's Roles	Roles of Materials
Suggestopedia	Rather conventional, although memorization of whole meaningful texts is recommended.	Learning occurs through suggestion, when learners are in a deeply relaxed state. Baroque music is used to induce this state.	To deliver advanced conversational competence quickly. Learners are required to master prodigious lists of vocabulary pairs, although the goal is understanding not memorization.	Ten-unit courses consisting of 1,200-word dialogues graded by vocabulary and grammar.	Initiatives, question and answer, role play, listening exercises under deep relaxation.	Must maintain a passive state and allow the materials to work on them (rather than vice versa).	To create situations in which the learner is most suggestible, and present material in a way most likely to encourage positive reception and retention. Must exude authority and confidence.	Consists of texts, tapes, classroom fixtures and music. Texts should have force, literary quality and interesting characters.
The Natural Approach	The essence of language is meaning. Vocabulary not grammar is the heart of language.	There are two ways of L2 language development: "acquisition"—a natural subconscious process, and "learning"—a conscious process. Learning cannot lead to acquisition.	Designed to give beginners and intermediate learners basic (oral / written) personal and academic communicative skills.	Based on a selection of communicative activities and topics derived from learner needs.	Activities allowing comprehensible input about things in the here-and-now. Focus on meaning not form.	Should not try and learn language in the usual sense, but should try and lose themselves in activities involving meaningful communication.	The teacher is the primary source of comprehensible input. Must create positive low-anxiety climate. Must choose and orchestrate a rich mixture of classroom activities.	Materials come from realia rather than textbooks. Primary aim is to promote comprehension and communication.
Communicative Language Teaching	Language is a system for the expression of meaning; primary function-interaction and communication.	Activities involving real communication. Carrying out meaningful tasks and using language which is meaningful to the learner to promote learning.	Objectives will reflect the needs of the learner. they will include functional skills as well as linguistic objectives.	Will include some/all of the following, structures, functions, notions, themes, tasks. Ordering will be guided by learner needs.	Engage learners in communication, involving processes such as information sharing, negotiation of meaning, and interaction.	Learner as negotiator and interactor who gives as well as takes.	Facilitator of the communication process. Needs analyst counsellor. Process manager.	Primary role of promoting communicative language use. Task-based materials. Authentic.

三、语言教学法对比分析

语言教学法的出现可以追溯到 19 世纪初。当时西欧各国的语言学家们提出语法翻译法，并使用该法教授希腊语和罗马语等已消亡的语言。人们通过翻译经典文学作品来学习这些语言。以此为目的的语法翻译法便主要以教授书面语为主，而较少关注口语。随着欧洲国家间交流的日益频繁，对外语学习，尤其是对外语口语能力培养的需求也提上了日程。语言学家和应用语言学家开始关注并寻求更有效的外语教学方法。作为对语法翻译法的一种改进方法，直接法在 20 世纪初受到了热烈的欢迎。第二次世界大战期间，美国政府决定为其军队提供精通不同语言的工作人员，随即要求美国大学为军队筹建外语课程，继而在 1942 年设立了陆军专业训练计划（ASTP）。听说法在这个军队语言培训项目中脱颖而出，并在美国学术界产生了很大的影响。该教学法很快在外语／第二语言教学中占据主导地位，并因其吸收了语言学和心理学的最新理论，被视为为语言教学提供了一条前进的道路。然而，当诺姆·乔姆斯基对语言由一系列句型结构组成，语言通过习惯形成而获得等听说法的核心观点提出质疑后，听说法的影响力开始减弱。在听说法衰落之后，语言教学领域在 20 世纪 70 年代进入了一个方法论多元化的时期，在这一时期出现了许多"创新方法"，如沉默法、社团语言学习法、全身反应法和暗示法。

20 世纪 80 年代，因对语言教学要培养学生交际能力这一观点的普遍关注，语言教学界又重新有了共识。大卫·A. 威尔金斯提出关注语言功能，并设计了功能意念教学大纲，为交际法奠定了首块基石，具有里程碑意义。随后，交际法成了大西洋两岸的主流语言教学法，并被视为当今语言教学最合理的教学法基础。在交际法提出的语言教学方法论基础上，第二语言教学的研究视角从寻找"最佳的语言教学方法"和"如何教一门语言"开始转向关注学习者的学习过程和"如何学习一门语言"。20 世纪 80 年代末到 90 年代，人们对语言学习过程的关注促进了语言教学领域的又一轮创新。新的教学方法提出，学生在使用语言进行互动时，语言学习才是最有效的。比如，使用语言完成一项任务，伴随着学科内容的学习来学习语言，或使用语言解决现实生活中的问题等，在这样的学习情境下，语言结构不是一个一个依次讲授的，而是在必要时提醒学生或为学生提供必要的语言形式。

到了 21 世纪，语言教学领域的变化开始受到来自外部领域的影响——科学技术的发展革新。基于网络的现代远程教育、计算机辅助学习、翻转课堂、慕课、SPOC 和 STEAM 等教学理念都是利用先进的教育技术和网络技术在教育学和语言教学领域的改革创新。

从对语言教学流派历史发展的梳理中可以看到语言教学作为一门学科，从无到有，不断发展壮大。这些语言教学法都是为适应当时社会需求及对以往教学法局限的思考和改进而创立发展而来。每一种教学法都为第二语言或外语教学与学习做出了重要贡献。

在语言教学理论体系建构方面，理查德和罗杰斯提出了比较分析语言教学理论与方法的框架，即三大层面，九个要素。三大层面是理论、设计和教学过程。理论层面涉及语言理论和学习理论，是语言教学实践与教学原则的基础。设计层面是教学法分析的层面，需要考虑：①教学法的教学目标是什么；②使用一种教学法时，如何选择和组织语言方面的教学内容，即教学法所包含的教学大纲；③教学法提倡的学习任务和教学活动的类型；④学习者的角色；⑤教师的角色；⑥教学材料（教材）的作用。教学过程（即实践）是描述一种教学法如何在课堂行为中实现其理论与设计的层面。包括根据特定教学法教授语言时所使用的实际的、即时的教学技巧、教学实践和教学行为。根据如上分析框架，我们编制了表 11-1，从理论和设计两个层面总结并对比了每种教学法的特色及异同（由于教学过程是涉及具体操作的细节性、实用性层面，在前面各章节中已经介绍过，因此，本章将不再涉及）。

表 11-1   不同语言教学法在理论和设计层面的比较

	语言理论	学习理论	教学目标	教学大纲	活动类型	学生角色	教师角色	教材作用
语法翻译法	书面语先于口语。"母语是学习第二语言得其参照的参照系"	语言学习就是记忆语法规则和语言事实，从而理解和掌握外语的词法与句法	学习一种语言是为了能够阅读其文学文献。从外语学习过程中，训练心智，发展智力	课文是从文学著作中节选的。语法点根据在课文中出现的顺序进行编排，并尽量做到系统有序	传统的课堂活动，如翻译、阅读理解、记忆、造句、填空和作文	学习者的角色非常传统。学习者应该按照教师的要求去做	教师是课堂的权威	教材来源于经典文学文献。教材是语言的经典范本，是教师教学和学生学习的依据
情景法（直接法）	语言是一套结构系统，语言与情境信息息相关	记忆理论；习惯形成理论	教授学生实际掌握语言的四项基本技能。自动、准确地掌握基本句型。口语先于写作	根据语法难度进行分级，列出语言结构及词汇表	重复、替换练习；避免翻译和语法解释；绝不允许学习者犯错误	听并重复、回答问题并按要求做；学习内容对学习者没有发言权；学习后以陈述观点，进行提问	在展示语言结构时做示范；进行语言操练；纠正语言错误，测试进度	依托教科书和实物教具；教材内容结构组织严密，分级推进
听说法	语言是一个由规则支配的层次结构体系	习惯形成理论，口语领先，读写跟上才能使语言的学习更加有效；进行类比而不是进行分析	控制语言音结构、语言形式和语序，掌握语言符号；目标是达到母语者语言掌握程度	划分音韵学、形态学和句法学，并进行分级。对比分析	对话及操练；重复和记忆；句型训练	学生是能通过富于技巧性的操练产生正确的反应有机体	教师为主导，为中心；教师设计教学模式，控制课程进度和节奏	以教师为主导。经常使用磁带、视频，也经常使用语言实验室
全身反应法	基本上是一种结构主义的、基于语法的语言观	二语学习与母语学习相同；先理解后表达，通过执行命令（右脑功能）形成语言内化；应减轻压力	教授口语能力，培养能与母语者顺畅交流的学习者	句本位大纲，语法和词汇主要关注语言内容和标准，注意语义而非形式	发出祈使类命令，引发身体动作行为反应	倾听者、表演者；对学习内容的影响力不大	直接指导学生表演，是学生演员的"舞台导演"	没有基本的文本教材；学习材料和教学媒介在后续教学中起着重要作用。教学的初始阶段，利用声音、动作即可和手势即可

续表

	语言理论	学习理论	教学目标	教学大纲	活动类型	学生角色	教师角色	教材作用
沉默法	每种语言都是由一些元素组成的，这些元素赋予了语言独特的节奏与特质。语言中的功能词汇和核心是理解语言实质的关键	学习第二语言的过程与母语学习截然不同。第二语言学习是一个运用智力的、认知的过程。顺应语言规律，沉默的意识得以激发	达到接近母语的流利程度；发音标准，具备第二语言实用语法知识。学习者要学会如何学习一门语言	大纲基本上是体现语言结构性特点的，围绕语法项目和相关词汇设置课程。大纲涉及的语言点按照语法复杂性进行编排	学习者对教师的指令、提问和实物线索提示进行反应。鼓励并开展不依赖于教师示范及语法解释的口头表达活动	学习是一个人成长的过程。学习者对自己的学习负责，并培养独立性、自主性和自信心	教师必须①教授、②检验测试、③让位。保持沉默。避免示范，纠正、辅指出错误接指出错误	独特的教具：彩色棒、彩色发音图、词汇表
社团语言学习法	语言是一个人际交流系统。它是一个社会过程，涉及"全人"过程，文化的过程、教育的过程、发展的过程等	学习涉及"全人"。它是一种社会性活动，好比幼儿从依赖到自主，再到独立的成长过程	没有具体的教学目标。达到四语者的熟练程度是学习目的	没有固定的教学大纲。课程设置与进度是基于话题的；话题由学习者提供。教学从学习者的学习意愿和教师的整理汇编中形成	翻译、小组合作、录音、誊写、反思、观察、聆听、自由对话等常规语言活动与创新语言活动相结合	学习者组成一个语言社团，他们都是这一社团的成员。学习不是由一个人完成的，而是通过合作来实现的	教师相当于咨询师或父母，为学生提供一个安全的学习和成长环境	没有教科书，因为教材书会抑制学生成长。教学材料随着课程的开展而形成
暗示法	虽然建议记住所有有意义的课文，但暗示法的语言观还是相对传统的	当学习者处于非常放松的状态时，学习是通过暗示进行的。可以使用巴洛克音乐导出放松的学习状态	快速形成高级会话能力。教学目标是理解而不是记忆，但仍需要学习者掌握大量的词汇	课程分为10个单元，每个单元是一篇包含1200个单词的对话。对话由词汇和语法项目编排而成	主动性、问答练习、角色扮演、深度放松状态下的听力练习	必须保持被动状态，并允许语言材料作用于其身（而不是相反）	创造最容易被暗示的情境，并以最有可能鼓励和保持的极接受和保持的方式呈现材料。必须呈现权威和信心	包括课文、磁带、教室设施设备和音乐。课文要有穿透力、兼具文学性和趣味性

续表

	语言理论	学习理论	教学目标	教学大纲	活动类型	学生角色	教师角色	教材作用
自然法	语言的本质是意义。语言的核心是词汇而不是语法	第二语言的发展有两种方式：习得（一种自然的潜意识过程）和学习（一种有意识的过程）。学习不能致习得	旨在为初学者和中级学习者提供个人生活和学术方面的基本（口头/书面）交流技能	根据学习者的需求选择交际活动和话题	开展基于此时此地、此情此景的可理解性语言输入活动。注重意义而不是形式	不应该试图进行常规意义上的语言学习，而应该尝试融入人有意义的交流活动中去习得语言	教师是可理解输入的主要来源。教师必须创造积极的、低焦虑的学习氛围，选择和安排丰富多彩的课堂活动	教学材料来源于现实，而不是教科书。教学材料的主要目的是促进理解和交流
交际法	语言是一个表达意义的系统；其主要功能是交流与互动	语言活动应涉及真实的交流；要执行有意义的任务，应使用对学习者有意义的语言来促进语言学习	教学目标应反映学习者的学习需求；教学目标要涵盖语言结构，也要包含功能意念项目	教学大纲包含语言结构、功能、意念、主题、任务等各领域的部分或全部内容，并根据学习者的需求进行分级和排序	教学活动应使学习者参与到交流过程中来，开展如交换信息，进行有意义的沟通与互动等课堂活动	学习者是参与者，也是互动者、交流者	教师是交流过程的促进者，学生需求分析者、教学过程管理者	教材教具的主要作用是使用语言，促进交际；可以是任务型材料，也可以是真实语言素材

4 The Development Trend of Second Language Teaching

The initiatives for changing programs and pedagogy may come from within the profession — from teachers, administrators, theoreticians, and researchers. Incentives or demands of a political, social, or even fiscal nature may also drive change, as they have in the past. Particular personalities and leaders in the field may also shape the future of language teaching. Change may also be motivated by completely unexpected sources. Based on the survey of various language teaching methods, Richards and Rodgers submitted the question "How do we feel about the language teaching profession will move ahead in the near, or even more distant, future?" and predicted the answer to the question. The factors[①] that have influenced language teaching trends in the past will continue to do so in the future.

Government policy directives. Increased demands for accountability on the part of funding agencies and governments have driven educational changes on a fairly regular basis for decades and are likely to continue to do so in the future.

Trends in the profession. The teaching profession is another source for change. Professional certification for teachers, as well as endorsement of particular trends or approaches by professional organizations and lobby groups promoting particular issues and causes, can have an important influence on teaching.

Guru-Led innovations. Teaching has sometimes been described as artistry rather than science and is often shaped by the influence of powerful individual practitioners with their own schools of thought and followers. Just as Gattegno, Lozanov, and Krashen inspired a number of teachers in the 1970s and 1980s, and as Gardner does today, doubtless new gurus will attract disciples and shape teaching practices in the future.

Responses to technology. The potential of the Internet, the World Wide Web, and other computer interfaces and technological innovations is likely to capture the imagination of the teaching profession in the future as it has in the past and will influence both the content and the form of instructional delivery in language teaching.

Influences from academic disciplines. Disciplines such as linguistics, psycholinguistics, and psychology have an impact on the theories of language and language learning and support particular approaches to language teaching. As new theories emerge in disciplines such as these, they are likely to have an impact on future theories of teaching. Just as in the past Audiolingualism and Communicative Language Teaching reflected linguistic theories of their day, so new insights from functional linguistics, corpus linguistics, psycholinguistics, or

---

① RICHARDS J C, RODGERS T S. 语言教学的流派 [M]. 2 版 . 北京：外语教学与研究出版社，2008：252–254.

sociolinguistics, or from sources now unknown, may play a dominant role in shaping language pedagogy.

Research influences. Second language teaching and learning is increasingly a field for intensive research and theorizing. Second language acquisition research provided impetus for the development of the Natural Approaches and Task-Based Language Teaching, and it will doubtless continue to motivate new language teaching approaches.

Learner-Based innovations. Learner-based focuses recur in language teaching and other fields in approximately 10-year cycles, as we have seen with individualized instruction, the learner-centered curriculum, learner training, learner strategies, and Multiple Intelligences. We can anticipate continuation of this trend.

Crossover educational trends. Cooperative Learning, the Whole Language Approach, Neurolinguistic Programming, and Multiple Intelligences represent crossovers into second language teaching of movements from general education and elsewhere. Such crossovers will doubtless continue because the field of language teaching has no monopoly over the theories of teaching and learning.

Crossovers from other disciplines. Encounters with cognitive psychology, psychotherapy, communication science, ethnography, and human engineering have left their imprint on language pedagogy and exemplify the way that such diverse disciplines can influence a field that is always looking for inspiration.

The coming of Post-Method Era changes in the status of approaches and methods, we can therefore expect the field of second and foreign language teaching in the twenty-first century to be no less a ferment of theories, ideas, and practices than it has been in the past.

四、第二语言教学法的发展趋势

课程的改革与教学法的创新可能来自专业内部——比如，来自教师、管理者、理论家和研究人员。而政治、社会、甚至是财政情况也能够激励并推动教学改革，在语言教学发展历史上就不乏这样的例子。在这个专业领域中的特殊人物和领袖也可能影响甚至引领语言教学的未来趋势。另外，有些改变也可能完全是由意料之外的因素引发的。理查德和罗杰斯基于对各种语言教学法的调查研究，提出了"在不久的将来，甚至是更遥远的未来，语言教学事业的发展趋势如何"这一问题，并预测了答案。他们认为曾经影响过语言教学发展趋势的因素还将在未来继续对这一事业产生影响。

政府政策指引。几十年来，政府和各种机构对教育事业进行资助，教育资助项目标准及要求的提高，推动了教育改革，其影响在未来也将持续。

行业趋势。专职教师是另一个推动教学改革的源泉。对教师专业的认证，专业培训机构和个体辅导组织对某一教学理念或教学法的认可和大力推行，都将对教学产生重要影响。

大师引领创新。教育有时被认为是一门艺术而不是一门科学，它常常受到有巨大影响力的教育实践者的影响，这些教育家有自己的思想流派和追随者，如加特诺、洛扎诺夫和克拉申，这些教育大师在 20 世纪 70 年代到 80 年代激励了许多教师。正如加德纳在当今社会产生的影响一样，毫无疑问，新的大师将吸引徒众，并在未来创新教学。

科学技术的影响。互联网、万维网和其他计算机接口与技术创新都有着巨大的潜力，很可能像过去一样，在未来继续吸引并激发教师的想象力与创造力，影响语言教学的内容与形式。

学科理论的影响。语言学、心理语言学和心理学等学科都对语言理论和语言学习理论产生过影响，并曾为语言教学法提供理论基础。随着这些基础学科领域新理论的产生，它们很可能会对未来的教学理论产生影响。正如前述听说法和交际法一样，两种教学法都反映了当时的语言学理论。因此，功能语言学、语料库语言学、心理语言学或社会语言学领域的新理论，以及其他未知领域的新见解，都可能在语言教育学的形成中起主导作用。

学术研究的影响。第二语言教学与学习已逐渐成为一个值得深入研究和理论建设的领域。第二语言习得研究为自然法和任务型教学法的发展提供了动力，无疑将继续推动新的语言教学法的产生和发展。

基于学习者的改革。正如我们所看到的，个性化教学、以学习者为中心的课程、学习者培训、学习策略和多元智能等以学习者为中心的教学现象以约十年为周期，在语言教学和其他领域再度兴起。可以预见这种趋势会继续下去。

教育学科内的跨专业交叉趋势。合作语言学习法、全语言法、神经语言程序法和多元智能法体现了第二语言教学与普通教育学及教育学其他专业领域的跨专业交叉。语言教学与研究这一领域并不故步自封，它对一切来自教与学的理论都开放兼容，因此这种交叉无疑将继续下去。

跨学科交叉趋势。与认知心理学、心理治疗学、传播科学、民族志和人类工程学等学科的交叉融合给语言教学留下了深刻的印记，并证明了这些不同学科可以对语言教学这个一直在寻找灵感的领域产生影响。

后方法时代的到来改变了教学法的地位，但我们可以预见，21 世纪的第二语言 / 外语教学领域仍将与过去一样，是一个理论、思想和实践的"百花地""争鸣场"。

○ **Activities and Exercises**

1. Please list the second language teaching methods and approaches you have learned.

2. Please review the emergence period of the following language teaching methods and mark them in the timeline.

- The Grammar-Translation Method
- The Direct Method
- The Audiolingual Method
- Total Physical Response
- The Silent Way
- Community Language Learning
- Suggestopedia
- Communicative Language Teaching
- Content-Based Instruction
- Task-Based Language Teaching

3. Please refer to the development of linguistics, psychology and second language acquisition theories in "Further Reading," analyze the theoretical basis of the following language teaching methods and fill in the form (Table 11-2).

Table 11-2　Theoretical Basis of Different Language Teaching Methods and Approaches

No.	Language Teaching Method	Theory of Linguistics	Theory of Psychology or Language Learning	Other Theories
1	The Grammar-Translation Method			
2	The Direct Method			
3	The Audiolingual Method			
4	Total Physical Response			
5	The Silent Way			
6	Community Language Learning			
7	Suggestopedia			
8	Communicative Language Teaching			
9	Content-Based Instruction			
10	Task-Based Language Teaching			

4. This is the table of "Comparison of different methods and approaches" from the Conclusion Section of Professor Diane Larsen-Freeman and Marti Anderson's book *Techniques and Principles in Language Teaching*. The teaching method or approach is hidden. Please complete Table 11-3 according to the information of each teaching method's characteristics and theoretical basis.

Table 11-3　Features of Different Language Teaching Methods and Approaches

No.	Method/ Approach	Language/Culture	Language Learning	Language Teaching
1		Literary language Culture: Literature and the fine arts	Exercise mental muscle	Have students translate from target language (TL) texts to native language
2		Everyday spoken language Culture: History, geography, everyday life of target language (TL) speakers	Associate meaning with the TL directly	Use spoken language in situations with no L1 translation
3		Sentence and sound patterns	Overcome native language habits: form new TL habits	Conduct oral/aural drills and pattern practice
4		Unique spirit/melody	Develop inner criteria for correctness by becoming aware of how the TL works	Remain silent in order to subordinate teaching to learning. Focus student attention; provide meaningful practice
5		Whole, meaningful texts; vocabulary emphasized	Overcome psychological barriers to learning	Desuggest limitations: teach lengthy dialogues through musical accompaniment, playful practice, and the arts

continued

No.	Method/ Approach	Language/Culture	Language Learning	Language Teaching
6		Created by a community	Learn nondefensively as whole persons, following developmental stages	Include the elements of security, attention, aggression, reflection, retention, and discrimination
7		Vehicle for communicating meaning; vocabulary emphasized	Listen; associate meaning with TL directly	Delay speaking until students are ready; make meaning clear through actions and visuals
8		Communicative competence Notions/ functions	Interact with others in the TL; negotiate meaning	Use communicative activities: information gaps, role-plays, and games
9		Language is a medium	Learn language through engaging meaningful content	Teach language and content at the same time have objectives and activities for both
10		Language is meaningful-useful for accomplishing certain tasks in the world	Learn by doing	Engage in tasks with clear outcomes

5. Syllabus is used to refer to the form in which linguistic content is specified in a course or method. Brown lists seven basic syllabus types — Structural, Situational, Topical, Functional, Notional, Skills-based, and Task-based, and these can usually be linked to specific language teaching approaches or methods. Please analyze and indicate the syllabus types of the following language teaching methods (Table 11-4).

Table 11-4 Syllabus Types of Different Language Teaching Methods and Approaches

No.	Language Teaching Method	Type of Syllabus
1	The Grammar-Translation Method	
2	The Direct Method	
3	The Audiolingual Method	
4	Total Physical Response	
5	The Silent Way	
6	Community Language Learning	
7	Suggestopedia	
8	Communicative Language Teaching	
9	Content-Based Instruction	
10	Task-Based Language Teaching	

6. The teaching objectives and syllabus of a language teaching method are attained through the instructional process, through the organized and directed interactions of teachers, learners, and materials in the classroom. Differences among methods manifest themselves in the choice of different kinds of learning and teaching activities and specific teaching techniques in the classroom. There are 30 specific teaching techniques followed. Please find out the language teaching method for each specific teaching technique (Table 11-5, Table 11-6).

Table 11-5   List of Language Teaching Activities

Specific Teaching Techniques		
Memorization	Complete the Dialogue	Reflective Listening
Translation	Question and Answer Exercise	Teacher's Silence
Chain Drill	Choose a New Identity	Antonyms/Synonyms
Action Sequence	Using Commands to Direct Behavior	Classroom Set-Up
Role Play	Reading Comprehension Questions	Information-Gap Task
Reading Aloud	Sound-Color Chart	Picture Strip Story
Repetition Drill	Word Chart and Fidel Charts	Passive Concert
Human Computer	Opinion-Gap Task	Process Writing
Substitution	Authentic Materials	Self-Correction Gestures
Cognates	Graphic Organizers	Fill-in-the-Blanks Exercise

Table 11-6   Teaching Activities of Different Language Teaching Methods and Approaches

No.	Language Teaching Method	Specific Teaching Techniques
1	The Grammar-Translation Method	
2	The Direct Method	
3	The Audiolingual Method	
4	Total Physical Response	
5	The Silent Way	
6	Community Language Learning	
7	Suggestopedia	
8	Communicative Language Teaching	
9	Content-Based Instruction	
10	Task-Based Language Teaching	

7. The success of a language teaching method may depend on the degree to which the teacher can provide the content or create the conditions for successful language learning. So the relationship/interaction between teacher and learner is one of the important characteristics of

language teaching methods. While the potential role relationships of learner and teacher in a real language class are many and varied. They may be relationships such as those of conductor to orchestra member, therapist to patient, coach to player, friend to friend, colleague to colleague, etc. Please mark "√" in the column of "Teacher-centered" or "Learner-centered" according to the roles of the teacher and learner in each following language teaching method, and describe the teacher-learner relationship/interaction of the corresponding teaching method if necessary (Table 11-7).

Table 11-7　Teacher-Learner Relationship of Different Methods and Approaches

No.	Language Teaching Method	Teacher-Centered	Learner-Centered	Specific Teacher-Learner Relationship/Interaction
1	The Grammar-Translation Method			
2	The Direct Method			
3	The Audiolingual Method			
4	Total Physical Response			
5	The Silent Way			
6	Community Language Learning			
7	Suggestopedia			
8	Communicative Language Teaching			
9	Content-Based Instruction			
10	Task-Based Language Teaching			

8. There are many methods and approaches in the history of second language teaching. Please classify them and give your reasons.

The Second Language Teachings Methods and Approaches:

- The Grammar-Translation Method
- The Direct Method
- Situational Language Teaching
- The Reading Method
- The Audiolingual Method
- The Silent Way
- Community Language Learning
- Total Physical Response
- Suggestopedia
- Cognitive Approach
- Communicative Language Teaching
- Content-Based Instruction

- Task-Based Language Teaching
- Cooperative Language Learning
- Competency-Based Language Teaching
- The Lexical Approach
- Multiple Intelligences
- The Natural Approach
- Neurolinguistic Programming
- Whole Language

9. In general, the Grammar-Translation Method, the Audiolingual Method and Communicative Language Teaching are the three of the most widely used teaching approaches in foreign language contexts. Please compare them from seven features which refer to the theories that support each approach, the reason that motivates the creation of these approaches, the resources, and techniques used for teaching a class within these approaches, as well as the role of teachers, learners, and the learners' mother tongue in the language teaching-learning process (Table 11-8).

Table 11-8 Comparison of Different Language Teaching Methods and Approaches

No.	Criteria and Parameters	Approaches			
		Grammatical	Audiolingual	Communicative	Alternative*
1	**Supporting Theories** Behaviorism or Conductism Krashen's Hypotheses about Second Language Acquisition Universal Grammar (Innatist) Socio-Cultural None				
2	**Creation Purpose** To teach classical languages To teach people who needed to travel/study in other countries To teach people from the army to communicate To teach European languages and allow Europeans to communicate To teach any person willing to learn				
3	**Materials Used** Realia Physical objects Observable actions Books Audio Visuals Audio-Visuals Language laboratory Worksheets Authentic materials				
4	**Techniques Used** Drills Translation Memorization Role-Plays				

continued table

No.	Criteria and Parameters	Approaches			
		Grammatical	Audiolingual	Communicative	Alternative*
4	Dialogues/Conversations Reading and comprehension activities Vocabulary exercises Games Hands-on activities Oral presentation Pair and group work Mind engaging tasks Listening activities				
5	**Teacher's Role** The teacher is accountable for creating an appropriate environment (full of comprehensible input) for language learning The teacher is the center of the class at certain grade The teacher is the center of the class All the class turns around him The Teacher is a guide				
6	**Learner's Role** Active learner Passive learner Goes from passive to active, depending on the stage of language learning				
7	**Learner's Mother Tongue Role** Students are banned from using it Students can use it as a support It is important in the learning process The teacher speaks only in the target language				

10. The following material is an English text. Please choose one of the language teaching methods or approaches you learned, make an instructional design. Pay attention to making the teaching objectives clear and having teaching procedures detailed.

Tour of London

Welcome to this short tour of London. This square is Trafalgar Square and it is the middle of London. We're standing opposite the National Gallery, a famous museum with lots of famous paintings. From here, we'll walk along the Red Street to Buckingham Palace. The Queen lives there.

Turn left and go to the Houses of Parliament and Big Ben. Opposite you can see the London Eye. It takes you 135 meters above the River Thames. You can see most of London on a clear day.

When you are tired, the best way to see London is by boat. You can get the boat near Big Ben. As you go along the river, the London Eye is on your right.

Get off the boat at Tower Bridge. Next to the bridge is the Tower of London. It's over 900 years old.

After visiting the Tower of London, take the boat back along the river to the railway station. When you get off the boat, go past the station and walk along the street. Turn left into King's Street and go past a church. You're now back at the square. And this is where we'll finish our tour.

○ Further Reading[①]

1. Theories of Linguistics

The study of language has a very long history. Although we are not sure when people began to show interest in the languages they were using, we are quite certain that, according to the records available, language study is at least more than 2500 years old. During the long history of linguistic study, a lot of theories and schools of thought emerged. Because of the limited space here, we will only introduce the theories of the following four schools.

(1) Traditional Linguistics

By traditional linguistics we mean the linguistic theory that comes directly from or is in line with the traditional study of language in ancient Greece. It has a tradition of more than 2000 years. In the fifth century B.C., the ancient Greeks began to make a serious study of language in the realm of philosophy. There were two famous controversies at that time. One was between the naturalists and the conventionalists on the relations between form and meaning. The naturalists argued that the forms of words reflected directly the nature of objects. They use onomatopoeia and sound symbolism as their evidence to justify their point of the contrary, while

---

① 舒白梅，陈佑林. 外语教学法 [M]. 北京：高等教育出版社，1999（8）：4-27.

the conventionalists thought that language was conventional and there was no logical connection between the form and meaning of words. The other was between the analogists and the anomalists on the regularities of language. The analogists claimed that language in general was regular and there were rules for people to follow. The anomalists maintained that language was basically irregular and that was why there were so many exceptions and irregularities in the Greek language. Although the two sides of the two controversies could not convince each other, their debate roused people's interest in language and led them to the detailed study of Greek. The direct result of this was that in the first century B.C., there came a book of *Greek Grammar* written by Dianysius Thrax. In this book he summarized the views and achievements of his predecessors and classified all the words of the Greek language into eight parts of speech. About three hundred years later, a Greek scholar called Apollonius Dyscolus made an extensive study of the syntax of Greek. He worked on the basis of Thrax's book and built his syntactic description on the relations between the noun and the verb. From then on, the model of language description set up by Thrax and Dyscolus was followed by different scholars at different times in their analyses of languages.

Traditional study of language was, to a large extent, practical in nature. People made a study of language in order to understand the classic works of ancient times and in order to be able to teach students, enabling them to understand and appreciate those classic works. These practical purposes, together with other factors such as the availability of written records, made traditional linguists believe that the written form of language was superior to the spoken form, which was regarded as the corrupted form of language. So in their study of language, they gave priority to the written form and took words as their starting point. When discussing the rules of language, they usually took a prescriptive approach, because they wanted to set up principles and standards for people to use language correctly.

(2) American Structuralism

American structuralism started at the beginning of the 20th century and was very popular and influential in the 1930s and 1940s throughout the world. The two forerunners of it were Franz Boas and Edward Sapir. Boas as an anthropologist, worked in the field for about 20 years at the turn of the century, recording the native languages and cultures of American Indians which were dying out very quickly. Since all of the American Indians' languages had no written forms, he had to make investigations into those languages before recording them. In his investigation, he found that the traditional grammatical model could not be used to analyse the structures of those languages. Therefore, he had to describe them as they were used. Sapir began to do the fieldwork in 1904 and recorded a dozen and half American Indians' languages. He found that although those languages had no written forms and were regarded as primitive, they were virtually very systematic and were very efficient in communications within their communities.

Leonard Bloomfield, a linguist in America, is regarded as the father of American structuralism. He accepted the theories and principles of behaviorism which was a dominant approach in psychology in that country. He agreed with the views of the psychologist John B. Watson that only things that could be observed publicly and objectively could be studied scientifically. So he held the position that if linguistics was going to be a science, it should only admit data that could be objectively verified. His adherence to objectivity was also reflected in his approach to the study of language. He maintained that linguists should describe instead of prescribe what people actually say and should take an inductive approach in analyzing data. He characterized language and language acquisition in terms of behaviorist terminology. For him, language was a habit of verbal behavior which consisted of a series of stimuli and responses. He argued that to acquire a language was to form a habit of verbal behavior and learning a second language was learning a new habit. Based on the anthropologists' fieldwork and his own research, he concluded that the proper object of linguistics was speech and he thought that speech was primary and writing was secondary, because for him, writing was a later development to represent speech. He stated, in agreement with Sapir's view, that each language had a unique system of its own and it was wrong to fit it into the established grammatical patterns of Greek. In 1933, he published the book *Language* which is a comprehensive statement of his ideas and principles of linguistic science. Soon after its publication, the book became the bible of linguistics and remained unsurpassed as an introduction to linguistics after more than 3 decades. During the years of World War II, a lot of American structuralists joined in the training of military personnel and they summarized the ideas and principles of structuralism and applied them systematically to the teaching of foreign languages. Their methods were so successful that they set a new approach to foreign language teaching on its course.

(3) Transformational-Generative Linguistics

The year 1957 saw the publication of Noam Chomsky's book *Syntactic Structures*, which started a revolution in the linguistic world and ushered in a new school — the Transformational Generative Linguistics. Although Chomsky was trained in the structuralist tradition, he was not satisfied with the theory of structuralism, which was inadequate in explaining some common linguistic facts and phenomena. For example, it would be very difficult for the structuralists to explain why children acquire their first language in a few years, and why the same structure can be used to express different meanings and different structures can be used to express the same meaning.

Chomsky assumes that children are born with a Language Acquisition Device (LAD). This LAD is made up of a set of general principles called universal grammar. These general principles can be applied to all the languages in the world. Once the child is born, the particular language environment will trigger the LAD. Chomsky assumes that the child will make hypotheses on the basis of the general principles, then he will test the hypotheses against the actual language data, then he will modify the hypotheses accordingly, test them again against the data. This hypothesis testing procedure will repeat again and again until the hypotheses agree with the actual grammar of the language. Children's language acquisition process completes when the Universal Grammar is successfully transformed into the grammar of a particular language. Only in this way is it possible to offer explanations for the facts that all children acquire their first language at roughly the same speed, that they will make mistakes that never occur in the adult language, and that they can understand or produce sentences they have never heard before.

Chomsky has also made the distinction between linguistic competence and linguistic performance. Linguistic competence refers to the internalized knowledge of the language that a native speaker of that language possesses. It includes the ability to understand and produce an infinite number of sentences, to detect ambiguity contained in sentences, to tell whether a sentence is grammatical or not, to understand the internal structure of sentences, and to detect paraphrases. Linguistic performance refers to the actual utterances produced by the native speakers. The native speaker may make mistakes or errors in his performance, but this does not mean that he has not got the ability to produce grammatical sentences. Similarly, when a man runs along a street, he may stumble if he is in a hurry, excited or exhausted, but this does not mean that he has not got the ability to run.

Chomsky opposes the structuralist position of taking classification and description of linguistic performance as the goal of linguistics and attacks the inductive approach the structuralists used in their research. According to Chomsky, the data they collected in the field is bound to be very limited because it is virtually impossible to collect all the sentences of a language, including those that have been produced and those that will be produced in the future. Comparatively speaking, what they can collect is just like a drop of water in the vast sea. So they are sure to have problems when they use the rules from their analysis of the limited data to account for all the sentence structures of a language. Chomsky holds the position that linguists should study the linguistic competence, not the performance, of the native speaker and try to set up a system of rules that will generate an infinite number of grammatical sentences of the language and none of ungrammatical ones, will demonstrate and explain the various kinds of relations including ambiguity among sentences, and will be able to characterize the creative property of language. In order to reach this goal, Chomsky argues, a deductive, hypothesis-testing approach should be taken. That is to say, linguists should form a hypothetical grammar, according to their observation of a given language, test the grammar against other observations, modify or revise it whenever necessary, test it again, and so on until it can account for all the facts and phenomena of the language. That is why Chomsky's theoretical model of Transformational-Generative Grammar is changing from time to time.

From the goal of Transformational-Generative Grammar, we can see that Chomsky is interested in the mental process and tries to describe the grammatical knowledge of the native speakers of a language. He believes that linguistic study and research can help explain what happens in the mind, and linguistics should be regarded as a branch of psychology.

(4) Functional Linguistics

The functional linguistics develops directly from the London School of Linguistics and the precursor of it was the anthropologist Bronislaw Malinowski. During the early years of the century, he did some ethnographic research among some Melanesian tribes of Eastern New Guinea. While he was doing his anthropological fieldwork in these tribes, he realized that it was very difficult to translate the native words and expressions into English. To understand an utterance, he had to resort to other sorts of knowledge, like the situation in which the utterance was spoken, and the proper setting of native culture. Therefore, he arrived at the conclusion that "the meaning of any single word is to a very high degree dependent on its context" and an utterance has no meaning at all if it is out of the context of situation.

Although the phrase "context of situation" was created and used by Malinowski, it was J. R. Firth who had made it a key concept in the technique of the London School of Linguistics. Malinowski was primarily an anthropologist and he tackled language problems from the point of view of anthropology. J.R. Firth, unlike Malinowski, was a linguist. The consequence of this was that he approached the context of situation from a different point of view and attempted to establish a descriptive framework for the analysis of language by the application of the context of situation to language events. He accepted Malinowski's view of the relations between language and society, and his definition of meaning as function in context. He held the position that all branches of linguistics are concerned with meaning, and the meaning of linguistic items depends on the context of situation. He set up sets of categories which could link the linguistic items with the context of situation, and which were, like grammatical categories, abstract in nature but at a different level from grammatical categories. Having worked out the categories, he then proceeded to develop a linguistic theory based on the notion of function in context. His main approach to this was by means of the concept of system. For Firth, a system is simply a set of choices within a specific context. Any linguistic item has got two sets of contexts: the context of the other possible choices in a system and the context where the system itself occurs. Since system is so important a notion in his theory, people refer to the theory as system-structure theory.

Although Firth attempted to combine the linguistic components with Malinowski's sociolinguistic insights and to develop a model of linguistic description accordingly, he was never able to work out his theory in detail. It is M.A.K. Halliday who has accomplished this task and made the London School of Linguistics one of the most competitive linguistic theories in the world. While he was developing and elaborating the theory of systemic linguistics, Halliday made remarkable progress in the study of context. He accepts Malinowski's statement that meaning is determined by the context of situation and he fully agrees with Firth that the context of situation must have an important position in a descriptive linguistic model. As early as 1961 when he was discussing categories of a grammatical theory, he made quite clear his point of view that linguistic events should be accounted for at three primary levels: substance, form, and context. The substance is the material of language which can be phonic or graphic. The form is the organization of the substance into meaningful events. And by context he meant the relation of the form to non-linguistic features of the situations in which language operates, and the relation of form to linguistic features other than those of the item under attention. In the same article, he claimed that language has formal meaning and contextual meaning. The formal meaning of a linguistic item is its operation in the network of formal relations while the contextual meaning of an item refers to its relation to extratextual features, i.e., the context.

In the 1970s, Halliday began to shift his research work to a more sociology-oriented perspective. He believes that language can be explained or described only when it is regarded as the realization of meanings inherent in the social system. He takes Firth's point that the context of situation should be interpreted as an abstract representation of the environment in terms of certain general categories, but he thinks that it will be necessary to represent the situation in still more abstract terms if it is to have a place in a general sociolinguistic theory; and to conceive of it not as situation but as situation type. He refers to a particular situation type as a semiotic structure which can be represented as a complex of three dimensions: the ongoing social activity, the role relationship involved, and the symbolic or rhetorical channel. He labelled these three dimensions as "field," "tenor," and "mode" respectively. For Halliday, these dimensions form a conceptual framework for representing the social context as the semiotic environment in which people exchange meanings. He maintains that if we are given an adequate specification of the semiotic properties of the context in terms of field, tenor, and mode, we should be able to predict the semantic properties of texts. He is convinced that there is a systematic relationship between the context and the text.

In recent years, Halliday has concentrated his attention on the investigation into the ways in which the context of situation works, and made an attempt to show how the dimensions of context are linked to the linguistic forms and to the ideational, interpersonal and textual functions of language.

2. Theories of Psychology

Quite a number of schools of psychology have emerged since 1879 when the German scientist Wilhelm Wundt at the University of Leipzig opened a laboratory of experimental psychology, which announced the official birth of science. Here we will only mention four of the schools that have direct or indirect influence over foreign language teaching.

(1) Gestalt Psychology

The 1920s saw the emergence of a new psychological school called Gestalt psychology. It was founded by a group of German psychologists such as Max Wertheimer, Kurt Koffka, and Kurt Lewin. Most of their early research was focused on the area of perception, aiming at the exploration of the relationship between parts and whole in people's perceptual experience. From their experiments, they found that people perceived objects and scenes as organized wholes before they noticed their component parts. For example, when people catch sight of a desk, they will recognize the desk as a whole before noticing its legs and other parts. That is why they used the word Gestalt, which means roughly "organized shape" or "whole form" in English, to name their school of psychology.

Later on, they did a lot of experiments on problem solving and they found out that solutions to problems came as wholes rather than in bits and pieces. Based on their studies, they argued that an object was not the sum of the individual parts. For example, an article is not the sum of individual words that make up the article. The meaning units of consciousness are whole, organized constructs which cannot be understood by an analysis of elementary judgments and sensations. That is to say, the mind must be understood in terms of a whole, not individual parts.

(2) Psychoanalysis

Psychoanalysis is a theory of the mind put forward by Sigmund Freud, who was a physician specializing in neurology. He began to work with patients in 1886 in Vienna. From his experiences with patients, he found that many of their mental problems originated from some disturbing events in their early childhood. In most of the cases, the patients could not recall consciously the memories of those disturbing events, but their abnormal behaviour made Freud believe that such memories did exist and they must be buried somewhere in the mind. The part of the mind which is out of the reach of consciousness was called by Freud the unconscious mind, which was the most important concept in psychoanalysis.

Freud divided the mind into a conscious and unconscious mind and he was the first psychologist that made a careful study of the latter. According to Freud, the conscious mind is only a very small part of the whole mind while the rest remains unconscious. The contents of the unconscious mind consist of buried memories and instinctive wishes or drives and will influence the activities of the conscious mind.

The basic approach of Freud was to analyse irrational behaviour of the patients, including their dreams and slips of the tongue, in order to detect clues for the discovery of the contents of their unconscious mind. In general, all the aspects of the irrational conscious behaviour and thought were regarded by Freud as evidence of the unconscious mind. Today, few psychologists will accept the full details of Freud's theory, but most of them will make no objection to his general view that unconscious mental processes influence conscious thought and action.

(3) Behaviorism

While the German Gestalt psychologists were busy working on the perceptual problem of part-whole relationships, a new approach in psychology emerged in America. It is known as behaviorism in the historical development of psychological science. In 1913, the American psychologist John B. Watson published an article entitled Psychology as the Behaviorist Views It, which was regarded as a formal introduction to behaviorism in the psychological world.

In the dozen years before 1913, Watson did a lot of experiments with nonhuman animals and he was impressed with what he could learn about animal's behavior without any consideration of the animal's mind. As a matter of fact, Watson believed that any consideration of animal's mental events such as knowledge, perception and decisions only made the explanation of predictable behavior more complex and confusing, because we had no direct way to observe the animal's mind. What we could observe publicly was the animal's behavior and the external environmental conditions. Therefore, Watson argued in his article that if psychology was going to be a science, it should study what could be observed publicly and objectively. Since only behavior, but not the mind, could be observed directly and objectively, it was the only proper subject of study in psychology. The appropriate goal of psychology set out in his article was to understand the environmental conditions that would cause an animal to behave in a particular way. According to Watson, there was no fundamental difference between human behavior and that of other animals. So the methods that were used to study nonhuman animals should be appropriate for the study of human beings.

These ideas stated in the article were responded to enthusiastically by most of the psychologists in America. During the next 10 years, behaviorism developed very fast and became a dominant school of psychology in that country. That dominant position of behaviorism was maintained for several decades until the mid-1960s.

One of the behaviorists that followed Watson, the most famous, was B.F. Skinner who was in fact regarded as the leader of behaviorism. He developed a new kind of apparatus for studying learning in animals and a new way of describing the learning process. What's more, he made further development and important modifications of Watson's learning theory. That is why people refer to Watson's theory as classic behaviorism while Skinner's neo-behaviorism.

The early behaviorists focused their attention on the topic of learning and they tried to characterize learning in terms of stimuli (observable events in the world that affect behavior) and responses (observable behavioral acts). As behaviorism developed, its main goal became that of identifying basic learning processes that could be described in terms of stimuli and responses. Skinner argued that learning processes could be divided into two kinds. One kind of learning processes is now called classical conditioning, by which a stimulus that did not elicit a response comes to elicit a response after it is paired several times with a stimulus that already elicit a response. For example, an infant may be afraid of sudden loud noises. He will cry when he hears a sudden loud noise. In such a case, we say that the stimulus (a sudden loud noise) elicits a response (the crying). The infant may not be afraid of rabbits and he may play with a rabbit happily. However, whenever the infant comes near to a rabbit, you suddenly produce a loud sound. Of course, each occurrence of the loud sound will elicit the infant's crying of fear. After this has been repeated a few times, then the infant will cry each time a rabbit comes near although the loud sound is not produced. That is to say, the rabbit has become a stimulus that will elicit a response (crying) which was previously elicited by the sudden loud sound.

The other kind of learning processes is now labelled as operant conditioning by which the occurrence of a response will be determined by the consequences of the response. For instance, we look up a word in a dictionary because we can find out the meaning of the word in it; we turn on the light because we want to see better; and we go to a shop because we can buy what we need there. Actually, a lot of our actions are performed simply because of their consequences.

(4) Cognitive Psychology

At the end of the 1960s, behaviorism began to descend from its dominant position, which was to be taken by a new approach called cognitive psychology. The term cognition means knowledge and "cognitive psychology can be defined as the study of people's ability to acquire, organize, remember and use knowledge to guide their behavior."

There are a number of factors that have made cognitive psychology the dominant approach in the world. The most important one is the development of the computer technology. It is so influential that people have changed their conception of the brain. The way the computer processes information helps psychologists assume that the brain works in a similar way to process information. A computer receives coded information, processes it and then sends it to the output system. All this is analogous to what the brain does. The brain receives information through senses, processes it and sends it out as behavioral actions.

Another factor which has made great contribution to the development of cognitive psychology is the work of a Swiss psychologist, Jean Piaget, whose focus of research was on the reasoning abilities of children. Based on the data collected in his experiments with children, Piaget claimed that while the child grows up, his capacity of reasoning would become more and more developed through different stages. He described the development of children's reasoning abilities at each stage in terms of hypothetical mental constructs which he called schemes.

Still another factor which influences cognitive psychology a great deal is the work of the American linguist Noam Chomsky. His publication of *Syntactic Structures* in 1957 not only started a revolution in linguistics, but also had an enormous impact on psychology. In this book as well as in his later publications, Chomsky argued that language should be viewed as a system of mental rules which are in part wired into the brain as a result of evolution. Many psychologists were very enthusiastic about his hypothesis and did a lot of experiments to test his idea, which brought a rapid growth of psycholinguistics.

From the above, we can see that Cognitive Psychology can not be regarded as a single approach, but as a cover term which describes the common feature of different approaches in today's psychology. Some cognitive psychologists make direct use of the computer analogy and some work along the line of behaviorism. However, all of them want to explain the observable behavior by reference to hypothetical mental structures, no matter what approach they are taking in their research.

The research results of the cognitive psychologists show that experimental subjects do not simply make passive, mechanic responses to stimuli. Rather, they are very active in identifying the meaning of stimuli and in expecting the consequences of their responses. Cognitive psychologists maintain that all the relationships among stimuli, responses and consequences are learned and are integrated into the animal's knowledge. That is to say, the animal under study makes a response simply because it has the knowledge or belief that in a particular situation, a particular response will have a particular effect. They have done a lot of experiments and collected a lot of evidence to support their theory.

As for the acquisition of knowledge, some cognitive psychologists like Piaget describe it in terms of cognitive structures. According to Piaget, there are two principal types of cognitive structures which he called schemas and concepts. The schemas refer to sets of rules that define particular categories of behavior and concepts are rules that describe properties of events and their relations with one another. Children acquire schemas and concepts by interacting with their environment with the help of two processes. Piaget called the two processes assimilation and accommodation. Assimilation refers to the process by which new items are added to a concept or schema, while accommodation refers to the process by which the existing concept or schema is changed on the basis of new information. For example, suppose that a child has a color concept of two categories: black and white. If he sees a grey color and calls it black, he has assimilated the new into an existing concept. However, if he decides or learns that a grey is a new kind of color, he will accommodate his color concept to include the new category. Now his color concept has been enlarged and consists of black, white and grey.

3. Theories of Second Language Acquisition

In the study of second language acquisition process, scholars in the world have proposed quite a few theories and hypotheses. The main ones will be introduced here.

(1) The Habit-Formation Theory

The habit-formation theory comes from behavioral psychology and was very popular in the 1950s and 1960s. It was put forward by a group of behaviorists with B.E. Skinner as their representative. According to behaviorists, language is regarded as a set of linguistic habits and the linguistic habits are formed through identifying and strengthening the associations between stimuli and responses. Learning a second language means the formation of a new set of linguistic habits. Imitation and practice play an important role in the process of habit-formation, because the behaviorists maintained that imitation will help learners identify the associations between stimuli and responses while practice will reinforce the associations and help learners to form the new linguistic habits.

Since the process of second language acquisition is regarded as a process of habit formation, the old habits — the mother tongue of the learner will either facilitate or get in the way of the second language learning. That is to say, if the mother tongue and the target language have the same linguistic habits, then positive transfers will occur and the target language learning process will be facilitated. However, when the mother tongue and the target language share a meaning but express it in different ways, the learner will transfer the ways of expression in the mother tongue to the target language. This is called negative transfer and the results of such transfers are realized by errors made by the learner. Therefore, according to the theory, errors should be avoided and should be corrected if they have been made, because they are indication of non-learning and have the danger of becoming bad linguistic habits. Since errors will interfere with the new habit-formation process and are the results of negative transfers, the best way to avoid the errors is to predict when they will occur and find ways to prevent the occurrence of them. Contrastive analysis is proposed as a valid means to predict potential errors. Some scholars believe that if a careful and detailed comparison between the mother tongue and the target language is done, then all the errors in the second language learning process can be predicted and avoided.

(2) The Hypothesis of Linguistic Universals

The hypothesis of linguistic universals originates from the study of linguistic universals in natural languages. It is acknowledged that there exist certain linguistic properties which are true to all the natural languages in the world. There are two most influential approaches to the study of linguistic universals. One is taken by Noam Chomsky, who is making a detailed study of a particular language in order to reveal the universals of language; the other is taken by Joseph H. Greenberg, who studies and compares different languages in an effort to determine the linguistic universals.

Chomsky divides the grammar of a natural language into core grammar and peripheral grammar. According to him, human beings are born with a language acquisition device which consists of a set of general principles. The core grammar of a natural language agrees with the inborn set of general principles while the peripheral grammar can not be governed by the language acquisition device. In research into the second language acquisition process, people have found that second language learners usually acquire the core grammar of the target language and then the peripheral grammar. This is simply because the core grammar agrees with the inborn general principles and is much easier to learn. They also believe that the core grammar of the learner's mother tongue will facilitate the development of the learner's interlanguage and will exert a positive influence on the acquisition of the target language.

(3) The Acculturation Theory

The acculturation theory originated in the late 1970s and was put forward by J. Schumann and R. Anderson. By acculturation they meant that individuals of one culture have to go through the process of modification in attitudes, knowledge, and behavior in order to function well in another culture. It involves not only social adaptation but also psychological adaptation. Schumann thinks that second language acquisition is just one aspect of acculturation and the relation between acculturation and second language acquisition is that the degree of the former will control the degree of the latter. That is to say, successful acculturation will bring about successful second language acquisition while poor acculturation will produce poor second language acquisition. When discussing the factors which determine the degree of acculturation success, Schumann maintains that the social and psychological distances play a decisive role. Social distance is created by the relations between the learner and members of the target social group, and psychological distance is the result of various affective factors of the learner. It is assumed that the shorter the distance, the better the learning environment, hence the better the language learning result.

Schumann thinks that a good language learning environment will be created by the following social factors:

① There is social equality between the first language and the target language group.

② Both groups desire assimilation.

③ The First language group is small and not cohesive.

④ The First language group's culture is congruent with the target language group.

⑤ Both groups have positive attitudes toward each other.

⑥ Both groups expect the first language group to share facilities.

⑦ The first language group expects to stay in the target language area for an extended period.

He describes language shock, culture shock, low motivation and high ego boundaries as negative psychological factors that will increase the psychological distance.

(4) The Discourse Theory

The discourse theory was established by E. Hatch in the late 1970s. This theory of second language acquisition was developed from M.A.K. Halliday's theory of first language acquisition. Halliday thinks that the process of first language acquisition is actually the process of learning how to communicate in that language. Hatch agrees with Halliday's views on first language acquisition and perceives little difference between the first language acquisition process and the process of second language acquisition — only through communication discourses can the learner acquires the second language. The main points of the discourse theory can be summarized as follows:

① In second language acquisition, the rules of grammar are acquired in a natural order.

② When communicating with a non-native speaker, the native speaker will adjust his discourse.

③ The strategies and means used in discourses and the adjusted language input will influence the speed and order of second language acquisition in the following aspects:

A. The order in which the learner acquires the second language grammar is consistent with the frequency of the grammatical structures appearing in the language input.

B. The learner acquires the usual structure patterns in the language input before he is able to analyze them into component parts.

C. The learner acquires the formation of cohesive discourse before he acquires the formation of single sentences.

D. Therefore, the natural order of second language acquisition is the result of the learner's learning to make discourse interactions.

From the above points of the discourse theory, we could see that Hatch focuses his research on the process of second language acquisition and he tries to describe the process by analysing the face-to-face communications.

(5) Krashen's Theory of Second Language Acquisition

The monitor theory, which is very popular among foreign language teachers in America, was put forward by Stephen Krashen in the late 1970s. The theory consists of the following five hypotheses.

① The Acquisition-Learning Hypothesis

Krashen claims that adult learners of a second language have two ways of developing their competence in a second/foreign language. One is acquisition, which refers to the subconscious process in which they develop their language proficiency through natural communications in the target language and it is very similar to the process children use in acquiring their first language. The other is learning, which refers to the conscious process in which they acquire the explicit knowledge of the rules of the target language. The basic distinction between language acquisition and language learning is whether the learner pays conscious attention to the rules of the target language. Generally speaking, language can be acquired in natural communication settings when learners pay attention to meaning instead of form, or in the classroom when the focus is on communication. Focusing on the form of the target language will only result in an explicit knowledge of the rules of the target language. In Krashen's point of view, conscious learning usually does not lead to acquisition.

② The Monitor Hypothesis

According to Krashen, acquisition and learning have different functions in the communication activities. Acquisition is responsible for the fluency of the utterances produced by speakers, while learning is responsible for the accuracy of the speeches or passages. That is to say, in natural communication settings, acquisition has a far more important role to play than learning, the only function of which is to monitor or edit what has been or is going to be produced according to the norms of the target language.

In order to perform this monitor function, language learners have to satisfy at least three conditions. The first condition is that the speaker must have sufficient time to monitor his productions. In normal conversations, the speaker usually does not have enough time to monitor his speeches.

However, if the learner is writing something in his spare time, he may have sufficient time to edit his production. The second condition is that the language performer must have his focus on form. In certain occasions, such as language examinations or preparation of a formal speech, accuracy becomes an important factor and if the learner has enough time, he will try his best to monitor what he is going to produce. The third condition is that the language performer must have an explicit knowledge of the rules of the target language; otherwise, the language performer won't be able to monitor his production.

③ The Natural Order Hypothesis

This hypothesis claims that foreign language learners acquire the rules of the target language in the same order no matter where, when and how they are learning the language. For example, one group of learners may learn a language in a natural communication setting and another group may be taught in the classroom. However, their order of acquisition of the language system will be the same. Krashen believes that this natural order of acquisition is independent of the order of rules taught in the classroom. In his point of view, language teaching cannot change the natural order of language acquisition. The only thing it can do is to facilitate the speed of acquisition. Although at the moment Krashen is sure that there is a natural order of language acquisition, he cannot explain with evidence what this order is. And he assumes that one task of applied linguistic research is to find out the true picture of this natural order.

④ The Input Hypothesis

Krashen uses the input hypothesis to explain the relationship between language input and language acquisition and to answer the question of how people acquire languages. According to Krashen, the only way for people to acquire a language is by understanding messages or receiving comprehensible input. They move from "i", their current level, to "i+1", the next level along the natural order, by understanding input containing "i+1" . That is to say, language is acquired by people's comprehension of input that is slightly beyond their current level. People understand input containing "i+1" because the situation, context, facial expressions, gestures, etc. will provide clues for their comprehension. Krashen maintains that input containing "i+1" will be provided automatically in natural communication settings, so it is not necessary for the language teachers to teach the next structure deliberately along the natural order.

⑤ The Affective Filter Hypothesis

The affective filter hypothesis attempts to account for the variation in speed of language acquisition among individuals of the same group. Research in second language acquisition shows that motivation, self-confidence, and anxiety are the three affective factors which determine the degree of success in second language acquisition. Generally speaking, learners with high motivation, self-confidence, and low anxiety will do much better than those that are unmotivated, lacking in self-confidence, and concerned too much with failure. The affective filter hypothesis is formed on the basis of such research and it claims that language acquirers with a low affective filter will get more input containing i+1 and they are able to make a better use of the input in their acquisition process, while learners with a high affective filter which will block the input will get less input and they won't be able to make the full use of the input in their language acquisition process. This explains why we do have individual differences among the same group of learners.

(6) The Cognitive Theory

The cognitive theory of second language acquisition originated from cognitive psychology and was put forward by scholars like Barry Mclaughlin in the 1980s. Cognitive psychologists regard learning as a cognitive process because they think it involves internal representations which offer regulation and guidance for the performance. The cognitive theory of second language acquisition claims that second language learning should be regarded as the acquisition of a complex cognitive skill, and its internal representations are based on the target language system and include procedures for selecting appropriate vocabulary, grammatical rules, and pragmatic conventions governing language use. Learners' language performance improves along with the restructuring of their internal representations. The task of language acquisition is very complex because it involves constant practice and integration of different aspects of the task until automaticity is reached. Therefore, in the cognitive theory, automaticity and restructuring are the most important notions.

According to McLaughlin, the process of language communication is a kind of information processing. When processing information, people usually use two different ways which are labelled as automatic and controlled modes of information processing. Comparatively speaking, automatic processing of information needs less time and energy than controlled processing. What must be dealt with through controlled processing can eventually be done through automatic processing if language performers have had sufficient practice. That is to say, teaching and practice will help the learner to acquire the automatic processing capacity.

However, the transition from controlled processing to automatic processing can not explain fully the second language acquisition process, because such a transition is realized within a specific framework of structural knowledge of the target language. Along with the increase of learning content, the internal representation of the language system will change and the structure of the knowledge framework must be restructured. In another word, when the existing internal representation cannot be used to account for the new information, then it is necessary for us to restructure the internal representation. Actually, the process of second language acquisition can be viewed as a process in which the internal representations are being restructured constantly.

As a complex cognitive skill, second language acquisition involves the processes of automaticity and restructuring. However, the two processes have different functions at different stages of learning. The cognitive theory holds that language learning at the beginning stage involves more of the process of automaticity while language learning at the advanced stage usually involves more of the process of restructuring.

Appendix: Other Language Teaching Approaches

附录：其他语言教学法

Contents

- Situational Language Teaching
- Multiple Intelligences
- The Lexical Approach
- The Natural Approach
- Cooperative Language Learning
- Competency-Based Language Teaching
- Project-Based Learning
- Flipped Classroom Approach

- 情景法
- 多元智能法
- 词汇法
- 自然法
- 合作学习语言法
- 能力导向型教学法
- 基于项目的教学法
- 翻转课堂教学法

1 Situational Language Teaching

Situational Language Teaching①

Situational Language Teaching is a term not commonly used today, but it is an approach developed by British applied linguists in the 1930s to the 1960s, and which had an impact on language courses which survive in some still being used today. This approach shares with the Direct Method the fact that they are both oral approaches except that the Situational Method is more systematic in terms of the principles and procedures that could be applied and the selection of the content of a language course. The focus of this approach was mainly on vocabulary and grammar control, and there was a tendency in the 1920s towards developing systematic principles of selection, gradation and presentation of materials to language learners. In the 1960s, there was an emphasis on the principle of introducing and practicing new language points situationally, and "it was then that the term situational was used increasingly to refer to the Oral Approach".

1.1 Approach, Design and Objectives

The structural view of language is the view behind the Oral Approach and Situational Language Teaching. Speech was viewed as the basis of language and structure as being at the heart of speaking ability. This was a view similar to American structuralists, such as Fries, but the notion of the British applied linguists, such as Firth and Halliday, that structures must be presented in situations in which they could be used, gave its distinctiveness to Situational Language Teaching.

The theory of learning underlying Situational Language Teaching is behaviorism, addressing more the processes, than the conditions of learning. It includes the following principles:

• Language learning is habit-formation.

• Mistakes are bad and should be avoided, as they make bad habits.

• Language skills are learned more effectively if they are presented orally first, then in written form.

• Analogy is a better foundation for language learning than analysis.

• The meanings of words can be learned only in a linguistic and cultural context. Objectives of Situational Language Teaching include the following:

• A practical command of the four basic skills of a language, through structure.

• Accuracy in both pronunciation and grammar.

• Ability to respond quickly and accurately in speech situations.

---

① RICHARDS J C, RODGERS T S. 语言教学的流派 [M]. 2 版. 北京：外语教学与研究出版社，2008：44-46.

• Automatic control of basic structures and sentence patterns.

The main characteristics of Situational Language Teaching were as follows:

① Language teaching begins with the spoken language. Material is taught orally before it is presented in written form.

② The target language is the language of the classroom.

③ New language points are introduced and practiced situationally.

④ Vocabulary selection procedures are followed to ensure that an essential general service vocabulary is covered.

⑤ Items of grammar are graded following the principle that simple forms should be taught before complex ones.

⑥ Reading and writing are introduced once a sufficient lexical and grammatical basis is established.

Besides, lessons in Situational Language Teaching class are hence teacher-directed, and the teacher sets the pace. Pittman summarizes the teacher's responsibilities as dealing with:

① Timing.

② Oral practice, to support the textbook structures.

③ Revision [i.e., review].

④ Adjustment to special needs of individuals.

⑤ Testing.

⑥ Developing language activities other than those arising from the textbook.

1.2 Procedures

Davies et al. give detailed information about teaching procedures to be used with Situational Language Teaching. The sequence of activities they propose consists of the following:

① Listening practice in which the teacher obtains his student's attention and repeats an example of the patterns or a word in isolation clearly, several times, probably saying it slowly at least once (where...is...the...pen?), separating the words.

② Choral imitation in which students all together or in large groups repeat what the teacher has said. This works best if the teacher gives a clear instruction like "Repeat," or "Everybody" and hand signals to mark time and stress.

③ Individual imitation in which the teacher asks several individual students to repeat the model he has given in order to check their pronunciation.

④ Isolation, in which the teacher isolates sounds, words, or groups of words which cause trouble and goes through techniques 1–3 with them before replacing them in context.

⑤ Building up to a new model, in which the teacher gets students to ask and answer questions using patterns they already know in order to bring about the information necessary to introduce the new model.

⑥ Elicitation, in which the teacher, using mime, prompt words, gestures, etc., gets students to ask questions, make statements, or give new examples of the pattern.

⑦ Substitution drilling, in which the teacher uses cue words (words, pictures, numbers, names, etc.) to get individual students to mix the examples of the new patterns.

⑧ Question-Answer drilling, in which the teacher gets one student to ask a question and another to answer until most students in the class have practiced asking and answering the new question form.

⑨ Correction, in which the teacher indicates by shaking his head, repeating the error, etc., that there is a mistake and invites the student or a different student to correct it. Where possible, the teacher does not simply correct the mistake himself. He gets students to correct themselves so they will be encouraged to listen to each other carefully.

Davies et al. also give sample lesson plans for use with Situational Language Teaching. The structures being taught in the following lesson are "This is a..." and "That's a..."

Teacher: (holding up a watch) Look. This is a watch. (2 ×) (pointing to a clock on wall or table) That's a clock. (2 ×) That's a clock. (2 ×) This is a watch. (putting down watch and moving across to touch the clock or pick it up) This is a clock. (2 ×) (pointing to watch) That's a watch. (2 ×) (picking up a pen) This is a pen. (2 ×) (drawing large pencil on blackboard and moving away) That's a pencil. (2 ×) Take your pens. All take your pens. (students all pick up their pens)

Teacher: Listen. This is a pen. (3 ×) This. (3 ×) Students: This. (3 ×)

A student: This. (6 ×)

Teacher: This is a pen.

Students: This is a pen. (3 ×)

Student: (moving pen) This is a pen. (6 ×)

Teacher: (pointing to blackboard) That's a pencil. (3 ×) That. (3 ×) Students: That. (3 ×)

A student. That. (6 ×) Teacher: That's a pencil.

Students: (all pointing at blackboard) That's a pencil. (3 ×) Student: (pointing at blackboard) That's a pencil. (6 ×)

Teacher: Take your books. (taking a book himself) This is a book. (3 ×) Students: This is a book. (3 ×)

Teacher: (placing notebook in a visible place) Tell me...

Student 1: That's a notebook.

1.3 Points of Criticism

① Focus was primarily given to speech which was regarded as the basis of language, and structure was viewed as being the heart of speaking ability. This led to less importance to other abilities, such as writing.

② This method has been criticized for being time-consuming. Its insistence on giving the meaning of words and structures through dramatization, demonstration and association without resorting to the mother tongue has led to the use of roundabout techniques which are time-wasting.

③ The learner is expected to deduce the meaning of a particular structure or vocabulary item from the situation in which it is presented, which might lead to confusion on the part of the learner and misunderstanding.

④ The learner is expected to apply the language learned in the classroom to situations outside the classroom. The problem here is that it is not guaranteed that learners will apply what they have learned, and even if they are willing to do so. It is not guaranteed that they will be able to do it, especially in countries where the language learned is not used frequently.

⑤ Errors are not tolerated. This could cause stress which may hinder the learning process.

⑥ Accuracy in both pronunciation and grammar are regarded as crucial.

⑦ There is no mention of communicative ability and appropriacy in this method.

1.4 Conclusion

Taking into consideration both the advantages and the disadvantages of this approach to language teaching, a competent teacher could make use of the earlier and avoid the later. It should be understood that, in language teaching, there is no one perfect approach or method. What could be successful is an approach that blends different approaches to yield the pros of each. Thus, this approach could be adopted, for example, in teaching pronunciation or vocabulary with beginners and avoided when it comes to teaching language for communicative purposes.

2 Multiple Intelligences

Study on Multiple Intelligences Theory①

2.1 The Background of Multiple Intelligences

Traditionally, intelligence can be measured by intelligence tests and figured by IQ (intelligence quotient). It restricts the definition of intelligence in a very narrow range as they only care one's performance in dealing with such paper tests mainly including math, logic and language items. As Ceci said:

"It is important to keep in mind that 'intelligence' is complex and that individuals have many kinds of abilities and strengths, not all of which are measured by IQ tests."

Howard Gardner, Professor of Education and Co-Director of Project Zero at the Harvard

---

① 代锦霞 . Study on Multiple Intelligences Theory [J]. 中国科技纵横 . 2010 (C1): 169.

Graduate School of Education, endeavored to define intelligence in a much broader way and put forward multiple intelligences theory with the publication of his treatise, *Frames of Mind*, in 1983.

MI theory challenges the traditional intelligence theory in three aspects: Firstly, it thinks the composition of intelligence is multiple. He thinks every human being owns all eight intelligences in varying amounts. So "each intelligence is of equal significance for everyone". Secondly, it connects intelligences with culture. Howard Gardner viewed:

"Intelligence is a bio-psychological potential to process information that can be activated in a cultural setting to solve problems or create products that are of value in a culture."

Student's intelligence is assessed in a certain cultural background. Individual's cultural experience should be taken into account. Thirdly, it describes the track of intellectual development. Gardner and Hatch think these intelligences can be nurtured and strengthened, or ignored and weakened. Every intelligence has its own developing track.

2.2 Description of Multiple Intelligences

Gardner put forward the notion of multiple intelligences and listed seven intelligences and has since added an eighth.

Verbal/Linguistic Intelligence refers to the sensitivity and ability of learning languages, and effectively using the language to accomplish some certain goals in social life, express ideas, describe things or events, converse with others to establish human relationships, etc.

Logical/Mathematical Intelligence consists of the ability to do mathematical calculations, think and analyze problems logically, deduce conclusions from facts, detect patterns, and investigate things scientifically.

Visual/Spatial Intelligence is the ability to perceive the external visual/spatial world, transform it into one's inner mind, and recreate/express it in the forms of lines, colors, pictures, and spatial positions, etc.

Bodily/Kinesthetic Intelligence is controlled by the motor nerves on the brain cortex which enable people to use their bodies skillfully to make a variety of gestures and movements in order to express mental activities, engage labor, and solve problems, etc.

Musical/Rhythmic Intelligence has the capacity to understand, appreciate and compose the musical patterns including pitches, tones, and rhythms, and people begin to exhibit this intelligence at earlier ages than any other intelligence does.

Interpersonal Intelligence indicates the ability to perceive the feelings, emotions, moods, desires, intentions, etc. of other people so as to communicate well, exchange ideas, and cooperate with others.

Intrapersonal Intelligence refers to the ability to understand and analyze the inner feelings and emotions of one's own. This helps people to have an accurate understanding and evaluation of themselves so as to adjust the moods, emotions, motivations to adapt to different environments.

Naturalist Intelligence enables people to observe, understand and recognize the creatures in the natural environment. This allows people to distinguish among, classify, and use features of the environment.

2.3 Principles of Multiple Intelligences

The following principles are a condensation of Richard and Rogers based on his study of Howard Gardner's theory:

① Intelligences are multiple.

② Every person is a unique blend of dynamic intelligences.

③ Intelligences vary in development both within and among individuals.

④ All intelligences are dynamic.

⑤ Multiple intelligences can be identified and described.

⑥ Every person deserves opportunities to recognize and develop the multiplicity of intelligences.

⑦ The use of one of the intelligences can be used to enhance another intelligence.

⑧ Personal background density and dispersion are critical to knowledge, beliefs, and skills in an intelligence.

⑨ All intelligences provide alternative resources and capacities to become more human, regardless of age or circumstance.

⑩ A pure intelligence is rarely seen.

⑪ Developmental theory applies to theory of multiple intelligences.

⑫ Any list of intelligences is subject to change as we learn more about multiple intelligences.

⑬ Teachers must seek ways to assess their students' learning in ways which will give all accurate overview of their strengths and weaknesses. And the assessment should also be dynamic with the development of students.

2.4 Procedure[①]

Christison describes a low-level language lesson dealing with description of physical objects.

– **Stage 1:** Awaken the Intelligence. The teacher brings many different objects to class. Students experience feeling things that are soft, rough, cold, smooth, and so on. They might taste things that are sweet, salty, sour, spicy, and so on. Experiences like this help activate and make learners aware of the sensory bases of experience.

– **Stage 2:** Amplify the Intelligence. Students are asked to bring objects to class or to use something in their possession. Teams of students describe each object attending to the five physical senses. They complete a worksheet including the information they have observed and

---

① RICHARDS J C, RODGERS T S. 语言教学的流派 [M]. 2 版 . 北京：外语教学与研究出版社，2008：122–123.

discussed (appendix-1).

Appendix-1   The Sensory Handout

Name of team _____
Team members _____
Sight _____
Sound _____
Feel _____
Smell _____
Size _____
What it's used for _____
Name of the object _____

– **Stage 3:** Teach with/for the Intelligence. At this stage, the teacher structures larger sections of lesson(s) so as to reinforce and emphasize sensory experiences and the language that accompanies these experiences. Students work in groups, perhaps completing a worksheet such as that shown in appendix-2.

Appendix-2   Multiple Intelligences Description Exercise

What am I describing?
Directions: Work with your group. Listen as the teacher reads the description of the object. Discuss what you hear with your group. Together, decide which object in the class is being described.
Name of the object
Object 1 _____
Object 2 _____
Object 3 _____
Object 4 _____
Object 5 _____
Next, have each group describe an object in the classroom using the formula given in Stage 2. Then, collect the papers and read them, one at a time. Ask each group to work together to write down the name of the object in the classroom that you are describing.

– **Stage 4:** Transfer of the Intelligence. This stage is concerned with the application of the intelligence to daily living. Students are asked to reflect on both the content of the lesson and its operational procedures (working in groups, completing tables, etc.).

This particular lesson on describing objects is seen as giving students opportunities to "develop their linguistic intelligence (for example, describing objects), logical intelligence (for example, determining which object is being described), visual/spatial intelligence (for example, determining how to describe things), interpersonal intelligence (for example, working in groups), and intrapersonal intelligence (for example, reflecting on one's own involvement in the lesson)".

3 The Lexical Approach

The Lexical Approach[①]

3.1 Introduction

A few decades ago, there was a predominant view in the linguistic circles that vocabulary was subservient to grammar. Linguists at that time strongly supported the dichotomy of grammar and vocabulary. Also, they were of the view that acquisition of a language is dependent on the mastery of grammatical rules of the language and vocabulary is of secondary importance. However, with the publication of the book *The Lexical Approach* in 1993, there was a shift from the traditional approaches of language teaching to a lexis-based approach which holds that the building blocks of language learning are not grammar or some other units of planning and teaching but lexis, that is, words and word combinations. The lexical approach believes that vocabulary is a collection of "lexical chunks." It is based on the idea that an important part of language acquisition is the ability to comprehend and produce lexical phrases as unanalyzed wholes, or "chunks" and by these chunks, learners perceive patterns of language which are traditionally thought of as grammar.

Lewis, who coined the term lexical approach, also suggests the following principles:

(1) Lexis is the basis of language.

(2) Lexis is misunderstood in language teaching because of the assumption that grammar is the basis of language. The mastery of the grammatical system is a prerequisite for effective communication.

(3) The key principle of the Lexical Approach is that language consists of grammaticalized lexis, not lexicalized grammar.

One of the central organizing principles of any meaning-centered syllabus should be lexis.

3.2 Types of lexical units

For the Lexical Approach, there is a distinction between vocabulary and lexis, which includes both separate words and word combinations stored in mental lexicons. Lewis argues that

---

① 王文静 . Lexical Approach [J]. 东方教育 , 2017 (5). 多处进行增改。

language consists of lexical units and treats them as belonging to five major categories:

① Words (e.g. pen, glass);

② Poly-words (e.g. upside down);

③ Collocations (e.g. to catch a cold);

④ Fixed expressions (e.g. If I were you);

⑤ Semi-Fixed expressions (e.g. Firstly...; Secondly...; Finally...).

Words and poly-words have been considered as essential vocabulary for learners to memorize. Collocations are understood as the way in which words typically occur with each other. Collocations and expressions are thought to be the most important types of lexical units. Language fluency and accuracy is achieved mainly by recalling and combining ready-made chunks of language.

3.3 The Lexical Approach in Language Teaching and Learning

It is clear that lexis plays an important role in a lexical approach in language teaching and learning. Teaching should be based on the idea that language production is the piecing together of ready-made units appropriate for a particular situation. Lewis holds that implementing lexical approach in the classroom would entail teachers paying more attention to: lexis of different kinds, specific language areas, listening and reading, the language learners may meet outside the classroom (films, books, Internet), preparing learners to chunk the language, creating a habit of using dictionaries as learning sources, etc.

The lexical approach recommends the learning of multi-word items as they aid the learner in producing the language without much effort. Lewis also emphasizes that the lexical approach does not undermine the importance of grammar. As he puts it, the Lexical Approach in no way denies the value of grammar, nor its unique role in language. Lewis suggests that language teaching should include the teaching of lexical phrases or chunks. Lexical chunks are characteristics of language use and language acquisition and present advantages for language teaching and learning.

Hill suggests that classroom procedures involve ① teaching individual collocations, ② making students aware of collocation, ③ extending what students already know by adding knowledge of collocation restrictions to known vocabulary, and ④ storing collocations through encouraging students to keep a lexical notebook.

Lewis gives the following example[①] of how a teacher extends learners' knowledge of collocations while giving feedback on a learner's error.

S: I have to make an exam in the summer.

---

① RICHARDS J C, RODGERS T S. 语言教学的流派 [M]. 2 版. 北京：外语教学与研究出版社，2008：138.

(T indicates mistake by facial expression.)

S: *I have to make an exam.*

(Writes "exam" on the board.)

T: *What verb do we usually use with "exam"?*

S2: *Take.*

T: *Yes, that's right. (Writes "take" on the board.)*

What other verbs do we use with "exam"?

S2: *Pass.*

T: *Yes. And the opposite?*

S: *Fail.*

T: *(Writes "pass" and "fail" on the board.)*

And if you fail an exam, sometimes you can do it again.

What's the verb for that? (Waits for response.)

No? OK, retake. You can retake an exam.

(Writes "retake" on the board.)

If you pass an exam with no problems, what can you say? I...passed.

S2: *Easily.*

T: *Yes, or we often say "comfortably." I passed comfortably.*

What about if you get 51 and the pass mark is 50?

What can you say? I...(Waits for response.)

No? I just passed. You can also just fail.

3.4 Conclusion

The Lexical Approach is worthwhile and beneficial for students, because they get involved in the process of becoming aware of lexical chunks, identifying, writing, distinguishing between high frequency and low-frequency lexical units. Counting lexical chunks as unanalyzed wholes will surely contribute to more efficient and fruitful English teaching and learning.

Besides, advances in computer-based studies of language, such as corpus linguistics, have provided huge databases of language including the Cobuild English Corpus, and the British National Corpus and so on, which examined patterns of language as they appear in various contexts as well as in spoken English. In particular, the corpus project at Birmingham university in England examined patterns of phrase and clause sequences as they appear in various texts as well as in spoken language. It aims at producing an accurate description of the English language in order to form the basis for design of a lexical syllabus. Some English courses attempt to develop a syllabus based on lexical rather than grammatical principles. In other words, the lexical approach originates from the research result of corpus linguistics.

The lexical approach can be implemented on the basis of Nattinger and Decarrico's research into lexical chunks. Their research has demonstrated that lexical chunks are important pans of language learning and teaching. Lexical chunks are not only the focus of language learning but also the basis of commanding grammar structure.

The development of cognitive linguistics and psycholinguistics has laid solid foundations for the development of the Lexical Approach. Schmitt theory can be more convincing. He claims that lexical chunks can be stored and processed in the human brain. When communicating, human beings can automatically use the lexical chunks stored in the human brain. In this case, people can easily accomplish the communication process.

4 The Natural Approach

Analysis on the Natural Approach in Foreign Language Teaching[①]

4.1 Introduction

The Natural Approach (NA) is proposed by Stephen Krashen and Tracy Terrel to develop teaching principles, which is usually regarded as the process of language acquisition in which the learners' skills to use the language are acquired in the non-formal settings and which is primarily designed to develop human basic communication skills. The NA occupies strong theoretical and practical basis, and therefore attracts a wide interest. It is one of the contemporary and prospective language teaching approaches. In this part, those theoretical bases and teaching principles will be reviewed. Then, comments on the advantages and disadvantages of the NA will be analyzed, to help the application of the NA in the process of foreign language teaching in the environment of China in a more reasonable and effective way.

4.2 General Review of the NA's Theoretical Basis

The theoretical assumptions of the NA focus on two factors: the nature of language and language learning.

(1) Theory of Language of the Natural Approach

Briefly speaking, the view of language of the NA consists of lexical items, structures and messages. Krashen and Terrel give much attention to messages, because messages are closely related to communication and meaning. They regard communication as the primary function of language and consider language as a vehicle for the communication of different meanings and messages. They stress the significance of vocabulary and hold that a language is essentially its lexicon. In the NA, grammar has only the function of determining how words are used to convey meaning and grammatical structure does not require explicit analysis or attention.

---

① LEI Q Q. Analysis on the Natural Approach in foreign language teaching [J]. Overseas English. 2012 (10): 132-134.

(2) The NA's Theory of Learning

The NA's learning theory consists of the following five hypotheses, which are collectively referred to as Krashen's language acquisition theory or the Monitor Model.

① Acquisition/Learning Hypothesis.

According to Krashen, there are two independent systems of second language performance: the acquired system and the learned system. The acquired system (acquisition) is the product of a subconscious process and it requires natural communication in which speakers concentrate not on the form of utterances, but on the communicative act.

② Natural Order Hypothesis.

In this hypothesis, it is believed that human's acquisition of grammatical structures proceeds progression that can be predicted. And the natural order in second language acquisition is similar. Second language learners would always acquire these rules in a certain order. What's more, whether in the classroom or in a natural environment, the order of rule acquisition one learns a language is the same.

③ The Monitor Hypothesis.

According to this hypothesis, language acquisition and language learning play different roles in second language learning. Learning has only a "monitor" function using conscious grammatical knowledge to determine the form of produced utterances. Acquisition can help speakers to produce utterances and it is responsible for fluency.

④ The Input Hypothesis.

This hypothesis is a central claim of Krashen. It claims that humans acquire language only by understanding messages or by receiving "comprehensible input," i.e., language that is heard and understood. According to this hypothesis, the input should be a little higher than the learners' current level. If a learner is at the stage i, the input conductive to acquisition should contain i+1. If the input at a higher or lower level (e.g. i or i+2), no acquisition will occur.

⑤ Affective Filter Hypothesis.

According to the hypothesis, learners need to be affectively disposed to "let in" the input they comprehend; comprehension is not sufficient. Krashen believes that a number of affective variables play a facilitative and formal role in second language acquisition, including motivation, self-confidence, and anxiety. Lack of motivation, low self-esteem, and a strong sense of anxiety can raise the affective filter. When the filter is up, it can create a mental block that prevents comprehensible input and prevents language acquisition.

4.3 Teaching Principles of the NA

The NA conforms to the naturalistic principles found in successful second language acquisition. Is it possible for teachers to apply the NA in the classroom foreign language teaching context? The answer is yes — it is likely to train students in a classroom to learn to communicate in the target language through the use of the NA. Four general principles are sketched to guide language teaching in the context of second language learning.

① Language instruction should focus on communicative competence rather than grammatical perfection.

In the NA, language is viewed as a vehicle for communicating meanings and messages. And the primary goal of the Natural Approach is to develop basic oral or written communication skills. On the contrary, the accuracy of linguistic knowledge is paid little attention to. Error correction is done only in written assignments that specially focus on form and never during communication.

② Comprehension precedes production; production emerges automatically.

The NA divides the foreign language learning process into comprehension stage and production stage. Specifically speaking, the ability to speak fluently can not be taught directly, because it can emerge independently, after the acquirer has comprehended messages that were heard or read. So the best way to teach speaking is to focus on listening and reading. Following that, the spoken fluency will occur.

③ Teachers should provide students with lots of acquisition activities to acquire language.

The core of the NA classroom is a series of acquisition activities which focus on meaningful communication rather than language form. The most important function of these activities is to provide comprehensible input, and in a sense, the main task is to develop listening skills, and the valuable by-product is the development of oral communication. There are four groups of activities: affective-humanistic activities, problem-solving activities, games, and content activities.

④ Affective filter should be lowered.

The affective variables play an important role in acquiring a second language, and that it is desirable to produce a lower affective filter to allow more necessary input. In a foreign language classroom, the teacher tries to bring down the affective filter to as a low level as possible. He does not ask students to speak the target language until they are ready. Students make their decisions on when to speak and what to speak about. If they make errors in language form, they are not corrected directly. A friendly and interesting atmosphere in a classroom is created as well.

4.4 Comments on the NA: Its Advantages and Disadvantages

Every coin has two sides and every teaching approach has its advantages and disadvantages. There is no exception in the NA. In the following part, let's look at the advantages and disadvantages of the NA.

(1) Advantages of the NA

① The NA applies the natural principle in the classroom situation and tries to create a native-like environment.

The NA suggests that the unconscious acquisition process involves the naturalistic development of language proficiency. It stresses the naturalistic language learning of the young children. As we know, the classroom is one important place for second language learning, so the acquisition activities organized during the classroom time are significant in creating a natural learning context, allowing them to contact more authentic materials, to communicate more and to practice more, and to improve more in the last.

② The NA is typical of modern language teaching ideas and it is a typically humanistic teaching approach.

Firstly, it stresses communication rather than grammatical structures. It regards communication as much more important and the entire class period is devoted to communication activities. Secondly, the NA is student-centered. In the NA classroom, the student is the center of all teaching programs. He/she is the processor of comprehensible input, is expected to assign meaning to the input, and decides when to speak and what to speak. As for the teachers, they are really the instructors, providing input and helping them to comprehend the input at last. But traditional learners are passive to believing what their teachers say, to do what their teachers ask them to do, and have a lot of rote learning. From this point, we can also see that this approach is also a humanistic one, considering learners' emotions and their needs. What is more, the NA pays attention to establish a low affective filter classroom, choosing interesting topics and allowing certain errors. The NA creates a humanistic classroom.

③ The NA stresses the comprehensible input.

It claims that learners must be exposed to as much comprehensible input as possible, i.e., input whose content is comprehensible to them but whose linguistic forms are slightly in advance of their current levels. No comprehension has no acquisition, and comprehension is the basis of mastering a second language. The situation, extra-linguistic information, the knowledge of the world and teachers' speech are provided to help students accomplish their comprehension. It is sensible to learn a second language in the process of comprehension.

(2) The Disadvantages of the NA

① The teaching object of the NA is limited to the beginners.

This approach is primarily designed to develop basic and essential communication skills, and is designed to help beginners to become intermediates. As for the students of high levels, they have mastered the basic skills and the NA is no longer appropriate for them. Take the graduate students for example. These students are expected to learn more specialized knowledge. Some of them take the linguistics as their major and need to pay more attention to the linguistic forms. Thus, the NA is not appropriate for students of high linguistic levels.

② It is hard to master the classroom full of acquisition activities for a teacher if the NA is employed.

If these activities are not organized well, it is likely to produce a loose classroom atmosphere. In a loose classroom, the students are hard to control, the teaching activities are hard to continue, and the effective learning is hard to accomplish. This bad situation is more likely to occur when the young students are being taught.

③ There are still many controversial problems in the NA.

The distinction between acquisition and learning seems to be reasonable, but it is hard to put into practice, because it is difficult for us to distinguish where the learners' knowledge comes from: the acquisition process or the learning process or both of the two processes; the NA emphasizes the importance of comprehensible input, but it is hard to define the so-called i+1 input and how to make the input comprehensible by every student; it also undervalues the importance of improving the quality of output; it is too simplified to explain the individual differences through the effective filter. Therefore, we can see that there still exist both conceptual problems and practical problems in the NA.

4.5 Conclusion

The NA belongs to a tradition of language teaching methods based on observation and interpretation of how learners acquire both first and second languages in nonformal settings. However, we must realize that this creative approach firstly occurs in American and is firstly applied in American. So if the NA is applied to China, a non-English environment, things will be different. To employ the approach well in China, it is necessary to create a native-like language learning environment. In our teaching practice, we should make our choice in accordance with the specific situations and then it will be of great significance to employ the NA in China to develop language communicative competence.

5 Cooperative Language Learning

Cooperative Language Learning: Increasing Opportunities for Learning in Teams[①]

5.1 Introduction: Cooperative Learning in Language Settings

During the past decade, "cooperative learning" seems to have attracted a lot of attention and became popular. This conceptual approach is based on a theoretical framework that provides general principles on how to structure cooperative learning activities in a teacher's specific subject area, curriculum, students, and setting. It is the one that teachers can use to stimulate students to acquire the knowledge as well as interpersonal and team skills. It helps promote student-student interaction via working in small groups to maximize their learning and reach their shared goal. As Johnson puts it, cooperation is not assigning a job to a group of students where

---

① WICHADEE S, ORAWIWATNAKUL W. Cooperative Language Learning: Increasing Opportunities for Learning in Teams[J]. Journal of College Teaching and Learning. 2012, 9, (2): 93–98.

one student does all the work and the others put their names on the paper. It is not having students sit side by side at the same table to talk with each other as they do their individual assignments as well. It is not having students do a task individually with instructions that the ones who finish first are to help the slower students. On the contrary, cooperative learning is a teaching strategy in which small teams, each with students of different levels of ability, use a variety of learning activities to improve their understanding of a subject. Each member of a team is responsible not only for learning what is taught but also for helping teammates learn, thus creating an atmosphere of achievement. Students work through the assignment until all group members successfully understand and complete it.

Cooperative learning is characterized by five common elements, including ① positive interdependence, where the group has a common goal and each member's contribution is important to the group's success; ② face-to-face group interactions in which each member is encouraged to participate, help others succeed, and learn from each other; ③ individual and group accountability in which members divide the work and are individually responsible for specific tasks; ④ development of small group social skills involving negotiating and use of group interaction skills; and ⑤ group processing, which involves students reflecting on the group's experience. To be cooperative, group members must promote each other's learning and success face-to-face, hold each other personally and individually accountable to do a fair share of the work, use the interpersonal and small group skills needed for cooperative efforts to be successful, and process as a group how effectively members are working together. These five essential components are needed for small group learning to be truly cooperative.

Cooperative learning has been implemented in many areas including language instruction. Olsen and Kagan strongly believe that Cooperative Language Learning (CLL) offers a chance for interaction among students and helps integrate content learning into language learning. CLL was founded from Dewey's humanistic educational philosophy which supported the notion that learners are the subject of education. CLL will be more efficient if students learn the meaning and function of the language at the same time. Activities and interaction among group members emphasize communicative skills, promoting them to practice language usage in various situations. Since CLL provides students with an opportunity to be responsible for learning, as well as helping one another to reach the goal, the supportive environment is meaningful to language learners. Basically, CLL is suitable to be used in the Thai education system because it serves the National Education Act for two main reasons. The first one is that this learning context emphasizes cooperation in helping each other to acquire knowledge. Cooperative learning activities have been employed with EFL students due to the fact that they can foster active participation, a sense of community, emotional support and provide more social interaction for students. This type of learning decreases competitiveness and individualism but increases opportunities to actively construct or transform the knowledge among students. Second, CLL creates student centeredness. As we know, teacher-centered approaches taking place in traditional classroom could not produce active recipients and resulted in fossilized language learning. It is not effective enough to promote language acquisition. Interaction among group members, therefore, is believed to produce communicative skills, enabling students to practice language skills in various situations.

5.2 Research Support for Cooperative Language Learning

A number of research studies on cooperative-based learning in all levels of education have been conducted, with most of them yielding positive results for a variety of cognitive and affective outcomes. Analyses of research can be drawn to the following conclusions:

(1) The Effect on Students' Social Relationship

Three pieces of research demonstrate that cooperative learning produced more positive social relationships among students.

(2) The Effect on Students' Learning Achievement

The results of three studies showed that the post-test scores, after learning English reading using cooperative learning, were higher than the pre-test scores at the .05 level of significance. Most of the samples displayed very good behavior in cooperating in their tasks.

(3) The Effect on Students' Critical Thinking Skills

A study was conducted to compare critical thinking skills of students who studied Business English I at Chiangrai Commercial School using the cooperative learning method with those of students using the traditional group work method. The post-test scores of students who were taught through the cooperative learning method were remarkably higher than the post-test scores of students who were taught through the traditional group work method at $P < .05$ level. Moreover, the unit post-test scores of the experimental group were higher than those of the control group as the statistical difference was significant at $P < .05$ level. The results of the questionnaire showed that students' opinions toward the cooperative learning were moderately positive.

(4) The Effect on Students' Self-Efficacy

A study examined the effects of cooperative learning using Student Team-Achievement Divisions (STAD) technique on self-efficacy. Results indicated that the students who studied through STAD had a higher self-efficacy after the treatment than before the treatment at the .01 level of significance. The students who studied through STAD had higher self-efficacy and English learning achievement than those students who studied through the conventional method at the .01 level of significance.

(5) The Effect on Students' Learning Anxiety and Language Proficiency

One study was done to examine the effectiveness of Cooperative Learning Approach in reducing foreign language anxiety and to investigate its impact on language proficiency of 40 sophomore students enrolled in EN 211 course in the second semester of academic year 2009 at Bangkok University. Three instruments employed were the standardized Foreign Language Classroom Anxiety Scale (FLCAS), two proficiency tests covering reading and writing skills, and a semi-structured interview. The pre- and post-scores from the questionnaire and the tests of the group were calculated for descriptive statistics and compared using a paired sample t-test measure. It was found that the students' top five sources of language classroom anxiety and overall language anxiety were significantly decreased. In addition, they obtained higher language proficiency scores for the post-test than the pretest at the significance level of .001 after learning through this approach. The students also had a favorable attitude toward cooperative learning as a whole.

5.3 Creating Cooperative Language Learning (CLL) Activities

Macpherson states that cooperative learning is a very formal way of structuring activities in a learning environment which includes specific elements intended to increase the potential for rich and deep learning of the participants. So, the appropriate cooperative learning models for language settings should be designed based on the following basic principles:

• Group tasks are designed to be suitable for group work.

• Positive interdependence is built in — cooperation is necessary for students to succeed.

• Attention and class time are given to interpersonal/cooperative skill building.

• Participants learn together in small (2–5 members) groups.

• Students are individually accountable for learning and participation.

• The instructor's role changes from being the "sage on the stage" to the "guide on the side."

Although there are many types of cooperative learning activities implemented in EFL class, four main activities are suggested as they provide more channels for students to get knowledge and information. These activities are not at all anxiety-provoking situations, but increase supportiveness among students.

The first activity "Think-Pair-Share" developed by Frank Lyman and his colleagues in Maryland, can be used to encourage student classroom participation without stress. This activity helps the students formulate individual ideas and share these ideas with other students. It involves a three-step cooperative structure. In the "think" step, the teacher provokes students' thinking with a question or a prompt. It should take a few moments for them to think about the question individually. In the "pair" step, students work in pairs talking about the answer each comes up with. They compare their written notes and identify the answers they think are best, most convincing or most unique. In the last step called "share" the teacher calls for pairs to share their thinking with other pairs and the rest of the class. Often, the teacher or a designated helper will record these responses on the board. Students are allowed to choose their own partners in doing pair work. This kind of activity covers different tasks and can be created to improve different skills as follows:

• Think-Write-Pair-Share: To increase individual accountability, have students jot down their ideas before turning to a partner to discuss them. The teacher can walk around the room and look at what they are writing to see who understands the concept. It also prevents students from adopting their partner's attitude easily or just sitting back and letting their partner do all the thinking.

• Spelling: The teacher calls out a word, has them think of the spelling, then designates one person to turn to their partner and whisper the spelling. The partner gives a thumbs-up to show agreement or corrects the spelling. The teacher can reveal the correct spelling by showing it on screen with PowerPoint.

In short, Think-Pair-Share provides an opportunity for all students to share their thinking with at least one other student, which, in turn, increases their sense of involvement in classroom learning.

The second group work activity the teacher can employ is "Numbered Heads Together". Its structure is derived from the work of Spencer Kagan. A team of four is established and each member is given numbers of 1, 2, 3, 4. Questions are asked of the group whose members work together so that all can verbally answer the questions. The teacher calls out a number and that number in each team is asked to give the answer. By doing this, everyone in the team must participate and be able to answer the question. This activity is usually conducted to enhance students' reading comprehension skill. One great benefit includes students being able to learn from each other. They must work together to ensure that everyone can understand and answer the question. This activity is one way to reduce anxiety in class.

The third activity is called "Circle the Sage" created by Kagan. First, the teacher polls the class to see which students have special knowledge to share. For example, the teacher may ask who in the class is able to solve a difficult math homework question, who has visited Mexico, who knows the chemical reactions involved in how salting the streets helps dissipate snow, etc. Those students (the sages) stand and spread out in the room. The teacher then has the rest of the classmates surround a sage, with no two members of the same team going to the same sage. The sage explains what they know while the classmates listen, ask questions, and take notes. All students then return to their teams. Each, in turn, explains what they have learned. Because each one has gone to a different sage, they compare notes. If there is disagreement, they stand up as a team. Finally, the disagreements are resolved.

The last activity, which fits the learner-centered approach, is called "Peer Review" — an activity requiring students to read each other's draft and give comments on it. Peer Review provides students with the opportunity to learn how to give and receive constructive feedback. The main goal of using peer review is to help both writers and commentators improve their writing. The benefits from doing peer feedback are that ① students who give feedback to peers will develop their critical thinking and ② students will become active learners. The Peer Review is usually conducted in pairs. The students are trained on the principles of peer correction and how to give feedback so that they would not encounter any difficulties when giving comments. Peer Review training should be available before the lesson officially starts. This means they will be taught how to follow the review procedure step by step, how to consult the dictionary when in doubt, how to write up a comment, etc. Through Peer Review activity, students will experience supportive peer feedback which helps increase their motivation and attitude toward studying English. The feedback from peers is less threatening than from teachers, so there is less anxiety in class.

5.4 Evaluation Used in Cooperative Language Learning

One problem of students' unwillingness to do cooperative learning is due to the grading. Low-achievers might learn harder, but high achievers might lose motivation when evaluation is done as a whole or as a group. Therefore, to encourage both groups to learn in order to make good progress, teachers should not only assess students' learning achievement by groups, but also evaluate them individually. Oxford proposes that teachers should grade students on how they improve, even though they are assigned to four-member learning teams that are mixed in performance level. During team study, group members may work cooperatively with provided worksheets and answer sheets. The function of the team is to prepare its members to do well on the quizzes. However, after one or two periods of team practice, each student individually takes a quiz on the material. Students are not permitted to help one another during the quizzes. Next, the teacher scores the papers using a scoring system that ranges from 0 to 30 points and reflects degree of individual improvement over previous quiz scores. That is, students' quiz scores are compared with their own past averages. Slavin uses the following scoring procedure to stimulate students' learning in STAD model:

Step 1: Establishing baseline (Each student is given a base score based on an average on past quizzes.)

Step 2: Finding current quiz score (Students receive points for the quiz associated with the current lesson.)

Step 3: Finding improvement score (Students earn improvement points to the degree in which their current quiz score matches or exceeds their base score, using the scale provided.)

The purpose of base scores and improvement points is to make it possible for all students to bring maximum points to their teams, whatever their level of past performance. It is fair to compare each student with his or her own level of past performance since all students enter a classroom with different levels of skills and experience in English. Therefore, whenever CLL takes place in class, students tend to have a positive attitude toward it.

Appendix-3   The Scale of the Scoring System

Quiz Score	Improvement Points
More than 10 points below base score	0
10 points below to 1 point below base score	10
Base score to 10 points above base score	20
More than 10 points above base score	30
Perfect paper (regardless of base score in Step 1)	30

5.5 Advantages of Cooperative Language Learning

Cooperative Language Learning is a good solution to any instructional problem. It is believed to be one of the best approaches as it promotes students to work in teams with cooperation to accomplish something of importance. Based on the author's experience of facilitating CLL in many classes, students developed themselves a lot in different aspects.

(1) The Increase in Motivation But Less Competition on Studying

A CLL class, compared with a teacher-centered class, is likely to be more beneficial in terms of producing supportive relationships among students. Therefore, cooperative learning can change students' learning behavior. Although some students are not concerned about grades or interested in participating in class, if a group's performance depends on each individual contributing, they have to come. They don't want to miss a class in which all assignments are handed out and they don't want to disappoint their teammates since they care about their peers. They know that members cannot work without them. Although some students are not much concerned about grades, they don't want to fail their group by missing the points from the quiz. That is, cooperative learning can dramatically improve students' attendance as well as motivation to learn.

(2) Students' Development in Thoughts

All members have a chance to think about the issues or problems that the teacher raises; they have a chance to discuss and determine the answer for the group. This can maximize the students' interaction in English and it can take away the big burden of running large classes. It solves the problem that one teacher cannot pay attention to all students. With this method, they receive attention not only from the teacher, but also from their friends.

(3) Better Perception on Other Group Members' Intention

When working together, each student can see how much effort their team members are making. Students possess a sense of community. CLL can solve the problems of isolation and alienation that are two predictors of failure. According to Tinto, two main reasons for dropping out of university are failure to establish a social network of friends or classmates and failure to become academically involved in classes.

(4) Reducing Students' Learning Anxiety

CLL provides a less anxiety-producing context in terms of discussing, creating, and thinking in a group rather than in a whole class. In such an atmosphere, students may feel more comfortable studying and trying out new ideas. Normally, students tend to be silent when they do not want to clarify their confusion. This concept is in accordance with Wei who demonstrates that speaking to a whole class is often a threatening experience to most students, but they are quite at ease talking to their group members. Further interaction occurred in group discussion and peer checking of worksheets since students exchange ideas and make corrections or improvements in collaboration instead of individual learning. Language acquisition can occur in a context that is supportive, friendly, motivating, communicative, developmentally appropriate, and feedback rich.

5.6 Putting Some Awareness on Cooperative Language Learning

Nowadays, CLL is employed in different parts of the world to enable active learning. The reason behind the frequent use of it is that this kind of learning offers a lot of opportunities for students to improve themselves in different aspects, such as knowledge, skill, attitude, and achievement as mentioned earlier. Although most research results offer positive perspectives of cooperative learning, some awareness should be taken into consideration when implementing it in language teaching. Based on the author's experience, most of the limitations of CLL came from not being able to implement the cooperative structure completely. First, it is time-consuming for students to learn materials in a cooperative way and to work together in groups. This might affect other contents which teachers need to cover. Therefore, teachers should be aware of time limitation in order to make group learning more meaningful. The class activities should be well-planned in advance to ensure the learning process is really based on cooperative learning. Second, the room with fixed chairs might not be suitable for doing cooperative learning activities. Also, the seats arranged in tiers and spaces narrowly apart make it difficult for group working. Third, CLL will never take place if students don't get clear instructions, so students have to be informed of what they are doing. They should be told what they are going to learn and why it is important so that they will realize they must pay careful attention during the class presentation because doing so will help them to do well on the quizzes which determine their team scores. They are obliged to help their members learn. After the material is presented by the teacher, the team meets to study worksheets or other material. Most often, they have to discuss the problems together, compare answers, and correct any misconceptions if teammates make mistakes. Lastly, most Thai students feel uncomfortable speaking English to their friends; for this reason, they do not take advantage of the chance to do so. To solve this problem, students should be encouraged to interact and converse with one another in English in order to practice the target language and absorb knowledge. Moreover, it will be better to have them prepare themselves or study the content in advance.

6 Competency-Based Language Teaching[①]

The Competency-Based Approach to English Language Education and the Walls Between the Classroom and the Society in Cameroon: Pulling Down the Walls[②]

6.1 Definitions of the Concept

The Competency-Based Approach (CBA) is also referred to as the pedagogy of integration or to an outcomes approach. This approach entails the putting together of all the knowledge, know-how and attitudes required for the solution of real life problems or situations. Put simplistically and with reference to language learning, using all the grammar, vocabulary, punctuation and pronunciation to communicate effectively in real time listening, speaking, reading and writing situations. Furthermore, it consists of knowing what to do, where, when and with whom; or, being linguistically, communicatively and sociolinguistically competent with the learned language. CBA, as earlier mentioned, seeks to bridge the wall between school or the classroom and everyday real life: seeking and giving information by interacting with people in the market, hospital, school, offices etc. through listening, reading, writing and speaking; in short, the point is communicating: CBA is thus interdisciplinary; for, to effectively solve problems in read life one has to deploy knowledge, know-how and attitudes drawn from several domains of life like history, science and mathematics. CBA therefore integrates theses domains in its approach.

① Richards and Rodgers hold that the Competency Based Approach focuses on the outcomes of learning. It addresses what the learners are expected to do rather than what they are expected to learn about. The CBA advocates defining educational goals in terms of precise measurable descriptions of knowledge, skills and behaviors that students should possess at the end of a course of study.

② Schneck views the CBA as an outcome-based instruction that is adaptive to the needs of students, teachers and the community. Competencies describe the students' ability to apply basic and other skills to situations that are commonly encountered in everyday life. Therefore, the competency based approach is based on a set of outcomes that are derived from an analysis of

---

① 能力导向型教学法（Competency-Based Language Teaching）是基于能力的方法（The Competency-Based Approach）在语言教学领域的具体应用。本着遵循原文的原则，拓展阅读在教学法名称上不另改正，两种表述同指能力导向型教学法。

② NKWETISAMA C M. The Competency Based Approach to English Language Education and the Walls between the Classroom and the Society in Cameroon: Pulling Down the Walls[J]. Theory and Practice in Language Studies, 2012, 2(3): 516–523.

tasks typically required of students in life role situations.

③ Savage holds that the competency-based model was defined by the U.S. Office of Education as a performance-based process leading to demonstrated mastery of basic and life skills necessary for the individual to function proficiently in the society. It is therefore a functional approach to education that emphasizes life skills and evaluates mastery of those skills according to actual learner performance.

④ Mrowicki holds that competencies consist of a description of the essential skills, knowledge, attitudes and behaviours required for effective performance of a real world task or activity. These activities may relate to any domain of life.

6.2 Components of the Competency-Based Approach

Weddel outlines the components of Competency-Based education and says that the approach consists of the following:

① An assessment of the learners' needs;

② The selection of the competencies;

③ The target instruction;

④ An evaluation of the competency attainment.

The four components do not function in isolation. The approach starts with the assessment of needs of the students, moves to the selection of the expected competencies, then to the target instruction from where it moves over to the evaluation of the rate of attainment of the competence, and then back to the assessment of the needs. It is thus a cyclical.

6.3 Features of the Competency-Based Approach

The Competency-Based Approach is characterized by the following:

① The competencies are stated in specific and measurable behavioral terms.

② The contents are based on the learners' goals, i.e., outcomes or competencies.

③ The learners continue learning until mastery is demonstrated.

④ The approach makes use of an unlimited variety of instructional techniques and group work.

⑤ It centers on what the learner needs to learn, which is the application of basic skills in life skill language context such as listening, speaking, reading or writing.

⑥ The approach makes extensive use of texts, media, and real life materials adapted to targeted competencies.

⑦ It provides learners with immediate feedback on assessment performance.

⑧ The instruction or teaching is paced to the needs of the learners.

⑨ It gets learners to demonstrate mastery of the specific competency statements or objectives.

The targeted skills are listening, speaking, reading and writing. The specific competency

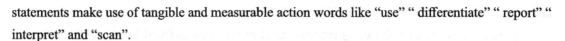

statements make use of tangible and measurable action words like "use" "differentiate" "report" "interpret" and "scan".

6.4 Integrating Language Segments in the CBA

Language segments can be broadly categorized into the larger holistic components like functions, topics, situations, notions or into the smaller ones like grammar, vocabulary and pronunciation. Meaningful Task-Based activity or a problem solving complex situation under any of the segments enables learners to be involved more intensively with the language associated with it. Since the Competency-Based model aims principally at the mastery of specific competencies and is learner-participant centred, the techniques used could include the print, audiovisual simulation models. Furthermore, the teaching/learning of pronunciation, vocabulary and grammar is most effective when they are also integrated into activities that use the target item meaningfully for a communicative purpose.

Whether we adopt the larger or smaller segment approach, we do not have to lose sight of the importance of the communicative acts and overall interactive context of language use by over stressing correct grammar and pronunciation.

Appendix-4　Integrating Language Segments

Situation	Topics	Notions	Functions	Grammar	Vocabulary
Getting to know some one	Tastes hobbies	Inquiring Informing Greeting	Offer, request, promise, advise, threat, instruct, apology, remind, express opinions, (making requests)	Interrogative forms, other verbs	Reading, swimming, past time and leisure activities
Reporting an incident	Road accident	Past time Narrating Describing		Past tense	Drive Car etc. road scenes
Shopping	Food stuff Clothes			Modals, would, could, might	Food stuff, clothes, adjectives of colour, size, tastes, etc.
Planning a trip	Travel Accommodation	Future time Predicting Suggestion		Future tense	Train, plane, bus, hotel, dormitory inn, etc.
Asking about or describing a job or profession	Jobs/profession Activities Equipment	Describing activities		Present tense, Yes/No questions	Teacher, carpenter, farmer, trader, etc. Jobs

The obviously binary functions are "offer" usually followed by acceptance or rejection; "request" followed by positive or negative response; "instruction" followed by some expression of comprehension; "apology" followed by acknowledgement.

All these have to be taken into consideration for competence sake.

The pronunciation column is empty because any aspect of it can be linked to a wide range of activities.

Competence can be applied to language learning and teaching in terms of accuracy and fluency in the language. Mastery of the language means the learner can understand and produce it both accurately (correctly) and fluently (receiving and conveying messages with ease).

The teaching of pronunciation, vocabulary and grammar is accuracy-oriented while focus on the holistic categories of topic, situations, notions, and functions is fluency-oriented. With fluency, emphasis is on producing appropriate language in context and equal importance is attached to form and message. This is then the case with the four skills of listening, speaking, reading and writing where emphasis is lowered on accuracy.

6.5 CBA Lessons

A CBA lesson plan calls for:

(1) Presentation of the Problem-Solving Situation

This is the discovery phase and it contains new notions to be discovered by learners. The teacher presents it and gives instructions to learners.

(2) Systematization

After examining and bringing out relationship between previously learned elements and elements found in the new problem solving situation, learners come out with rules (hypothetical). This is done with the help of the teacher.

(3) Application

Here, the teacher gives tasks where learners apply the new knowledge.

(4) Partial Integration Activities

The teacher presents a new complex situation that will necessitate the exercise of the skill to solve a problem which is similar to the competence/skill the learners used at the beginning of the lesson. Note that this has to be a concrete real life situation.

It should be noted also that partial integration activities are not done systematically at the end of every lesson.

The lesson plan in the table portrays implicit and explicit use of cognitive strategies like noticing or observing, emitting hypotheses and testing them, problem solving and restructuring. This is in opposition to the traditional approach which stressed on structures and functions.

Appendix-5   Lesson Fromat Based on the Competency-Based Approach

Stages	Intermediary Pedagogic Objectives	Teachers Activities	Learners Activities
① Discovery (presentation of the problem solving situation)	-To clearly restate the problem	-Presents the problem solving situation through statements, drawing, questions, actions, mimed, etc. -Ensures that everybody understands the problem. -Gives instructions.	-Get acquainted with the situation by reading or by listening. -Ask questions if any.
② Research (Individually or in groups seek solutions to problems) Hypotheses are put forth and analysed	-To posit and verify hypotheses	-Recalls the instruction so as to elicit the emission of hypotheses. -Goes round the groups to help and encourage learners.	-Give hypotheses. -Work individually, and then in groups, compare their findings. -Call teachers attention in case of conflict.
③ Comparison and validation of findings or results	-To present -To justify the results -To validate	-Recalls the instructions once more. -Puts away wrong answers and retains justifiable answers which tie with the objectives.	-Give the answers or solutions. -Justify their answers or solutions. -Get the final opinion or say of the teacher.
④ Institutionalization and formulating the new knowledge (generalization)	-To formulate the new knowledge	-Generalizes one case. -Identifies new knowledge. -Introduce new vocabulary (concept).	-Use what they already know to come up with new knowledge.
⑤ Consolidation (application)	-To use the new knowledge	-Gives exercises (written or oral) to verify if objectives have been attained.	-Get used to new knowledge by using it accordingly.
⑥ Partial integration activities	-To put together the new knowledge and know how to solve a complex problem situation	-Gives complex problem solving situations to verify the level of development of the skill.	-Get acquainted (more familiar) with the new leanings and use them in solving real life problems.
⑦ Remediation activities	-To tackle cases of incomprehension	-Explains over and over that which was not understood.	-Discover their errors and rectify them.

7 Project-Based Learning

A Literature Review on the Definition and Process
of Project-Based Learning and Other Relative Studies[①]

7.1 Introduction

The National Standards of Teaching Quality for Undergraduate English Majors lays great emphasis on cultivating the students' overall competence to use English language proficiently, and think critically and innovatively. Under the guidance of the national standards, English teaching is entering into a new era. Meanwhile, English teachers must make efforts to figure out new and effective ways to improve students' language proficiency in order to meet the new standards. In fact, the ultimate objective of English learning is to use English in real life or authentic contexts. Thus, it is suggested that Project-Based Learning (PBL) should be taken into consideration. It can render help in achieving the objectives, especially enhancing the use of English in practical communication. Meanwhile, a survey of western studies is necessary and meaningful since it may shed light on the relevant studies or practices in China. This part gives a review of the research of PBL from different aspects, including the definition of PBL, the process of PBL and its relative studies.

7.2 Definition of Project-Based Learning

The PBL has been part of the educational practice approximately at the beginning of the 1980s and it was greatly influenced by the communicative approach. Nowadays, as an appropriate and effective method, it is widely used in the teaching of English as a second language.

The history of PBL can be traced back to the progressive tradition advocated by John Dewey. Dewey insisted on the idea of "learning by doing." He argued that the classroom should be a kind of society and the students should be encouraged to become the center in the learning process.

Legutke and Thomas define project work as a learner and task-centered mode of teaching and learning which results from a joint process of discussion between all participants.

Project is an extended task which usually integrates language skills through a number of activities. It involves a number of features: the use of authentic English language materials, an emphasis on integrity and student-centered activities, the importance of students' participation and the use of different skills. It is also defined as "an instructional approach that contextualizes learning by presenting learners with problems to solve or products to develop". Project work

---

① DU X M, HAN J. A Literature Review on the Definition and Process of Project-Based Learning and Other Relative Studies [J]. Creative Education, 2016 (7): 1079–1083.

encourages creativity, critical thinking, collaboration, self-study, and other study skills.

PBL is a very effective approach that allows the students to throw out opinions about the topics covering fields of interest, to ask questions, to estimate, to develop theories, to use different tools, to use the skills acquired in the context of a real and meaningful life, and allows learners to solve problems and answer questions in a creative way in the classroom and outside.

Thomas adopts five criteria to define PBL: ① "Projects are central, not peripheral to the curriculum"; ② "projects are focused on questions or problems that 'drive' students to encounter (and struggle with) the central concepts and principals of the discipline"; ③ "projects involve students in a constructive investigation"; ④ "projects are student-driven to some significant degree"; and ⑤ "projects are realistic, not school-like." Collaboration, as a matter of fact, should also be included as a sixth criterion of PBL.

Stoller defines PBL as: ① having a process and product; ② giving students (partial) ownership of the project; ③ extending over a period of time (several days, weeks, or months); ④ integrating skills; ⑤ developing students' understanding of a topic through the integration of language and content; ⑥ collaborating with other students and working on their own; ⑦ holding students responsible for their own learning through the gathering, processing, and reporting of information from target language resources; ⑧ assigning new roles and responsibilities to students and teachers; ⑨ providing a tangible final product; and ⑩ reflecting on both the process and the product. Thus, it is different from traditional English teaching in that it lays great emphasis on the communicative and functional aspect of language learning and it also pays attention to the integrity of language and content learning.

It is obvious that the definition of PBL is changing from time to time. This diversity of defining features coupled with the lack of a universally accepted model or theory in PBL has finally led to a variety of PBL researches and development activities, which rendered great complexity to this issue. Fortunately, there are still some overlaps in these design features.

7.3 The Process of Project-Based Learning

Papandreou maintains that every project is the result of a series of activities conducted by the students and these activities are organized into a process. That is to say, every project is composed of certain stages. Wrigley argues that most project works cover the following steps: topic selecting, planning, researching and products-making. Studies on the process of PBL vary from each other; however, they share certain core features or steps.

There are a variety of approaches to present the PBL in English teaching classrooms. Fried Booth argues that a project actually covers three stages: beginning in the classroom, moving out into the world, and returning back to the classroom. This model later develops into the eight stages of development.

Papandreou in *An Application of the Projects Approach to EFL* introduces a model which illustrates the process of project work in six steps:

Step 1: Preparation. In this period, the teacher introduces the topic to the students, and asks them to discuss and ask questions.

Step 2: Planning. In this period, the teacher and the students determine the mode for collecting and analyzing information, and different work is assigned.

Step 3: Research. In this part, the students work individually or in groups gather information from different sources.

Step 4: Conclusions. The students draw conclusions based upon their analysis of the collected data.

Step 5: Presentation. The students are supposed to present their final product to the whole class.

Step 6: Evaluation. In this part, the teacher makes comments on the students' endeavor and efforts.

In this model, Papandreou adds a new step into the whole process, namely evaluation, which is apparently a new initiative to the traditional model. And this model is similar to the six-step model undertaken by Kaptan.

Here are steps for implementing PBL, which are detailed below:

Step 1: Stating the subject and sub-subjects, organizing the groups.

Students explore the resources and in order to create a frame for the project they state questions.

Step 2: Groups creating projects.

Group members make a project plan. They ask questions like "Where are we going?" "What will we learn?" etc. They choose their roles in the project.

Step 3: Application of the project.

Group members are organized and analyze the data and information.

Step 4: Planning of the presentation.

The members define the essential points in their presentation and then decide on how to present the project.

Step 5: Making the presentation.

Presentations can be made in any place.

Step 6: Evaluation.

Students share the feedback of everyone on their project. Both the students and the teacher share the project(s) with everyone.

Based upon the above models, Stoller puts forward his initial eight-step framework, which is, to some extent, an improvement to the previous studies. In order to keep pace with time, this model is revised later. Stoller summarized the revised ten-step process in "maximizing the benefits of project work in foreign language classrooms."

Step 1: Students and instructor agree on a theme for the project.

Step 2: Students and instructor determine the final outcome.

Step 3: Students and instructor structure the project.

Step 4: Instructor prepares students for the language demands of information gathering.

Step 5: Students gather information.

Step 6: Instructor prepares students for the language demands of compiling and analyzing data.

Step 7: Students compile and analyze information/data.

Step 8: Instructor prepares students for the language demands of the culminating activity.

Step 9: Students present final product.

Step 10: Students evaluate the project.

In this revised framework, steps 4, 6 and 8 are newly designed to differentiate it from the traditional one. The two models are different in that the language demands related to each step are taught in a different way.

The revised model is easier to handle and manage, which may help the teachers and students in the real application of the project. Thus the students' language skills, creative thinking and content learning can be facilitated. The final objective of the project work can be achieved.

7.4 Other Relative Studies

Apart from the theoretical studies on the definition and the process of PBL, there are a large number of research regarding the application of PBL in English language teaching, including academic papers, dissertations, textbooks and monographs.

The first paper on the application of PBL in English teaching probably is "A Project Course in Spoken English" by Roslyn Eslava and Peter Lawson. In this course, a short episode of "silence movie" is adopted to engage the EFL students in the analysis of the film and the students are asked to produce a final dialogue based upon the situation. Although the research did not provide any empirical data, it is without any doubt that in this process, the students' motivation, autonomy, creativity and interest in English have increased.

Similarly, in Washington, D.C., research on the students from John Easton Elementary School found that nothing pulls the students' speaking and presentation skills together as effectively as PBL. The study also demonstrated that PBL helps students in critical thinking, collaboration and communication.

Similar studies also proved the effectiveness of PBL in improving critical thinking, problem-solving and overall skills. For instance, a study of PBL revealed "a positive effect on low-ability students, who increased their use of critical-thinking skills including synthesizing, evaluating, predicting, and reflecting by 46% while high-ability students improved by 76%".

Meanwhile, there are some articles in the literature in which the authors found that PBL is a challenge for language teachers, especially for those who have never used PBL before, which may result in the teachers' frustration, disappointment and other negative feelings. For instance, Ladewski, Krajcik and Harvey enlist the following challenges and conflicts encountered in the implementation of PBL: ① Should time be most effectively used to allow students to pursue their own investigations or to cover the state-prescribed curriculum? ② Should activities be designed to allow students to seek their own answers or be teacher-controlled so that (all) students obtain the same "correct" results? ③ Should students be given the responsibility for guiding their own learning or should the (more knowledgeable) teacher take responsibility for directing activities and disseminating information in the classroom?

In addition, Mar et al. demonstrate the teachers' problems and obstacles in implementing PBL as follows: ① projects were time-consuming; ② classrooms felt disorderly; ③ teachers could not control the flow of information; ④ it was difficult to balance giving students independence and providing them supports; ⑤ it was difficult to incorporate technology as a cognitive tool; ⑥ authentic assessments were hard to design.

7.5 Conclusion

Based upon the review above, it is easy to draw the conclusion that PBL exerts a great positive and beneficial effect on the students' academic achievements, namely the language skills, critical thinking and knowledge acquirement. Meanwhile, PBL is also a great challenge for the English teachers and students who are in need of help and support. Though there are many challenges and obstacles, the benefits without any doubts outweigh the disadvantages. The teacher should take all the possible factors related to the successful enactment into consideration, such as time, place, resources, students, technology and possible training.

8 Flipped Classroom Approach

Flipped Classroom Approach[①]

8.1 Introduction

In the century we are in, rapidly developed technologies affect the education training field as they do in all fields. In parallel to the speed of development in technology, education conditions develop as well and different learning demands come out. In order to compensate for these demands that come out with this transformation, technological innovations are among the prior responsibilities of education systems. That is why a qualified education system should

---

① OZDAMLI F., ASIKSOY G. (CYPRUS). Flipped classroom approach [J]. World Journal on Educational Technology, 2016, 8 (2): 98–105.

not limit learning and transform traditional structure into modern structure with technological opportunities. As changing in knowledge and technology is so fast, education also keeps up with it and continues its development with innovative learning approaches. This change and transformation in the education training field takes out the existence of a new strategy that is a flipped classroom system in education. Flipped Classroom Approach, which is accepted as the most popular and active-based approach, is a special type of blended learning. This approach firstly attracted the attention of educators in 2007 with chemistry teachers Jonathan Bergmann and Aaron Sams from Woodland Park High School recording live lessons and broadcasting them on-line for the students that missed those lessons. The main aim of this new learning approach is to provide preparation of students for the subject before the course and during course applying activities that increase the quality of face to face education.

There are many definitions regarding flipped classroom in literature. According to Bishop and Verleger, flipped classroom is a student-centred learning method consisting of two parts with interactive learning activities during lessons and individual teaching bases directly on the computer out of calss. Mull defined it as a model that provides students prepare themselves for the lesson by watching videos, listening to podcasts and reading articles. According to Milman, it is an approach aims at the efficiency of lessons by transferring knowledge to students via videos and podcasts as well as by discussions, group works and applications during the course. Toto and Nguyen expressed that flipped classroom is an approach that increases active learning activities and gives the students opportunity to use their knowledge in class with guidance of the teacher. Hamdan and others explained that flipped classroom is not a defined model; instead, it is a model that teachers use as compensating the demands of students by using different equipments. Since the educators in different countries use flipped classroom with various methods, this caused changing of flipped classroom concept to flipped classroom approach. It is emphasized that this new approach can be used with different learning methods.

In literature there are many studies regarding the usage of flipped classroom approach and its results in many fields such as Science, Maths and Healthcare training.

8.2 Flipped Classroom Approach

With its simplest definition, Flipped Classroom Approach is expressed as "what is done at school done at home, homework done at home completed in class".

In this approach, before the course, the students watch the theoretical part of the lesson via multiple equipments such as online videos, presentations, and learning management systems, take notes, and prepare questions about the parts that they do not understand. During the course they achieve supporting activities such as finding answers together to the questions they prepared before lesson, group working, problem solving, discussion and making an inference. Flipped classroom is an approach that transfers learning responsibility from teacher to students.

Flipped Classroom Approach has four different elements. It is expressed that in order for teachers to achieve this approach, they have to take these four elements into consideration. The properties of this approach which its English correspondence is "Flip" are explained like this by referring first letters: F ("F"lexible Environment): It indicates provision of time and place flexibity of learning. L ("L"earning Culture): In traditional teacher-centered approach, the source of knowledge is the teacher. In Flipped Classroom Approach, there is a transition from teacher-centered approach to student-centered approach. I ("I"ntentional Content): Flipped classroom educators both think about how education is used to provide fluency and how they can develop cognitive understanding of students. P ("P"rofessional Educator): The responsibility of flipped classroom educators is greater than the ones using the traditional approach. Flipped classroom educators continuously observe students during the course, evaluate their studies and make feedback.

(1) What Is or What Is Not Flipped Classroom Approach

Bergmann, Overmyer and Wilie made explanations below about what is or what is not Flipped Classroom Approach. Flipped Classroom Approach is a system that provides increased interaction time between the teacher and the students, presentation of a condition in which students take their own learning responsibilities, transition of the role of the teacher into a guidance, blending of constructivist learning with teaching method, each student taking individual education, consistency of learning by repetitions and preventing students from falling behind in class for any reason that they cannot come to class.

Flipped Classroom Approach is not synonym with online videos. The important point is the interactive activities done during the time when the teacher and students are face-to-face. It is not using a video instead of teacher. It is not working unsystematically for students. It is not students spending all course period in front of a computer. It is not a student studying alone.

(2) Technology of the Flipped Classroom

In order to apply a flipped classroom model, it is not necessary to be a professional video producer; it is possible to use any source that explains the subject (PDFs, recorded sounds, websites). Although Tucker expressed that flipped classroom educators don't need to prepare their own videos; instead, they can get access to lecture videos from Internet sites such as Khan Academy, YouTube or Ted, while most of the educators and researchers prefer to prepare their own videos. Some equipment that is necessary to form and broadcast lecture videos, are presented below:

Video forming equipment: Screen-Cast-O-Mattic, Camtasia PC, TechSmith Relay, Office Mix, Adobe Presenter.

Video Hosting: After forming the video, it should be placed online for access of students. Some of video sites are: YouTube, TeacherTube, Screencast.com, Acclaim, GoogleDrive.

Video interaction Softwares: These are softwares that provide teachers to access some information such as which student watched which lecture video, how long he watched, how he answered the questions in the video. Some softwares that can be given as example are: EduCanon, EdPuzzle, Zaption, Office Mix, Verso, TechSmith Relay, Adobe Presenter, Google Apps for Ed.

Learning Management: As created videos can be sent to video hosting sites, they can be presented to access by using Learning Management System (LMS). LMS are not only broadcast videos, they can also provide interaction with students. Moodle, Sakai, Blackkboard, VersoApp, Schoology, canvas, My Big Campus, Haiku Learning, Google Classroom can be given as examples for Learning Management Systems (LMS).

(3) The Role of Teachers

The most important factor in Flipped Classroom Approach is the role of teachers. The roles of Flipped Classroom educators are presented below.

• Creating learning condition based on questioning.

• Instead of transferring knowledge directy, being a guide to make learning easy.

• Making one to one interaction with students.

• Correcting misunderstandings.

• Individualizing learning for each student.

• Using technological equipments suitable for learning condition.

• Creating interactive discussion conditions.

• Increasing participation of students.

• Sharing lecture videos as out of class activity.

• Providing feedback by using pedagogical strategies.

(4) The Role of Students

In Flipped Classroom Approach, students are transformed from passive receivers of knowledge to active promoters of knowledge. In this approach, the roles of students are expressed below;

• Taking their own learning responsibilities;

• Watching lecture videos before the course and preparing for the course by using learning materials;

• Learning at his own learning speed;

• Making necessary interactions with his teacher and friends, taking and giving feedback;

• Participating discussions within class;

• Participating team working.

8.3 Flipped Classroom Models

In order to apply Flipped Classroom Approach, there are different models. If the condition of class is taken into consideration in choosing these models, the results will be more effective.

(1) Traditional Flipped Classroom Model

Bergmann and Sams explained traditional Flipped Classroom model as "what is done at school done at home, homework done at home completed in class." In traditional Flipped Classroom Approach, students come to class by watching the lecture video of the previous night. The lesson starts with short questions and answers. If there are points in lectures that are not understood, they are explained comprehensively. In the rest of time, the teacher makes activities based on questioning and gives one to one support to students. In this kind of class structure, the lessons are always given as lecture video format out of course period and the teacher never teaches lessons directly. Accordingly, students are given the opportunity to learn by discussing. In this approach, it is not a teacher-centered class but a student-centered class and the teacher is in class as just a guide. In Flipped Classroom Approach, time is restructured. However, in traditional approach, teaching of a subject takes the most of course time. Class activity periods in traditional approach and class activity periods in Flipped Classroom Approach are given in Appendix-6.

Appendix-6   Comparison of Within Class Activity Periods of Traditional Approach and Flipped Classroom Approach

Traditional Classroom	Time	Flipped classroom	Time
Warm up	5 min	Warm up	5 min
Homework checking of previous lesson	20 min	Answering lecture video questions	10 min
Teaching of new subject	30–45 min	—	—
Exercises or labarotory applications	20–35 min	Exercises or laboratory applications	75 min

(2) Partial Flipped Classroom Approach Model

Partial Flipped Classroom structure is the less strict of traditional Flipped Classroom structure. Gwyneth Jones made the perfect application of partial Flipped Classroom Model in Murray Hill Secondary School. Jones encouraged his students watching the videos out of course period. In addition to this, he did not punish the ones that could not watch the videos or the ones that could not watch because of lackness of equipment. Although Jones expressed his method as Flipped Classroom, this method is the part of traditional Flipped Classroom Model of Sams and Bergman.

(3) Holistic Flipped Classroom Model

Chen et al added 3 structures (Progressive Activities, Engaging Experiences, and Diversified Platforms) to four structures of Flipped Classroom Approach (Flexible Environments, Learning Culture, Intentional Content, and Professional Educators) and formed Holistic Flipped Classroom (HFC) model. HFC is a model that contains total of home, mobile and physical classrooms synchronously. In contrast to traditional Flipped Classrooms where students are only supervised by instructors in the physical classroom and their home activities are not recorded and monitored, and hence cannot be analyzed, all learning spaces in HFC are treated in classrooms because all of them are supported and monitored. By logging on to the platform in HFC, students can preview/review course lectures, attend synchronous class sessions, discuss course content with the instructor and classmates, and offer reflections. All these tasks can be done seamlessly, and all their learning activities are recorded in the platform's system log. The lessons that has to be watched and materials that has to be examined before each synchronous class could be conducted in one of the Mobile or Cloud or Asynchronous classroom environments. To attend the synchronous class, students would log on to the learning platform and conduct synchronous classroom activities under the instructor's guidance. In the synchronous classroom, the instructor could require the students to conduct various hands-on activities, such as conducting research on Cloud, uploading reports to the asynchronous classroom or taking online quizzes. Appendix-1 shows the working of Holistic Flipped Classroom Model. (Appendix-6)

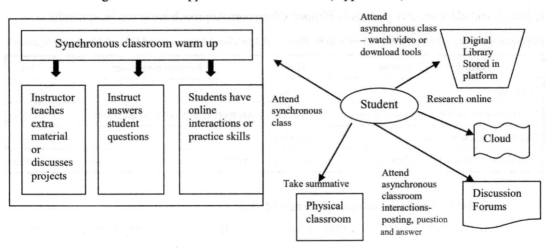

Appendix-6　Holistic Flipped Classroom Model

8.4 The Advantages and Limitations of Flipped Classroom Approach

(1) Advantages

There are many advantages of Flipped Classroom Approach. The most important one is it increases the interactive period within the class. By means of lecture videos the teacher uses the time for the interaction between teacher and students rather than for teaching. Accordingly, the teacher can spare more time to fulfill the learning and emotional demands of students. In Flipped Classroom Approach, the students can find the opportunity to discuss with their teachers which is not a possible situation in traditional approach.

According to Milman, the most important benefit of Flipped Classroom Approach is to support team work within the class. The advantages that Fulton expressed are: students can access lecture videos whenever and wherever they want and it enables students to learn at their own speed. The students that are educated with this approach are encouraged to think both within and out of class. It is available to be used with various teaching strategies. Parents can follow the courses of students and help their children is another advantage of it. In addition to all these advantages, Herreid and Schiller reported that Flipped Classroom Approach provides students with more time to make inventive research.

(2) Limitations

Despite all these positive sides, there are negative opinions about the method. Students may be stubborn at the beginning and may come to class without preparation. Also, lecture videos should be prepared carefully in a way to prepare students for the course. It is hard to prepare such good quality videos and it takes time. Springen expressed that teaching design models that are going to be applied in the teaching process are limited.

Kordyban and Kinash attracted attention to the point as a difficulty that how teachers are certain if the students do their responsibilities out of class well, and Bristol expressed the difficulties in case the students come to class without preparation. Also, the obstacles that prevent the usage of approaches are expressed as students lack sth equipment such as smart phones, tablets or computers and have Internet problems.

The biggest disadvantage for teachers is not preparing or broadcasting lecture videos but preparing class activities and integrating them to Flipped Classroom Approach. In contrast to what is known, this method increases the duty of teachers instead of relieving it.

8.5 Conclusion and Future Work

In order to compensate for the educational demands of the 21st-century students, it is important to use innovative approaches in education. This study can attract the attention of educators about the potential of approach and can form a point of view on how to use it in their courses. For the expanding of Flipped Classroom Approach in educational institutions, it is thought that the approach has to be cognitively and practically presented. Accordingly, the skills of teachers in designing materials by using multiple equipments and to transform these materials with learning management systems, have to be developed. The positive development in desire, interest and motivation of educators using technological equipments will be effective in spreading of this approach. In future studies the applications of Flipped Classroom Approach in different education levels can be analysed.

References

参考文献

［1］ADAMSON B. Fashions in language teaching methodology[C]//DAVIES A, ELDER C. The handbook of applied linguistics. London: Blackwell, 2004.

［2］ASHER J J. Learning another language through actions: the complete teacher's guide book[M]. 2nd ed. Los Gatos, Calif.: Sky Oaks Productions, 1982.

［3］BLOOMFIELD L. Language[M]. New York: Holt, 1933.

［4］BREEN M. Learner contributions to task design[C]//CANDLIN C N, MURPHY D F. Language Learning Tasks. London: Prentice Hall, 1987.

［5］BRINTON D M, SNOW M A, WESCHE M. Content-based Second Language Instruction[M]. New York: Newbury House, 1989.

［6］BROOKS N. Language and language learning: theory and practice[M]. 2nd ed. New York: Harcourt Brace, 1964.

［7］BROWN H. Teaching by Principles: An interactive approach to language Pedagogy[M]. 2nd ed. New York: Longman, 2001.

［8］BYGATE M P, SKEHAN P, SWAIN M. Task-based learning: language teaching, learning, and assessment[M]. Harlow, Essex: Pearson, 2000.

［9］CHOMSKY N. Syntactic structures[M]. The Hague: Mouton, 1957.

［10］CROOKES G. Task classification: a cross-disciplinary review (Technical report No. 4.)[C]// Center for second language classroom research. Honolulu: University of Hawaii at Manoa, 1986.

［11］CURRAN C A. Counseling-Learning: A whole-Person model for education[M]. New

York: Grune and Stratton, 1972.

[12] ELLIS R. Task-based language learning and teaching[M]. Oxford: Oxford University Press, 2003.

[13] ELLIS R, SKEHAN P, LI S F. Task-based language teaching: theory and Practice[M]. Oxford: Oxford University Press, 2003.

[14] FINOCCHIARO M, BRUMFIT C. The functional-notional Approach: from theory to practice[M]. New York: Oxford University Press, 1983.

[15] FIRTH R. Papers in linguistics: 1934–1951[M]. London: Oxford University Press, 1957.

[16] GATTEGNO C. Teaching foreign languages in schools: the silent Way[M]. 2nd ed. New York: Educational Solutions, 1972.

[17] GRUBE P. The silent way–a method for the german classroom[M]. Munich: Grin Verlag, 2013.

[18] HALLIDAY M A K. Categories of the theory of grammar[J]. Word, 1961, 17(3):37–94.

[19] HALLIDAY M A K. Learning How to Mean: explorations in the development of language[M]. London: Edward Arnold, 1975.

[20] HALLIDAY M A K. Language as social semiotic: the social interpretation of language and meaning[M]. London: Edward Arnold, 1978.

[21] HARMER J. Practice of english language teaching[M]. New York: Pearson Education ESL, 2015.

[22] HOWATT A P R, WIDDOWSON H G. A history of english language teaching[M]. New York: Oxford University Press, 2004.

[23] HYMES D. On communicative competence[C]// Pride J B, Holmes J. Sociolinguistics. Harmondsworth: Penguin, 1972.

[24] LARSEN-FREEMAN D, ANDERSON M. Techniques and principles in language teaching[M]. Oxford: Oxford University Press, 2011.

[25] LEWIS M. Implementing the lexical approach[M]. London: Language Teaching Publications, 1997.

[26] LEWIS M. Teaching Collocation: Further developments in the Lexical Approach[M]. London: Language Teaching Publications, 2000.

[27] LIGHTBOWN P M. Focus on content-based language teaching: research-led guide examining instructional practices that address the challenges of Content-Based Language Teaching[M]. New York: Oxford University Press, 2014.

[28] LITTLEWOOD W. Communicative Language Teaching[M]. Cambridge: Cambridge University Press, 1981.

［29］LITTLEWOOD W T. Communicative Language Teaching[M]. Cambridge: Cambridge University Press, 2013.

［30］LONG M H. The role of the linguistic environment in second language acquisition[C]// Ritchie W C, Bahtia T K. Handbook of second language acquisition. New York: Academic Press, 1996.

［31］LOZANOV G, GATEVA E. The foreign language teacher's suggestopedic manual[M]. New York: Gordon and Breach, 1988.

［32］LYSTER R. Content-Based Language Teaching[M]. London: Routledge, 2017.

［33］MALINOWSKI, B. The problem of meaning in primitive languages[C]// Ogden C K, Richards I A. The meaning of meaning. New York: Harcourt Jovanovich, 1923.

［34］NUNAN D. Designing tasks for the communicative classroom[M]. Cambridge: Cambridge University Press, 1989.

［35］NUNAN D. Task-based language teaching[M]. Cambridge: Cambridge University Press, 2004.

［36］PENNY U R. A course in english language teaching[M]. Cambridge: Cambridge University Press, 2012.

［37］PRABHU N S. Second language pedagogy[M]. Oxford: Oxford University Press, 1987.

［38］PRTER G. Psychology[M]. New York: Worth Publishers, Inc, 1991.

［39］RICHARDS J C, RODGERS T S. Approaches and methods in language teaching[M]. 2nd ed. Cambridge: Cambridge University Press, 2001.

［40］RICHARDS J C, SCHMIDT R W. Longman dictionary of language teaching and applied linguistics[M]. London: Routledge, 2010.

［41］SKEHAN P. A framework for the implementation of task-based instruction[J]. Applied Linguistics, 1996a, 17(1): 38-61.

［42］SKEHAN P. Second language acquisition research and task-based instruction[C]// Willis J, Willis D. Challenge and change in language teaching. Oxford: Heinemann, 1996b.

［43］SKEHAN P. A Cognitive approach to language learning[M]. Oxford: Heinemann, 1998.

［44］STRYKER S, LEAVER B. Content-based instruction in foreign language education[M]. Washington, D.C.: Georgetown University Press, 1993.

［45］SWAN M. Communicative language teaching[M]. Cambridge: Cambridge University Press, 1981.

［46］SWAN M. A critical look at the communicative approach[J]. English Language Teaching Journal, 1985, 39(1): 2–12.

［47］THORNBURY S. Scott Thornbury's 30 language teaching methods[M]. Cambridge:

Cambridge University Press, 2017.

［48］VYGOTSKY L. Mind in society[M].Cambridge, MA: Harvard University Press,1978.

［49］WIDDOWSON H. Teaching language as communication[M]. Oxford: Oxford University Press, 1978.

［50］WILKINS D A. Linguistics in language teaching[M]. Strasbourg: Cambridge: MIT Press, 1972.

［51］WILKINS D A. Notional syllabuses[M]. Oxford: Oxford University Press, 1976.

［52］WILLIS J. A flexible framework for task-based learning[C]// WILLIS J, WILLIS D. Challenge and change in language teaching. Oxford: Heinemann, 1996.

［53］WILLIS J. Doing task-based teaching[M]. New York: Oxford University Press, 2007.

［54］H. H. 斯特恩 . 语言教学的基本概念 [M]. 刘振前，宋青，庄会彬，译 . 北京：商务印书馆，2018.

［55］RICHARDS J C. 交际语言教学的新发展 [M]. 北京：人民教育出版社，2007.

［56］RICHARDS J C, RODGERS T S. 语言教学的流派 [M]. 2 版 . 北京：外语教学与研究出版社，2008.

［57］BROWN H D. 语言学习与语言教学的原则 [M]. 北京：外语教学与研究出版社，2002.

［58］UR P. 语言教学教程：实践与理论 [M]. 北京：外语教学与研究出版社，2000.

［59］BRUMFIT C J, JOHNSON K. 交际法语言教学 [M]. 上海：上海外语教育出版社，2000.

［60］HARMER J. 怎样教英语 [M]. 北京：外语教学与研究出版社，2000.

［61］鲁子问 . 英语教学方法与策略 [M]. 上海：华东师范大学出版社，2008.

［62］刘珣 . 对外汉语教育学引论 [M]. 北京：北京语言大学出版社，2000.

［63］武和平，武海霞 . 外语教学方法与流派 [M]. 北京：外语教学与研究出版社，2014.

［64］吴勇毅 . 对外汉语教学法 [M]. 北京：商务印书馆，2019.

［65］舒白梅，陈佑林 . 外语教学法 [M]. 北京：高等教育出版社，1999.

［66］章兼中 . 国外外语教学法主要流派 [M]. 福州：福建教育出版社，2016.

［67］朱志平 . 汉语第二语言教学理论概要 [M]. 北京：北京大学出版社，2007.